Comparative Perspectives on Afro-Latin America

UNIVERSITY PRESS OF FLORIDA

Florida A&M University, Tallahassee
Florida Atlantic University, Boca Raton
Florida Gulf Coast University, Ft. Myers
Florida International University, Miami
Florida State University, Tallahassee
New College of Florida, Sarasota
University of Central Florida, Orlando
University of Florida, Gainesville
University of North Florida, Jacksonville
University of South Florida, Tampa
University of West Florida, Pensacola

Comparative Perspectives on Afro-Latin America

Edited by Kwame Dixon and John Burdick

FOREWORD BY HOWARD WINANT

UNIVERSITY PRESS OF FLORIDA

Gainesville Tallahassee Tampa Boca Raton
Pensacola Orlando Miami Jacksonville Ft. Myers Sarasota

First cloth printing, 2012
First paperback printing, 2013

Library of Congress Cataloging-in-Publication Data
Comparative perspectives on Afro-Latin America / edited by Kwame Dixon and John
Burdick ; foreword by Howard Winant.
p. cm.
Includes bibliographical references and index.
ISBN 978-0-8130-3756-1 (cloth: alk. paper)
ISBN 978-0-8130-4962-5 (pbk.)
1. Blacks—Latin America. 2. Blacks—Caribbean Area. I. Dixon, Kwame. II. Burdick,
John, 1959–
F1419.N4C65 2012
305.896'08—dc23   2011037509

The University Press of Florida is the scholarly publishing agency for the State University
System of Florida, comprising Florida A&M University, Florida Atlantic University,
Florida Gulf Coast University, Florida International University, Florida State University,
New College of Florida, University of Central Florida, University of Florida, University of
North Florida, University of South Florida, and University of West Florida.

University Press of Florida
15 Northwest 15th Street
Gainesville, FL 32611-2079
http://www.upf.com

Contents

Figures

Foreword

A New Hemispheric Blackness

When President George W. Bush asked Fernando Henrique Cardoso, then president of Brazil, "Do you have blacks too?" (Pedreira 2002),[1] he was reflecting more than his own provincialism. He was expressing the ignorance of the vast majority of the U.S. population about Afro-Latin America. How many North Americans know that Brazil has the second-highest black population of any country in the world? How many know that of the approximately 15 million Africans who survived the tortures of the Atlantic slave trade, roughly 85 percent were transported to Latin America and the Caribbean (Curtin 1972) and only about 15 percent arrived alive in the North American colonies and early United States? How many North Americans know of the vast contributions Afro-Latin Americans have made to the economic, political, and cultural development of the modern world?

Economically, Afro-Latinos were the world's first industrial workers, toiling in the *engenhos* (sugar factories) of the Brazilian Recôncavo, the Haitian *moulins* (James [1963] 1989), and the Cuban *ingenios* (Moreno Fraginals 1976) to establish sugar as the world's most extensively traded international commodity (Mintz 1985). Afro-Latinos were the gold miners, coffee pickers, and plantation workers who made the circulation of capital possible in the sixteenth through the nineteenth centuries. Indeed, Afro-Latino workers also played a major role as the age of import-substitution industrialization dawned in Latin America in the 1930s, especially in São Paulo but in other Latin American metropoles as well (Andrews 1991; see also Andrews 2004).

How many are aware of the political centrality of Afro-Latin slave revolutions in shaping not only black freedom movements around the world but also in inventing modern anticolonialism and indeed modern democracy and popular sovereignty?[2] The first modern anti-imperial movements occurred throughout the Western Hemisphere and depended in large measure on the armed struggles of emancipated (and self-emancipated) slaves of African descent.[3] Whole regions of Latin America and the Caribbean were liberated territory occupied by *cimarrones*, maroons, or *quilombo* communities, quasi–nation-states comprised of people who had emancipated themselves from colonial slavery and defended themselves by force of arms (Price 1996). Many were crushed, of course, but some survived into the era of emancipation. Some continue even today.

And how many recognize the importance of Afro-Latin culture, notably of the treasure-house of African music that has shaped the blues, reggae, salsa, merengue, samba, and cumbia? Without Afro-Latinidad, would we even have jazz, hip-hop, or rock and roll? Would we have the "primitivism" of Picasso, Stravinsky's *The Rite of Spring*, or the sculptures of Giacometti?

These all-too-brief points suggest the tremendous importance of *Comparative Perspectives on Afro-Latin America*, which is more than a title for the vital book you hold in your hands. For the themes addressed in that title contribute in a central way to the new understanding of race and racism that is developing today. This text takes its place within a growing literature of *new racial studies*. Theoretically informed and empirically grounded, the work collected here signals a shift in race scholarship that is long overdue: from the world's North to its South, from the limited focus of American studies to something that is not just hemispheric but global, from the disciplinary confinement of various social sciences and humanities fields to a fully multidisciplinary and historically attuned cultural studies and (once again) a new racial studies. Perhaps most important, the work collected here honors the vast legacy of freedom struggles that African-descended people continue to present to the world.

The Atlantic slavery system produced a contradictory legacy. In the main it was a bottomless abyss of human horror, a taker of numberless souls, a *shoah* or *nakba* all its own. But it was also the antithesis of genocidal disaster. The predation of Africa and the framework of "blackness" that were the outcomes of European imperialism and the Atlantic slavery system also gave rise to modernity (Gilroy 1993), to revolutionary self-activity, and to the demand for a universal popular sovereignty that is shared in a broad sense by all the wretched of the earth. So blackness in the Western Hemisphere has a contradictory valence, both in the historical past and in the present day: the Africanizing of the Western Hemisphere was both deracinating (that is, it dug up African peoples from their roots) and radicalizing (that is, it permitted or forced them to dig deep new roots elsewhere). The mass transport (and mass murder) of African people that founded the modern world also produced new peoples: peoples that were both more authentic and more marginalized than any other Americans. It generated sociopolitical regimes that were both more western and white supremacist than had ever existed before and that were simultaneously more unstable and illegitimate, more despotic and prone to permanent revolt than any others in the modern world.

While it has not yet achieved the scholarly attention that North American blackness has received, the new hemispheric blackness embodied in Afro-Latin

America has nevertheless been the subject of continuous study. This volume both continues and alters a long tradition of attention to Africans in the Americas based in the social sciences and the humanities (Thornton 1998; Thompson 1983). The case-specific ethnographic and theoretical studies assembled here are the latest iterations of that tradition. They succeed earlier generations of research on colonial rule and abolition, modernization and revolution, dictatorship, and *abertura*. They build upon long-standing politically and culturally oriented analyses of the black experience in the Americas. They also alter that legacy in numerous ways, notably through a deepened commitment to blackness at the grassroots level, a greater attentiveness to women's praxis, and a heightened ability to hear and understand the voices of everyday Afro-Latinos. So while these essays flow from the work of earlier periods, they also challenge and transform the tradition. By validating the experiences and insights—the self-activity—of contemporary black people in Latin America, these works also update the great work that has come before: the sociology of Florestan Fernandes, for example (1978), the anthropology of Melville Herskovits (1966), and the work of many other giants in the field who must be recognized.

World War II, I have argued, began to establish a new global racial system, one characterized by new contradictions: on the one hand, it generated a higher degree of inclusion of black people (as well as other racially identified groups) than had existed earlier, but on the other hand, it gave rise to mendacious claims that race had been transcended and democratic inclusion at long last extended to peoples of color around the world. Our various contemporary "commonsense" notes of race derive from the contradictory outcomes of that war: ideas of "colorblindness," "racial democracy," "nonracialism," and the like (Winant 2001). Thus, in our time we are required to account for racial conditions that are largely (if not totally) unprecedented: recognizable "progress" from despotism to racial justice combined with reinforced and newly ratified patterns of "structural racism."[4]

Needless to say, these transformations did not occur as a result of the benevolence of ruling groups. Instead they were an uneven response to the achievement of greater political power on the part of colonized and racially oppressed nations and communities around the world. The mobilizations of these peoples during and after World War II and the enormous demographic transformations that occurred over the same period allowed black people to achieve higher levels of cultural awareness and political autonomy than had generally been available to them before.

Inspired by parallel anticolonial and antiracist struggles around the world and drawing more deeply on their own legacies of resistance, rebellion, and revolution, Afro-Latin peoples too began to assert their own identities in new ways, both culturally and politically. This process of course drew on many earlier precedents and "rehearsals": on slave revolts, *marronage*, abolitionism, and fitful and partial democratizations across the whole historical sweep of Afro-diasporic history and Afro-modernity (Hanchard 1999; see also Hanchard 2006). Afro-Latin movements were subject to many painful and sometimes brutal setbacks, but I would like to argue here that by the time of the demise of the most recent (and hopefully the last) wave of right-wing dictatorships in Latin America in the 1980s and 1990s, the black communities of meso-America were poised to make a giant step forward politically. They were striving everywhere to achieve greater collective self-awareness and greater political power as black communities. Black power: the term might have a familiar ring. . . .

Indeed, Latin American blacks have achieved parallel and sometimes greater political gains than their North American sisters and brothers: notably the development of quota-based affirmative action and land redistribution in Brazil, the emergence of black political formations and parties, and the enactment of reforms variously characterized as racial or ethnic reforms in many countries.

Culturally, politically, and in state-based institutions as well these processes continue to advance, not without inspiring significant reaction, of course, but still quite inexorably. Their core energy, as every author in this volume makes abundantly clear, is popular and comes from the bottom up: the continuing vitality of black struggles to assert and legitimate identity, both personal and collective. These efforts make use of a wide variety of cultural forms, most notably music (as has been true historically as well), but also a vast range of other expressions: it's going on, friends, in all the arts, in scholarly work, in mass media, and in cultural politics. Black movement organizations are active everywhere in Latin America and the Caribbean, linked not only to these culturally oriented activities, but to active challenges to the racial state and white supremacy at all levels, from the local to the national to the diasporic.[5] Of course there are numerous currents, wide disagreements, and differences among various movement groups—often rooted in class and gender tensions—but the underlying recognition of the depth of the black presence throughout the continent is not generally in question. What a significant change from generations past!

A certain amount of state-based support of racial justice can also be discerned—for example, affirmative action policies, land title transfers to traditional *quilombo-* and *mocambo*-based communities, and efforts to spur access to education and other social and political resources. These achievements remain uneven, however; they are often more symbolic than substantive. Huge racial disparities continue: in literacy and incarceration rates, in access to health care, and in "life chances" in general—economic opportunity, income distribution, and life expectancy.[6] Reformist racial policy, where it exists, is driven in large measure by the social movement activity and cultural ferment discussed in these pages. There is still a long way to go.

It is tempting to end these brief remarks with the standard disavowal: *plus ça change, plus c'est la même chose.* But in my view, and as this book makes clear, Afro-Latin conditions do not merit that cynical judgment. Despite the tremendous journey that still lies ahead, great strides have already been taken: the movement toward respect for racial difference and for the enormous achievements of black people in Latin America proceeds. Complete citizenship, full democracy, and racial equality still lie ahead. We *norteños* have a lot to learn from our sisters and brothers across the hemisphere.

Howard Winant

Notes

1. The White House reacted with indignation to Pedreira's account of this event, it should be noted, dismissing it as "total crap" (Kamen 2002). Pedreira, who was a close friend of the Brazilian president, stuck by his story, however.

2. The Haitian Revolution is the grand example of this, of course. Haiti made the French Revolution possible. Haiti sheltered Simón Bolívar, a slave-holding *criollo,* and led him to accept abolitionism as a necessary condition for an independent Gran Colombia. Slave uprisings and revolutions were endemic throughout Latin America and laid the groundwork for the decolonization of both the continent and the Caribbean. Emancipation was as volatile an issue in the Latin American anticolonial wars as it was in the North American one; it played almost as central a role in the largest armed conflict ever to occur on the continent, the Guerra do Paraguai (1864–1870), as it did in the contemporaneous U.S. Civil War. Slavery was a principal issue in the U.S.-Mexico war of 1846 to 1848: newly independent Mexico had abolished slavery, which provoked slaveowners such as Sam Houston to seize Texas and reimpose the practice there. U.S. interventions in mid-nineteenth-century Central America were led by pro-slavery pirates (called "filibusters") under contract with U.S. interests. U.S. slavocracy was deeply involved with Brazil as well, perpetuating the African slave trade there (and in Cuba too) long after it had been officially banned. Indeed, because emancipation came to Brazil so late (1888), some U.S. southern slaveholders moved there after the Civil War's end in an irredentist effort to perpetuate their ancien régime on Brazilian soil (Horne 2007). Hence the territorial contours of the United States and the dawn of its imperial relationships with Latin America—two rather major features of the modern world—may be traced back to its efforts to impose or perpetuate African slavery on much of the continent.

3. This is true not only of the Haitian Revolution but of the North American Revolution, the first Mexican and Bolivarian revolutions, and others as well. The U.S. Civil War may be counted in this number too, a claim that originates with Du Bois ([1935] 1998).

4. This concept has become familiar in the U.S. antiracism literature. It designates the continuity and automaticity of racist practices over time, whether or not active discrimination is practiced or conscious prejudice is present in the minds and hearts of racism's perpetrators. See Winant 1998.

5. Both the Afro-Latin presence at the 2001 UN World Conference against Racism in Durban and the subsequent effects of that conference in many Latin American nations demonstrated how deeply Afro-diasporic connections have taken hold in recent years.

6. For what is probably the most advanced demographic treatment of these matters, see

Telles 2003 and 2005. That work on Brazil will undoubtedly soon be matched by parallel research in other Latin American countries.

Bibliography

Andrews, George Reid. 1991. *Blacks and Whites in São Paulo, Brazil, 1888–1988.* Madison: University of Wisconsin Press.

———. 2004. *Afro-Latin America, 1800–2000.* New York: Oxford University Press.

Curtin, Philip D. 1972. *The Atlantic Slave Trade: A Census.* Madison: University of Wisconsin Press.

Du Bois, W.E.B. (1935) 1998. *Black Reconstruction in America: An Essay toward a History of the Part which Black Folk Played in the Attempt to Reconstruct Democracy in America, 1860–1880.* New York: Free Press.

Fernandes, Florestan. 1978. *A Integração do Negro na Sociedade de Clases.* 2 vols. São Paulo: Atica.

Gilroy, Paul. 1993. *The Black Atlantic: Modernity and Double Consciousness.* Cambridge, Mass.: Harvard University Press.

Hanchard, Michael. 1999. "Afro-Modernity: Temporality, Politics, and the African Diaspora." *Public Culture* 11 (1): 245–268.

———. 2006. *Party/Politics: Horizons in Black Political Thought.* New York: Oxford University Press.

Herskovitz, Melville. 1966. *The New World Negro: Selected Papers in Afroamerican Studies.* Ed. Frances S. Herskovits. Bloomington: Indiana University Press.

Horne, Gerald. 2007. *The Deepest South: The United States, Brazil, and the African Slave Trade.* New York: New York University Press.

James, C.L.R. [1963] 1989. *The Black Jacobins: Toussaint L'Ouverture and the San Domingo Revolution.* New York: Vintage.

Kamen, Al. 2002. "What Did He Say and When Did He Say It?" *The Washington Post.* June 5.

Mintz, Sidney W. 1985. *Sweetness and Power: The Place of Sugar in Modern History.* New York: Viking.

Moreno Fraginals, Manuel. 1976. *The Sugarmill: The Socioeconomic Complex of Sugar in Cuba, 1760–1860.* Trans. Cedric Belfrage. New York: Monthly Review Press.

Pedreira, Fernando. 2002. "A Retumbante Ignorância." *Estado de São Paulo,* April 28.

Price, Richard, ed. 1996. *Maroon Societies: Rebel Slave Communities in the Americas.* Baltimore, Md.: Johns Hopkins University Press.

Telles, Edward E. 2003. *Racismo à Brasileira: Uma Nova Perspectiva Sociológica.* Rio de Janeiro: Relume-Dumará.

———. 2005. *Race in Another America: The Significance of Skin Color in Brazil.* Princeton, N.J.: Princeton University Press.

Thompson, Robert Farris. 1983. *Flash of the Spirit: African and Afro-American Art and Philosophy.* New York: Random House.

Thornton, John. 1998. *Africa and Africans in the Making of the Atlantic World, 1400–1800.* 2nd ed. New York: Cambridge University Press.

Winant, Howard. 1998. "Racism Today: Continuity and Change in the Post-Civil Rights Era." *Ethnic and Racial Studies* 21 (4): 755–766.

———. 2001. *The World Is a Ghetto: Race and Democracy since World War II.* New York: Basic Books.

Acknowledgments

Comparative Perspectives on Afro-Latin America is the work of many diverse individuals, and three common threads wove it together and made it possible: first is Amy Gorelick, editor-in-chief at the University Press of Florida; second is my coeditor and colleague, John Burdick at Syracuse University; and third are the volume contributors.

The first thread was in 2007 when I received an e-mail from Amy Gorelick, then acquisitions editor at the University Press of Florida. At this time, I was preparing to attend the Latin American Studies Association Conference in Montreal, Canada. She asked if I would like to meet while in Montreal to discuss my research and the possibility of collaborating with UPF. I wondered why she had chosen me of all the people at the conference, what I might say to her during the meeting, and how to frame my research on Latin America. After much preparation and thinking, I explained that I wanted to edit a volume on Afro-Latin America that would offer comparative perspectives with deep regional coverage focused on key themes. While the single-authored volume is the gold standard in the academy, I argued that an edited volume focused on Afro-Latin America was desperately needed. The edited volume, I argued, would not only bring together some of the leading scholars in the field but would present a nuanced narrative of some of the critical issues facing Afro-Latin America. Thus, I chose what was actually needed in the field over my own narrow ambitions. Amy agreed, and this project was set into motion. Throughout the process she has been extremely supportive, and her experience and advice have been invaluable. Also, special thanks to Shannon McCarthy, Amy's assistant, who handled a lot of the last-minute but crucial details. And special thanks to our copy editor, Kate Babbitt, for a job well done.

The second thread was my colleague John Burdick in the Maxwell School of Citizenship at Syracuse University. John Burdick needs no introduction, as he is a well-known intellectual, teacher, and activist. He has written extensively on Brazil, and his book *Blessed Anastacia: Women, Race, and Popular Christianity in*

Brazil remains a seminal work in the field. I explained to John that I had been approached by UPF to do an edited volume on Afro-Latin America and wanted him to be the co-editor. John agreed immediately, and from the start his substantial knowledge, vision, and sharp editorial eye added a great deal to the project. I could not have done it without him, and he would not have done it without me. Also, special thanks to Rogerio Caldas, the graduate assistant who proofread, organized, and compiled all of the chapters.

The third thread was the agreement with our current contributors. John and I were very lucky, as we were able to recruit an exceptionally talented group that brought well-known senior scholars together with emerging junior scholars. We sought gender balance and disciplinary range as well as scholars from the region in order to give the volume textural richness. We believe the contributors have all in some way made significant contributions to the field of Latin American Studies while addressing with sophistication many of the key debates unfolding across the black Americas. Simply put, without them it would not have been possible.

In closing, it is important to thank the Program in Latin American and Caribbean Studies (PLACA), the African American Studies Department, and the Dean's Office in the College of Arts and Sciences at Syracuse University for their generous support. Finally, I wish to thank my family in Madrid, who stood by me during the project, for their patience and understanding.

Kwame Dixon

Introduction

KWAME DIXON AND JOHN BURDICK

Over the past decade, the acceleration across Latin America of state- and social-movement-led initiatives to remedy five centuries of racial injustice has rendered increasingly urgent the need for an examination of Afro-Latin America that is geographically broad, comparative, and analytically focused. *Comparative Perspectives on Afro-Latin America* is our effort to address this need, by engaging in a single volume key intellectual and political debates currently unfolding across the black Americas. Our understanding of these debates has led us to divide the volume into three main sections: Part 1 examines the processes and politics of black identity; Part 2 analyzes black political mobilization; and Part 3 addresses state responses to that mobilization.

The volume seeks to provide a range of disciplinary perspectives, in-depth regional coverage, and cutting-edge analyses of Afro-descendant peoples in Latin America and the Caribbean. In recent scholarship, considerable attention has been paid to indigenous social mobilization across Latin America (e.g., Warren 1998; Yashar 2005; Becker 2008; Lucero 2008), and a comparable degree of attention has begun to be paid to the recent political mobilizations of the region's populations of African descent (e.g., Sawyer 2005; Dixon 2008; Mullings and Marable 2009; Pinho 2010). Informed and challenged by this scholarship, this volume investigates how the region's Afro-descendants are reconfiguring notions of citizenship, territory, race, gender, belonging, and nation.

For many years the image in the scholarship about Latin America and the Caribbean was of a region where antiracism movements were weak or nonexistent (e.g., Wright 1993; Wade 1993; Hanchard 1994). For many scholars, class rather than race explained socioeconomic inequality, racial oppression was rare, and black identities were overshadowed by powerful ideologies of racial democracy. Today, these perspectives have been fundamentally challenged by a growing awareness among scholars that a new balance of forces has emerged in the growing network of civil society organizations and social movements, and the uneven growth of state legislation to correct centuries of discrimination. Building on this surge of scholarship (Reiter and Mitchell 2010; Davis 2007; Dzidzienyo and Oboler 2005; Andrews 2004), we seek to enrich theory about race in Latin America by exploring the region's various forms of black consciousness and identity, distinct kinds and levels of political mobilization, and the nature of state responses to these. The continent is currently witnessing a sea change with regard to all of these dimensions and we have sought to capture this change by focusing on new democratic spaces opening up for Afro-descendants to construct citizenship, intensify political participation, and claim rights. Most broadly, in this volume we trace how people of African descent are making their presence felt in new ways.

What follows is a summary of the key arguments developed in the volume's three sections.

Part 1: Blackness and Cultural Difference

In order to contextualize Afro political mobilization in Latin America we begin with what "being black" means in the region. For us, "being black," "black identities" or "blacknesses" (we use the terms interchangeably) refer to bundles of ideas and meanings held by particular actors in particular societies about people who are socially defined as "black" ("*negro*") or "afro-descended" (Wade 2008a; Jackson 2005). Blackness is, variously, a form of consciousness among black people, a deliberate project to produce such consciousness, and ideas about blacks held by nonblacks (Hartigan 2010, 117). Throughout the hemisphere, consciousness and projects of blackness cluster around the ideas of common descent from Africa, a common history of enslavement and emancipation, and common experiences of social oppression (Wade 2008b), while ideas nonblacks have about black people center on racist stereotypes that articulate white fears of loss of dominance (ibid., 118). The contents of each of the categories—"Africa," slavery, emancipation, oppression, fear, and dominance—and how these concepts cluster together vary from place to place and context to context.

In order to understand the patterns of blackness specific to Latin America, we must begin by drawing a broad contrast with blackness as black consciousness as it developed in the "other" major empire of the hemisphere—that of Great Britain. Paul Gilroy's notion of the Black Atlantic (1993a, 1993b) articulated the view that the collective experiences of diaspora, enslavement, and emancipation among Africans caught up in the British system of Atlantic slavery generated a consciousness among blacks that was simultaneously infused by the values of the African homeland and the ideals of liberty, equality, and citizenship celebrated by Europeans (Gilroy 1993a; see also Parker 2009). While admiring

Gilroy's work, scholars of Spanish and Portuguese Latin America have long sensed that his model does not perfectly fit the societies they know best. The ideals of liberty, equality, and citizenship developed differently in these societies than they did in the British and French empires. This was generally the result of four forces: the anti-liberal political traditions of Spain and Portugal; the peculiarities of the transatlantic slave trade in the nineteenth century to Brazil and Spanish Latin America; the existence of organizations of slaves and ex-slaves that were approved by the Catholic Church; and the strong political identification of Afro-descended people in Brazil and Cuba with African homelands.

These are admittedly sweeping generalizations to which scholars will promptly find important exceptions. Still, as an overall pattern, we propose that rather than developing "double consciousness" as Afro-descended peoples arguably did in the British ex-colonies (Gilroy 1993a; Du Bois [1903] 2005; Parker 2009), people of African descent in the Spanish and Portuguese societies of the hemisphere evolved a distinctively hybrid set of consciousnesses—and consequently blacknesses—that we loosely gather under the rubric "Latin American blackness." It is our goal in the first section to offer accounts that illustrate these multiple forms of blackness and to begin to explain them as specific outcomes of political arrangements and power relationships. For the purposes of this volume, and without any claim to exhaustiveness, we have selected five key ways blackness has been socially constructed in Latin America: the Latin black Atlantic; the Latin black Pacific; blackness as class oppression; blackness as commodity; and blackness as white fear and fantasy. We do not regard these patterns as mutually exclusive; we are sure that in many cases one would find elements of all these patterns overlapping and interlocking. We have simply located strong examples of each pattern and argue that each reveals distinctive arrangements of social power.

Patricia Pinho's chapter offers a glimpse of the Latin black Atlantic. Here we note two major ideological features that distinguish this blackness from Gilroy's black Atlantic. First, in the Spanish and Portuguese territories that border on the Atlantic, people of African descent regularly and publicly recognized, valued, and enacted cultural practices traceable to specific locations on the African continent. The Latin black Atlantic thus involves an interest on the part of people of Nagô, Bantu, Yoruba, Kikongo, and Fon descent to engage in boundary negotiations with each other (see Nishida 2003; Pinho 2010; Matory 2005). Second, for Afro-descended people in these societies, the ideals of citizenship deriving from the British and French revolutions were looked upon more skeptically than they were by people of African descent in the British Empire. While admiring these lofty ideals, Afro-descended people living with the legacies of Spanish and Portuguese rule have tended to have less confidence that nonblack people would ever feel moved by idealism to concede genuine rights to black people. Consequently, for black people in the Latin black Atlantic, sources of political identity beyond their African ethnic groups derived not as much from the values of European citizenship as from cultural values embedded in African political and religious traditions and from struggles rooted in the rejection of domination (Scott 1985, 1990). Thus, in the Latin black Atlantic, the experience of inhabiting white-dominated societies forged, alongside specific African-based ethnic identities, both pan-African solidarities and broad-based identification with the oppressed.

Pinho's analysis of Bantu blackness in Bahia, Brazil, illustrates these dynamics. A major question here is on what ideological basis self-identified Bantu activists have come to claim the high ground of political universalism, declaring themselves to be committed not only to people of Bantu descent and not only to all people of "afro" descent but to *all* people suffering from any kind of marginalization. Here, where Gilroy may have seen the influence of European republicanism, we detect other forces. Bantu activists' position that they can remain deeply committed to Bantu identity while simultaneously expressing a strong commitment to the broader "afro" identity has been generated by two specific forces that have little to do with European republicanism: the fact that the Bahian state defines the key resources it wishes to allocate not in "Bantu" but in "afro" terms and the fact that evangelical Christians' attacks on both the Bantu and the Yoruba have thrown the two groups into each others' arms. But why do the Bantu wish to benefit the poor in general? One reason is a specific African spiritual ethos. Bantu Candomblé, Pinho tells us, teaches its adherents to *feed the spirits and each other,* a philosophical stance that nurtures a sense of identification with broader—and universal—humanity. Beyond this, Pinho argues, we must consider the specific historical experience of the Bantu: they have been marginalized not only by whites but also by blacks (i.e., the Yoruba), a fact that has made them very sensitive to marginalization, whoever experiences it. Overall, the political views of Bantu activists highlight a key feature of the Latin black Atlantic: though it is based in a core of specific African ethnicity, it is less directly influenced by European republicanism and hence develops its own political logic as a response to a mix of each group's internal cultural ethos and external challenges, oppositions, and injustices.

On the Atlantic coast, we are in the presence of well-established, dense, publicly self-identifying populations of African descent. This is not the case on the Pacific seaboard (with several key exceptions). Here, people of African descent arrived in a second migration, cut off from the demographic and cultural density of the African-descended populations of the Atlantic coast and the Caribbean. In societies where powerful assimilative ideologies of *mestizaje* and *criollismo* have left little room for recognizing African cultural survivals; where people of African descent have not settled together in large, visible concentrations that might serve as refuges of black culture; where archival and oral resources offer only the sparsest of evidence of cultural continuities to Africa; and where African-based religions have never developed—here, cultural and political activists are obliged to build blackness from the bottom up, as it were, piecing together the shards where they can find them and when necessary reaching out to non-African traditions to assist in the reconstruction.

Enter Heidi Feldman's important notion of a "black Pacific"—the cluster of ideological elements that activists have begun to identify as components of a revival of blackness in the wide swath of societies on the Pacific seaboard. Feldman suggests three ideological elements of this blackness. First, activists on the Pacific coast, distanced from African roots, turn instead to the closer, more readily available traditions of Cuba and Brazil, claiming that any cultural resemblance between these countries and those of the Pacific coast must be due to a common African source. Second, black Pacific activists posit that African cultural "memory" has been sustained not by intergenerational social learning but by being lodged within the very bodies of people of African descent. While bodily essentialism is also present in the black Atlantic, it generally occurs there alongside a belief in the mechanism of cultural transmission, a belief rendered plausible by the existence of large, visible African-descended communities. And third, the black Pacific, unable to find much in the way of African cultural resources, turns instead to the other non-European cultural resource at hand—that of indigenous Americans—and redefines it as "African." Feldman's analysis of this ideological cluster opens a new path of understanding blackness in Latin America (and elsewhere) by drawing our attention to the creative, agentive role of activists in framing identities (see McAdam and Snow 2000; Escobar 2008). Some identities—in our case, some blacknesses—require more framing work than others. A key question that the contrast between the black Atlantic and black Pacific raises is how successfully these blacknesses have resonated with their targeted constituencies at the grassroots. It would not surprise us to learn that the black Pacific has had a harder time of it. We look forward to future analyses that conduct careful, detailed comparisons of the relative capacity of the two blacknesses to mobilize constituencies.

While a common feature of Atlantic and Pacific blacknesses is their invocation of Africa, it is important to recall that such invocations are secondary among many populations of African descent in Latin America. Indeed, phenotype itself is not always a primary marker of identity among people of visibly African descent, especially when they live side by side with people of no such visible descent inside the sprawling, explosively growing cities of the continent (Streicker

1995; Burdick 2009; Ferreira da Silva 2005). The third chapter in this section, by Sujatha Fernandes, exemplifies this pattern: for many people of African descent who live in the shantytowns, peripheries, and *favelas* of the continent, the logic of "being black" is not so much about descent from Africa but about connecting phenotype to the identity of living in poverty in socially marginalized places. For the rappers Fernandes studies, the term "*negro*" connects phenotype directly to poverty and marginalization. The primary identity reference for these rappers is the streets of the barrios, places that are very racially mixed. Hence, they are reticent about embracing the term "Afro-Venezuelan," as they are less interested in invoking common descent than in drawing attention to the oppressions of the barrio that affect everyone who lives there. El Gordo and Ochoa prefer "*negro*" to "Afro-descendant" because their everyday reality is that all people suffer equally in the barrios; they wish to use a term that "open[s] the possibility of building broader solidarities among the racially diverse urban poor."

While this blackness thus has considerable political potential, Fernandes challenges us to see its limitations. While rappers may denounce the misery of the barrios, their analysis of this misery and what is to be done about it often remains bound to the realm of the immediate. This is a blackness that is class-oriented and place-based but is immersed in the politics of "voice" and "experience." For the rappers Fernandes describes, like rappers in other Latin American societies (see Burdick 2009; Pardue 2004, 2008), the solutions often remain individual—altering the company one keeps, renouncing drugs, developing inner peace—while collective solutions remain vague, abstract, and distant. Venezuelan rappers are thus carving their own hybrid path of blackness: uninterested in black nationalist or pan-African identity politics and unprepared for structural or class analysis, they gravitate to NGO projects based in poor neighborhoods, celebrating voice and looking for a shred of opportunity that might lead to upward mobility.

A very different pattern may be found in contexts where blackness has been discovered as a commodity in the international tourism circuit. In such places (e.g., Pinho 2010; Wade 2005) blackness is passing through a process of complex public redefinition, and the components of it that receive publicity, legitimacy, and authorization are the ones that developers and investors believe will bring maximum market share and minimum controversy. In contexts with robust preexisting black communities, the effort to commoditize blackness leads to a complex compromise between forces (see Collins 2007 for Brazil), but in places with relatively weak preexisting black communities, the forces of commodification enjoy the upper hand. Mexico is a case in point. Throughout Mexican history, the massive availability of indigenous labor meant that African slaves in Mexico never grew very numerous or influential. Thus, Mexico's nationalist ideology of *mestizaje* could keep blackness invisible (Vinson 2009), and when migrants from the Caribbean in the twentieth century created an "Afro" region along Mexico's Caribbean coast that was impossible to ignore, white elites promptly characterized it as "non-Mexican." Then the power of commoditization entered the scene. The discovery of Mexico's coastal "Afro" population as a legitimate—though, to be sure, distinctly *regional*—identity took off in the 1990s, when investors, boosters, and government officials found in it the possibility of attracting tourists. As Angela Castañeda argues in her contribution, the blackness offered to tourists on the Vera Cruz coast is a reassuring, unthreatening one: in it the spirituality of Santería has been sanitized of its controversial aspects such as animal sacrifice and spirit possession and reduced to dance, beads, and colorful costumes.

Yet the pattern of commodifying blackness at work in Vera Cruz is a complex one, in which dialectical forces are working themselves out. The revalorization of blackness as a commodity does not necessarily contradict nationalist ideologies of *mestizaje* (Wade 2008c), but it can, by opening up new discursive spaces for reflection, lead to new identities that may not fit neatly into authorized blackness. A glimpse of this hybridity (Escobar 1998; Canclini 1995) is suggested by Castañeda's argument that opening up Caribbean blackness for public consumption unleashed a rediscovery of Mexico's African past, leading the Vera Cruz community of Yanga to begin celebrating its history as a runaway slave community. While appealing to tourists, this narrative may also lead to increased recognition of the presence of Africans in Mexico.

So far we have been considering blackness as black consciousness, but we also need to understand what whites think about people of African descent (cf. Bonilla Silva 2003; Caldwell 2007). Here the patterns are complex: whites' ideas about blacks in Latin America vary according to the political circumstances of each country—the balance of power between whites and blacks, how fearful whites feel about losing their power, and the extent to which whites can fit people of African descent into their nation-building projects and ideologies (Applebaum, Macpherson, and Rosemblatt 2007; Thomas 2004; Williams 1993). Whites' images of black slaves in nineteenth-century Cuba, for example, as analyzed by Elizabeth Morán through the paintings of Victor Landaluze, were shaped by slaveholders' nervous desire to reassure themselves that faced with slaves' growing numbers and organization, they had little to fear from them. That is why, Morán argues, the paintings show blacks as childlike, effeminate, sexualized, and unworthy of being taken seriously. In the nineteenth century, Cuban whites had no clear long-term vision of their nation that could incorporate people of African descent as citizens, due, in part, to white Cubans' inability to trust mulattos: the experience of the Haitian Revolution, which was led by mulattos, was simply too close and too raw. The experience of Brazil offers an instructive contrast. In the 1920s, Brazilian middle-class whites had come to feel quite unthreatened by Afro-Brazilians, having cowed them into submission by the massive importation of European labor. Indeed, by the 1920s Brazil's middle-class whites had come to see themselves as influential on the world stage. They thus began to rebel against European insinuations that miscegenation rendered them and their nation inferior (Skidmore 1993) and began instead to construct images of Afro-Brazilians (and their blood) as carriers of a rich and meritorious culture at the heart of a distinctive national identity independent of Europe (Vianna 1999).

But we must always be mindful of the contradictory dialectics of history. Cuban whites' images of blacks were undoubtedly part of the process of sustaining white supremacy, but they were also, ironically, the cause of constant white stress and, ultimately, political fragility. Cuban whites' self-affirming fantasies undoubtedly allowed them to achieve psychological calm in the face of a restless black population, yet the fantastic images of blacks white ideologues such as Landaluze created ensured that the elite remained dangerously ignorant of blacks' true sentiments. This ignorance led many white Cubans to assume that little harm to their interests could be done by allowing slaves to own property and perform their religious rituals. By not taking African ritual seriously and by failing to understand how landholding increased black power, white Cubans destined themselves to generation after generation of challenge from below and to at least one near-revolution. In contrast, by conceding, at least rhetorically, that people of African descent had helped build the nation and that their culture helped enrich it, Brazilian whites forged a national ideology to which generation after generation of Brazilian blacks have consented. Blackness in the white Latin American imagination, while serving in one way or another to uphold white supremacy, does so in ways that vary according to differing degrees of whites' security in their social power.

Part 2: Afro Social Movements and Political Mobilization

The second section of the volume situates Afro mobilization and grassroots protests within the broader frame of Latin American social movements. Over the past two decades there has been a sharp uptick in social movements organized at the grassroots across the Americas. These movements—as new formulations of activism—contest the region's political and economic systems and challenge narrowly constructed definitions of citizenship, democracy, and participation. As they contest power and policy these mobilizations call into question traditional rule by the dominant classes and the politicians who enable it (Vanden

2003). These social actors and the networks they create are commonly referred to as new social movements because they seek to define a new relation to the formal realm by fundamentally reworking relations of power (Stahler-Sholk, Vanden, and Kuecker 2008, 2). However, in sharp contrast to traditional guerilla movements or expressions of the electoral left in Latin America, new social movements are not organized to seize power (ibid., 12). Their main objective is to put maximum pressure on the state in order to extract specific demands. New social movements have the following characteristics: 1) a tendency to seek autonomy from conventional/hierarchical political institutions; 2) horizontal and participatory decision making; and 3) a quest for solidarity derived from notions of social justice linked to shared identities such as race, ethnicity, and/or gender (Hellman 1995).

Many new social movements (hereafter referred to as social movements) originate in civil society, nongovernmental organizations, and from "below." And while many social movements promote agendas of social justice, not all social movements are progressive. What is absent from the current discussion of social movements in Latin America is the role played by Afro social movements and their struggles to address centuries of neglect and social discrimination. This volume places Afro social movements in the larger context of these "new" social movements, and by doing so, fills a gap in the social movement literature.

Afro-Latin mobilizations for self-defense and against oppression in Latin America and the Caribbean have a long history, including maroon communities during slavery, the Haitian Revolution, the slave revolts in Bahia in 1835, and the Cuban Independent Party of Color (1908), to name only a few (Safa 1998). At times, blacks in Latin America formed their own independent formations such as runaway slave communities, black militias, religious confraternities and sodalities, and mutual aid societies. At other times, they forged tactical alliances with whites, Indians, and mestizos to create multiracial movements that had a profound effect on the region. The independence armies, the national liberal parties of the 1800s and early 1900s, the labor unions of the same period, and the popular parties of the mid-1900s were all broad-based interethnic coalitions that were supported and sustained by Afro-Latin Americans (Andrew 2004, 8).

Today in Latin America and the Caribbean vibrant Afro social movements are on the rise. Throughout the Americas black social movement groups are using increasingly sophisticated strategies and tactics to challenge racial and gender inequality. A new landscape has emerged as blacks are demanding more political and cultural space to advance social, cultural, and economic rights and are simultaneously articulating oppositional racial discourses (Dixon 2008). Clearly, more works focused on Afro-Latin social movements that explore the implications of race, gender, citizenship, and democracy are urgently needed.

Equally important are works rooted in black feminist perspectives that explore the cultural politics in the region (Dixon 2008).

Part 2 analyzes black political mobilization in three countries (Colombia, Ecuador, and Brazil) with distinct social and political histories. The reader should pay close attention to the process of citizenship construction and the ways social movements in these countries claim the right to full and equal citizenship. Citizenship construction is the process by which the excluded build a legal and social framework that recognizes and accepts them, transforming them from noncitizens into citizens. This political transformation is rooted in concepts such as cultural citizenship, new citizenship, and active citizenship, each of which offer legitimation to claims of rights, space, and belonging in the dominant society. By challenging racialized, gendered, and class structures and by developing strategies of empowerment, Afro social movements are expanding citizenship and opening new democratic possibilities. Each essay situates Afro movements within local, regional, or transnational networks.

Peter Wade's and Bettina Ng'weno's essays explore struggles for land rights in Colombia. These two chapters shed light on the how Afro-Colombians are negotiating collective rights and repositioning black identity within the new language of multiculturalism and pluralism. Wade highlights the constitutional reforms of the 1990s and current Afro-Colombian mobilization. He points out that organizing in Cali and elsewhere evolved through dense and sometimes contradictory ideological networks and that violence on the Pacific coast may be changing the meaning of Afro-Colombianness. He examines why the Colombian government is interested in opening up black landholding and discovers that this has to do with the routinization of relations with the state, delimitation of boundaries, taxation, and transnational pressures.

Along the same lines, Bettina Ng'weno examines how Afro-Colombians are claiming lands under the constitutional reforms of the 1990s and in light of newly created social spaces. She argues that the practices and claims of Afro-Colombians and Afro-Latin Americans profoundly challenge what it means to be a citizen in Latin America. According to Ng'weno, Afro-Colombians moved from legally invisible silenced racial groups to legally visible ethnic groups. She argues that the process of claiming territory is a form of citizenship negotiation and affirmation because Afro communities must negotiate new political relations with other ethnic groups (indigenous), economic interests (mining, coffee), and governments (local, regional, national, and transnational). Ng'weno points out that these claims open up new spaces for politics in a variety of ways. Silenced, invisible, and marginalized as black, rural, and poor, claimants are struggling for meaningful political participation and government recognition. Territories are essential for achieving this recognition.

Here we believe it may be useful to think back to the volume's first section and draw a theoretical connection between the political dynamics of black identity in the black Pacific, and the trajectories of black mobilizations in Colombia. We have suggested that black identities on the Pacific coast tend to be more readily hybrid and receptive to synthesis with indigenous identity. Seizing upon the issue of land as a basis for mobilization has multiple origins, yet clearly its plausibility in Colombia must be understood in the context of a blackness that is ready to see a deep commonality, even overlap, with indigenous peoples. Recent work among *quilombos* in Brazil (French 2009) suggests that Afro-Brazilians face a steeper uphill ideological battle in making claims modeled on indigenous land rights.

On the other hand, in contrast to Brazil and Cuba, people of the black Pacific have tended not to base their common identity on religious or spiritual grounds. One consequence of this may be a certain fragility of black mobilization when faced with co-optation and the divide-and-conquer tactics of the nonblack political system. These tensions are well illustrated in the chapters on Afro-Ecuador. Ollie Johnson's and Jean Rahier's chapters focus our attention on Ecuador's burgeoning black social movements. In complementary ways Johnson and Rahier illustrate some of the deep problems faced by Afro groups as they seek to frame issues of social discrimination in the context of newly elaborated constitutions. In 1998 Ecuador adopted its first multicultural constitution, which for the first time awarded collective rights to indigenous peoples and, in a less obvious way, to Afro-Ecuadorians.

Ollie Johnson's piece situates Afro-Ecuadorian social movements within the broader frame of Ecuadorian national politics and indigenous social movements. Unlike the traditional narrative where the movements triumph at the end of the day, Johnson's piece highlights the sharp tensions, organizational problems, and ideological issues facing Afro-Ecuadorian social groups. In his view, despite many years of hard work, Afro-Ecuadorians have not been able to create effective social movements and have not been able to mobilize adequate resources to give themselves substantial power. Rahier examines the process leading to Ecuador's multicultural Constitution of 2008. He provides a close textual reading of this new constitution and how it inscribes Afro-Ecuadorians into Ecuador's national identity. Rahier and Johnson demonstrate that these new social spaces for Afro-Ecuadorian organization and mobilization must be placed in the context of international pressures placed on the Ecuadorian state by donor agencies.

Turning to Brazil, we are in the presence of a rather different style of political mobilization. Here, we witness the convergence of blackness as class with the Latin black Atlantic, articulated with gender politics. Keisha-Khan Perry turns our attention to the urban struggles over land rights—but struggles driven by a rather different conception of land—among black grassroots activists led mainly by women in Salvador, Bahia (Brazil). Black movements in Brazil have struggled since the early 1980s to influence state policies affecting black women's lives. Keisha-Khan Perry builds a gendered analysis of Afro women's grassroots urban movements that articulate racial and class-based claims to urban space. In her examination of black women activists' resistance to displacement, eviction, and uneven urbanization practices, Perry shows how black urban spaces in Salvador are racialized and gendered terrains of domination and how black women's resistance unites class, space, and gender politics. We suggest that black women's movements in Salvador neatly illustrate the power of black mobilizations that are intersectional—those that synthesize a black identity rooted in class and gender, are invigorated by spirituality, and are concretely organized around high-stakes issues of urban space.

Part 3: State Responses

The final section of the volume is dedicated to the analysis of state responses to Afro-descendants' pressures from above and below for greater social and political inclusion and for cultural recognition. In the 1990s many Latin American states implemented multicultural citizenship reforms that established collective rights for indigenous and Afro communities. It is generally recognized that indigenous collective rights (land, language, cultural identity) are more comprehensive than those of Afro-descendants (Hooker 2005). However, despite the differences in the scope and range of rights afforded, Afro-descendants have been granted an impressive set of social rights that include collective land titles, cultural recognition, affirmative action measures, and antidiscrimination laws.

Responding to transnational pressures from above (multilateral agencies) and domestic pressures from below (social movements), Latin American states over the last decade have been pushed from the notion of a homogenized *mestizo* identity to various forms of multiculturalism. How are multicultural polices being implemented? Does multiculturalism mean "more equal," and if so, in what way? The pieces in this section suggest that even when new laws are being fashioned in response to antiracist pressure, a great deal of work remains to be done to ensure that law translates into the building of antiracist societies. As recent work on Brazil's major antiracist policy initiatives suggests (Htun 2004), and as Wade has suggested for Colombia (Wade 2009; cf. Hale 2005), the motivations of the state in framing and implementing antiracism policies may have more to do with neutralizing radical political tendencies, retaining and extending state control, and scoring public relations points domestically and internationally than with seeking to fundamentally challenge the privilege and supremacy of white/mixed populations. Mindful of these cautions, the last section of the book conceptualizes the terrain of state action as a contradictory one, in which state initiatives simultaneously open up new spaces from which to challenge white/mixed supremacy while actually working in more or less visible ways to reinscribe it.

Judith Morrison's essay explores how Afro-descended populations have established national and regional organizations to combat discrimination. She emphasizes the role of civil society organizations and their unyielding pressure on the state and the role of regional and transnational organizing networks while highlighting some of the specific legislation enacted in several countries. It is an important synoptic essay that provides a continent-wide context for assessing the responses of different states in the region to these pressures.

Juliet Hooker's chapter analyzes how Afro-descendant Creoles in Nicaragua are currently reimagining their collective identities in the context of multicultural polices that extend collective rights to indigenous and Afro peoples. She examines the process of negotiation as English-speaking Creoles inscribe their identities within the boundaries of Nicaragua's national identity, which is constructed as overwhelmingly *mestizo* or Indo-Hispanic. She traces the shifting conceptions of Creole identity in relation to the changes in the Nicaraguan model of multiculturalism.

Shane Greene's chapter examines these questions in Peru, by discussing how Peruvian civil servants, in the wake of a new multicultural Constitution, continue to articulate the intersection of history and race in ways that were hegemonic before the new Constitution. Greene analyzes how Peruvian government officials have responded to Afro-Peruvians' race-based claims by striving to weaken them. He points out that even as the Peruvian Constitution declares a new day in indigenous and Afro-Peruvian rights, government officials perpetuate hackneyed ideas of "the Inca" as defining Peruvian national identity. At the same time, this discourse complicates the narrative for Afro-Peruvians who are portrayed in it as failing to contribute to Peru's national civilization.

Antônio Guimarães's piece argues that the major policy positions on race that have been influential in Brazil since the 1920s reflect changing national contexts, the influence of European and North American political thought, and the impact of anti-racist and social activism. He places Brazil's current heated policy discussion about affirmative action in historical perspective, revealing how long-existing theoretical debates on race, racial identity, and racial inequality are once again defining sides in a major political debate.

But not all the societies of the hemisphere have been touched by the influence of antiracist organizing and mobilization. The Dominican Republic is one glaring example. As a way of reminding the reader just how much remains to be done, we end the book with an essay on the continuing policy and legal injustices to which the Haitian population of the Dominican Republic are subjected. Ernesto Sagás' chapter examines the current official status of Afro-Dominicans and Haitian immigrants and the ways that social whiteness is inscribed in the Dominican Republic through law and policy.

The contributors to this volume all address the fluid interplay of culture and politics. They demonstrate how "blackness" is constructed with a specific set of cultural, social, and political meanings. The texture and range as well as the contradictions of blackness are highlighted: from "Bantu-ness" as a specific form of black consciousness in Brazil to the "black Pacific," where Afro-descendants in Peru reinterpret indigenous cultural forms as African, to hip-hop in Venezuela as a critique of neoliberal policies, to social movements in Colombia, Ecuador, and Nicaragua. Blackness across the Americas is clearly a social construction with various meanings, class-based representations, gendered structures, and spiritual significances. Each chapter presents Afro-Latin populations as history-making agents of social change. It is against this backdrop that students and activists may be able to see the current struggles of Afro-Latin Americans through a new lens and appreciate how they are based in different blacknesses that challenge outdated notions of national identity, forge new forms of democratic participation, and grapple with the contradictions of states that continue to struggle to protect the interests of white or mixed elites. The narrative we uncover here is neither linear nor simple; it is rather a cluster of narratives, in which people of African descent continue to find new ways to struggle and increase their capacity to shape their own destinies across the hemisphere.

Bibliography

Andrews, George Reid. 2004. *Afro Latin Americans Today*. New York: Cambridge University Press.

Applebaum, Nancy, Anne S. Macpherson, and Karin Rosemblatt, eds. 2007. *Race and Nation in Modern Latin America*. Chapel Hill: University of North Carolina Press.

Becker, Marc. 2008. *Indians and Leftists in the Making of Ecuador's Modern Indigenous Movements*. Durham, N.C.: Duke University Press.

Bonilla Silva, Eduardo. 2003. *Racism without Racists: Color-Blind Racism and the Persistence of Racial Inequality in the United States*. Lanham, Md.: Rowman and Littlefield.

Burdick, John. 2009. "The Singing Voice and Racial Politics on the Brazilian Evangelical Music Scene." *Latin American Music Review* 30 (1): 25–55.

Caldwell, Lia Lilly. 2007. *Negras in Brazil: Re-Envisioning Black Women, Citizenship, and the Politics of Identity*. New Brunswick, N.J.: Rutgers University Press.

Canclini, Nestor. 1995. *Hybrid Cultures: Strategies for Entering and Leaving Modernity*. Minneapolis: University of Minnesota Press.

Collins, John. 2007. "The Sounds of Tradition: Arbitrariness and Agency in a Brazilian Cultural Heritage Center." *Ethnos* 72 (3): 383–407.

Davis, Darien, ed. 2007. *Beyond Slavery: The Multi-Layered Legacy of Slavery in Latin America and the Caribbean.* Lanham, Md.: Rowman and Littlefield.

Dixon, Kwame. 2008. "Afro-Colombian Transnational Social Movements." In *Latin American Social Movements in the Twenty-First Century: Resistance Power, and Democracy,* ed. Richard Stahler-Sholk, Harry Vanden, and Glen David Kuecker, 181–195. Lanham, Md.: Rowman and Littlefield.

Du Bois, W. E. B. [1903] 2005. *The Souls of Black Folk.* New York: Simon and Schuster.

Dzidzienyo, Anani, and Suzanne Oboler, eds. 2005. *Neither Enemies nor Friends: Latinos, Blacks, Afro-Latinos.* New York: Palgrave Macmillan.

Escobar, Arturo, ed. 1998. *Cultures of Politics, Politics of Cultures: Re-Visioning Latin American Social Movements.* New York: Westview.

———. 2008. *Territories of Difference: Place, Movements, Life, Redes.* Durham, N.C.: Duke University Press.

Ferreira da Silva, Denise. 2005. "'Bahia Pêlo Negro': Can the Subaltern (Subject of Raciality) Speak?" *Ethnicities* 5 (3): 321–342.

French, Jan Hoffman. 2009. *Becoming Black or Indian in Brazil's Northeast.* Chapel Hill: University of North Carolina Press.

Gilroy, Paul. 1993a. *The Black Atlantic.* Cambridge: Harvard University Press.

———. 1993b. *Small Acts: Thoughts on the Politics of Black Cultures.* London: Serpent's Tail.

Hale, Charles. 2005. "Neoliberal Multiculturalism: The Remaking of Cultural Rights and Racial Dominance in Central America." *PoLAR: Political and Legal Anthropology Review* 28 (1): 10–28.

Hanchard, Michael. 1994. *Orpheus and Power: The Movimento Negro of Rio de Janeiro and São Paulo, Brazil, 1945–1988.* Princeton, N.J.: Princeton University Press.

Hartigan, John. 2010. *Race in the 21st Century: Ethnographic Approaches.* New York: Oxford University Press.

Hellman, Judith. 1995. "The Riddle of New Social Movements: Who They Are and What They Do." In *Capital, Power, and Inequality in Latin America,* ed. Sandor Halebsky and Richard L. Harris, 165–183. Boulder, Colo.: Westview Press.

Hooker, Juliet. 2005. "Indigenous Inclusion/Black Exclusion: Race, Ethnicity, and Multicultural Citizenship in Latin America." *Journal of Latin American Studies* 37 (2): 285–310.

Htun, Mala. 2004. "From 'Racial Democracy' to Affirmative Action: Changing State Policy on Race in Brazil." *Latin American Research Review* 39 (1): 60–89.

Jackson, John L. 2005. *Real Black: Adventures in Racial Sincerity.* Chicago: University of Chicago Press.

Lucero, José Antonio. 2008. *Struggles of Voice: The Politics of Indigenous Representation in the Andes.* Pittsburgh, Pa.: University of Pittsburgh Press.

Matory, James Lorand. 2005. *Black Atlantic Religion: Tradition, Transnationalism, and Matriarchy in the Afro-Brazilian Candomblé.* Princeton, N.J.: Princeton University Press.

McAdam, Doug, and David Snow, eds. 2000. *Readings on Social Movements: Origins, Dynamics and Outcomes.* Oxford: Oxford University Press.

Mullings, Leith, and Manning Marable, eds. 2009. *New Social Movements in the African Diaspora: Challenging Global Apartheid.* New York: Palgrave.

Nishida, Mieko. 2003. *Slavery and Identity: Ethnicity, Gender, and Race in Salvador, Brazil, 1808–1888*. Bloomington: Indiana University Press.

Pardue, Derek. 2004. "Putting *Mano* to Music: The Mediation of Blackness in Brazilian Rap." *Ethnomusicology Forum* 13 (2): 253–286.

———. 2008. *Ideologies of Marginality in Brazilian Hip Hop*. New York: Palgrave Macmillan.

Parker, Christopher. 2009. *Fighting for Democracy*. Princeton, N.J.: Princeton University Press.

Pinho, Patricia. 2010. *Mama Africa: Reinventing Blackness in Bahia*. Durham, N.C.: Duke University Press.

Reiter, Bernd, and Gladys Mitchell, eds. 2010. *Brazil's New Racial Politics*. London: Lynne Rienner.

Safa, Helen. 1998. "Race and National Identity in the Americas." *Latin American Perspectives* 25 (3): 3–20.

Sawyer, Mark Q. 2005. *Racial Politics in Post-Revolutionary Cuba*. New York: Cambridge University Press.

Scott, James. 1985. *Weapons of the Weak: Everyday Forms of Peasant Resistance*. New Haven, Conn.: Yale University Press.

———. 1990. *Domination and the Arts of Resistance: Hidden Transcripts*. New Haven, Conn.: Yale University Press.

Skidmore, Thomas. 1993. *Black into White: Race and Nationality in Brazilian Thought*. Durham, N.C.: Duke University Press.

Stahler-Sholk, Richard, Harry Vanden, and Glen David Kuecker, eds. 2008. *Latin American Social Movements in the Twenty-First Century: Resistance, Power, and Democracy*. Lanham, Md.: Rowman and Littlefield.

Streicker, Joel. 1995. "Policing Boundaries: Race, Class, and Gender in Cartagena, Colombia." *American Ethnologist* 22 (1): 54–74.

Thomas, Deborah. 2004. *Modern Blackness: Nationalism, Globalization, and the Politics of Culture in Jamaica*. Durham, N.C.: Duke University Press.

Vanden, Harry E. 2003. "Globalization in a Time of Neo-Liberalism: Politicized Social Movements and the Latin American Response." *Journal of Developing Societies* 19 (2–3): 308–333.

Vianna, Hermano. 1999. *The Mystery of Samba: Popular Music and National Identity in Brazil*. Chapel Hill: University of North Carolina Press.

Vinson, Ben. 2009. *Black Mexico: Race and Society from Colonial to Modern Times*. Albuquerque: University of New Mexico Press.

Wade, Peter. 1993. *Blackness and Race Mixture: The Dynamics of Racial Identity in Colombia*. Baltimore, Md.: Johns Hopkins University Press.

———. 2005. "Rethinking *Mestizaje*: Ideology and Lived Experience." *Journal of Latin American Studies* 37: 239–257.

———. 2008a. "African Diaspora and Colombian Popular Music in the Twentieth Century." *Black Music Research Journal* 28 (2): 41–56.

———. 2008b. "Población negra y la cuestión identitaria en América Latina." *Universitas Humanística* 65: 117–137.

———, ed. 2008c. *Raza, etnicidad y sexualidades: Ciudadanía y multiculturalismo en América latina*. Bogotá: Universidad Nacional de Colombia.

———. 2009. "Defining Blackness in Colombia." *Journal de la Société des Américanistes* 95 (1): 37.

Warren, Kay B. 1998. *Indigenous Movements and Their Critics*. Princeton, N.J.: Princeton University Press.

Williams, Brackette. 1993. *Stains on My Name, War in My Veins: Guyana and the Politics of Cultural Struggle.* Durham, N.C.: Duke University Press.

Wright, Winthrop. 1993. *Cafe con Leche: Race, Class, and National Image in Venezuela.* Austin: University of Texas Press.

Yashar, Deborah. 2005. *Contesting Citizenship in Latin America: The Rise of Indigenous Movements and the Postliberal Challenge.* Cambridge: Cambridge University Press.

PART
I

Blackness and Cultural Difference

I

Nurturing Bantu Africanness in Bahia

PATRICIA DE SANTANA PINHO

Food became a very important symbol in this moment of our journey. The cosmo-
vision of African origin establishes a transcendental relationship with food. In this
manner, *food was the motivating instrument in the struggle for citizenship* and in the continuity of steps in the direction of the neediest in the neighborhood, independently
of religion, ethnicity/race, personality.

"ACBANTU e Rede Kôdya: Breve Balanço das Atividades,"
NKAANDA, June 29, 2007, 2, emphasis in the original.

Food is at the heart of Candomblé, a religion that envisions the world as a "giant
mouth" where "everything and everyone eats" (Lody 1995, 65, quoted in Johnson
2002, 36). Food is offered in rituals to the gods and goddesses both in temples
and at natural sites that correspond to their essences. Food is also handed out in
abundance to devotees and visitors during the sacred festivals of any Candomblé
terreiro.[1] Grounded in the logic that food distribution is central to Candomblé,
the Cultural Association for the Preservation of Bantu Heritage (ACBANTU)
persuaded the Brazilian federal government that Candomblé *terreiros* should
become key participants in Fome Zero, the highly successful Zero Hunger program implemented by the Lula administration to reduce starvation in one of the
world's most unequal countries.[2] In 2003, approximately 46 million of Brazil's
approximately 170 million people (Belik and Del Grossi 2003) were living in a
situation of food insecurity.[3] As a partner of the Zero Hunger program since
2004, ACBANTU has distributed over a thousand tons of beans, rice, corn,
manioc flour, sugar, and other foods received monthly from the federal government, food that has benefited over 30,000 families in the greater Salvador area.[4]

Feeding the hungry has been one of ACBANTU's major purposes since
its creation in December 2000. The association views this task as twofold. On
the one hand is the concrete need to reduce famine by distributing food to the
malnourished. On the other it is about filling another kind of void besides the

empty bellies of individuals: the widespread unawareness of the Bantu presence in Brazil. Thus, to feed the hungry is also a metaphor for the group's goals of informing, teaching, and raising awareness about *other* black identities that have been marginalized in Brazilian history and society.

This chapter examines the reconstruction of Bantu identity and the reinvention of the meanings of Bantu culture in Bahia in the last decade. This is not a historical analysis of the Bantu peoples in Brazil, nor is it strictly an anthropological approach to studying black culture. Employing cultural studies theories, I shed light on discourses about and representations of Bantu tradition by focusing specifically on the work carried out by ACBANTU.[5] My purpose here is not to examine the "accuracy" of the term Bantu or its "loyalty" to African origins. Instead, I seek to demonstrate how the current reinvention of Bantu culture has served to empower a segment of the Afro-Brazilian population. Stemming from Candomblé *terreiros* yet extending beyond the realm of religion, a recent employment of the term Bantu has taken place in Brazil, more specifically in Bahia, where *capoeira* schools, *quilombos* (settlements of runaway slaves), and music and dance groups have joined forces with several Candomblé *terreiros* in order to celebrate their Bantu origin in a context dominated by the glorification of Yoruba culture, language, and religion. I look at the discourses and representations produced at the heart of ACBANTU as permeated by the material circumstances of the daily lives of the people with whom the association works and for whom it seeks social inclusion. More than intimately connected realms, the material and the symbolic constitute one and the same reality in the work of ACBANTU.

Bantu Africanness in Bahia

The terms "Bantu" or "Yoruba" are not meant here to be precise designations of identity groups on the African continent or in the Americas. Both terms have been used to refer to groups that spoke the same language or languages within the same linguistic family. Scholars of slavery and black culture in Brazil divided the enslaved African peoples brought to the country into two main generic designations: Bantu and Sudanese (Freyre 1990; Rodrigues 1932 and 1935; Ramos 1940, among others). According to this division, the Bantu include Central and Southwestern African groups that speak "Bantu languages," a broad label that includes over 400 dialects considered to share a linguistic core.[6] Among these languages, Kimbundo and Kikoongo were the ones that lent the greatest number of words to the *terreiros* of Bantu origin and to the Portuguese language spoken in Brazil. The label Sudanese was used to define groups that inhabited the regions known today as the countries of Sudan, Nigeria, Benin, Togo, and

Ghana. The Yoruba were considered to be a subgroup of the Sudanese, but the two terms gradually began to be used interchangeably.

Although speakers of a same language might have shared roughly similar religious and cultural traditions, they did not see themselves as sharing a common identity. The labels "Bantu" and "Yoruba" did not start to become associated with identity groups until members of these groups experienced slavery in the Americas. Because it brought together and mixed peoples of different cultural backgrounds, one of the consequences of slavery was that the enslaved and their descendants reorganized themselves through new forms of identification. According to Matory (2005, 9), "The late 18th and 19th centuries were in fact a time when both American territorial units (such as Brazil, Cuba, and British colonial North America) and transoceanically dispersed black ethnic groups (such as the Nagô, Jeje, Angola, and Congo) were becoming 'nations' for themselves." Thus, Bantu and Yoruba, as dealt with in this chapter, refer to identities that emerged in the New World and, to a great extent, in contrast to one another. In Brazil, this distinction has played out most significantly among the *terreiros* of Candomblé and the classification of *terreiros* into nations.[7]

Candomblé is the most well-known of the Afro-Brazilian religions. Candomblé *terreiros* have historically functioned as sites of black resistance, mobilization, and mutual aid practices for the enslaved and their descendants. While there is great diversity among the different *terreiros* in terms of doctrine, rituals, and liturgy, there is undeniably a set of "vectors of signification" that allow for intelligibility and communication among Candomblé practitioners (Johnson 2002, 35). These key vectors include the worshipping of the Orixás (a Yoruba term that roughly corresponds to the Nkisi among the Bantus); the belief in *axé*, the transforming power of the Orixás; and the classification of the *terreiros* into "nations."

While the concept of African "nations" was previously used to indicate a specific "ethnic origin" of a particular Candomblé, the term gradually became used to claim a social identity constructed within the *terreiro*. "African nation" today has a more political than theological meaning (Lima 1976). Among the most well-known nations of Candomblé are Jeje (Ewe-Fon), Angola (Bantu), and Nagô and Ketu (both Yoruba). "Nagô" is a generic designation given in Brazil to the Yoruba-speaking African groups that came from the former nation of Dahomey and from southern Nigeria (Dantas 1988, 34).[8] Also centered on language, the term "Bantu" (or Banto) was employed to designate the enslaved who spoke Bantu languages. Bantu *terreiros* in Brazil include the "nations" of Bantu/Congo, Angola, and Amburaxó. In other parts of Latin America, such as in Cuba, "Congo" roughly corresponds to what has been defined as "Bantu" in Brazil.

Several scholars have highlighted the hegemonic role that Yoruba cultural expressions attained in the classification of "things African" in Brazil (Dantas 1988; Capone 2004, Matory 2005, among others). Since the early twentieth century, the religion of Candomblé has had great importance in the invention of the Brazilian nation. It is not a coincidence that this process was intensified as Brazil began to be "narrated" (Bhabha 1990) as a racial democracy, in which cultural elements from Africa and Portugal allegedly blended with those of the indigenous populations to form Brazilian *mestiçagem*.[9] But if the colors, symbols, and iconic beauty of Candomblé were borrowed to embellish this national narrative, these elements were not drawn from just any kind of Candomblé. The Nagô (Yoruba) nation was chosen to represent Brazil's Africanness to the detriment of other Candomblé nations.

Scholars and politicians played an important role in establishing the notion that Yoruba culture was superior to other African cultures in Brazil. Several reasons account for this hierarchy that places the Yoruba—interchangeably referred to as Nagô or Sudanese—at the top and the Bantu (or Angola) at the bottom. Among these reasons are the residues of evolutionist theories among academics who studied Afro-Brazilian religions (see especially Rodrigues 1932, 1935); the arrival of a large number of Yoruba-speaking enslaved Africans in the final period of the slave trade and their residency in predominantly urban areas (see Verger 1987); and the negotiations that later took place between religious leaders and anthropologists and politicians. Yoruba priests played a special role in establishing the supremacy of their religion, supported, according to Matory (2005), by their travels between Bahia and West Africa and their competency in the English language.

To justify Yoruba superiority, scholars described Bantu groups as "backward" in comparison to the more "advanced" Yoruba. Religious, linguistic, and even aesthetic features were used in this hierarchy that devalued and stigmatized Bantu cultures. Roger Bastide (1971, 1978), Gilberto Freyre (1990), Pierre Verger (1987), Juana Elbein dos Santos (1976), Lydia Cabrera (1986), and Fernando Ortiz ([1951] 1981) were among the most influential scholars who contributed to the belief in Yoruba superiority in Latin America. Freyre directly associated Yoruba culture with a greater capacity for political organization among the Sudanese (Yoruba): "Unlike the Bantu, a sweeter and more adjustable people, the Sudanese slave or slave of Sudanese origin, the most conscious [among all slaves] of the value of his culture and, because of that, the most insubordinate . . . proved his capacity of organizing against the whites" (1990, 73).[10] Also contributing to the establishment of this hierarchy, although in another site of the African diaspora, was eminent Cuban anthropologist Fernando Ortiz. Based on an evolutionist notion that as blacks "evolved" they would leave behind their belief in magic, Ortiz stated that "the Congo [Bantu] are the least sophisticated religious rites in Cuba. . . . Those blacks that in Cuba are called 'lucumís' [Yoruba] have a more elevated religion than the Congo, and their rituals are more distant from magic" (Ortiz [1951] 1981, 168, 170).[11]

In Brazil, the responsibility of scholars for disseminating the idea of Yoruba superiority should be understood in connection to the role played by Candomblé priests and priestesses. Unlike Matory, who argues that recent scholarship on the topic has overlooked or denied the agency of Afro-Brazilian clerics, I argue that several authors have in fact highlighted the processes of negotiation that took place between the different social actors involved. Beatriz Góis Dantas (1988), for instance, does not argue that Nagô religion was reinvented according to the arbitrary standards of white patrons, nor does she suggest that the notion of "Nagô purity" was applied to specific *terreiros* based only on scholars' definition of Africanness, as Matory claims (Matory 2005, 45). Dantas shows that *alliances* between Candomblé leaders, on one hand, and politicians and anthropologists, on the other, were the main reason for the resignification of Candomblé as symbolically important for the Brazilian nation and for the superior status the Yoruba acquired.

As a consequence of this hierarchy, Bantu-based Candomblés have suffered double marginalization: first, for being composed of black individuals in a society marked by a preference for whiteness and *mestiçagem*, and second, for being stigmatized as the least developed among black groups. These demeaning representations have negatively affected Bantu-based groups, weakening their capacity for political articulation and action in the public sphere. Having frequently lacked the support of intellectuals, politicians, and other members of the ruling classes, Bantu groups were marginalized and to a great extent overshadowed in the public images of Bahia and Brazil. Nonetheless, these groups have continuously resisted exclusion and marginalization.

Im/mobilizing Bantu Culture

The last decade has witnessed a revitalization of Bantu cultural organizations in Brazil. In the case of Bahia, one organization in particular, ACBANTU (Associação Cultural de Preservação do Patrimônio Bantu; Cultural Association for the Preservation of Bantu Heritage) has taken on a leading role. Founded in December 2000, ACBANTU operates as an umbrella association; it is the organizer of a network that assembles over 3,800 organizations of Bantu culture from different parts of Brazil, including Candomblé *terreiros*, "Angola" *capoeira* schools, *quilombo* communities, neighborhood associations, associations of artisan fishermen,[12] and music and dance groups including the Association of Samba Dancers (Associação dos Sambadores e Sambadeiras de Roda), and several *jongos* and *congadas*.[13]

ACBANTU is a prime example of Bantu-organized resistance and mobilization. The association was founded in response to the twofold situation of being marginalized in mainstream society and othered within blackness. Among its major goals is the promotion of greater visibility for Bantu culture in Brazil. According to ACBANTU's newsletter *NKAANDA*, the contributions of Bantu peoples in the Americas are like "treasures that have been kept hidden in large trunks," and this includes musical instruments, musical rhythms, cuisine, and vocabulary. The same text outlines ACBANTU's purpose of not only preserving Bantu culture but also of "*innovating* the forms of preserving, revitalizing, and transmitting the African Matrix Civilizational Heritage while simultaneously promoting the insertion of the Afro-descendant communities in search of ethnic and racial equality, and proposing governmental policies of social inclusion."[14]

One example of innovation in "preserving culture" is ACBANTU's project to "recover" the Bantu languages spoken in Brazil. This project has led AC-BANTU to carry out several challenging tasks: gathering the vocabulary and terms that are scattered in several Candomblés and *quilombos* around the country, writing and documenting what has so far been an oral culture in Brazil, and teaching the Bantu languages Kikoongo and Kimbundu to "traditional Bantu communities." Among these communities are Candomblé *terreiros*, *capoeira* schools, and *quilombos*. The language classes include grammar, colloquial expressions, prayers, songs, and, according to an ACBANTU brochure, "Bantu ways of comprehending life." Although referring to a quite different context, Raymond Williams's (1958) analysis of culture applies well to the work carried out by ACBANTU since it defines culture as simultaneously traditional and creative, as objectified representations, and as "a whole way of life." In its work to recover Bantu languages, the association is dealing with culture as "known meanings." However, ACBANTU approaches linguistic cultural traditions in an innovative way, and in this sense it also engages with culture as the production of new meanings.

Project Nzuumba, established in 2005, is another initiative that combines the "known meanings" of tradition with an innovative approach to immaterial culture since it seeks to simultaneously fulfill the goals of transmitting to youth the knowledge of their elders while qualifying them for the job market.[15] The youth are taught courses on Bantu Afro embroidery and traditional Bantu cuisine not only so they can learn about the general history of Bantu groups in Africa and Brazil but also so they can acquire these specific skills that may help them generate income. The abstract notion that it is necessary to preserve tradition is thus merged with the concrete need to fight poverty: "Ancestral knowledge is the reference for the construction of forms of production, creation, and generation of income and employment."[16] The fact that men are not banned from participating in the courses is also innovative, and although they do not enroll in large numbers in the embroidery course, their presence is increasing in the course on Bantu cuisine. At the same time, despite Project Nzuumba's inventive characteristics, it safeguards the idea that traditions are to be preserved, in proof of which it has contributed to the "rescue" of the nearly extinct artistic forms of needlecraft practiced by elderly female Candomblé devotees by transmitting this knowledge to a younger generation.

The notions of recovery, protection, preservation, and transmission of culture will certainly sound essentialist to postmodern scholarship on culture, and not without reason. The recognition that culture is more than a mere set of symbols or practices has become commonplace even in more structuralist-oriented scholarship. This recognition is especially significant in the analysis of black cultures in the Americas since they have necessarily undergone processes of creolization, hybridization, and reinvention. Nonetheless, while ACBANTU's ambitious strategies of social inclusion are grounded in a questionable logic of preservation of cultural practices, the association has simultaneously treated culture as ever-changing and dynamic. Although using a language that seems at times to *immobilize* culture by reducing it to a collection of symbols, traditions, and practices, the association is continuously using culture to *mobilize*. The work with Bantu languages is a case in point: while ACBANTU collects words and expressions from the various *terreiros* and *quilombos*, its language courses also constitute a venue where culture circulates and people congregate.

ACBANTU's projects are clear examples of the indissolubility between discourse and materiality and between material and immaterial cultures. In addition, the organization has been "employing culture" for economic and political purposes. George Yúdice (2003) argues that as globalization intensifies, grassroots organizations have begun to conceive of culture as more than just a way of life but as a resource that is increasingly connected with political and economic dimensions. According to Yúdice, culture has become an expedient in the context of globalization, and it has been instrumentalized in the pursuit of such different, but interconnected, goals as economic growth, the reduction of unemployment, the elevation of self-esteem, and the fight against racism. While the instrumentalization of culture reveals the penetration of the logic of capital in every domain of life, disenfranchised groups have astutely managed this trend for their own benefit. This argument applies well to ACBANTU's reinvention of African traditions, as the association has reinvented Africanness as a source of empowerment for black subjects in a context marked by racism, inequality, and exclusion.

Probably the most emblematic illustration of ACBANTU's use of culture as an expedient is the strategic employment of the tradition of Candomblé *terreiros* as centers of food distribution for the poor to validate its partnership with the federal government. The Zero Hunger program was created by the Brazilian federal government in 2003, shortly after Luiz Inácio Lula da Silva's inauguration. The goal of Zero Hunger is to assure food security and meet the human right to adequate nourishment through initiatives geared toward the most vulnerable members of Brazilian society. Among the program's goals is the engagement of different sectors of civil society, thus recognizing that food security is not just connected to greater economic justice, but that it is also connected to the need to reduce racial and gender inequalities (Presidência da República Federativa do Brasil 2006).

Because of its active engagement in the Zero Hunger program, in March 2007 ACBANTU received the UN's Food and Agriculture Organization Medal in recognition of its commitment to the fundamental human right to nourishment. The award ceremony was an important demonstration of ACBANTU's participation in Brazilian political culture because it brought the minister of social development, Patrus Ananias, and the UN's FAO coordinator, Jacques Diouf, to the usually unnoticed Bantu Candomblé *terreiro* Mansu Dandalunda Kokuazenza, located in a poor neighborhood in the outskirts of Bahia's capital Salvador.

Besides bringing recognition to this religious community, which is also an urban *quilombo*, the award ceremony served as the backdrop for the donation of 50 tons of beans to 150 religious communities of African origin (*comunidades religiosas de matrizes africanas*), which, in turn, distributed the food to 7,200 families facing hunger in the greater Salvador region, including the Recôncavo area and the islands in the Bay of All Saints.[17] It was also at this event that ACBANTU inaugurated the Rede Kôdya, the Kôdya Network, also called Organized Communities in the African Diaspora for Public Policies and Social Inclusion of Black Populations (Comunidades Organizadas da Diáspora Africana por Políticas Públicas de Inclusão Social para a População Negra). The main goal of Kôdya is to provide financial support for "traditional communities of Afrodescendants." The unemployed members of these communities can access a network of over 600 *terreiros*, 53 *quilombo* communities, and 11 associations of fishermen and female shellfish harvesters. With several projects funded by the federal government, Kôdya benefits thousands of families by providing them with adult literacy classes, preparation for the job market, and food security (Fundação Cultural Palmares, 2006).

ACBANTU's partnership with the Zero Hunger program currently involves four methods of food distribution: 1) the Ministry of Social Development and Hunger Prevention (Ministério de Desenvolvimento Social e Combate à Fome) distributes food via ACBANTU five times a year to 1,000 families located in Salvador; 2) the same method is employed three times a year to distribute food to 3,000 families located in Santo Amaro da Purificação that are victims of environmental racism;[18] 3) the federal government sends food to the National Food Supply Company (Companhia Nacional de Abastecimento) six times a year to be distributed to 9,000 families throughout Bahia; 4) the Federal Government Food Purchase Program (Programa de Aquisição de Alimentos do Governo Federal) requires the federal government to buy vegetables produced by several Candomblé *terreiros* and distribute it to 2,600 families in Salvador and the Recôncavo region. In order to carry out all this work, ACBANTU relies on the labor of 500 volunteers who are responsible for analyzing the situation of the families in need in order to prioritize those who are considered to be in situations of emergency, such as the victims of droughts and floods. Once the families are selected, ACBANTU's volunteers, who are usually based in Salvador, mobilize another set of volunteers from within the communities that will receive the food. This facilitates the process of distribution and helps build local leadership. The families are then invited to receive the food in a *terreiro*, where they attend a meeting to discuss the difficulties they have been facing. The beneficiaries also sign a document that functions both as proof of the delivery of the food and as an instrument to quantify the number of people who have been benefited.[19]

Another important example of the expedient use of culture has been ACBANTU's participation in the struggle led by the Bahian Federation of Afro-Brazilian Cults (Federação Baiana do Culto Afro-Brasileiro, FEBACAB) to ensure that elderly Candomblé priests and priestesses are entitled to a retirement pension. Article 5 of item 9 of Brazil's Social Security Regulation (Regulamento da Previdência Social) establishes that religious clerics are entitled to retirement pensions paid by the federal government, even if they have never paid a tax to the retirement fund. However, so far only Catholic priests had taken advantage of this regulation because of the fact that Candomblé was for a long time considered a "cult" and not a "religion." Responding to this hierarchical representation, and arguing that Candomblé clerics spend most of their lives serving their communities and therefore deserve to be taken care of during their old age, FEBACAB, supported by ACBANTU, argued that Article 275 of the Bahian Constitution recognizes Candomblé as a religion and that therefore its clerics should be entitled to the same benefit afforded to Catholic priests. The Ministry of Social Security ultimately approved this claim in 2000, and since then several Candomblé priests and priestesses have been receiving pension checks.

ACBANTU's fight to secure a retirement pension for Candomblé clerics reveals that despite the belief in the supernatural power of the priests and priestesses, the association is aware of the mundane needs to which priests and priestesses must also attend. While constantly referring to a magical past and to the divinized ancestors (Bakulu), ACBANTU is at the same time pragmatically operating in the present. Its Bantu-based discourse, filled with magical allusions to an African essence—such as the connection of Bantu people to divine entities (Bankisi)—is coupled with a practical day-to-day struggle for access to education, health care, and income generation for Afro-descendants.

The cultural action of Bantu groups in Bahia has also been undeniably political. As Bantu groups have fought against social exclusion and political marginalization, the reconstruction of their identity has necessarily transformed power relations in mainstream Brazilian society. Whether culture is conceived of as a way of life or as objectified representations, it is produced in a hierarchical world in which some of its versions become hegemonic. Culture is political because meanings are constitutive of the processes that seek to transform or preserve the given hegemonic order (Wade 1999). As ACBANTU's president Raimundo Konmannanjy has stated, "We know that our religion has served not only to bring comfort in the many moments of pain suffered by our ancestors, but it has functioned, above all, as the main source for our political organization and mobilization for citizenship in a country marked by a long history of racism and social exclusion."[20]

Recognition and Redistribution

From their beginnings, Candomblé *terreiros* in general and Bantu-based religion in particular have functioned as sources of social and political mobilization for Afro-Brazilians. While in the past the religion was mainly directed inward toward the community—for example, promoting dignity and carrying out processes of healing—nowadays Bantu culture and religion has also been directed outward, toward achieving social and political ends. ACBANTU's discourse explicitly connects recognition with redistribution, demanding that municipal, state, and federal governments acknowledge the presence of Bantu-based groups in Brazil and include them in the allocation of resources. There has been an increasing interdependence between the struggle for recognition—the need to repair cultural prejudice—and redistribution—the need to repair socioeconomic injustice (Fraser 1997).

The fight for recognition takes place mainly in the realm of communication between different groups within a given society, thus requiring the production and circulation of new cultural representations that will allow for the reinterpretation of the image of the subjugated group. Redistribution is sought mainly by demanding the establishment of new public policies that can be legitimatized only if new representations of the oppressed groups successfully challenge previously hegemonic notions. Therefore, recognition and redistribution are not two separate spheres but are intrinsically connected realms. In their struggles for social justice, grassroots organizations seek both components at once. The interconnection between recognition and redistribution is presented in a discourse in which tradition does not oppose modernity, as is made clear in the statement of Ana Maria Placidino, educator and co-founder of ACBANTU: "We have a whole heritage to protect. We're traditional communities . . . that carry out traditional activities in the ways we collect food, fish, and cook, for instance. . . . But we also want to have access to public policies."[21]

As part of its work to improve the participation of impoverished black communities in governmental processes of decision-making, ACBANTU is a member of important Conselhos de Controle e Participação Social (Councils of Social Control and Participation) at the municipal, state, and federal levels. The *conselhos* are democratic instruments that represent the interface between the state and civil society, allowing for the latter to participate in the process of creating public policies. Most *conselhos* were established in Brazil shortly before the 1988 Constitution, in the period commonly referred to as the "re-democratization" of Brazilian society after the military dictatorship. In the early days, the *conselhos* played only an advisory role, providing the state with suggestions for the implementation of public policies. After the founding of the Novo Conselho Nacional de Saúde (New National Health Council) in 1990, however, the *conselhos* began to have legal, normative, and deliberative functions. ACBANTU participates in several of these *conselhos*, including Food and Nutrition Security, Health, Environment, and Genetic Heritage,[22] among others. The association also provides legal aid for traditional Afrodescendant communities, including *quilombos* that are struggling for land tenure.

As Alvarez, Dagnino, and Escobar (1998) explain, the "new" social movements that have emerged in Latin America since the late 1980s have combined mobilization for material resources with the production of new cultural representations. Grassroots organizations have been fighting not only for access, incorporation, participation, and inclusion in their respective countries but have also been participating in the very definition of the nation and the political system. Thus, the quest for the empowerment of the disenfranchised has taken place both in the realm of *cultural politics*, where disembodied struggles over meanings and representations take place, and the realm of *political culture*, the dimension of what counts as "political" in every society, the domain of practices and institutions that are carved out of the totality of social reality. Politics encompasses wider struggles of power that include (but are not limited to) the specific activities of voting, campaigning, and lobbying. In order to bring about social transformation, these recognizably political acts must be coupled with the construction of new narratives and representations (ibid.).

Thus, the production of knowledge has been a crucial element in the processes of empowerment of oppressed groups. Aware of the need to re-narrate a history that has marginalized the Bantu presence in Brazil, ACBANTU has linked its social mobilization to its construction of new representations of Bantu culture and identity. One method ACBANTU has used to achieve this has been through gathering information about the past and present history of Bantu groups in the country. The association is currently engaged in a collaborative research initiative with the Federal University of Bahia to develop an Inventory of the Communities of African Heritage in Salvador (Inventário das Comunidades de Matriz Africana em Salvador). The goal of the inventory is to determine how many urban *quilombos* exist in Bahia and research their ethnic backgrounds in order to better assist them in their struggles for land tenure.[23]

ACBANTU thus challenges the boundaries of class not only by fighting for material gains for the disenfranchised but also by increasing the cultural capital of disenfranchised groups. Instead of being exclusively an *object* of the research of anthropologists and sociologists, ACBANTU has worked *together with* researchers, thus exercising its agency as subject and knowledge producer.

Conscious of how scholars helped establish the notion of Yoruba superiority, members of ACBANTU have decided to both forge personal links with researchers and, even more important, to develop their own intellectual production. Bantu Candomblé *terreiros* in Bahia are very aware of the hierarchy that has placed the Yoruba at the top and the Bantu at the bottom, and they have felt its consequences firsthand. In an interview for a local newspaper, one of ACBANTU's directors, Raimundo Dantas, stated that Yoruba Candomblés are the most showcased by the Brazilian media, and this happens because of prejudice against Bantu Candomblé.[24]

On the other hand, while protesting the lack of attention given to Bantu Candomblé by mainstream society, ACBANTU has understood this marginalization as to some extent positive, since it has served to protect the treasured secrecy of their *terreiros*. Bantu groups have reinterpreted the negotiations carried out by Yoruba Candomblé clerics with members of the Brazilian elite as a sign of disloyalty to the concealment deemed necessary for the preservation of Candomblé. Accordingly, if in the past these connections favored Yoruba groups, they may have also served to detach them from the allegedly original African culture.

The notion of Yoruba disloyalty, however, has not created unbridgeable differences among Candomblé nations. ACBANTU members constantly participate in and promote events, seminars, and meetings where they peacefully and cheerfully congregate with members of Nagô and Kêtu Candomblés. I have witnessed instances of friendly teasing and joking among members of different Candomblé *terreiros* in events ACBANTU promoted. On one occasion, ACBANTU hosted a reception to showcase Bantu culture to African American tourists in their headquarters in Pelourinho. At the event, an artisan and acquaintance, a member of a Nagô *terreiro,* showed up uninvited and began to sell his handcrafted jewelry to the well-off tourists.[25] An ACBANTU member teased him, saying, among laughs, "*tinha que ser iorubá mesmo pra já chegar negociando!*" which roughly translates to "it had to be a Yoruba to negotiate right from the start!" Amused with the comment, the artisan laughed and carried on selling his work.

The distinction between Bantus and Yorubas has led to an emphasis on contrast, but not to the extent of promoting conflict. In fact, the notions that Yorubas are good negotiators and more outgoing and that the Bantus are more introspective and better at preserving ancestral knowledge have served to assign tasks and responsibilities when these groups work together. According to Ana Maria Placidino:

> The relationship between Bantus and Yorubas, while marked by timeless tribal prejudice, also became, in the conditions of the diaspora, characterized by links of solidarity and mutual support. Proof of which is that many Jeje, Ketu, and Nagô terreiros participate in the network organized by ACBANTU. Instead of intensifying the differences, we try to optimize them; for example, Kitaanda Bantu (a project that brings together community entrepreneurs) is coordinated by individuals of the Ketu nation due to their great capacity for doing business. On the other hand, our Environment Department is coordinated by individuals of the Angola nation due to their vast knowledge of leaves, roots, etc. In other states, too, ethnicity determines the type of work individuals will develop in the organization. (e-mail communication with author, September 29, 2009)

Likewise, a discourse based on contrast and secrecy surrounds the distinction between "Angola *capoeira*" and "regional *capoeira*." It is very common to hear, especially among black activists, the claim that "Angola *capoeira*" (i.e., of Bantu origin) has not received the same recognition as "regional *capoeira*" because the former, in contrast to the latter, did not build alliances with white elite Brazilians. This discourse builds an analogy with the myth of "Nagô purity" but adds an interesting twist since it establishes that while the lack of patronage contributed to the secondary status of "Angola *capoeira*," it has also allegedly preserved its purity. Because it has become "mixed"—meaning not only that it has incorporated foreign martial arts moves but also that it has negotiated white participation—"regional *capoeira*" has been represented in this discourse as "impure." This idea corresponds with the notion that Bantu power in Brazil stems from its secrecy and distance from the dominant sectors of society.

Thus, visibility is understood as a two-edged sword: on the one hand, it generates recognition and respect, but on the other hand, it is perceived as a risky business where oppressed groups may "lose their identity." This explains why ACBANTU seeks to maintain control over the process through which Bantu culture becomes visible. As part of its strategy to enhance visibility, in 2003 ACBANTU carried out a research project called Kizoonga Bantu, which had the goal of discovering the genealogical origins of Bantu communities in Bahia. Another important example of ACBANTU's intellectual activism was the research it conducted in partnership with the State University of Bahia, which resulted in the designation by UNESCO of *samba de roda*[26] as an Oral and Intangible Heritage of Humanity. *Samba de roda* is described in UNESCO's proclamation as "choreography. . . . often improvised and based on the movements of the feet, legs and hips. One of the most typical movements is the famous belly push, the umbigada, a testimony of Bantu influence, used by the dancer to invite her successor into the centre of the circle." Using the discourse of the preservation of traditions, UNESCO's text explains the importance of conferring the title of Oral and Intangible Heritage of Humanity upon *samba de roda*: "The influence of mass media and competition from contemporary popular music have contributed to undervaluing this Samba in the eyes of the young. The ageing of practitioners and the dwindling number of artisans capable of making some of the instruments pose a further threat to the transmission of the tradition" (UNESCO 2009).

Based on the same logic of the need to preserve cultural practices, ACBANTU also lobbied for a municipal law aimed at preserving African cultural heritage in Salvador. Approved by the municipal government as Law No. 7216/2007 in January 2007, the law establishes that all cultural productions of African origin, of both material and immaterial character, shall be considered the historical and cultural heritage of Afro-descendants. This includes forms of expression, documents, monuments, buildings, and sites where cultural and artistic manifestations take place as well as the locations inhabited by *quilombos* and Afro-Brazilian religious *terreiros*. The law also includes state protection and preservation of historical buildings. Commenting enthusiastically on the law's approval, ACBANTU's president Konmannanjy stated that it was a fundamental victory for Afro-descendants in Bahia because "it will guarantee that black culture will not be *distorted* by those who do not have *real knowledge* about *our culture*. Our songs, our traditions, and our religion will be respected, and will no longer be transformed into folklore or used for commercial and tourism purposes" (Fundação Cultural Palmares 2007, emphasis added).

The law's unspecific wording that "all cultural production of African origin" is supposed to be preserved puts its very viability in question. Yet even if the law had a more specific language, it would not be able to "guarantee" how black culture would be used, by whom, and with what intentions. Because culture cannot be bounded, it cannot be reduced to a limited realm of objects or expressions, nor can it be effectively appropriated by a specific group. On the other hand, the passage of the law reveals that there is a dispute over the ownership of black cultural expressions. As Yúdice correctly points out, the employment of culture as an expedient does not mean that culture is becoming more materialized. One of the consequences of its uses as an expedient is, in effect, the nonmaterialization of culture, witnessed in the rise of cultural property rights, the decision of "native tribes" to patent their culture, and the struggles over how to define cultural heritage. This is especially true in Bahia, where a powerful tourism industry focuses heavily on black culture and frequently exploits black cultural producers.[27]

Because of its successful partnership with the federal government, AC-BANTU has been able to challenge the prevailing dependence of Bahian black cultural organizations on the tourism industry. More important, the association has also been able to rise above the clientelism that more often than not characterizes the relationship between cultural groups and politicians in Brazil. Instead of depending on the patronage of specific politicians, ACBANTU has become an official participant in projects developed at the interface of state and civil society. The gains obtained in such conditions are not limited to the measurable material benefits of food, jobs, and land; they also include the inestimable values of autonomy and legitimacy achieved by a grassroots organization.

Conclusion

ACBANTU's struggle for visibility and recognition has been based on a sense of ownership of black culture and on the notion that there is a correct way of practicing African traditions. To make matters even more complicated, this happens in a context of passionate dispute among black groups over who has been more faithful to the original Africanisms brought to Brazil. Nonetheless, what frequently strikes researchers as an essentialist attitude on the part of social movements and grassroots organizations may actually be a possessive use of culture by groups who have felt historically dispossessed. In recognizing the role dispossession has played, I am not supporting the notion that we should understand culture as property as a way to compensate for material deprivation. Elsewhere I have argued against the proposal put forward by some scholars and activists in Brazil that it is necessary to "regain black culture for black people" (Pinho 2010, 161). The logic behind that notion is that in order to fight the myth of racial democracy it is necessary to "extricate" black culture from nonblacks.

I contend that it is not possible to "reclaim" *samba, capoeira,* Candomblé, and other Afro-Brazilian cultural expressions as "black things" that should be practiced only by "black people" because culture is not circumscribed within neat and clear-cut boundaries. Whether we define culture as a way of life or as objectified representations, its irreducibility and collective nature make it impossible to erect fences around it. Even though objectification is necessary for culture to circulate, ultimately culture is not a thing. It is not possible to disentangle or purify black culture by prohibiting nonblacks from partaking in it.

Interestingly, despite ACBANTU's rather exclusive discourse about Bantu culture, its daily practices and interactions have been quite inclusive. The group is aware that its actions benefit Afro-descendants in general, not just those who claim Bantu ancestry. Furthermore, unlike black organizations that practice "race-first" politics, ACBANTU's work has favored, above all, the poor. Although actively working to promote a distinctively black identity, the association does not select only those who are deemed black to receive food, language courses, training for the job market, or legal assistance.

In my view, the racially inclusive practice of ACBANTU stems from two interconnected realms: Candomblé *terreiros* and the ordinary racial conviviality of daily life in Brazil, especially among the poor. Although frequently dismissed as a mystifying feature of the myth of racial democracy, racial conviviality has been in fact a very important aspect of Brazilian racial politics. Although it does not automatically promote "racial harmony" or prevail over anti-black beliefs and practices, racial conviviality helps explain some of the challenges faced by those organizations and movements that have revolved around a clear-cut definition of races.[28]

In addition, while engaged in the nitty-gritty of identity politics, ACBANTU's work is at the same time informed by the universalistic character of Candomblé, an element that unifies the practices of Bantus and Yorubas. In fact, one of the reactions to the attacks of neo-Pentecostalists on Candomblé *terreiros* and devotees has been the strengthening of an oppositional identity based on the idea that if neo-Pentecostalists are prejudiced and narrow-minded, Candomblé folks are tolerant and open-minded. This contrast to neo-Pentecostalists has strengthened the bonds between Bantu and Yoruba *terreiros.*

An oft-cited example of the tolerance of Candomblé is the fact that the *terreiros* of any nation, when "feeding the hungry," do so "independently of religion, ethnicity/race, or personality," as stated in the quote that opens this chapter. This does not mean that skin color has been of no importance for the members of Bantu organizations, but it has not been more significant than poverty, and it has not been weighty enough to fragment the class-based elements that bond the group's members to one another and stimulate their joint mobilization against a common source of oppression. Because they are unrestrained and rebellious, black cultures in the diaspora do not obey the delineations established by intellectuals and activists. As a result, the nurturing of Bantu Africanness in Brazil has borne fruit not only for those of supposedly Bantu origin or just for those of African descent but for a vast population of disenfranchised Brazilians.

Notes

I am very grateful to ACBANTU's members for the information they have shared with me about the tremendous work that they carry out to overcome poverty and racism. I offer my special thanks to Ana Maria Placidino for her constant patience and generosity in answering my many questions.

1. I find the term "temple" insufficient to represent the idea of a *terreiro* of Candomblé. Translated literally as "plot of land," *terreiro* includes the plants, animals, streams, soil, air, and wind; in sum, the natural elements necessary for the perpetuation of the *axé* (energy) of the Orixás. A "temple" refers only to a building, while *terreiro* refers to a location that includes the buildings and also the natural surroundings where Orixá worship takes place.

2. When President Lula took office in January 2003, there were 49 million Brazilians classified as "Class E," that is, those whose family's monthly income ranges from R$0 to R$705 (US$0–US$415). As we approach the end of Lula's second turn in office, not only has this number dropped to 28.8 million but also during this same period almost 30 million Brazilians joined "Class C" (those whose monthly income ranges between R$1126 and R$4854, or US$663–US$2,862) (Neri 2010). The currency conversion is that of October 25, 2010 (US$1 = R$1.69).

3. FAO defines "food insecurity" as "a situation that exists when people lack secure access to sufficient amounts of safe and nutritious food for normal growth and development and an active and healthy life. It may be caused by the unavailability of food, insufficient purchasing power, inappropriate distribution, or inadequate use of food at the household level. Food insecurity, poor conditions of health and sanitation, and inappropriate care and feeding practices are the major causes of poor nutritional status. Food insecurity may be chronic, seasonal or transitory." See the FAO's definition of food insecurity at its online glossary: http://www.fao.org/FOCUS/E/SOFI00/sofi007-e.htm.

4. "ACBANTU e Rede Kôdya: Breve Balanço das Atividades," *NKAANDA* June 29, 2007, p. 2.

5. I have known and interacted with the co-founders of ACBANTU since 2001. Thus, my analysis is grounded on conversations with them and observations of the association's work over these years. In the summer of 2007 I had the opportunity to work closely with ACBANTU when I led a study-abroad tour to Salvador, Bahia. Most of the practical activities of the course were carried out with ACBANTU, including field trips to Candomblé *terreiros* and urban and rural *quilombos* and meetings with Afro-Brazilian activists. For the purpose of writing this chapter I have also researched online news, ACBANTU's website, and their newsletter, *NKAANDA*.

6. According to Nurse and Philippson (2003), it is difficult to state with certainty the exact number of Bantu languages, especially because of the frequent confusion between the definitions of language and dialect. Different students of the topic have come up with totals varying between 300 and 680.

7. The contrast between Yoruba and Bantu (or Congo) identities is also visible in the Cuban religious realm. Palmié (2002) shows that the meanings of Yoruba-based Lucumí and Congo-based Palo Mayombe stem not only from their distinct African origins but also from hierarchical notions developed in Cuba that associate the former with having a moral ethos and the latter with a lack thereof.

8. On the interchangeability of the terms Nagô, Quêto/Ketu, and Yoruba in Africa and the diaspora, see Matory (2005, 21): "Nowadays, the West African cognates of 'Quêto'—'Kétou' or 'Kétu'—refer to a specific Yoruba-speaking town in the People's Republic of Benin and to a kingdom that cuts across the border of Nigeria and the People's Republic of Benin. The West African cognates of 'Nagô'—'Nagôt,' 'Nagô,' or 'Anàgó'—refer either to a specific Beninese Yoruba group or, in Beninese parlance, to the Yoruba speakers as a whole. In Brazil, too, both 'Quêto' and 'Nagô' have come to be equated consciously with the inclusive Yoruba ethnic group. Cubans identify the same inclusive Yoruba group, including its Latin American diaspora, as 'Lucumí.'"

9. The Portuguese term *mestiço* shares similarities with the Spanish term *mestizo*, since both indicate racial mixture. However, there are also several differences between the two. First, the ideologies of *mestizaje* in Spanish America, and *mestiçagem* in Brazil, are quite distinct from country to country. Second, while *mestizo* usually refers to a mix between a white and an indigenous partner, *mestiço* in Brazil almost always refers to a racial mixture that includes a black counterpart, even though one can dispute the conditions of that "inclusion."

10. This is my own translation of Freyre's text: "*Ao contrário do bantu, gente mais doce e acomodatícia, o escravo sudanês ou de origem sudanesa, consciente como nenhum dos valores de sua cultura e, por isso mesmo, mais insubmisso . . . deu provas de sua capacidade de organizar-se contra os brancos*" (1990, 73).

11. This is my own translation of Ortiz's text: "*Los congos son en Cuba los ritos de religión menos avanzada. . . . Los negros que en Cuba decimos 'lucumís' [Yorubas] son de religión más elevada que la de los congos y sus ritos están algo más apartados de la magia*" (Ortiz [1951] 1981, 168, 170). I am grateful to Cubanist scholar Robin Moore for sharing this information with me.

12. "Artisan fishermen" is the term employed in Bahia to define those who perform traditional forms of fishing such as the *puxada de rede*, a practice in which large nets are thrown into the sea and later dragged out onto the sand. Although this practice is not necessarily defined as having African origin, ACBANTU has included it among the traditions to be preserved because it has historically been carried by "traditional Afrodescendant communities." The same applies to the practice of *mariscagem* (shellfish harvesting).

13. *Jongos* are dance and music expressions considered to be one of the origins of samba. They are danced in a circle where the dancers take turns going to the middle to display their abilities. *Congadas* are theatrical dances invented by African slaves and their descendants in Brazil that represent the crowning of the queen and king of Congo.

14. "Bakulu Etu," *NKAANDA*, June 29, 2007, p. 1, my italics.

15. The effort to preserve material culture has taken place through community-based eco-museums, in which sacred trees are protected and utensils, clothes, books, and documents that attest to the endurance of Bantu culture in Brazil are preserved.

16. "Projeto Nzuumba: Compartilhamento de Conhecimentos," *NKAANDA*, June 29, 2007, p. 3.

17. Text box, *NKAANDA*, June 29, 2007, p. 3.

18. The term "environmental racism" refers to those situations in which environmental injustice disproportionately affects specific ethnic groups. This characterizes the Bahian town of Santo Amaro da Purificação, where hundreds of inhabitants were contaminated by lead and cadmium from 1960 to 1993 by the Companhia Brasileira de Chumbos (COBRAC), a subsidiary of the French company Penarroya Oxide AS. The factory left a devastating legacy in the region, including a wide range of diseases that have affected a huge number of individuals.

19. I am grateful to Ana Maria Placidino for sending me, via e-mail, this detailed description of how the process of food distribution is carried out by ACBANTU.

20. Author's interview with ACBANTU's president.

21. N.a., "Comunidades Tradicionais," *Pravda*, August 29, 2005, available at http://port.pravda.ru/news/cplp/brasil/29-08-2005/8530-5.

22. The Brazilian Ministry of the Environment defines as genetic heritage the information pertaining to the genetic origin of vegetal and animal specimens collected in Brazil's national territory. The Council on the Management of Genetic Heritage (Conselho de Gestão do Patrimônio Genético) seeks to control and regulate the access to the genetic heritage related to the cultural practices of indigenous and local communities.

23. This inventory is important because in order to apply for land tenure, *quilombo* communities must comply with Convention 169 (Indigenous and Tribal Peoples Convention, 1989) of the International Labour Organization. To officially own the land where they live, the community must self-identify as "indigenous" or "tribal" and request the land title from the federal government through Fundação Cultural Palmares. The process requires a researcher (historian, geographer, or anthropologist) to produce an "anthropological report of the historical, economical, environmental and social-cultural characterization of the identified quilombo area.").

24. N.a., "Sucursal da Africa," *Correio da Bahia*, December 9, 2002.

25. For more on African American roots tourism in Brazil, see Pinho 2008.

26. *Samba de roda* was declared an Oral and Intangible Heritage of Humanity on November 25, 2005.

27. For more on the intricate relationship between black culture, local politics, and tourism see Pinho 2008 and 2010.

28. For more on this discussion, see Pinho 2010, esp. 1–22.

Bibliography

Alvarez, Sonia, Evelina Dagnino, and Arturo Escobar, eds. 1998. *Cultures of Politics/Politics of Cultures: Re-Visioning Latin American Social Movements*. Boulder, Colo.: Westview Press.

Bastide, Roger. 1971. *As Religiões Africanas no Brasil. Contribuição a uma sociologia das interpenetrações das civilizações*. São Paulo: Pioneira.

———. 1978. *O Candomblé na Bahia. Rito Nagô*. São Paulo: Nacional.

Belik, Walter, and Mauro Del Grossi. 2003. "O Programa Fome Zero no contexto das políticas sociais no Brasil." Texto preparado para o painel "Políticas de Combate à Pobreza: Segurança Alimentar, Nutrição, Renda Mínima e Ganhos de Produtividade na Agricultura," realizado no dia 30 de julho de 2003 no XLI Congresso da SOBER em Juiz de Fora.

Bhabha, Homi. 1990. *Nation and Narration*. London: New York: Routledge.

Cabrera, Lydia. 1986. *Anagó: vocabulario lucumí (el yoruba que se habla en Cuba)*. Miami, Fla.: Ediciones Universal.

Capone, Stefania. 2004. *A Busca da África no Candomblé. Tradição e poder no Brasil*. Rio de Janeiro: Pallas.

Dantas, Beatriz Góis. 1988. *Vovó Nagô, Papai Branco. Usos e abusos da África no Brasil*. Rio de Janeiro: Graal.

Fraser, Nancy. 1997. *Justice Interruptus: Critical Reflections on the Postsocialist Condition*. London: Routledge.

Freyre, Gilberto. 1990. "Luiz Vianna Filho e seu estudo sobre o negro na Bahia." In Freyre, *Bahia e Baianos. Textos reunidos por Edson Nery da Fonseca*. Salvador: Empresa Gráfica da Bahia.

Fundação Cultural Palmares. 2006. "Relatório destaca atendimento a comunidades de terreiro baianas." August 3. Available at http://www.palmares.gov.br/?p=1618.

———. 2007. "Lei garantirá preservação da cultura africana e afro-brasileira em Salvador." February 2. Available at http://www.palmares.gov.br/?p=1854.

Johnson, Paul Christopher. 2002. *Secrets, Gossips, and Gods: The Transformation of Brazilian Candomblé*. New York: Oxford University Press.

Lima, Vivaldo da Costa. 1976. "O conceito de nação dos Candomblés da Bahia." *Afro-Ásia* 12: 65–90.

Lody, Raul. 1995. *O povo santo*. Rio de Janeiro: Pallas.

Matory, James Lorand. 2005. *Black Atlantic Religion: Tradition, Transnationalism, and Matriarchy in the Afro-Brazilian Candomblé*. Princeton, N.J.: Princeton University Press.

Neri, Marcelo Côrtes, ed. 2010. *A Nova classe média: O lado brilhante dos pobres*. Report prepared by the Fundação Getúlio Vargas, Rio de Janeiro. Available at http://www.fgv.br/cps/ncm. Accessed October 25, 2010.

Nurse, Derek, and Gérard Philippson, eds. 2003. *The Bantu Languages*. London and New York: Routledge.

Ortiz, Fernando. (1951) 1981. *Los bailes y el teatro de los negros en el folklore de Cuba*. Havana: Editorial Letras Cubanas; New York: Distribuido por Ediciones Vitral.

Palmié, Stephan. 2002. *Wizards and Scientists: Explorations in Afro-Cuban Modernity and Tradition*. Durham, N.C.: Duke University Press.

Pinho, Patricia de Santana. 2008. "African-American Roots Tourism in Brazil." *Latin American Perspectives* 35 (3): 70–86.

———. 2010. *Mama Africa: Reinventing Blackness in Bahia*. Durham, N.C.: Duke University Press.

Presidência da República Federativa do Brasil. 2006. "Fome Zero." Available at http://www.fomezero.gov.br/o-que-e. Accessed June 12, 2011.

Ramos, Arthur. 1940. *O Negro Brasileiro*. São Paulo: Companhia Editora Nacional.

Rodrigues, Raymundo Nina. 1932. *Os Africanos no Brasil*. São Paulo: Companhia Editora Nacional.

———. 1935. *O Animismo Fetichista dos Negros Bahianos*. Rio de Janeiro: Civilização Brasileira.

Santos, Juana Elbein. 1976. *Os Nagôs e a Morte*. Petropolis: Vozes.

UNESCO. 2009. "Safeguarding Intangible Cultural Heritage." Available at http://www.unesco.org/culture/ich/index.php?cp=BR&topic=mp#14, 09/07/2009. Accessed March 18, 2011.

Verger, Pierre. 1987. *Fluxo e refluxo do tráfico de escravos entre o golfo do Benin e a Bahia de Todos os Santos: dos séculos XVII a XIX*. São Paulo: Editora Corrupio.

———. 2002. *Orixás, Deuses Iorubás na África e no Novo Mundo*. Salvador: Editora Corrupio.

Wade, Peter. 1999. "Working Culture: Making Cultural Identities in Cali, Colombia." *Current Anthropology* 40 (4): 449–472.

Williams, Raymond. 1958. "Culture Is Ordinary." In *The Raymond Williams Reader*, ed. John Higgins. Oxford: Blackwell, 2001.

Yúdice, George. 2003. *The Expediency of Culture: Uses of Culture in the Global Era*. Durham, N.C.: Duke University Press.

2

Strategies of the Black Pacific

Music and Diasporic Identity in Peru

HEIDI CAROLYN FELDMAN

Peru has not collected census data about racial and ethnic identity since 1940. Reaffirming this decision in 1961, Census Director Pedro Gutierrez stated, "The question about race has been omitted because there is no racial problem in Peru" (*La Prensa* 1961, 5).

Decades later, in 2009, a taxi driver in Lima questioned me about the recent election of the first African American president of the United States, Barack Obama. "Pardon my frankness," he said, "but how is it that a country like yours, with such racial problems, succeeded in electing a black president?" Implicit in his statement was a comparison between Peru (where presidential elections in the 1990s had foregrounded the ethnic backgrounds of Japanese Peruvian Alberto Fujimori, nicknamed "El Chino," and mestizo Alejandro Toledo, known as "El Cholo") as a country with "no racial problem" versus the United States, with its history of legalized segregation and institutionalized discrimination against blacks in housing, restaurants, buses, employment, and other forms of public life (see Oboler 2005).[1]

For Afro-descendants in Peru, all is not what it seems. Anthropologist Marisol de la Cadena (1998) explains that Peruvian national ideology long has held that there is no such thing as race, while at the same time members of non-European groups are excluded from membership in the educated and "decent" classes, creating an environment of silent racism. Afro-Peruvian scholar José Campos, similarly, explains that "racism in Peru is felt but not seen" (quoted in Portocarrero 2000, 208; see also Sims 1996). Isolated protests have highlighted less subtle forms of discrimination: the use of blackface on a 1988 televised drama about slavery (R. Santa Cruz 1988); the demeaning and racist stereotypes presented by the Peruvian comedic TV character "Negro Mama" (taken off the air after protests by Afro-Peruvian organizations in 2010) (Quiroz 2010); the 2004 Lima phonebook cover juxtaposing the image of a black bellhop carrying luggage with images of a white doctor, nurse, and home repair technician (Bridges 2004); charges in 2007 that a nightclub refused to admit blacks (*Living in Peru*, 2007); the 2009 commercial by the major Peruvian newspaper *El Comercio* that depicted Afro-descendants as cannibals (aired shortly after the Peruvian government's official apology to Afro-Peruvians for discrimination) (Peru.com 2009); the persistence of racial stereotypes in advertising and product displays on billboards and in stores (Becerra 2010); and so on.

In the twenty-first century, Afro-Peruvian NGOs are challenging frequently cited estimates that blacks make up less than 3 percent of the country's population, highlighting the detrimental consequences of black social invisibility in Peru, where many blacks live in poverty and few are found in white-collar jobs or high-ranking professional positions. Published estimates of Peru's black population vary in the absence of scientific measures and/or agreement about what constitutes "blackness" in Peru. The 1940 Peruvian census designated Afro-Peruvians as 0.47 percent of the population (quoted in Glave 1995, 15), and in 2010, the CIA's World Factbook stated that 3 percent of Peru's population was "black, Japanese, Chinese, and other" (World Factbook 2010). Yet, in 1995 José Luciano and Humberto Rodriguez Pastor described the Afro-Peruvian population as an estimated 6 to 10 percent of the population (Luciano and Rodriguez Pastor 1995, 271), and in 2002, Peru's Commission on Andean, Amazonian, and Afro-Peruvian Peoples (CONAPA) estimated the Afro-Peruvian population to be 3 million, or 13.5 percent of the country's total population (Congreso de la República, Comisión de Amazonía, Asuntos Indígenas y Afroperuanos 2002, 4). The commission criticized the lack of ethnic data in the national census for its role in the continued social invisibility and sublimation of Afro-Peruvians, stating, "Afro-Peruvians do not figure in the poverty map created by the government to establish its investment priorities, so they find themselves abandoned. Even if being on the coast means possibilities for access are more feasible than in an indigenous community high in the Andes, they have no dependable infrastructure that allows them to mobilize themselves.[2] Programs to alleviate poverty do not consider the coast to be a critical poverty zone, nor do they consider Afro-Peruvians a vulnerable group" (ibid., 5).[3]

To be sure, this critical condition is not limited to Peru. Throughout Latin America, people of African descent tend to be invisible, and ideologies of *mestizaje* and whitening to "improve the race" mask the persistence of racializing practices that keep people of color in positions of poverty and low social prestige (see Andrews 2004; Dzidzienyo and Oboler 2005; Minority Rights Group 1995; Wade 1997; Whitten and Torres 1998).

However, a closer look at the experience of Afro-descendants on the Pacific coast suggests that something is different in what I call the black Pacific

(Feldman 2005, 2006). While Afro-descendants struggle against social invisibility all over Latin America, in Peru and neighboring countries they seem to be *more* invisible, making efforts to fight racism more difficult. In international scholarship on the African diaspora, Peru has maintained a low profile at best. Few studies of slavery or blackness in the Americas even mention Peru, and maps of slave routes often completely omit the Pacific coast. Thus, many people (both Peruvians and non-Peruvians) are unaware of the existence of African-descended people or cultural traditions in Peru.

In 1993, African diaspora studies were enlivened by Paul Gilroy's model of the black Atlantic, a cultural world made up of citizens of Africa, Europe, and the Americas who share a transnational community linked by waterways and commerce, expressive culture forms, and "structures of feeling" (Williams 1977). Gilroy's black Atlantic model rejects the classic notion of the African diaspora as a one-way relationship between a center (the African homeland) and periphery (those longing to return), instead proposing a multidirectional, postnational cultural flow. Opposing Afrocentric models, Gilroy locates the birth of black Atlantic culture and the social construction of black racial identity in the trans-Atlantic slave trade. Building upon the work of W. E. B. Du Bois ([1903] 1994), Gilroy describes the double consciousness of blacks in the New World, who identify with both premodern Africa and the modern "West," resulting in what Gilroy calls a black "counterculture of modernity" (Gilroy 1993).

Some critics, while embracing Gilroy's emphasis on hybridity and multidirectionality, have sought to move beyond the Anglocentric nature of his examples (Fox 2006; Oboe and Scacchi 2008; Williams 1995). However, most efforts to address the omission of the Afro-Latin American experience from Gilroy's model retain his exclusive focus on the Atlantic.

My research in Peru suggests that while Gilroy's black Atlantic model reinvigorated the way scholars think about the African diaspora, it left unexplored the lesser-known communities of African descendants in countries along Latin America's Pacific coast. In an effort to map previously uncharted African diasporic territories on the margins of the black Atlantic, I locate what I call the black Pacific (Feldman 2005, 2006) in Peru and (tentatively) other areas along the Andean Pacific coast (Ecuador, Bolivia, Chile, and Colombia) where the history of slavery, and even the persistence of people and cultural expressions of African descent, is unknown to many outsiders. I imagine the black Pacific as a second diaspora on the margins of the black Atlantic because of its geographical location along the Pacific coast and the second journey made by enslaved Africans that severed them from the shared structures of feeling and waterways of Gilroy's black Atlantic. After some enslaved Africans crossed the Atlantic

Ocean, they were re-exported (legally or illegally), generally continuing on to Peru from Cartagena by sea (via Panama).[4] Colonial Peru's market then became an important supplier of enslaved Africans for the Pacific coast (Bowser 1974, 26–51, 54–55).

Within their respective countries, black Pacific people tend to be socially invisible and their sense of African diasporic identity is sometimes dormant.[5] With few or no visible surviving African-descended cultural forms, black Pacific populations appear to be no longer "very African" in Herskovits's terms (1941), especially compared with black Atlantic cultures such as Cuba or Brazil. This loss of cultural heritage has led to several revivals of African-derived culture and accompanying struggles over how to reclaim forgotten and largely undocumented history. In the isolated black Pacific, revival leaders search for African heritage in unconventional places, remapping "center" and "periphery" in the African diaspora and inventing traditions to restore a link with the African past (Hobsbawm and Ranger 1983). Whereas for Gilroy, black Atlantic double consciousness results from dual identification with premodern Africa and the modern West, the black Pacific negotiates ambiguous relationships with local *criollo* and indigenous culture and with the black Atlantic itself.

The Afro-Peruvian music revival (1950s–1970s) and its legacy provide an excellent example of the black Pacific condition and its strategies to recover African diasporic identity. As the following examples demonstrate, these strategies suggest new ways to map the African diaspora, and they bring into relief the difference between citizens of black Pacific and black Atlantic worlds.

Excavating Africa in the Black Atlantic

In early-twentieth-century urban Peru, few cultural traditions remained that were considered Afro-Peruvian. Race was perceived as changeable, whiteness was equated with social mobility, and, as Raúl Romero explains (1994), Peruvians of African descent typically were not viewed as a separate ethnic group because they identified culturally, along with the descendants of Europeans, as *criollos*, a term that originally described the children of Africans born into slavery and later included European descendants born in Peru. After independence, the word *criollo* came to describe a set of cultural practices that were believed to be of European origin, including *música criolla*, or Creole music. At Lima's *jaranas* (multi-day, invitation-only social gatherings involving the communal affirmation of shared *criollo* culture through food, drink, humor, music, and dance), ethnically diverse *criollos* performed *música criolla*, especially the *marinera*, on the guitar, *cajón* (box drum), and other instruments.[6] Those who did not play an instrument sang, danced, or performed the special rhythmic handclap patterns unique to each musical genre, affirming the participatory character of creating and maintaining a shared culture. Although the performers were of mixed ethnic backgrounds, by the middle of the century this music was considered to be of strictly European origin (Romero 1994).

Before the Afro-Peruvian revival, many blacks in Peru identified with *criollo* culture, yet they were denied the social benefits afforded white *criollos*. In the 1960s, while African independence movements and the U.S. civil rights movement sought to overturn colonialism and racism, respectively, in Peru, music and dance were the first successful arenas for the politics of black resistance. Whereas for some critics, staged music and dance might seem an unlikely format for collective protest, the first step for Afro-descendants in the isolated black Pacific was to make themselves visible as a group by organizing around a newly embraced collective, ethnic, and diasporic identity before they could unite in a political struggle for civil rights. In the Afro-Peruvian revival, black Peruvians began by mounting staged performances that reinscribed forgotten and ignored black culture in Peruvian official history, starting with times of slavery (plantation settings, slave dances, and so on). The leaders of the Afro-Peruvian revival reconstructed lost black Peruvian music and dances for theatrical performances and recordings, musically promoting racial difference to challenge the prevailing ideology of *criollo* unity without racial equality.

Many Peruvian musicians date the beginning of the revival to 1956, when Peruvian scholar José Durand (a white *criollo*) founded the Pancho Fierro company, which presented the first major staged performance of reconstructed Afro-Peruvian music and dance at Lima's Municipal Theater.[7] Several black Peruvians who participated in Durand's company formed their own groups in the 1960s, including the charismatic siblings Nicomedes and Victoria Santa Cruz. Perú Negro, the only group from the revival still existing in the twenty-first century, was founded in 1969 by former protégés of Victoria Santa Cruz.

Nicomedes Santa Cruz (1925–1992), an internationally renowned poet, folklorist, record producer, theater director, television and radio personality, journalist, and composer, is considered by many to be the father of the Afro-Peruvian revival (see Figure 2.1). Nicomedes Santa Cruz and his sister Victoria Santa Cruz (b. 1922) were born into a family of black intellectuals, artists, and musicians whose contributions to Peru's cultural life went back six generations (O. Santa Cruz n.d.). The Santa Cruz siblings were inspired to create a black theater company when they saw a 1951 performance by the U.S.-based Katherine Dunham Company at Lima's Municipal Theater (Santa Cruz 2000). Dunham, an African American choreographer and anthropologist, studied African-derived cultural expressions of the Caribbean and translated them to staged and stylized choreographies. Nicomedes Santa Cruz later described Dunham's show as the

Figure 2.1. Nicomedes Santa Cruz and his wife, Mercedes Castillo. Courtesy of Caretas Ilustración Peruana.

first staged performance in Peru to present blackness in a positive light (Santa Cruz 1973, 24).

In 1958, Santa Cruz founded the theater company Cumanana, which he used as a vehicle to bring his recited *décimas*, collected Afro-Peruvian songs and re-created Afro-Peruvian folklore to the public stage.[8] In 1963, Santa Cruz made a life-changing trip to Brazil, where he immersed himself in Afro-Brazilian culture and conferred with noted scholars of Afro-Brazilian folklore. Shortly after his return from Brazil, in 1964, Santa Cruz produced the ethnographic album *Cumanana*. This 2-LP boxed set, recorded by Santa Cruz and his company of the same name, contains the first recordings of many Afro-Peruvian genres that Nicomedes Santa Cruz had collected, reconstructed, and/or re-created, along with a 100-plus-page booklet on Afro-Peruvian music. *Cumanana* exerted a lasting influence on contemporary ideas about the black musical past in Peru; photocopies of the booklet circulate to this day as underground black history texts.

The most influential (and controversial) theory promoted in the booklet accompanying *Cumanana* (see Figure 2.2) demonstrates Santa Cruz's turn to the black Atlantic as a surrogate for Africa. Santa Cruz affirmed that an Angolan couple dance called *lundú,* featuring a pelvic bump in its descriptions by European chroniclers, became the Peruvian *landó,* a forgotten dance formerly performed by Africans and their descendants in Peru (Santa Cruz remembered seeing his grandparents perform the *landó* before it disappeared from practice, and he remembered his mother singing fragments of the verses). According to Santa Cruz, the African *lundú* also gave birth to over fifty couple dances found throughout Portugal, Spain, and the Americas, all featuring the pelvic bump "leitmotif" as part of their choreography. Santa Cruz's central piece of evidence for the persistence in Peru of a dance descended from the African *lundú* is the description, originally published in 1790 in the newspaper *Mercurio Peruano* and later cited by Manuel Fuentes in his influential book *Lima* ([1867] 1925), of an unnamed "indecent" erotic dance performed by enslaved Africans in eighteenth-century Lima (Santa Cruz [1964] 1970b, 18–20, 47). Santa Cruz further argued that the *landó* was the progenitor of the *marinera,* claiming African, not just European, heritage for Peru's most revered *criollo* dance. He supported this claim by citing elements of the *marinera's* choreography that, he affirmed, were survivals of the *lundú's* leitmotif: the requirement that the man and woman face each other and perform in a coquettish fashion throughout the dance, the use of the handkerchief, a "simulated pelvic bump" in the final figure, and so on (Santa Cruz [1964] 1970b, 20).

Where did Santa Cruz learn of the African origin of the Peruvian *landó?* Apparently he based his theory on a transposition of Brazilian scholars' writings

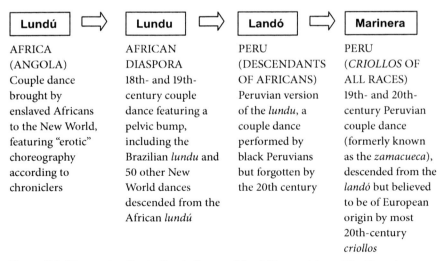

Lundú ⇨	**Lundu** ⇨	**Landó** ⇨	**Marinera**
AFRICA (ANGOLA) Couple dance brought by enslaved Africans to the New World, featuring "erotic" choreography according to chroniclers	AFRICAN DIASPORA 18th- and 19th-century couple dance featuring a pelvic bump, including the Brazilian *lundu* and 50 other New World dances descended from the African *lundú*	PERU (DESCENDANTS OF AFRICANS) Peruvian version of the *lundu,* a couple dance performed by black Peruvians but forgotten by the 20th century	PERU (*CRIOLLOS* OF ALL RACES) 19th- and 20th-century Peruvian couple dance (formerly known as the *zamacueca*), descended from the *landó* but believed to be of European origin by most 20th-century *criollos*

Figure 2.2. Nicomedes Santa Cruz's theory of the African origins of the Peruvian *marinera.*

about the Afro-Brazilian dance called *lundu*. There is no historical evidence to date that a dance called *lundú* (the Angolan progenitor of the Brazilian *lundu*) existed in Peru. However, Edison Carneiro and Luis da Cámara Cascudo (scholars Santa Cruz met in Brazil and whose books he cites in *Cumanana* in support of his theory) both wrote about the Brazilian *lundu*, a well-documented dance of Angolan origin (Carneiro 1961; Cascudo 1962). In *Cumanana*, Santa Cruz affirmed that the Peruvian *landó* must have had the same origin and choreography as the Brazilian *lundu*. His evidence for this correlation appears to come primarily from Cascudo's entry about the *lundu* in his *Dictionary of Brazilian Folklore*, which states that the African *lundú* gave birth to a series of Brazilian dances as well as to the Peruvian, Chilean, and Argentinean *samba cueca* (Cascudo 1962, 434–435; Santa Cruz [1964] 1970b, 18). In connecting the Brazilian *lundu* with the Afro-Peruvian *landó*, it appears likely that Santa Cruz relied on the similarity of the names of two lost dances, *landó* and *lundu*, that originated in black populations of different countries, making a significant assumption about the unity of all African diasporic dances described as "erotic" by chroniclers, colonizers, and other biased observers.

It is interesting to note that in the 1930s and 1940s, Peruvian scholar Fernando Romero had made a very similar argument (not cited in *Cumanana*), positing that the Peruvian *zamba*, a dance of African origin, had evolved into the *zamacueca* and later the *marinera* (Romero 1939a, 1939b, 1940, 1946a, 1946b). Romero stated that the Peruvian *zamba* was descended from the African *quizomba* (from Angola) because of similar choreographic traits, especially the *golpe de frente* (pelvic bump) or Bantú *m'lemba*, which simulated sexual intercourse. According to Romero, the pelvic bump was at one time performed as the epilogue of the Peruvian *zamacueca*, demonstrating the survival of an African trait (Romero 1940, 99).

However, while Romero noted that dances performed by black couples in colonial Peru were described in the eighteenth and nineteenth centuries as containing an "indecent" pelvic bump, he did not mention a dance called *lundú*. Rather than attributing this commonalty to a single origin dance, Romero indicated that black Peruvian dances seemed to display tendencies shared by a number of African dances, including those that made their way to Brazil. The *landó* does not figure in Romero's genealogy at all, though he does refer in passing to a variant of the samba called *samba-lundú* (Nicomedes and Victoria Santa Cruz later described the *zamba-landó* as the progenitor of the *landó*) (see Romero 1939a, 1939b, 1939c, 1939d, 1940, 1946a, 1946b, 1947).

With his album *Cumanana*, Nicomedes Santa Cruz—whose grammar school education prohibited his admission to the elite category of *gente decente* (whites and honorary whites; see De la Cadena 1998)—was able to popularize and disseminate his theory of the African *lundú* so widely that, decades later, most Peruvians who know anything about Afro-Peruvian music are aware of it. Many Peruvians positively state that the *landó* came from an African dance called *lundú* and that these dances are the basis of the *marinera*. Black musicians and dancers often say that the *landó* is the mother of all black music and dance in Peru and that all black rhythms come from the *landó*. Javier León observes that this public repetition of Santa Cruz's theory over a period of several decades has "transformed something that could be plausible into an incontrovertible fact" (León Quirós 2003, 106). Whether or not the theory is historically accurate, the fact that so many people *believe* it is true is an important element of the construction of Peruvian blackness by way of the black Atlantic in the twentieth century.

Nicomedes Santa Cruz made the first recording of a *landó*, "Samba Malató," for the album *Cumanana* in 1964. Santa Cruz began with a verse fragment remembered by his mother ("*la samba se pasea por la batea, landó, samba malató, landó*") (Santa Cruz y su Conjunto Cumanana [1964] 1970b, 47). Working with guitarist Vicente Vásquez, he elaborated a new musical arrangement, with guitar and percussion parts inferred from the basic rhythm of the surviving melody fragment. In order to support Santa Cruz's thesis that the *landó* was of African origin and that it later developed into the *criollo marinera*, the re-created "Samba Malató" had to sound both "African" and similar to the *marinera*. Several elements of Santa Cruz's arrangement are reminiscent of the *marinera*, especially the instrumental core of guitar and *cajón*. Elements of the recording that are commonly associated with West African music and its derivatives include the use of Afro-Latin percussion instruments (*bongó* and bell) and call and response between a soloist and chorus.

But Santa Cruz tried to make "Samba Malató" sound even more "African" in the second verse. In this added section, Santa Cruz embellished the fragment his mother remembered with what he later called "arbitrary Afroid wordage" (Santa Cruz [1964] 1970b, 47): "*Arambucurú, e loñá, loñá; a la recolé, uborequeté; babaloríchá, arambucurú; oyo cororó, oyo cororó; a la mucurú, e loñá, loñá; a la recolé, e kiri kiri; babaloríchá, e mandé, mandé; oyo cororó, oyo cororó ;e arambucurú . . . landó!*" (Santa Cruz y su Conjunto Cumanana [1964] 1970a). Some of these words are, or resemble, names of people or places in Africa (for example, Oyo was a kingdom in Yorubaland, or present-day Nigeria, and the Mande are a West African ethnic group descended from the kingdom of Mali), some are Spanish or Portuguese adaptations of Yoruba words used in Afro-Brazilian and Afro-Cuban religions (for example, "*babaloríchá*"), while others are of unknown origin.

In the third edition of *Cumanana*, Santa Cruz publicly repented for this artistic license, and he asked other recording artists to banish the added verse from the repertoire (N. Santa Cruz [1964] 1970b, 47). However, few Peruvians are aware of Nicomedes Santa Cruz's retractions, and other groups continue to perform and record the song with its Africanesque lyrics to this day. In fact, several Peruvians have told me that the lyrics are an African survival from ancient times. Thus, as was the case with the *lundú* theory, whether or not Nicomedes Santa Cruz's extrapolations from the Afro-Brazilian experience accurately characterize the "real" Afro-Peruvian past, they invented a version of the past that many Peruvians believe to be true. Santa Cruz's excavation of Peru's missing African heritage in "more African" black Atlantic cultures came to be one of several definitive strategies of the Afro-Peruvian revival that emphasize the marginalization of the black Pacific. Revival artists also borrowed musical instruments and chants from Cuba and Brazil, along with references to African-derived religions and Cuban singing styles. Thus, Cuba and Brazil (where many retentions from West African cultural practice could be found) became surrogates for Africa in the effort to restore a sense of diasporic identity and African cultural heritage to Afro-descendants in Peru.

Remembering Africa with the Body

Like her brother, Victoria Santa Cruz looked toward the black Atlantic to forge a transnational diasporic identity for black Peruvians, transplanting musical instruments and cultural expressions in revival productions (see Figure 2.3). But Victoria Santa Cruz's most celebrated legacy in Peru is her idiosyncratic deployment of "ancestral memory" as the cornerstone of a choreographic technique that enabled her to "return" to Africa by looking deep within her own body for the residue of organic ancestral rhythms.

Victoria Santa Cruz worked with her brother Nicomedes as co-director of Cumanana from 1959 until 1961. She studied in Paris and then returned to found her own company, Teatro y Danzas Negras del Perú (1966–1970s).[9] Later, she became director of Peru's Conjunto Nacional de Folklore (1973–1982). In these and other capacities, Victoria Santa Cruz trained a young generation of dancers to use her method to reclaim their African heritage, creating a lasting role for ancestral memory as a choreographic strategy in Afro-Peruvian dance (see Feldman 2006, 65–79; León Quirós 2003, 284–287, 305–310; León Quirós 2007, 143).

Explaining what she means by "ancestral memory," Victoria Santa Cruz writes: "What is ancestry? Is it a memory? And if so, what is it trying to make us remember? . . . The popular and cultural manifestations, rooted in Africa, which I inherited and later accepted as ancestral vocation, created a certain disposition

Figure 2.3. Victoria Santa Cruz. Courtesy of Octavio Santa Cruz Urquieta.

toward rhythm, which over the years has turned itself into a new technique, 'the discovery and development of rhythmic sense' . . . I reached my climax . . . when I went deep into that magical world that bears the name of rhythm" (Santa Cruz 1978, 18). Elsewhere, she said: "Having discovered, first ancestrally and later through study and practice, that every gesture, word, and movement is a consequence of a state of being, and that this state of being is tied to connections and disconnections of fixed centers or plexus . . . allowed me to rediscover profound messages in dance and traditional music that could be recovered and communicated. . . . The black man knows through ancestry, even when he is not conscious of it, that what is outwardly elaborated has its origin or foundation in the interior of those who generate it" (V. Santa Cruz 1988, 85).

Victoria Santa Cruz has spent her adult lifetime developing the philosophical approach to life and well-being that she calls "Discovery and Development of the Sense of Rhythm" (see Santa Cruz 2004). During the revival, she used this method to guide young Afro-Peruvians to discover their ancestry. Later in life, convinced that she had discovered something with cosmic ramifications, she used her method to teach students at Carnegie-Mellon University in the United States, where she was a tenured professor in the 1980s and 1990s.

A basic tenet of Victoria's method is the presumption that a sense of rhythm is innate in all black people by way of ancestry. "From an ancestral memory of Africa," she explains, "without knowing of the existence of an African continent; I learned the foundations of rhythm. Rhythm, without the intellectual connotation of 'time and beat.' Rhythmic combinations inherited, and in the passage of my life, recreated by me, awakened those inherent qualities of the human being. Qualities which taught me to discover the door that suffering hides, whose secret is not to exit but: To Enter" (e-mail communication with the author, July 25, 2003). Victoria Santa Cruz believes that the African origin of all black people is an organic culture with an inherent knowledge of the secret of rhythm. This does not mean that all black people are in touch with their ancestral memory. It means that through the method Victoria has discovered, they can reconnect with the knowledge that lies dormant within them, using the tool of rhythm. "Long ago," explains Victoria, "Africa discovered the secret of rhythm, the secret of movement. The black man vibrates to silence" (Santa Cruz 1979, 7).

This placement of ancestral memory in the black body is both compelling and problematic, seeming to support biological determinism and stereotypical assertions that rhythm, dance, and other essential qualities are in the blood of black people. While leading scholars of race and ethnicity (e.g., Appiah 1992; Gilroy 1993, 2000) take issue with such essentializing notions, arguing that "racial" behavior is learned, not inherent, and that "race" itself is an invention, I affirm that it is important to recognize the emic discourse of citizens of the African diaspora such as Victoria Santa Cruz (see also Scott 1991, 262). As Peter Wade observes, black and Native American participants in "new" social movements (that is, movements focused on identity politics) frequently organize around essentialist views of their own identity and history. As a result, scholars such as myself, whose training encourages us to identify the social constructedness of racial or ethnic identity, sometimes find that our analyses conflict with the beliefs of the people we represent. In an important passage that helped me sort out the disjuncture between my academic training, on the one hand, and what I have learned from Victoria Santa Cruz, on the other, Wade writes, "When academics deconstruct these historical traditions or more generally when they show how 'essentialisms become essential,' they may be weakening those identities and claims" (Wade 1997, 116). Because Victoria Santa Cruz helped mobilize a new sense of racial identity in a generation of Afro-Peruvians by using her concept of ancestral memory, I maintain that we must recognize both the empowering and the essentializing aspects of her approach.

Victoria Santa Cruz is famous in Peru for her use of ancestral memory as a means to re-create forgotten Afro-Peruvian dances, especially the *landó*. She writes: "One of my most important choreographic works was the creation of the 'disappeared' *landó* dance, which had disappeared as a form, but was alive in my ancestral memory" (Santa Cruz 1995). Victoria Santa Cruz first became acquainted with the Peruvian *landó* when she was a child. She recalls, "The first time I heard this beautiful and simple melody was from the lips of my mother's sister when I was barely six years old; this was one of the clues that moved in me unforgettable memories related to ancient ancestral connections" (ibid.). In this melody's rhythm, years later, she found the blueprint for its choreography. She writes, "Just as I discovered that all melodic lines implicitly carry their own harmony, I also rediscovered that the rhythmic combinations in a rhythmic phrase or unit also generate their respective movement and gesture, provided that we find a level of psychic connection" (ibid.).

Victoria Santa Cruz believes that through her choreographic re-creation of the *landó*, she recovered a musical memory of her ancestral homeland that is more "African" than contemporary Africa. She has been to Africa, and she perceives Africans who lived under colonialism as more European than African (Santa Cruz 2000). Thus, her Afrocentric re-creation of the *landó* creates an "island of time" (Assman 1995) by skipping over the Middle Passage entirely to recover a direct link with the Africa that preceded the Atlantic slave trade and colonialism.

Although Victoria Santa Cruz is unanimously credited with having rescued the *landó*'s choreography from obscurity, Afro-Peruvian musicians and scholars disagree about whether or not the choreography performed as *landó* since the revival—a dance featuring laundresses carrying washbasins and wringing clothes to dry—is the one she re-created.[10] When I asked Victoria Santa Cruz herself, her answer was elusive. She responded that "choreography" is simply a word that describes movements and figures that are the result of a process. That process is what is important and should be remembered (Santa Cruz 2000).

In addition to re-creating the lost *landó*, Victoria Santa Cruz used her ancestral memory to restore the "correct" manner of performing the *zamacueca* (a couple dance similar to the *marinera*), to choreograph African-inspired possession rituals, and so on. As director of Peru's national dance ensemble during the military revolution of the 1970s, she helped craft the ideology, training methods, and content of Peru's national folklore. Years later, Victoria Santa Cruz and her idiosyncratic method are generally acknowledged as pivotal in the struggle to reclaim the forgotten Afro-Peruvian past and elevate black arts to the stage in Peru.

Why was Victoria Santa Cruz's method so widely accepted? Perhaps because of the black Pacific's diasporic isolation and the lack of research and publicly available resources about Peru's actual African heritage, ancestral memory may have been perceived as one of the only available routes to recovering the remote African past. Further, in a country where people of African descent faced the double predicament of being invisible as an ethnic group but discriminated against as individuals, locating Africa in one's own body is likely to have been a tremendously empowering act for Victoria Santa Cruz's protégés, and a disarming one for critics (see Feldman 2006, 58–72). As Victoria Santa Cruz herself might say, while the choreographies she re-created became enduring symbols of African heritage, they are only end results of what is more important—the process that resulted in their creation.

Relocating Africa in Peru

About two hours south of Lima by car, a dirt road leads inland from the Panamerican Highway to several small districts in the province of Chincha, where blacks settled after abolition and continued to perform agricultural labor. The districts of El Carmen, San Regis, El Guayabo, and San José are known for their high concentration of black residents, their folklore and music traditions, and their rural lifestyle. Roads are unpaved and most residents lack plumbing or telephones. In the 1960s and 1970s, urban revival artists (including the Santa Cruzes) flocked to rural Chincha in search of surviving African-descended music. Scholars soon learned that Chincha was the source of the rural music and dance staged by the new urban black folklore and they began to write about its traditions (Tompkins 1981; Vásquez Rodríguez 1982). Tourists began to flood the El Carmen district in Chincha at certain times of year, when the residents performed the traditions that put Chincha on the map as Peru's recreated "Africa" in the black Pacific.

By the time I arrived on the scene to begin my doctoral research in the 1990s, Chincha was widely considered to be the center of black musical heritage in Peru and a full-fledged tourist attraction. The legend of Chincha was disseminated through tourism offices and brochures, newspaper articles, cab drivers, scholars, films, and television, all of which prepared visitors for an enclave of African survivals. As a result of this buildup, when I visited Chincha, I was surprised at how *Andean* (meaning expressive of indigenous or mestizo highland culture) some of the local traditions seemed. Appearing to negate common perceptions of deep-seated antagonism between black and indigenous Peruvians (see Greene 2007), the afromestizo nature of Peru's black expressive culture demonstrates what may be another distinguishing feature of the black Pacific—the relatively high level of mixture of indigenous and African-descended cultural traditions and peoples, a condition not found in black Atlantic regions such as Cuba and Brazil (where hybridity and creolization tend to be framed in terms of black-white mixture and where a smaller percentage of the population is of indigenous descent).[11] Why did certain public discourses about Chincha seem to ignore these comparisons to Andean traditions?

As cultural critic George Yúdice notes (2003), in the global era, elites and subaltern groups increasingly convert culture into a resource that connects local citizens to global economies. Exemplifying Yúdice's notion of cultural expediency, Chinchanos and their global co-producers have used blackness as cultural capital since the 1970s. On any given weekend at the modest home of the Ballumbrosios, El Carmen's designated family of culture bearers, one is likely to find a crew of international tourists, artists, scholars, filmmakers, and others who wish to document, analyze, or simply experience black Peru's rural origins. The public emphasis on the African over the Andean side of Chincha's multiethnic heritage converts local black culture into a resource for both tourism and the commerce in "authentic" rural Afro-Peruvian music. This phenomenon is particularly apparent in the festivals widely deemed to be most representative of the area's African-descended culture: the *yunza* and Black Christmas.

The *yunza* is a group dance performed throughout the Peruvian Andes at the end of Carnival. Each year a host decorates a tree with fruits, candies, gifts, balloons, toilet paper, and other adornments. Locally popular music styles are played, and the community performs a circle dance around the tree. Periodically, a couple dances in the center of the circle and then uses an axe to chop at the tree. Traditionally, the couple that knocks the tree down must host the following year's *yunza*.[12]

Despite the African "hype," the *yunza* appears to be an Andean survival in black Peru. The main difference between El Carmen's *yunza* and its Andean counterparts is the music, which in El Carmen includes Afro-Peruvian styles popularized during the urban revival. A typical *yunza* band in El Carmen prominently features the *cajón* (the quintessential symbol of black music since the revival) along with two or more guitars, singers, and small percussion. However, according to Miki González, a rock musician who lived in El Carmen in 1978, there were no *cajones* in El Carmen until *after* the revival (González 2000). If this is true, the "black" music that separates El Carmen's *yunza* from its Andean counterpart was borrowed from the urban revival rather than preserved in El Carmen and staged in the revival. In fact, at a meeting I attended in El Carmen's Centro Cultural Afroperuano San Daniel Comboni in 2009, community elders stated that the *marinera* (a graceful and intricate couple dance with handker-chiefs) was traditionally danced at the *yunza* until the late 1970s, when the style changed to faster and more "indecent" dances popularized in the revival, such as the *festejo*.

Another feature that marks El Carmen's *yunza* as "black" for many tourists and some urban Afro-Peruvians is the eroticism of the couple dances, recon-structed as an African retention since the revival. Exemplifying Yúdice's notion of cultural expediency, in 2000 the *yunza* was part of the fifteenth annual Black Summer festival, organized by the municipality of Chincha to promote tourism. T-shirts and posters displaying caricatures of large-lipped, voluptuous, danc-ing black women were sold in the street (see Figure 2.4). This strategic ethnic marketing relies on the Peruvian cultural stereotypes that Deborah Poole (1997) has described that separate the sexualized black female body from the virginal Inca maiden in the national imagination. At the *yunza* that I witnessed in 2000, most couples that danced in the center of the circle of onlookers conformed to expectations of eroticism, with suggestive, low-to-the-ground moves and body-hugging proximity. However, all is not what it seems, as I discovered when I showed my videotape of the *yunza* to Adelina Ballumbrosio, matriarch of El Carmen's "first family" of Afro-Peruvian music and dance, who had not ventured out of the house to see the *yunza* in several years. As she watched, she began to laugh. When I asked her to explain what was funny, she told me that nearly everyone dancing around the tree was a tourist from Lima, while the residents of El Carmen sat and watched the tourists.

Like the *yunza*, El Carmen's Catholic festival known as Black Christmas, or the Festival of the Virgin of El Carmen, has Andean parallels. The structure of events mirrors that of Catholicized Andean ritual festivals that re-create and present for worship particular saints and icons that represent the Virgin Mary and Jesus (see Mendoza 2000). During the festival, groups of young boys and men, called *hatajos de negritos*, perform Spanish Christmas songs honoring the Virgin and Jesus, suggesting images of both slavery and Christianity (see Figure 2.5). Groups of black *negritos* once were widespread throughout the region, but the *hatajo* of El Carmen is one of the few remaining black groups. The *negritos* carry rope whips and mark beats with handbells, and between sung verses they perform unison *zapateo* (tap dancing) steps in two parallel line formations, man-aged by a *caporal* (foreman).

There is much about this music to suggest Andean influence, if not origins. The use of the violin and the full-footed dance stomp are often described as reminiscent of typical Andean traditions (C. Ballumbrosio 2000; Sandoval 2000). Further, as William Tompkins points out (1981, 338), some of the songs and their vocal performance style resemble the popular Andean *huayno* genre.

Figure 2.4. Poster for the 2000 Black Summer Festival. Author's collection.

Figure 2.5. *Hatajos de negritos.* Courtesy of Caretas Ilustración Peruana.

Dances called *negritos* are also performed in many festivals in Peru's indigenous and mestizo highland communities, allegedly having originated when Spanish colonialists obligated Native Peruvian nobles to perform imagined versions of black dances in religious festivals (Salas Carreño 1998, 110). Michelle Bigenho writes that in Lucanas, Ayacucho, Native Peruvians—wearing black masks, carrying whips and shaking handbells—dance in two parallel lines, directed by a "foreman" and accompanied by violin and other instruments (Bigenho 1998).

Is the *negritos* repertoire of Chincha an Andean survival in which Afro-Peruvians imitate an imitation of themselves? Or is it the only remnant of the prototype imitated by indigenous and mestizo Peruvians? While I have no answer to this question, I am impressed by the readiness with which public discourse in Peru affirms an African origin myth without providing historical documentation or explanations for Andean parallels. Surely this is a strategy of the black Pacific, where the mixture of African and indigenous cultures is more common than in the black Atlantic and where that mixture is nevertheless constructed as "black" or "African," not in the essentializing manner of the so-called one-drop rule but rather as a strategic substitute for "more African" retentions such as those found in the black Atlantic.

Noticing the Andean qualities of Chincha's traditions casts a different light on Chincha's role as the legendary site of origins for the urban Afro-Peruvian revival. Ironically, Chincha's traditions sometimes appear less stereotypically African than the re-created ones they inspired. For example, Rony Campos, who succeeded his late father, Ronaldo Campos, as director of Perú Negro, the leading Afro-Peruvian company from the revival, told me that after early Perú Negro members collected black music and dances in Chincha young dancers learned the steps. When the company mounted them as staged dances, Rony said, "my father made them blacker" (Campos 2000). Thus, while Chincha became Peru's "Africa" in the discourse of revival artists, Chincha's music and dance traditions may better represent the multiethnic origins of Afro-Peruvian culture.

Building an Afro-Peruvian Social Movement: Music and Politics

The power of music to affect social change is often underestimated; music is often seen as a mere soundtrack to social movements that involve politics, power, and identity. Social movement scholarship tends either to ignore music altogether or to describe it only in passing (usually focusing only on lyrics or on songs as part of social action events). This may be because social movement theorists initially insisted upon the dominance of structural explanations, minimizing issues such as emotion, culture, creativity, leadership, and the creation of norms and values linked to new visions of subjectivity (see Barker, Johnson, and

Lavalette 2001; Della Porta and Diani 1999; Jasper 1997; Killian 1973; McAdam 1994; Weber 1946). In fact, American studies of social movements have only in recent decades moved beyond structuralism to acknowledge the agency of the actors in social movements (see Della Porta and Diani 1999; Eyerman and Jamison 1995; Jasper 1997). So-called new social movements, a category that generated an explosion of scholarship in the 1980s and 1990s, focus on the politics of identity (racial, ethnic, gender, etc.) and resist Marxist and structuralist modes of analysis. In new social movements, music often serves as a powerful agent of identity formation.

For the marginalized community of Afro-descendants in Peru, beginning in the late 1950s, music was the catalyst that launched the political struggle for civil rights. In the absence of a prominent political movement for black rights, the revival served as the primary means of promoting an African diasporic identity in Peru, elevating performers of African descent to Lima's grandest stages and challenging the invisibility of blacks in Peru by staging the culture of Peru's enslaved Africans and their descendants. Later, music's identity-building work opened the door for more overt political organizing through the formation of several Afro-Peruvian political and social organizations.[13] These groups grew from meetings held in the 1960s and 1970s that were directly inspired by young Afro-Peruvian intellectuals' interviews with Nicomedes Santa Cruz and by the U.S. civil rights and Black Power movements (one group emulated the Black Panthers in dress), and members of these groups included the artists who were active in the revival (Millones 2000; Rojas 2007, 146–148).[14] In the 1980s, Afro-Peruvian university students, some of whom had participated in the groups formed in the 1960s and 1970s, created the Institute of Afro-Peruvian Investigations (INAPE) with the intention of promoting research, analysis, and public lectures about the problems and conditions blacks in Peru faced. However, these early organizations did not attract a broad-based constituency or financial resources (although INAPE did receive initial funding from the Ford Foundation and the National Council of Sciences and Technology [CONCYTEC]), so they were short lived (Rodríguez Pastor 2008, 36; Thomas 2009, 16).

Movimiento Negro "Francisco Congo" (MNFC), which was founded in 1986 and was named for a runaway slave who led a resistance movement in Peru, became the first major grassroots organization to fight for black civil rights and political justice in Peru. This group included in its leadership members of the highly respected Afro-Peruvian Vásquez family, whose patriarch, Don Porfirio Vásquez, had been a major consultant for both José Durand and Nicomedes Santa Cruz during the revival. Nicomedes Santa Cruz himself is said to have attended some of the group's early meetings (Thomas 2009, 18). In its manifesto (Movimiento Negro Francisco Congo 1987), the leaders of the organization specifically refer to the roles of the Vásquez and Santa Cruz families in pre-serving black music. One of the group's major activities was the re-mounting of the Afro-Peruvian street dance *el son de los diablos* during Carnival. But the manifesto moves beyond recognition of black culture to "promote a platform of ethnic-cultural revindication." It enumerates the conditions resulting from racial prejudice against blacks and outlines a detailed platform for social action, including efforts to promote equal opportunities in work and education, efforts to intervene against drug addiction and delinquency among black Peruvian youth at risk, and so on (Movimiento Negro Francisco Congo 1987, 7–9). The organization attracted funding from Oxfam and the London-based Minority Rights Group. But in the 1990s, internal conflicts led some members of MNFC to form their own organization, Palenque, which lasted until 1995. Around 1999, Movimiento Negro Francisco Congo changed its name to Movimiento Nacional Afroperuano Francisco Congo (MNAFC), reflecting an ideological shift from "black" to "Afro-Peruvian" in the organization's focus.

While Movimiento Negro Francisco Congo dominated the political scene in the 1980s and most of the 1990s, by 2005, according to John Thomas III, at least fifteen Afro-Peruvian organizations were in operation (Thomas 2009, 21).[15] Some organizations involved new actors, but many emerged as the result of the splintering of existing organizations (especially MNFC) into different groups and offshoots in response to internal conflicts.[16] Some capitalized on newly available funding from international organizations interested in supporting the development of Afro-Latin communities and culture (see Rojas 2007, 206–208, 211).[17] Responding in part to the interest areas of foreign funding agencies, orga-nizations began to focus on specialized areas (e.g., women's issues, youth, rural versus urban, specific regions and neighborhoods, blacks and the Church, etc.). In the 1990s, Lima-based organizations tried to broaden their bases, incorporat-ing both urban and rural black populations by holding "*encuentros*" (meetings) in various regions hosted by MNFC (Greene 2007, 469n4; Rodríguez Pastor 2008, 425–429; Thomas 2009, 19). The Foro Afroperuano (Afro-Peruvian Fo-rum), founded in 2002, coordinates and serves as a clearinghouse for the en-deavors of many of these organizations, maintaining an informational website at http://www.cimarrones-peru.org/foro.htm.

The Peruvian government also created organizations that claimed to address the condition of Afro-Peruvians and other oppressed populations, but these initiatives were fraught with problems. In 2001, taking advantage of a $5 mil-lion loan from the World Bank intended for the development of impoverished black coastal communities in Peru, Peruvian president Alejandro Toledo's wife, anthropologist Eliane Karp, spearheaded an initiative to promote policies in support of the rights of Peru's multicultural citizens. The first institution to result from this initiative was the National Commission of Andean, Amazonian, and Afro-Peruvian Peoples (CONAPA). This organization, now defunct, was the subject of a scandal over alleged misuse of funds and failure to adequately represent indigenous and Afro-Peruvian citizens (the organization did not even include Afro-Peruvians in its name or personnel at first, despite the World Bank's specific criteria that the funds be used to promote development of that community) (see Greene 2007, 2008; Rojas 2007, 288). In 2004, it was replaced by the National Institute for the Development of Andean, Amazonian, and Afro-Peruvian Peoples (INDEPA), which inspired its share of criticism for lack of true representation of the people whose rights it ostensibly championed (see Greene 2007; Rojas 2007, 288–289). Government-initiated recognition of Afro-Peruvian culture was achieved through Congresswoman Martha Moyano's Mesa Afroperuana, which, among other achievements, successfully passed legislation making Nicomedes Santa Cruz's birthday (June 4) the Day of Afro-Peruvian Culture and convened the First National Afro-Peruvian Congress in 2004, in conjunction with the Sesquicentennial of Emancipation (Greene 2007, 464; Thomas 2009, 23).[18]

Several of the Afro-Peruvian organizations formed in the 1990s and 2000s recognize the liberating work of revival artists such as Nicomedes and Victoria Santa Cruz, both specifically and indirectly (one is even named LUNDU), and they continue to promote black Peruvian music and dance as a form of cultural preservation and pride. Enabled by the identity-building work of the music and dance revival, these organizations have taken the struggle a step further. While much remains to be accomplished to achieve social justice for Afro-descendants in Peru (see Rojas 2007 and Thomas 2009 for interesting discussions regarding these challenges), this phase of the struggle has allowed many black Peruvians to step out of the Afro-Peruvian revival's folkloric frame (which emphasized the slave past in order to reinscribe blacks in Peruvian history) and shine a spotlight on the visibility and social conditions of contemporary blacks in Peru.[19]

Conclusion: The Black Pacific Region

While the black Pacific strategies employed during the Afro-Peruvian revival (that is, borrowing from other parts of the diaspora, promoting the concept of embodied ancestral memory, presenting cultural traditions of mixed origins as "black," and using music as the first step in the social movement to promote black identity) occur in isolation elsewhere in the African diaspora, the composite picture created by these and other black Pacific strategies brings the black Pacific condition into sharper focus. Citizens of the black Pacific use these types of strategies because of their extreme social invisibility and their isolation from what they see as "more African" regions of the diaspora. Black Pacific citizens are heirs of the second journey that cut their ancestors off from the African diaspora's mainstream, and if and when they strive to reawaken their dormant diasporic identity and extricate blackness from local creole culture, they find that few resources or traditional strategies for building black identity and recovering lost history are available. Thus, they reinvent traditions and they look for Africa and its legacy in nontraditional locales (other parts of the diaspora, the body, and afromestizo cultural blends).

I offer this model of the black Pacific as a way to better understand the diasporic condition of Afro-descendants in Peru, adding a new dimension to Gilroy's important work on the black Atlantic. On a deeper level, if the black Pacific model resembles the experience of other communities beyond Peru (such as Ecuador, Chile, Colombia's Pacific coast, or Bolivia), it may provide a more nuanced understanding of the larger African diaspora(s).[20]

Notes

Some material in this chapter was published previously in my book, *Black Rhythms of Peru: Reviving African Musical Heritage in the Black Pacific*, and in my article "African or Andean? Origin Myths and Musical Performance in the Cradle of Black Peru."

1. It is common in Peru for people with any Asian ancestry to be called *"chino"* or *"china,"* whether or not they are of Chinese heritage, and Fujimori was labeled "El Chino" despite his Japanese ancestry. "*Cholo*" refers to an indigenous, rural person in the process of becoming urban and mestizo. Toledo was called "Cholo" because he was the first president with visibly indigenous ancestry, following Japanese American president Fujimori and a long line of European-descended *criollos*.

2. Peru's Afro-Peruvian population is concentrated along the coast, living in close proximity to the descendants of Europeans. Highland regions are primarily populated by Peru's indigenous peoples, although the great migration waves of the mid-twentieth century brought many indigenous and mestizo peasants to urban coastal areas.

3. This translation is mine, as are all others in this chapter, unless otherwise noted. I will discuss CONAPA in greater detail later in the chapter.

4. According to Scheuss de Studer, some enslaved Africans were taken through the interior from Rio de la Plata by land via Chile (1958, 222–224, 237).

5. There are many possible reasons for the prevalence of the notion that blacks "disappeared" from Pacific coastal countries: the smaller numbers of enslaved Africans and lesser participation in the late years of the slave trade in those countries, national ideologies encouraging "whitening" through miscegenation and targeted immigration, the larger presence of indigenous populations, and social conditions promoting a higher rate of assimilation into coastal creole culture (such as smaller plantations and the prevalence of urban and domestic slavery).

6. Typical *jaranas* lasted from four to eight days and nights, during which time the door was locked so that no one could leave before the official *despedida* (farewell) (Bracamonte-Bontemps 1987, 233; Tompkins 1981, 93).

7. Although Durand's Pancho Fierro company is acknowledged as a milestone, a few smaller

theatrical initiatives had already introduced black Peruvian music to the concert stage in Lima. Beginning in 1936, Samuel Márquez's Ricardo Palma company performed a mixture of *música criolla* and a few "old black songs" in a theatrical performance (Tompkins 1998, 500). In the 1940s, Rosa Mercedes Ayarza de Morales (a white *criolla* pianist/composer) transcribed, staged, and published symphonic and chamber music arrangements of black Peruvian songs performed for her by the elderly Ascuez brothers, who were revered for their knowledge of disappearing black Peruvian musical traditions. Pancho Fierro company member Nicomedes Santa Cruz viewed Durand's company as an extension of the Pampa de Amancaes, the site of an annual Lima festival of folkloric and *criollo* music and dance that was discontinued shortly before the Pancho Fierro company was founded in the 1950s (Nicomedes Santa Cruz quoted in R. Vásquez Rodríguez 1982, 37).

8. The Spanish *décima* is a poetic form based on ten-line strophes that came to the Americas with the Spanish conquest. In Peru, rural black and indigenous populations adopted the *décima*. Nicomedes Santa Cruz revitalized the *décima* and used it as a vehicle of negritude and political protest, performing it on stage, on television, and in recordings.

9. In Paris, Victoria Santa Cruz studied at the Université du Théâtre des Nations and École Supérieure d'Études Chorégraphiques. During this period, she also visited Africa for the first time as a member of a student theater group that toured Tangiers, Marrakesh, and Casablanca as well as Spain, Italy, Belgium, and Portugal (Revollar 1967, 7). The exact content of Victoria Santa Cruz's studies and cosmopolitan experiences in Paris and their impact on her later work in Peru is an area where further research is needed.

10. During the Afro-Peruvian revival, two *landós* were collected from elders in the Afro-Peruvian community and mounted for staged performance: "Samba Malató," which was re-created by Nicomedes and Victoria Santa Cruz with Cumanana, and "Samba *Landó*," which was collected in rural El Guayabo and stylized by the music and dance company Perú Negro. Each of these songs features a distinct choreography (see Feldman 2006, 73–74, 109–115, 274–275n22; León Quirós 2003, 214–215; Tompkins 1981, 296–298).

11. In Peru, it is commonly asserted that blacks and indigenous Peruvians historically have been separate, and even opposed, populations. Blacks in Peru are said to have fought against indigenous Peruvians. For example, the free colored militia helped suppress the largest indigenous revolt against the Spanish, the Túpac Amaru rebellion, in the 1780s (Bowser 1974, 7, 333). As anthropologist Shane Greene notes, twenty-first-century efforts by the Peruvian state to promote a multicultural agenda tend to "privilege indigeneity over blackness, culturalizing Indians and racializing blacks" (Greene 2007, 467). However, it is important to note that separate racial terminology developed in colonial Peru to describe and document the numerous children born of black-native unions (*zambos/as*), and that several prominent leaders of the Afro-Peruvian musical and political movements, including the late Amador Ballumbrosio of Chincha, were/are of mixed black and indigenous heritage (E. Ballumbrosio 2000; Thomas 2009, 7n16). Further, William Tompkins notes that especially along the northern coast, there is significant cross-fertilization between native and black Peruvians in music and dance (1981, 375–376). In contrast, in Cuba, as in many parts of the Caribbean, the indigenous population was decimated soon after European colonization, leaving little cultural legacy. While indigenous populations with distinct cultural traditions do survive in Brazil, discourses surrounding creolization, hybridity, and *mestizaje* in Brazil and other black Atlantic nations tend to be about mixtures involving "black" and "white," making the afro-indigenous mix in the black Pacific stand out as distinctive.

12. This practice has been discontinued in El Carmen.

13. While little has been published at this writing about the development of Afro-Peruvian political organizations, John Thomas III conducted research on this topic in 2005 and 2009 and his MA thesis on the subject is forthcoming (see also Thomas 2009).

14. An older group that was active in the 1960s was Grupo Harlem, which may have been founded by Victoria and Nicomedes Santa Cruz's father. Raúl Romero states that Grupo Harlem began in the 1930s (1994, 321). Grupo de los Melomodernos was a group consisting primarily of lawyers and academics, founded by Afro-Peruvian lawyer Juan Tasayco. Two organizations emerged in the 1960s and 1970s among the younger Afro-Peruvian population: the Cultural Association for Black Peruvian Youth (ACEJUNEP) and its sister organization El Tribú (The Tribe). These groups held "Soul Parties" for Afro-Peruvian youth, with Afro-Peruvian music, salsa, and U.S. black popular music (Rodríguez Pastor 2008, 36; Romero 1994, 321; Thomas 2009, 15–16).

15. These organizations (with establishment dates listed according to formal recognition by the Peruvian national registry) are: Movimiento Negro Francisco Congo (est. 1986); Asociación Negra de Defensa de los Derechos Humanos (ASONEDH; est. 1990); Mundo de Ebano and Centro de Desarrollo de la Mujer Negra Peruana (CEDEMUNEP; est. 1993); Cimarrones (est. 1998); Centro de Desarrollo Etnico (CEDET) and Perú Afro (both est. 1999); Mujer Negra y Desarrollo, Margarita, and Ciudadanos Negros (all est. 2000); Mamaine, Asociación Cultural Promoción de Desarrollo—Todas las Sangres, and Lundú (all est. 2001); Asociación Plurietnica Impulsora del Desarrollo Comunal y Social (APEIDO) and Organización para el Desarrollo e Identidad del Rimac (ODIR) (both est. 2002); Organización de Desarrollo Afro-Chalaco, Makungu, and Orgullo Afroperuano (all est. 2004); and Las Mesas Técnicas de la CONAPA and La Mesa de Trabajo Afroperuano (both est. 2005) (Thomas 2009, 33).

16. During the 1990s, the MNFC founded an NGO called the Asociación Negra de Derechos Humanos (ASONEDH), which dedicated itself to attracting international funding for Afro-Peruvian development issues. It also founded the Centro por el Desarrollo Etnico (CEDET), which attracted funding from German organizations in support of MNFC's organizing in the provinces (Thomas 2009, 19–20).

17. MNFC worked with Afro/America XXI, a regional alliance based in Washington, D.C., that sought to unite Afro-Latin movements and lobby for their funding. Interest also was generated by the participation of several groups in the 2001 Third World Conference Against Xenophobia, Racism and All Forms of Discrimination in Durban, South Africa (Thomas 2009: 20, 22). Monica Rojas attributes the flourishing of Afro-Peruvian organizations in part to Alberto Fujimori's neoliberal policies (1990–2000), which promoted a flood of investment and foreign aid in Peru from international organizations (Rojas 2007, 213).

18. Martha Moyano is one of three black members of Congress elected in Peru in 2001 (the others were Cecilia Tait and José Luís Risco).

19. After conducting a study among Afro-Peruvian organizations in the 2000s, John Thomas III concluded that the organizations had not achieved a successful strategy for social change, instead displaying disunity, division, failure to engage the community at a grassroots level, and a lack of coherent goals. John Thomas III's research also shows that over half of the Afro-Peruvian organizations active in 2005 were self-funded (Thomas 2009, 22, 35).

20. The work of several other scholars suggests that communities outside Peru may display characteristics of the black Pacific. Peter Wade, for example, has examined the cultural politics separating the black populations of Colombia's Atlantic and Pacific coasts (1993, 1998), and Michael Birenbaum Quintero has produced a dissertation (2009) and forthcoming work on music

in Colombia's black Pacific. In Bolivia, Robert Templeman (1998) documented how the forgotten *saya* was revived as the soundtrack of the black identity movement in the 1970s, resulting in disputes regarding whose re-created version was authentic. Jonathan Ritter (1998) has explored how the 1970s folklore revival of the Afro-Ecuadorian *marimba* tradition carved out a new public space for "blackness." The black Pacific might also be envisioned as a metaphorically, rather than geographically, bordered community, possibly including some culture groups not located on the Pacific coast. Bobby Vaughn (2005) and Angela Castañeda's (2004) work on Afro-Mexican culture, along with Lise Waxer's work on Cali, Colombia (2002) and the large body of literature on the Mardi Gras Indians of New Orleans, Louisiana (Berry, Foose, and Jones 2003; Lipsitz 1990; Sakakeeny 2002) might all constitute examples of cultures that share strategies and conditions with the black Pacific, despite their distance from the Pacific coast.

Bibliography

Andrews, George Reid. 2004. *Afro-Latin America, 1800–2000*. New York: Oxford University Press.

Appiah, Kwame Anthony. 1992. *In My Father's House: Africa in the Philosophy of Culture*. New York: Oxford University Press.

Assman, Jan. 1995. "Collective Memory and Cultural Identity." *New German Critique* 65 (Spring–Summer):125–133.

Ballumbrosio, Camilo. 2000. Interview with the author. Lima, Perú, March 16.

Ballumbrosio, Eusebio. 2000. "Mira el negro cómo está en el campo: los Ballumbrosios." In *Lo africano en la cultura criolla*, 169–176. Lima: Fondo Editorial del Congreso del Perú.

Barker, Colin, Alan Johnson, and Michael Lavalette, eds. 2001. *Leadership and Social Movements*. New York: Manchester University Press.

Becerra, Miguel Angel. 2010. "Stereotypes of Afro-Peruvians through the Media: The Case of the Peruvian Blackface." MA thesis, University of California, Santa Barbara.

Berry, Jason, Jonathan Foose, and Tad Jones. 2003. "In Search of the Mardi Gras Indians." In *Where Brer Rabbit Meets Coyote: African-Native American Literature*, ed. Jonathan Brennan, 197–217. Urbana: University of Illinois Press.

Bigenho, Michelle. 1998. "El baile de los negritos y la danza de las tijeras: Un manejo de contradicciones." In *Música, danzas y máscaras en los Andes*, 2nd ed., ed. Raúl R. Romero, 219–252. Lima: Pontificia Universidad Católica del Perú and Instituto Riva-Agüero.

Birenbaum Quintero, Michael. 2009. "The Musical Making of Race and Place in Colombia's Black Pacific." PhD diss., New York University.

Bowser, Frederick P. 1974. *The African Slave in Colonial Peru, 1524–1650*. Stanford, Calif.: Stanford University Press.

Bracamonte-Bontemps, Laura. 1987. "Dance in Social Context: The Peruvian Vals." MA thesis, University of California, Los Angeles.

Bridges, Tyler. 2004. "Long after Slavery, Inequities—and Some Progress—Seen." *Miami Herald*, August 1.

Campos, Rony. 2000. Interview with the author. Lima, Perú, March 16.

Carneiro, Edison. 1961. *Samba de umbigada*. Rio de Janeiro: Ministerio da Educaçao e Cultura Campanha de Defesa do Folclore Brasileiro.

Cascudo, Luís da Câmara. 1962. *Dicionário do folclore brasileiro*. 2nd ed. Rio de Janeiro: Instituto Nacional do Livro.

Castañeda, Angela Nicole. 2004. "'Veracruz también es Caribe': Power, Politics, and Performance in the Making of an Afro-Caribbean Identity." PhD diss., Indiana University, Bloomington.

Congreso de la República, Comisión de Amazonía, Asuntos Indígenas y Afroperuanos. 2002. "Plan de trabajo." Legislatura 2002–2003, aprobado en sesión del 26-08-02. Lima, Perú. Available at http://www.congreso.gob.pe/comisiones/2002/asuntos-indigenas-afro/PLAN-DE-TRABAJO.pdf. Accessed May 4, 2011.

De la Cadena, Marisol. 1998. "Silent Racism and Intellectual Superiority in Peru." *Bulletin of Latin American Research* 17 (2): 143–164.

Della Porta, Donatella, and Mario Diani. 1999. *Social Movements: An Introduction*. Malden, Mass.: Blackwell.

Du Bois, W.E.B. (1903) 1994. *The Souls of Black Folk*. Chicago: A. C. McClurg & Co.; repr., New York: Dover Publications.

Dzidzienyo, Anani, and Suzanne Oboler, eds. 2005. *Neither Enemies nor Friends: Latinos, Blacks, Afro-Latinos*. New York: Palgrave Macmillan.

Eyerman, Ron, and Andrew Jamison. 1995. "Social Movements and Cultural Transformation: Popular Music in the 1960s." *Media, Culture, and Society* 17 (3): 449–468.

Feldman, Heidi Carolyn. 2005. "The Black Pacific: Cuban and Brazilian Echoes in the Afro-Peruvian Revival." *Ethnomusicology* 49 (2): 206–231.

———. 2006. *Black Rhythms of Peru: Reviving African Musical Heritage in the Black Pacific*. Middletown, Conn: Wesleyan University Press.

———. 2009. "African or Andean? Origin Myths and Musical Performance in the Cradle of Black Peru." *Diagonal: Journal of the Center for Iberian and Latin American Music* 2. Available at http://www.cilam.ucr.edu/diagonal/issues/2006/.

Fox, Patricia D. 2006. *Being and Blackness in Latin America: Uprootedness and Improvisation*. Gainesville: University Press of Florida.

Fuentes, Manuel Atanasio. (1867) 1925. *Lima: Apuntes históricos, descriptivos, estadísticos y de costumbres*. Paris: F. Didot, Frères, Fils & Cie; repr., Lima: E. Moreno.

Gilroy, Paul. 1993. *The Black Atlantic: Modernity and Double Consciousness*. Cambridge, Mass.: Harvard University Press.

———. 2000. *Against Race: Imagining Political Culture beyond the Color Line*. Cambridge, Mass.: The Belknap Press of Harvard University Press.

Glave, Luis Miguel. 1995. "Origen de la cultura afroperuana." In *De cajón Caitro Soto: El duende en la música afroperuana*, ed. Bernardo Roca Rey Miró Quesada, 13–29. Lima: Servicios Especiales de Edición S.A. del Grupo Empresa Editora El Comercio.

González, Miki. 2000. Interview with the author. Lima, Perú, February 23.

Greene, Shane. 2007. "*Entre lo indio, lo negro, y lo incaico*: The Spatial Hierarchies of Difference in Multicultural Peru." *Journal of Latin American and Caribbean Anthropology* 12 (2): 441–474.

———. 2008. "On Being Black and Becoming Visible in Peru." *ACAP Magazine* (June). Available at http://www.acap-peru.org/june/on-being-black-and-becoming-visible-in-peru. Accessed May 4, 2011.

Herskovits, Melville. 1941. *The Myth of the Negro Past*. New York: Harper & Brothers.

Hobsbawm, Eric, and Terence Ranger, ed. 1983. *The Invention of Tradition*. Cambridge: Cambridge University Press.

Jasper, James M. 1997. *The Art of Moral Protest: Culture, Biography, and Creativity in Social Movements*. Chicago: University of Chicago Press.

Killian, Lewis M. 1973. "Social Movements: A Review of the Field." In *Social Movements: A Reader and Source Book*, ed. R. R. Evans. Chicago: Rand McNally College Pub. Co.

La Prensa. 1961. "En el censo no preguntarán la raza; No hay problema racial en el Perú." May 13, p. 5.

León Quirós, Javier Francisco. 2003. "The Aestheticization of Tradition: Professional Afroperuvian Musicians, Cultural Reclamation, and Artistic Interpretation." PhD diss., University of Texas at Austin.

————. 2007. "The 'Danza de las Cañas': Music, Theatre and Afroperuvian Modernity." In *Musical Performance in the Diaspora*, ed. Tina K. Ramnarine, 127–155. New York: Routledge.

Lipsitz, George. 1990. "Mardi Gras Indians: Carnival and Counter-Narrative in Black New Orleans." In *Time Passages: Collective Memory and American Popular Culture*, 233–253. Minneapolis: University of Minnesota Press.

Living in Peru. 2007. "Peru: Miraflores Night Club Denies Racism Charges." June 12. Available at http://www.livinginperu.com/news/4052. Accessed September 21, 2010.

Luciano, José, and Humberto Rodriguez Pastor. 1995. "Peru." Trans. Meagan Smith. In *No Longer Invisible: Afro-Latin Americans Today*, ed. Minority Rights Group, 271–286. London: Minority Rights Publications.

McAdam, Doug. 1994. "Culture and Social Movements." In *New Social Movements: From Ideology to Identity*, ed. E. Laraña, H. Johnston, and J. R. Gusfield, 36–57. Philadelphia, Pa.: Temple University Press.

Mendoza, Zoila S. 2000. *Shaping Society through Dance: Mestizo Ritual Performance in the Peruvian Andes*. Chicago: University of Chicago Press.

Millones, Luis. 2000. Interview with the author. Lima, Perú, March 21.

Minority Rights Group, ed. 1995. *No Longer Invisible: Afro-Latin Americans Today*. London: Minority Rights Publications.

Movimiento Negro "Francisco Congo." 1987. "Manifiesto, Plataforma, Estatutos." Lima, Perú: Movimiento Negro Francisco Congo.

Oboe, Annalisa, and Anna Scacchi. 2008. *Recharting the Black Atlantic: Modern Cultures, Local Communities, Global Connections*. New York: Routledge.

Oboler, Suzanne. 2005. "The Foreignness of Racism: Pride and Prejudice among Peru's Limeños in the 1990s." In *Neither Enemies nor Friends: Latinos, Blacks, Afro-Latinos*, ed. Anani Dzidzienyo and Suzanne Oboler, 75–100. New York: Palgrave Macmillan.

Peru.com. 2009. "Diario 'El Comercio' pide disculpas por comercial racista que ofende a afroperuanos." December 1. Available at http://www.peru.com/noticias/portada20091201/69121/Diario-El-Comercio-pide-disculpas-por-comercial-racista-que-ofende-a-afroperuanos-. Accessed September 21, 2010.

Poole, Deborah. 1997. *Vision, Race, and Modernity: A Visual Economy of the Andean Image World*. Princeton, N.J.: Princeton University Press.

Portocarrero, Gonzalo. 2000. "Comentario." In *Lo africano en la cultura criolla*, 207–212. Lima, Perú: Fondo Editorial del Congreso del Perú.

Quiroz, Carlos A. 2010. "Racism Media in Peru Causes Protests over TV Characters That Are Offensive to Indigenous and Afro Peruvians." *Peruanista*, April 8. Available at http://peruanista.blogspot.com/2010/04/racism-in-peru-media-causes-protests.html. Accessed September 21, 2010.

Revollar, Pilar. 1967. "Victoria Santa Cruz y la danza prohibida." *Ella* 43 (October 28): 6–7.

Ritter, Jonathan Larry. 1998. "La Marimba Esmereldeña: Music and Ethnicity on Ecuador's Northern Coast." MA thesis, University of California, Los Angeles.

Rodríguez Pastor, Humberto. 2008. *Negritud: Afroperuanos: Resistencia y existencia*. Lima, Perú: CEDET.

Rojas, Monica. 2007. "Docile Devils: Performing Activism through Afro-Peruvian Dance." PhD diss., University of Washington.

Romero, Fernando. 1939a. "Como era la zamacueca zamba." *Turismo* 140: n.p.

———. 1939b. "Instrumentos musicales en la costa zamba." *Turismo* 137 (March): n.p.

———. 1939c. "La zamba, abuela de la marinera." *Turismo* 141: n.p.

———. 1939d. "Ritmo negro en la costa zamba." *Turismo* 135 (January): n.p.

———. 1940. "De la 'samba' de Africa a la 'marinera' del Perú." *Estudios Afrocubanos* 4 (1–4): 82–120.

———. 1946a. "La evolución de 'la marinera'" (Part 1). *IPNA* 6 (May–August): 29–33.

———. 1946b. "La evolución de 'la marinera'" (Part 2). *IPNA* 7 (September–December): 11–21.

———. 1947. "La evolución de 'la marinera'" (Part 3). *IPNA* 8 (January–April): 12–20.

Romero, Raúl. 1994. "Black Music and Identity in Peru: Reconstruction and Revival of Afro-Peruvian Musical Traditions." In *Music and Black Ethnicity: The Caribbean and South America*, ed. Gerard H. Béhague, 307–330. Miami: North-South Center Press, University of Miami.

Sakakeeny, Matt. 2002. "Indian Rulers: Mardi Gras Indians and New Orleans Funk." *The Jazz Archivist* 16: 9–23

Salas Carreño, Guillermo. 1998. "Representación de la esclavitud en danzas peruanas." In *I Convocatoria Nacional "José María Arguedas" Avances de Investigación—Danza*. Lima: Biblioteca Nacional del Perú and Pontificia Universidad Católica del Perú.

Sandoval, Lucho. 2000. Interview with the author. Lima, Perú, March 1.

Santa Cruz, Nicomedes. (1964) 1970a. *Cumanana*. With Conjunto Cumanana (Kumanana). 3rd ed. LP. Philips/El Virrey Industrias Musicales S.A., P6350 001/002.

———. (1964) 1970b. "Cumanana: Antología afroperuana." Booklet to accompany the *Cumanana* LP, revised ed. for 3rd ed. of boxed set. El Virrey Industrias Musicales S.A., P6350 001/002.

———. 1973. "De Senegal y Malambo." *Caretas* 479 (June 21–July 5): 22–24.

Santa Cruz, Octavio. n.d. "Familia Santa Cruz." Web Site. Available at: http://espanol.geocities.com/familiasantacruz/. Accessed 2002.

Santa Cruz, Rafael. 1988. "Un 'Matalaché' blanco." *La República*, September 8. Manuscript copy provided by Rafael Santa Cruz.

Santa Cruz, Victoria. 1978. "Negritud en América Latina." *Folklore: Reencuentro del hombre con sus raíces* 1: 18–19.

———. 1979. "Descubrimiento y desarrollo del sentido rítmico." *Folklore: Reencuentro del hombre con sus raíces* 2: 4–7.

———. 1988. "La danza." In *Signo e imagen: La marinera*, ed. Willy F. Pinto Gamboa, 84–85. Lima: Banco de Crédito del Perú.

———. 1995. *Ritmos y aires afroperuanos*. CD and liner notes. Discos Hispanicos del Perú S.A., RH.10.0044.

———. 2000. Conversations with the author. Lima, Perú, February 21, February 28, March 29.

———. 2004. *Rhythm . . . the Eternal Organizer*, trans. Susan G. Polansky. Lima, Perú: PetroPerú.

Scheuss de Studer, Elena F. 1958. *La trata de negros en Rio de la Plata durante el siglo XVIII*. Buenos Aires: Libros de Hispanoamérica.

Scott, David. 1991. "That Event, This Memory: Notes on the Anthropology of African Diasporas in the New World." *Diaspora* 1 (3): 261–284.

Sims, Calvin. 1996. "Peru's Blacks Increasingly Discontent with Decorative Role." *New York Times*, August 17, 2.

Templeman, Robert. 1998. "We Are People of the Yungas, We Are the Saya Race." In *Blackness in Latin America and the Caribbean: Social Dynamics and Cultural Transformations*, vol. 1, ed. Norman E. Whitten Jr., and Arlene Torres, 426–444. Bloomington: Indiana University Press.

Thomas, John, III. 2009. "Theorizing Afro-Latin Social Movements: The Peruvian Case." Unpublished paper presented at the Comparative Politics Workshop, University of Chicago, May 28. Quoted with the author's permission.

Tompkins, William David. 1981. "The Musical Traditions of the Blacks of Coastal Peru." PhD diss., University of California, Los Angeles.

———. 1998. "Afro-Peruvian Traditions." In *The Garland Encyclopedia of World Music*. Vol. 2, *South America, Mexico, Central America, and the Caribbean*, ed. Dale A. Olsen and Daniel E. Sheehy, 491–502. New York: Garland Publishing.

UNHCR. 2008. "Peru—Afro-Peruvians." In World Directory of Minorities and Indigenous Peoples. Internet source. Available at http://www.unhcr.org/refworld/docid/49749ccca.html. Accessed June 8, 2009.

Vásquez Rodríguez, Rosa Elena (Chalena). 1982. *La práctica musical de la población negra en Perú: La danza de negritos de El Carmen*. Havana, Cuba: Casa de las Américas.

Vaughn, Bobby. 2005. "Afro-Mexico: Black Indigenas, Politics, and the Greater Diaspora." In *Neither Enemies nor Friends: Latinos, Blacks, Afro-Latinos*, ed. Anani Dzidzienyo and Suzanne Oboler, 117–136. New York: Palgrave Macmillan.

Wade, Peter. 1993. *Blackness and Race Mixture: The Dynamics of Racial Identity in Colombia*. Baltimore, Md.: Johns Hopkins University Press.

———. 1997. *Race and Ethnicity in Latin America*. London: Pluto Press.

———. 1998. "The Cultural Politics of Blackness in Colombia." In *Blackness in Latin America and the Caribbean: Social Dynamics and Cultural Transformations*, vol. 1, ed. Norman E. Whitten, Jr., and Arlene Torres, 311–334. Bloomington: Indiana University Press.

Waxer, Lise A. 2002. *The City of Musical Memory: Salsa, Record Grooves, and Popular Culture in Cali, Colombia*. Middletown, Conn.: Wesleyan University Press.

Weber, Max. 1946. "The Sociology of Charismatic Authority." In *From Max Weber: Essays in Sociology*, ed. H. H. Gerth and C. W. Mills, 245–252. New York: Oxford University Press.

Whitten, Norman E., Jr., and Arlene Torres, eds. 1998. *Blackness in Latin America and the Caribbean: Social Dynamics and Cultural Transformations*. Bloomington: Indiana University Press.

Williams, Brackette F. 1995. "Review of *The Black Atlantic: Modernity and Double Consciousness*, by Paul Gilroy." *Social Identities* 1 (1): 175–192.

Williams, Raymond. 1977. *Marxism and Literature*. Oxford: Oxford University Press.

World Factbook. 2010. "Peru." Available at https://www.cia.gov/library/publications/the-world-factbook/geos/pe.html. Accessed September 21, 2010.

Yúdice, George. 2003. *The Expediency of Culture: Uses of Culture in the Global Era*. Durham, N.C.: Duke University Press.

3

Malandreo Negro

Gangsta Rap and the Politics of Exclusion in Venezuela

SUJATHA FERNANDES

> Guerrilla Seca represents
> Misery, hunger, poverty, shit.
> This is the reality that can happen to you,
> What I live is *malandrismo*, real history.
>
> Guerrilla Seca, "Malandreo Negro"

"Malandreo Negro" (Black Malandrismo) is the title of a song by the Venezuelan rap group Guerrilla Seca. The title alludes to rappers' conceptions of blackness as constructed by class and place, and the resort to crime, or *malandrismo*, as an unfortunate consequence of the triage of misery, hunger, and poverty. Images of blackness in hip-hop represent both an everyday understanding of race as integrally connected to poverty and a developing consciousness related to the sharpening inequalities that occurred during the neoliberal decade of the 1990s. This stands in contrast to long-standing dominant invocations of Venezuela as a mixed-race or *café con leche* society. This understanding of race is also distinct from the more academic constructions of race in Venezuela that privilege terms such as Afro-Venezuelan and from rural over urban experiences.

At the same time, the popularity of rap in Venezuela, particularly gangsta rap, has been tied to the rise of a neoliberal consumer culture, where the good life is viewed in terms of access to material goods. Gangsta rappers have shown a proclivity for individual advancement and gain that has inhibited the development of a progressive racial politics, as was the case with hip-hop in countries such as Brazil and Cuba. Although some more black nationalist–oriented groups have emerged in recent years, they are still a relatively new phenomenon that is beyond the scope of this chapter.

In this chapter I explore the development of hip-hop as a musical form in

Venezuela, but I also address the distinct ways that rap music has taken shape in this context. The sharp divisions of race and class in neoliberal Venezuela gave way to realities of crime and violence that devolved the functions of maintaining justice and order to street gangs and urban mafias. Venezuelan rappers draw inspiration from American gangsta rappers, but at the same time they draw on a plurality of strategies and images as they construct new ways of belonging in the contemporary period.

Blackness and Racial Politics in Venezuela

Venezuelan rap emerged from a distinct set of conditions brought about by a growing process of urban segregation, a deterioration in the conditions of the urban infrastructure, and a crisis in state governance. The introduction of neoliberal economic measures in Venezuela led to spontaneous protests, rioting, and looting around the country on February 27, 1989, followed by a massive crackdown by police and the military. The gradual insertion of Venezuela into a neoliberal global order required new forms of efficiency and competition that put pressure on the state-based development model that previous governments had pursued. The shift of resources away from infrastructure, health care, education, and other social services led to a sustained increase in social inequality during this period (Predrazzini and Sanchez 2001). These changes were also racialized, with those at the bottom of the social scale—mostly black, indigenous, and mixed-race Venezuelans, who form the majority of the population—hit hardest by the changes. The social disjunctures, atomization, and crisis in governance that began in 1989 led to a spiraling in violence, crime, and urban tension. Ana María Sanjuán (2002, 87) comments that in 1999, the homicide rate in Venezuela increased 20 percent from the previous year. This number was greater in Caracas, where sometimes as many as 100 people were victims of homicides on weekends. In this context of general disorder and crisis of authority, alternative systems of justice such as street gangs and urban mafias grow in importance, contributing to a growing cycle of violence.

The period of the early 1990s also saw the growth of local popular movements in the barrios, or shantytowns, that ring the hillsides of Caracas. These nonpartisan movements reached a peak in 1998 when the Polo Patriótico, an alliance led by Hugo Chávez Frías, won the general election and came into power on the basis of promises to fight corruption, break away from the U.S.-supported neoliberal agenda, and rewrite the constitution. The political mobilization Chávez fostered has led to a deepening societal divide, as the lower classes increasingly identify along race and class lines. Highlighting his own mestizo features and dark complexion, Chávez has encouraged new forms of cultural identity based on blackness and indigeneity. Juan Carlos Echeandía, a Venezuelan rap producer, said in an interview that the emergence of rap music in Venezuela coincided with the increasing importance of the popular masses in the political process of the country: "In some ways, the popular masses begin to have voice and vote. . . . They begin to have much more importance in politics and society. And this is also what happens via the discs."[1] The appearance of a racially and politically conscious discourse in Venezuelan rap has been partly related to the emergence of a marginalized minority that is demanding its social and political rights.

Yet the forms of consciousness that are reflected and created through Venezuelan rap are related to an urban reality of crime, extreme poverty, and death by gang violence. On Echeandía's Venezuela Subterránea label (Venezuela Underground), two of the main groups are Guerrilla Seca and Vagos y Maleantes. In interviews, rappers Colombia and Requesón, members of Guerrilla Seca, talk about their musical inspiration as coming from African American gangsta rappers such as Tupac. Although Colombia and Requesón do not understand the English lyrics, they say that it is the dark and ominous tones of American gangsta rap that speak to their experiences of a kind of gang life that breeds nihilism, vacancy, and despair among youth in the barrios. In Venezuela rap music has also given voice to a new kind of racial consciousness among black youth. For instance, Requesón argues for the superiority of the black race: "We are a great race, I think we are a superior race."[2] In a shift from popular historical views of race that denied the existence of racial divisions in Venezuela and placed more importance on national than racial identity (Wright 1990), rappers have begun to reclaim black identity.

Despite the language of racial democracy that has dominated political rhetoric in Venezuela, rappers point to the underlying racism that exists in Venezuelan society and is now the basis for the politicization of racial and class cleavages. However, these reflections on race do not become demands for racial equality, as people of color in Venezuela still do not tend to see themselves as distinct groups, much less political groups. These differences are related to distinct histories, particularly the absence of race-based organizing in postcolonial Venezuela. While in contexts such as Cuba, there were several experiments in racial mobilization, such as the Partido Independiente de Color, formed in 1908, in Venezuela there were no corresponding organizations. This may be due to the fact that slavery ended in Venezuela much earlier than in other countries such as Cuba and Brazil. While slaves in Cuba and Brazil developed coherent religious systems such as Santería and Candomblé, free blacks in urban areas of Venezuela began to absorb European culture and habits. Given the myth of a mixed-race or *café con leche* society during the postcolonial period, black identity was submerged even further.

During the 1980s, several movements emerged among urban barrio communities that sought to reconstruct a notion of black culture and history. Williams Ochoa and Edgar "el Gordo" Pérez from La Vega, Totoño Blanco from San Agustín, and Jesus "Chucho" García from Caricuao began to travel to rural areas where [ex-slave communities] were concentrated to do research on traditional musical forms, drums, and fiestas. These investigations were connected to efforts to rediscover African heritage. Ochoa told me, "We realized that there were a lot of black people participating in the religious fiestas and these fiestas came from Afro-communities. It occurred to us that this was an 'Afro' culture that had been silenced."[3] Ochoa and El Gordo set up cultural organizations to promote the study and transmission of black cultures, while Chucho García founded a political group known as the Fundación Afroamérica (Afro-American Foundation). Once Chávez was elected, the Fundación Afroamérica, along with other groups such as the Unión de Mujeres Negras (Union of Black Women) under an umbrella organization Red de Organizaciones Afrovenezolanas (Network of Afro-Venezuelan Organizations), began to lobby the Chávez administration to make strong efforts to include Afro-Venezuelans in the multiethnic character of the republic (García 2005, 34). Although the group was not recognized in the 2000 Constitution, the Red has continued to lobby for the historical, political, and cultural recognition of Afro-descendants, rights to land for slave descendants, and laws prohibiting racism.

While the Red has played an important role in raising awareness about racial discrimination and advocating for the rights of Afro-descendants, it still is marginalized in terms of everyday understandings of race as articulated in rap music and other cultural forms. The term "Afro-Venezuelan" is perceived by many to be highly intellectual and disconnected from the vernacular uses of "*negro*" as a term of endearment. For example, El Gordo made the following humorous observation: "For us, the word 'negro' has a connotation of affection. I'll say to my woman, '*negra*, give me a kiss.' I can't say to her, 'Afro-descendant, give me a kiss.'"[4] For El Gordo and others, the redefinition of blackness is still organically connected with vernacular usages. Further, identifications of blackness are often used to refer to a shared condition of marginality and poverty rather than physical characteristics or lineage. It is also unclear how the concept of Afro-Venezuelan—which is often applied to the rural inhabitants of the coastal communities of former slaves in Barlovento—might relate to the more racially mixed inhabitants of the urban barrios. This is another reason why El Gordo and Ochoa prefer the concepts of "blackness" or "black culture" to the term "Afro-descendant"—their terms open the possibility of building broader solidarities among the racially diverse urban poor.

In the following sections, I explore the distinct forms and experiences of hip-hop culture in Venezuela. My analysis is based on ethnographic fieldwork and interviews with rap artists and producers carried out during several trips to Venezuela from 2004 to 2007 and to textual analysis of lyrics and media analysis.

Malandros as the New Urban Guerrillas

> While there is no employment, education, or constructive activities; while they continue eliminating basketball courts; while there are no spaces for socialization of the kids; what we have is a boiling pot of *malandros*, of people who are going to become violent, because it's the only form of expression available to them in the face of so much anger, impotence. "They didn't accept me to the school." "I was kicked out of school because I don't go regularly since my dad doesn't have money to pay for books." "I don't have bus fare to get to my high school." "I'm not eating properly." All these factors create social resentment and, of course, generate violence. They have to generate violence.
>
> *Cultural activist Williams Ochoa, La Vega, interviewed July 31, 2004*

> We don't promote violence, we live violence. We sing what we feel, and what we feel is the pain of a life of delinquency, drugs, and violence.
>
> *Colombia, rapper*

> If you're sane,
> they put you in jail.
> If you work,
> they put you in jail.
> If you're a student,
> they put you in jail.
> They made you a guerrilla.
>
> *Street children, Rap song[5]*

The structural conditions of marginality and exclusion described above have led to the emergence of a new generation of urban guerrillas in Venezuelan society. As opportunities for education and employment decline, many young people are forced to the streets in search of means to support themselves and their families.

José Roberto Duque and Boris Muñoz (1995, 160) report that in 1991 and 1992, more than 413,000 children were forced to abandon their basic education because of the pressures of survival. Often forced into the illegal and underground economy due to lack of opportunities, these young people are subject to constant harassment and torture by urban security forces. The Venezuelan rap group Guerrilla Seca, formed in 1999, takes its meaning from this reality: as member Requesón says, "This is a time when everyone is '*enguerrillado*' [becoming guerrillas], and we come as guerrillas, straight up, without buying into anything." The emergence of guerrillas and *malandros* as subjects is related to the criminalization of barrio youth, new conditions of informality and illegality, and the growing ethics of consumerism and individualism.

Contemporary street culture in Latin American urban centers has been variously described as a "culture of urgency" (Predrazzini and Sanchez 2001), a "male oppositional culture" (Goldstein 2003), and a "hidden culture of resistance and subversion forged in the same violence that generates exclusion" (Salas 2001). The *malandro* has emerged as a central figure of this culture, an embodiment of everyday violence (Ferrándiz 2004, 111). The *malandro* is similar to the "badman" in North American black working-class culture, a symbol of rebellion, alienation, and anti-assimilation (Quinn 2005; Kelley 1996). Francisco Ferrándiz argues that the *malandro* is the dominant form of masculinity available to barrio men. The model of a rough, rebellious, cool, and sexually voracious male is appealing to young men coming of age at a time when other masculine roles such as worker, provider, and professional are less readily available. Yet this image also functions as a stereotype that sentences barrio men to violent futures: according to Ferrándiz (2003, 116), it turns young men "into potential targets of systematic discrimination, arrest, torture, and violent death by the state and its agents." Whether young urban males are students, workers, or ordinary residents, being from a barrio or a marginal zone automatically confers on them the stigma of being a delinquent.

The figure of the *malandro* attained a central place in popular culture in the 1970s and 1980s. Beginning in the 1970s, there was a boom in testimonial literature about prisons and criminality. Autobiographies, testimonies, and first-person narratives such as *Retén de Catia* (Catia Prison), *Soy un delincuente* (I Am a Delinquent), and *40 años en el delito* (40 Years in Crime) became bestsellers. According to Elio Gómez Grillo (2000, 10), the novel *Retén de Catia*, a narrative about life in a notorious penitentiary in Caracas, produced "editions and re-editions that are still read and sold" and converted the unknown author into a phenomenon.

During this period, practitioners of the María Lionza cult, a popular spirit possession cult that focuses on healing, began to incorporate the figures of the *malandro*, the Viking, the guerrilla, and the African into the cult. In the cult, mediums, or *materias*, embody the spirits of historical figures such as Negro Primero, Simón Bolívar, and Guaicaipuro, people who have died and come back to give their counsel to the living. Ferrándiz (2004, 113) reports that with the growth of violence in Venezuelan society during the 1980s and 1990s, the images of dead *malandros* began to appear in statues in the devotional shops (or *perfumerías*) and on printed prayer cards and they inhabited the bodies of *materias* during possession ceremonies. Among barrio youth, these spirits became increasingly popular. The *malandro* figures include old and new *malandros* such as Petróleo Crudo (Crude Oil), Luis Sánchez, Pez Gordo (Fat Fish), Ismael, and Freddy. Along with the incorporation of the *malandro* into the Maria Lionza cult by practitioners, there has also occurred what Salas (1998, 267–274) calls an "africanization of the spirits," with divinities taken from Cuban Santería and other Afro-Caribbean religions, and practitioners' inclusion of warriors as figures in the cult, such as Vikings and guerrillas. Salas points out that these spirits began to gain importance during the "pacification," or the disarming of urban guerrilla movements initiated under President Raúl Leoni in the late 1960s. Guerrilla warfare moved into the symbolic realm where it could be played out in the bodies of *materías* rather than on the streets. But these spirits of guerrillas and *malandros* were fortified within the cult as urban violence grew in magnitude, attesting to their growing strength in the popular imagination.

The *malandro*, or urban guerrilla, has also been a central trope within hip-hop, which began to gain popularity among youth in the barrios during the 1980s and 1990s. Young black and mestizo youth growing up in the barrios learned about hip-hop through the music that came on the commercial airwaves and via global entertainment networks. They were also listening to Spanish-language hip-hop such as that recorded by Puerto Rican rapper Vico C, who had major hits in 1989 and 1992. The first compilation CD released in 2001, *Venezuela Subterránea* (Venezuela Underground), reached national and middle-class audiences. But its largest distribution was among urban barrio youth, who accessed the music through the so-called black or underground market. The market in pirated disks, which vendors copied and sold, accounts for about 75 percent of total sales. Pirated disks sell for around 3,000 bolívares (US$1.40),[6] as compared with regular disks that sell in stores for about 15,000 bolívares (US$7.00). The underground market has made the music available to barrio youth who cannot afford the expensive retail prices.

Budu and El Nigga, rappers in the group Vagos y Maleantes, grew up in barrio San José de Cotiza. "I began to get interested in hip-hop in '83, '84, when this genre arrived in Venezuela," Budu told me. Budu was originally a member of a break-dance crew, and later he began writing music with El Nigga. They were inspired by early Venezuelan rap groups such as El Corte. After one failed attempt to record with producer DJ Trece, the rappers decided to sell drugs to pay for their own recordings. "One day we thought, there's no one who'll support us, nobody can pay for a studio for us," said Budu. "Well, let's sell drugs to pay for our own production. So we took turns in standing on the street corner below and they'd say, 'Hey, deliver this for me,' and so on. And in this way we recorded six songs, paying for them ourselves, until the day that Juan Carlos Echeandía came with his proposal of a documentary, *Venezuela Subterránea*. He must have been sent by God, because we were practically ready to go into jail."[7] After the success of the documentary film and the compilation CD, Vagos y Maleantes went on to produce another disc with Echeandía in 2002 entitled *Papidandeando* (Partying).

The group Guerrilla Seca had a similar trajectory. When member Requesón was twelve years old, he was part of the rap group AracnoRap, who would meet at Parque del Oeste and rhyme in the street. Several members of the group were lost to drug addiction or were imprisoned, and Requesón continued on his own. He later formed another duo with a rapper from the group La Realeza, but that rapper was wrongly convicted of murder and imprisoned shortly thereafter. It was then that Requesón met fellow group member Colombia, the son of Colombian immigrants, at a club in 23 de Enero, and they began to perform together. After winning a rhyming competition at a club in the middle-class neighborhood of Las Mercedes in 1999, Requesón and Colombia formed the group Guerrilla Seca. They would freestyle together in the large avenue of historical monuments known as Los Próceres, where they were eventually introduced to Echeandía. They recorded three songs on his compilation CD, and then in 2002 they produced their own album, *La Realidad Más Real* (The Reality More Real).

The music of Vagos y Maleantes and Guerrilla Seca deals with the continuing urban reality of crime, extreme poverty, and death by gang violence. In my interviews with the members of Guerrilla Seca, rappers Colombia and Requesón talked about their musical inspiration as coming from African American rappers such as Tupac and Nas. Although Colombia and Requesón do not understand the English lyrics, they say that it is the dark and ominous tones of American gangsta rap[8] that speak to their experiences of a kind of gang life that breeds nihilism, vacancy, and despair among youth in the barrios. In this sense, rap lyrics are a form of what Robin Kelley (1996, 121) calls "a street ethnography of racist institutions and social practices." But more than just reflecting the reality of life in the barrio, gangsta rap creates a culture and an ethos that is an integral part of the new oppositional culture of the streets.

The *malandro* is depicted in rap music as emerging from a deteriorated social fabric. Compared with earlier depictions of urban working-class areas as a respite from wage labor and the brutality of work, Loïc Wacquant (2001, 125) notes that working-class areas in conditions of advanced marginality have come to be seen by insiders and outsiders as "social purgatories, urban hellholes where only the refuse of society would accept to dwell." The stigma of place is added to the stigma of race and poverty, producing enclaves of misery that cannot be escaped. The song "Boca del Lobo" by Vagos y Maleantes expresses this sense of the barrio as urban nightmare. The song refers to the notorious Calle Carabobo in Budu's barrio of San José in Cotiza, which has earned the nickname *boca del lobo*, or "mouth of the wolf." The song begins with voices of people in the street evoking the scene of the barrio, followed by a discordant and ominous riff. The rapper begins rapping in a low growl:

Welcome to the mouth of the wolf	*Bienvenidos a la boca del lobo*
Where in less than a second anything can happen	*Donde en menos de un segundo aquí puede pasar de todo*
Murders, attacks, that is daily life	*Muertes, atracos, lo que se vive a diario*
in my barrio, day and night, night and day	*En mi barrio, día y noche, noche y día*

Calle Carabobo is a place ruled by gangs, where the *malandro* is king, "only my laws apply," and no other gang would dare to enter the territory. But at the same time it is a prison, a "labyrinth without exit." In another song, "Historia Nuestra" (Our History), rapper Budu from Vagos y Maleantes relates that he was "raised in the barrio, better known as hell." In the Guerrilla Seca song "La Calle" (The Street), the rappers depict a bleak urban reality where nobody cares about anybody else: "Careful if you fall, here nobody will pick you up." The world inhabited by the rapper is ugly and obscene: "The world is shit and I'm addicted to this shit."

In contrast to the principled *malandros* of the past, what one young barrio man calls "a real *malandro*, a gentleman" who participates in crime for the benefit of his family and his community, what dominates in contemporary street culture is the *malandro* as *chigüirismo*, or the *malandro* who kills for money without regard for the other members of the barrio (Duque and Muñoz 1995, 108). In "Puro Lacreo" (Real Dog),[9] Guerrilla Seca describe this latter *malandro* as a cold-hearted, malevolent individual:

In the business of drugs and money	*En negocios de droga y dinero*
There are no friends or nothin'	*No hay panas ni nada,*
This is delinquency, pure trouble.	*Esto es malandreo, puro lacreo.*

| The one who you least suspect'll kill you for cash, homie, | *El que menos ti piensas te mata por pana,* |
| this is delinquency, this is what I see. | *esto es malandreo, es lo que veo.* |

This *malandro* is motivated by a desire for consumer goods and a jealousy of those who have more than him. *Malandros* will kill one another for money, fashionable clothes, and Nike shoes. In their negotiations over drugs nobody can be trusted, and the *malandro* has no friends, as this world is dominated by cruelty and self-interest. Kelley (1996, 124) notes that in the case of L.A.'s gangsta rappers, the absence of socially responsible criminals is related to the structural absence of job opportunities rather than to a pathological culture of violence. Yet he acknowledges that at times these distinctions between socially conscious and malevolent gangsters is blurred, and the same voices describing "black-on-black" crime may also call for action against dominant institutions. Similarly, Guerrilla Seca states in Puro Lacreo: "I have my morals high, assaulting banks and leading the way." Compared with the *malandro* who steals from his own community and would even assault his neighbor, the rapper targets wealthy institutions and rich people in this part of the song, like a modern-day Robin Hood.

But at the same time, rappers seek to reclaim the identity of the *malandro* and the *maleante*, or criminal. The name of the group Vagos y Maleantes comes from a 1956 law entitled Ley sobre vagos y maleantes (Law for Vagrants and Criminals). This law was passed during the military regime of Marcos Pérez Jiménez so dissidents and opponents of the regime could be imprisoned, but the law came to be used as a way of incarcerating those the authorities considered "undesirables" (Márquez 1999, 229). Vagos y Maleantes appropriate this name as a way of revindicating themselves and their lifestyle. As Echeandía said, "In Venezuela, blacks are *malandros* or delinquents, and the rappers via their discs and their music say that: 'Yes, we are, and here we express it, here we scream it.'"[10] Both Vagos y Maleantes and Guerrilla Seca have images of parental advisory labels on the covers of their CDs. On the cover of Guerrillas Seca's CD *La Realidad Más Real*, an English-language label reading "Parental Advisory, Explicit Lyrics" is superimposed over the tip of Colombia's middle finger, which is being raised in an obscene gesture. On the Vagos y Maleantes disc *Papidandeando* there is a label in Spanish that reads "Pendiente Activo, Grado Maloso" (Active Attention, Bad Rating). These labels, which originated in North America after Senate committee hearings that required the labels for all nationally distributed hardcore rap albums (Quinn 2005, 88), have come to provide a stamp of authenticity or street credibility in the Venezuelan context.

Rappers proclaim their status as urban gangsters, guerrillas, and warriors as a way of playing with dominant stereotypes. In their song "Llegó la Hampa" (The Delinquents Have Arrived), an upbeat all-female chorus announces "Murderers, murderers, the murderers have arrived." In contemporary public discourse, the phrase "Plomo contra el Hampa," or "War Against Delinquency," has become common and has justified the use of severe punishments for acts of juvenile crime. Speaking to official pronouncements that dehumanize and stigmatize young men of color by painting them as murderers and killers, the rappers playfully present themselves as the murderers. In a fast-paced rap, they begin, "Die! Don't mess with us because we are guerrillas." Exposing widespread stereotypes about blacks and the dreaded *cerros*, or hillside shanties, the rappers observe, "It makes you full of nerves when you see this black coming down from the hills shooting" and "You know that I am your nightmare." The song ends with the chorus, "Nobody escapes from Guerrilla Seca, / Careful, the delinquents have arrived!" As Kelley (1996, 139) argues in the case of L.A. gangsta rap, negative stereotypes of black men are recontextualized in these songs: "white fear of black male violence becomes evidence of black power."

The Informal Economy and Consumer Culture

The *malandros*, along with other social actors who emerged from the crisis of the 1990s and the restructuring of Venezuelan society, came to constitute a parallel power structure, an alternative to the official state apparatus. Leeds (1996) defines parallel power structures as drug gangs and local entrepreneurs who provide informal-sector activities and services in the absence of the state. In their song, "Malandrea Negro" (Black Delinquency), Guerrilla Seca suggests that it is the poverty, hunger, and desperation of the barrios that leads to drug dealing as a means of survival. For unskilled black youth, finding meaningful work is practically impossible: "I go on desperately, looking for work is a joke." Even for those who want to find work in the formal economy there are few opportunities: "I look for legal cash, but destiny is changing me." If one needs money and there are no legal opportunities, then the turn to crime and the informal underground economy is the only path, according to the rapper, especially when one has children to support. Similarly in their chronicle of street life, "Historia Nuestra" (Our History), Vagos y Maleantes relates that they began dealing drugs, "*empecé en el jibareo*," at the age of seventeen. While the parents of the rapper dreamed that he would become an engineer, he dreamed of being a criminal.

The drug dealer is often portrayed as a self-styled entrepreneur or hustler. Budu and El Nigga from Vagos y Maleantes adopt this aesthetic on the back cover of the album *Papidandeando*. The rappers appear as elaborately decked-out hustlers in pin-striped suits, gold chains, dark sunglasses, designer sneakers, and expensive watches. The "cocaine capitalist" is a particularly strong trope in urban street culture; according to Quinn (2005, 57), it represents "the meteoric rise of the fledgling entrepreneur; the rejection of traditional notions of communal responsibility in an age of individualism; the 'ruthless' startup business organization; and the marketing and distribution of a 'dangerous' product." In "Puro Lacreo," Colombia describes his drug business:

I have the drug, the bicarbonate, it's weighed and ready to pour into foil and paper.	*Yo tengo la droga, el bicarbonato, el pesao' y listo para sacar las galletas en aluminios y papeletas.*
We have the coolest business,	*Tenemos la merca mas fina*
And it's us who direct the kitchen.	*Y nos dirigimos directo a la cocina.*

The dealers are managers who own and oversee the entire business; they are intimately familiar with the production process. As compared with the degradation of wage labor or service work, the dealers themselves direct their business. They are concerned with many aspects of a start-up business. There is much demand, "everyone wants cocaine and rocks," but they need to establish a good name for themselves in the barrio and protect themselves against crackdowns by the police. As long as they have control over their zone and are street-smart about how they do business, no one will mess with them. The song ends with guns being fired into the air, emphasizing that in the end it is violence and the cartel's monopoly of the means of violence in the barrio that maintains their control over trade.

In addition to the rise of parallel power structures associated with neoliberal market reforms, the rise of a consumer culture has fostered what John Gledhill (2004, 340) has called the "neoliberalization of everyday life." Gledhill argues that neoliberalism represents an ideology of a period where capitalism seeks to "commoditize the most intimate of human relations and the production of identity and personhood." Personal worth is increasingly measured in terms of consumption and status symbols such as brand-name cars, clothing, and accessories. Venezuelan rappers also connected their sense of self-worth to the possibility of upward social mobility. For Requesón, "We live in bad conditions and we want to move ahead, climb to a different level because we want to take our mothers out of this place."[11] The rappers from Guerrilla Seca define their desire for a better life in terms of material goods and opportunities.

Rappers are attracted by the promise of material gain and reward, as demonstrated in the song by Guerrilla Seca, "Voy a Hacer Plata" (I'm Going to Make Money). The song begins with a chorus:

I'm going to make money	Voy a hacer plata.
From when you're born till when you die, that's what it's about	Desde que naces hasta que mueres, de eso se trata
So that finally my life is a little happier,	Para que el final mi vida se torne un poco más grata,
I'm going to make money.	Voy a hacer plata.
So that they treat me like a person not like a rat	Para que me traten como persona no como rata
I'm going to make money, whore.	Voy a hacer plata, puta.

For the rapper, life is all about money, and his happiness, dignity, and self-worth will depend on him being able to make money. He may be treated like a worthless rat by society, but if he can make money, he can be somebody. The denigrating term "whore," used in the last line of the chorus, emphasizes the connections between the enterprise of making money and the rapper's masculinity, based on his assertion of male dominance. He raps, "To be a poor villain is the worst because you always have to take shit, and if you have a lot of money others eat your shit." The mobility to which he refers is one that keeps intact a model of social hierarchy, where there is always someone at the bottom. The rapper acknowledges that "money is not everything in life, but it is everything in the world." He goes on to say:

If I could make five million dollars a month I'd be a real millionaire	Si yo me ganara cinco millones al mes sería demasiado millonario
I wouldn't live in the delinquency the barrio, I'd be a real businessman.	No viviera en el malandrón del of barrio, fuera tamaño empresario.
I'd get gold teeth and I'd adorn myself in gold all over	Me cambiara los dientes de oro y también de oro fuera todo mi escapulario,
I'd have a ton of Rolex, rings, chains for daily use.	Tuviera demasiado Rolez, anillos, cadenas para usar a diario.
Bodyguards to protect my life and defend me from all those against me.	Guardaespaldas para que me cuida ran la vida y las espaldas de todo lo contrario.
I want to be owner of everything: boats, yachts, motors, cars, businesses, mansions	Yo quiero ser dueño de todo: barcos, yakí, motos, carros, empresas, mansiones
and I would have earned it all from my skills on the mike.	Y que todo me lo hubiera ganado rimando los microfonos.

For all his pride in his underworld drug dealings and businesses, the rapper would prefer to leave behind the world of the barrio and be a real businessman.

Gold teeth, Rolex watches, and bodyguards, all of which successful North American rappers have, are visible symbols of status and the achievement of wealth and happiness. A crucial point for this rapper is that it is through his music, his "skills on the mike" that he has earned all of these privileges. Given the lack of opportunities for social mobility through regular work, particularly for black and marginalized youth, music and sports offer alternative roads to upward mobility. But notably, the solution for the rapper is individual rather than collective; he will be able to take himself and his family out of the barrio, but the realities of poverty and inequality will not change.

In some ways, rappers realize that the fantasy of wealth is unattainable, and they play with these fantasies in the kinds of inversions also found in popular cultural forms such as Carnival (Bakhtin 1968; Stallybrass and White 1986). The song "Papidandeando" (Partying) begins with a sample from Eddie Palmieri's "Café . . . Tostao y Colao." Vagos y Maleantes imagine themselves in a grand mansion with a view of the stars, drinking Cristal and driving a Lamborghini. In this fantasy, it is wealthy American magnates such as "Rocafeller" (a reference to John D. Rockefeller), Donald Trump, and Bill Gates who are performing the menial labor in the rapper's house. It is generally these American figures, rather than domestic ones, who function as entrepreneurial icons in the public imagination, given the extensive circulation of U.S. culture in Venezuela.

I have Rocafeller washing in the kitchen,	*Tengo Rocafeller lavando en la cocina*
Donald Trump is cleaning the pool,	*Donald Trump limpiando la piscina*
Bill Gates is parking my limousine.	*Bill Gates estacionando la limosina.*

The humor of the song lies in the absurdity of these images of Trump or Gates as pool boy or chauffeur. While the rich people are stuck with the chores, Vagos y Maleantes are raking in the cash: "I am higher and higher in my mountain of money that keeps growing and growing." For Vagos y Maleantes, it is international crime rings that will make them their millions, as they travel around the world creating a mafia of Latino criminals. The ridiculous images of "bank accounts in Spain and Switzerland with connections in Cotiza" are a comment on the fraud and corruption of an elite class that would never be available to the ordinary barrio resident. In "3 Dueños" (3 Owners), Vagos y Maleantes refer to former president "Carlos Andrés Pérez, who wanted to be a millionaire," who was impeached in 1994 for corruption, and Carlos Menem, a former Argentinian president indicted on charges of corruption and embezzlement. For the rapper, these are the "teachers of school in Venezuela." The desire for quick wealth comes from the models available to barrio youth, that of their corrupt politicians.

Through their music, rap musicians are parodying but also reinforcing dominant ideologies of entrepreneurship, consumerism, and mobility. As Phillipe

Bourgois (2003) argues in his study of drug dealers and street criminals in Harlem, "In their pursuit of success they are even following the minute details of the classical Yankee model for upward mobility." The Vagos y Maleante's song "Historia Nuestra," which details the hardships of the rapper's life that brought him into a life of crime, ends with his "making it" with a rap career, when rap producer Juan Carlos Echeandía "took us out of the darkness / and made us into his friend / to create, Aha! an underground business." A career in rap music is seen along the same lines as the other underground activities of the informal economy—it requires work, taking risks, and luck and can lead to fame and wealth. But unlike the informal economy, music is seen as one of the only avenues out of the ghetto. While the crack economy pulls youth closer to destruction of themselves and their communities, music can be a way to garner fame and leave poverty behind.

Modes of Urban Life and Protest

Can we consider the *malandro* a figure of social protest? Yves Pedrazzini and Magaly Sanchez R. (2001, 139) argue that the "militant or revindicative mentality" of workers organized in unions is no longer relevant to barrio youth, who do not have the option of sustained and long-term wage work but must rather rely on low-paying service work or the informal economy in order to earn an income. Corporatist bodies such as unions and established political parties have been unable to address the interests of a largely informal impoverished majority in an increasingly polarized society (Roberts 2003, 61). Protests such as the 1989 riots known as the Caracazo were not organized or channeled by political parties or trade unions; they were coordinated by actors from the informal economy.

The Caracazo also brought to the fore a critical awareness that was implicit in urban street culture. Although gangsta rappers do not demonstrate a social justice approach in their lyrics, they are aware that what underlies the problems of the barrios is the shortcomings of the political system under which they live. In an interview, rapper Budu criticized the kinds of short-term solutions to poverty such as the televised charity event Telecorazón:

> What about the kids in prison? What about the kids in the streets? Here they organized an event called Telecorazón. And ask me if after this event I've stopped seeing kids in the street. I see double as many, so what happened to the money? All the groups who participated in this event did it for free. There were thousands of people, they surpassed the numbers they were hoping for. And what happened? I don't understand. I'm in the

streets and I still see kids selling flowers. In my barrio there's a kid whose not even 10 and he's on crack.[12]

The solution is rather, as Budu puts it, that "we need more sources of work, what we want is for our children to have an education." In street kids' rap, the same sentiment is there: "I am repenting / the robbing and killing I did / I don't want to be a vagabond / or money or applause / Look, look my friend / what I want is a profession / I want to study / and do the best I can." These kinds of statements by rappers are poignant but rare, as earlier working-class dreams of social mobility and advancement through work and education have largely been shattered. Hopes for assimilation and integration are replaced by the realities of exclusion from society.

The racialized nature of this exclusion intensified after the Caracazo, as young barrio residents were identified as looters, criminals, and thugs. The images below from two mainstream daily newspapers, *El Universal* and *El Nacional*, illustrate the fears of the "black threat from the *cerros*" that animated dominant discourse. In Figure 3.1, taken from *El Universal*, a thief with dark skin, black features, a baseball cap, and baggy pants runs away with a large number of purses. The angry look on his face evokes the terror of the largely middle-class readership of this newspaper, who carry racialized stereotypes of criminals. Figure 3.2, from *El Nacional*, accompanies an article entitled "List of Maggots of the Barrio Is Done with the Cooperation of Neighbors." This image is also clearly racialized and consists of a young boy with black features, his lips and nose accentuated, who is dressed in a basketball shirt, baggy shorts, and sneakers. He is slouched over in a lazy posture, one foot dawdling behind the other to show his supposedly careless attitude. The description of the young boy as a "maggot" is related to an "epidemic" and "pathology of delinquency" that the city is suffering and that needs to be eradicated. The article even gives a profile of what neighbors should look for:

Age: Between 18 and 23 years.
Stature: Between 170 and 172 centimeters.
Composition: Thinner than usual. Short hair in "Jordan" style.
Dress: Shirt and brand name jeans, expensive shoes.
Origin: Generally children of parents who have come from the countryside and have established their homes in the metropolis. They are part of waves of illegal migrants who were situated in the poorest areas of the city.
Habits: Until the evening they stay at home while their woman (concubine, mother or sister) works. They come out at night to intercept those who are returning to the barrio.

CONTACTO DIRECTO

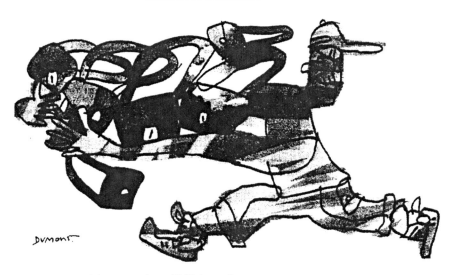

Figure 3.1. Racial cartoon from *El Universal.*

The language criminalizes all black youth, severing them from context and demanding their removal. Fernando Coronil and Julie Skurski (1991, 323) argue that after the Caracazo, the barrios were seen as a source of subversion and "their population became the enemy to be controlled, driven back, and broken." The bonds formed between rulers and the people in an earlier populist period were broken, and the people became a threat to private property and a source of terror.

Immiseration, restructuring of the workforce, and the fragmentation of society have increased economic and racial cleavages. The anxieties reflected in these media representations are related to the erosion of the myths of class harmony and racial democracy that have been hegemonic for a long time in many countries of Latin America. In a shift from popular historical views of race that denied the existence of racial divisions in Venezuela and placed more importance on national than racial identity (Wright 1990), rappers have begun to reclaim black identity. According to Requesón:

At one time, when they oppressed the black, they didn't see it as: "Shit, he's from here, he's from our same country." No, they didn't see it like that. They saw it as: "He's a black and we're gonna fuck him over cos' he's black, he's not from our nation." That's why I think we're blacks. All blacks, each one, are first blacks, then they're from the nation they're from.[13]

Figure 3.2. Racial cartoon from *El Nacional*.

In a direct challenge to the language of a racial democracy that has dominated political rhetoric in Venezuela, Requesón points to the underlying racism that exists in Venezuelan society. Alongside the growth in racialized poverty and the overt racism of the media, there has been the development of new kinds of racial consciousness among black youth, such as what we see in Venezuelan gangsta rap. The figure of the *malandro* as a figure of social protest differs from that of the traditional union-based worker not only in terms of his individualism, abandonment of political demands, and focus on consumption rather than production, but also in his adoption of a race-based cultural identity that speaks to a changing landscape of social struggle.

Conclusion

The debt crisis and neoliberal economic restructuring during the period of the 1990s reshaped the contours of Venezuelan society. As the state retreated from its earlier role of welfare provision and as market-driven growth replaced protectionist policies, poverty and inequality increased, leading to a growing cycle of violence and state repression. The growing informalization of the economy meant that more workers were concentrated in low-paying, unskilled jobs and were subject to physical harassment by the authorities. Over the 1980s and 1990s, the marginalized majority suffered major defeats as they found their share of national income decreasing markedly, their standard of living in decline, and their hopes of attaining a better life curtailed. The gunshots in the barrios are a reminder of the ongoing warfare in urban zones and the violent futures to which large numbers of young barrio men are condemned by virtue of where they are born.

At the same time, these processes of economic restructuring gave rise to new figures of social protest. Urban street culture and the informal economy are the incubators of forms of consciousness and social critique that shape novel kinds of political intervention and organization. The elements of racial consciousness in rap music have been found in a host of popular cultural movements across the city, in contrast to the more intellectual strands of the Afro-Venezuelan movement. But at the same time, the gangsta rappers of Caracas are strikingly different from the black nationalist and socially conscious rappers of Cuba, Brazil, or Colombia. They are not concerned with a more dramatic restructuring of society or with challenging of gendered relations of power. Contesting hierarchical social relations may call for deeper questions about available development models than these actors are prepared to ask.

Notes

1. Interview with Juan Carlos Echeandía, Caracas, January 14, 2004.

2. Interviews with Colombia and Requesón, Caracas, January 14, 2004.

3. Interview with Williams Ochoa, Caracas, July 31, 2004.

4. Interview with El Gordo, Caracas, January 17, 2004.

5. *Cancionero de niños de la calle*, Museo Jacobo Borges. All subsequent references to rap lyrics by street children are taken from this disc.

6. At the official 2004 exchange rate of 2,100 bolívares = $US1.00.

7. Interview with Budu and El Nigga, Caracas, January 15, 2004.

8. Gangsta rap is a musical genre that originated in the mid-1980s in black working-class communities in North America.

9. The original meaning of "*lacra*" is lumpen, vagrant, or a stain on society. But youth in the barrios reclaim this term, using "*lacreo*" to refer to those who do "*lacras*," meaning consuming drugs, going to a party to look for women or getting into fights. Thanks to José Roberto Duque for explaining these meanings.

10. Interview with Juan Carlos Echeandía.

11. Interview with Colombia and Requesón, Caracas, January 14, 2004.

12. Interview with Budu.

13. Interview with Requesón.

Bibliography

Bakhtin, Mikhail. 1968. *Rabelais and His World.* Translated by Helene Iswolsky. Cambridge, Mass.: MIT Press.

Bourgois, Phillipe. 2003. *In Search of Respect: Selling Crack in El Barrio.* Cambridge: Cambridge University Press.

Coronil, Fernando, and Julie Skurski. 1991. "Dismembering and Remembering the Nation: The Semantics of Political Violence in Venezuela." *Comparative Politics in Society and History* 33 (2): 288–337.

Duque, José Roberto, and Boris Muñoz. 1995. *La ley de la calle: Testimonios de jóvenes protagonistas de la violencia en Caracas.* Caracas: Fundarte.

Ferrándiz, Francisco. 2003. "Malandros, María Lionza, and Masculinity in a Venezuelan Shantytown." In *Changing Men and Masculinities in Latin America,* ed. Matthew Gutman, pp. 115–133. Durham, N.C.: Duke University Press.

———. 2004. "The Body as Wound: Possession, Malandros and Everyday Violence in Venezuela." *Critique of Anthropology* 24 (2): 107–133.

García, Jesús. 2005. *Afrovenezolanidad e inclusión en el proceso bolivariano venezolano.* Caracas: Ministerio de Comunicación y Información.

Gledhill, John. 2004. "Neoliberalism." In *A Companion to the Anthropology of Politics,* ed. David Nugent and Joan Vincent. London: Blackwell Publishing.

Goldstein, Donna. 2003. *Laughter out of Place: Race, Class, Violence, and Sexuality in a Rio Shantytown.* Berkeley: University of California Press.

Gómez Grillo, Elio. 2000. *Apunte sobre la delincuencia y la cárcel en la literatura venezolana.* Caracas: Monte Ávila Editores Latinoamericana.

Kelley, Robin. 1996. "Kickin' Reality, Kickin' Ballistics: Gangsta Rap and Postindustrial Los Angeles." In *Droppin' Science: Critical Essays on Rap and Hip Hop Culture,* ed. William Eric Perkins, 117–158. Philadelphia, Pa.: Temple University Press

Leeds, Elizabeth. 1996. "Cocaine and Parallel Polities in the Brazilian Urban Periphery: Constraints on Local-Level Democratization." *Latin American Research Review* 31 (3): 47–83.

Márquez, Patricia. 1999. *The Street Is My Home: Youth and Violence in Caracas.* Stanford, Calif.: Stanford University Press.

Pedrazzini, Yves, and Magaly Sanchez R. 2001. *Malandros, bandas y niños de la calle: Cultura de urgencia en la metropoli Latinoamericana.* Caracas: Vadell Hermanos Editores.

Quinn, Eithne. 2005. *Nuthin' but a "G" Thang: The Culture and Commerce of Gangsta Rap.* New York: Columbia University Press.

Roberts, Kenneth. 2003. "Social Polarization and the Populist Resurgence in Venezuela." In *Venezuelan Politics in the Chavez Era: Class, Polarization and Conflict,* ed. Steve Ellner and Daniel Hellinger, 55–72. Boulder, Colo.: Lynne Rienner Publishers.

Salas, Yolanda. 1998. "Nuevas subjectividades en el estudio de la memoria colectiva." In *Venezuela: Tradición en la modernidad.* Caracas: Fundación Bigott.

———. 2001. "Morir para vivir: La (in)certidumbre del espacio (in)civilizado." In *Estudios Latinoamericanos sobre cultura y transformaciones sociales en tiempos de globalización II,* ed. Daniel Mato, 241–249. Buenos Aires: CLACSO.

Sanjuán, Ana María. 2002. "Democracy, Citizenship, and Violence in Venezuela." In *Citizens of Fear: Urban Violence in Latin America,* ed. Susana Rotker, 87–101. New Brunswick, N.J.: Rutgers University Press.

Stallybrass, Peter, and Allon White. 1986. *The Politics and Poetics of Transgression*. London: Methuen.

Wacquant, Loïc. 2001. "The Rise of Advanced Marginality: Notes on Its Nature and Implications." *Acta Sociologica* 39 (2): 121–140.

Wright, Winthrop. 1990. *Café con Leche: Race, Class, and National Image in Venezuela*. Austin: University of Texas Press.

4

Performing the African Diaspora in Mexico

ANGELA N. CASTAÑEDA

Much has been written about Mexico's rich indigenous heritage and its major role in the colonial expansion of the Americas. Until recently, Mexico's contribution to the study of Afro-Latin populations was largely missing from this discussion. Where is the Afro-Mexican population located? How is the Afro-Mexican identity defined or constructed? And what makes Afro-Mexicans different from other African-descended groups in Latin America? This chapter will address these questions through an analysis of representations of Afro-Mexican cultural identity in cultural performances.

History of Africa in Mexico

The history of Africans in Mexico dates back to the colonial period when an estimated 200,000 to 300,000 enslaved Africans were introduced to the area via the trans-Atlantic slave trade. Most of them were taken to the port city of Veracruz in the Gulf of Mexico, but other port cities in this region received slaves, including Tuxpan and Campeche, followed later by Acapulco on Mexico's Pacific coast (Cruz-Carretero 2005, 73).

However, questions about the number of Africans brought into Mexico remain unanswered. Given the incomplete documentation available from slave ships, the number of undocumented slaves that were transported on pirate ships and through other means, and other factors, it is difficult to accurately estimate how many slaves arrived at any given port in the Americas. Gonzalo Aguirre Beltrán notes in his seminal work *Cuijla: Esbozo etnográfico de un pueblo negro* (*Ethnographic Outline of a Black People*) that "blacks in Mexico were a minority group; they represented from 0.1 to 2 percent of the colonial population; the numbers introduced were not more than 250,000 individuals during the course of three centuries" (Aguirre Beltrán 1958, 8). However, Adriana Naveda Chávez-Hita's work emphasizes the lack of accuracy associated with the slave trade in Veracruz, "The real numbers might never be understood because there weren't any complete registries of the slaves brought legally through the Port of Vera-cruz, not to mention the evidence that suggests the extended presence of an ille-gal commercial operation" (Naveda Chávez-Hita 2001, 32). The Spanish census for 1810 further complicates these numbers by showing "635,461 Afro-Mexicans in Mexico, or 10.2 percent of the total" (Vincent 1994, 258). We can contrast this figure with the numbers produced by Minority Rights Group, which recorded the minimum and maximum estimates of the Afro-Mexican population for the early to mid-1990s: the minimum is 474,000, or 0.5 percent, and the maximum is 9 million, or 10 percent of the entire Mexican population (1995, xii).

Along with the trans-Atlantic slave trade, Naveda Chávez-Hita points to other more recent migrations of people of African descent to Veracruz. She notes that many soldiers who fought with the United States during the Mex-ican-American War (1847) and with France during the Pastry War (1838) in-cluded people of African descent who ultimately stayed in Veracruz after their battles. Additionally, economic reasons led to an increased African presence in Veracruz. During the Porfiriato, or presidential term of Porfirio Díaz, which lasted from 1876 to 1911, many workers from the Caribbean, mainly Jamaica, were brought to help build railroads in this state (Naveda Chávez-Hita 2001, 41).

From their initial arrival, African slaves were forced not only into agricul-tural activities such as sugar cane cultivation and cattle ranching but also into all aspects of economic and social life in the Americas. New historical research suggests that "the single greatest oversight created by this picture of slavery in New Spain is the underestimation of the importance of Afro-Mexican slave labor to the *obrajes de paños* [woolen textile mills] during the middle part of the colonial period (1630–1750)" (Proctor 2003, 35). This suggests that a large and stable workforce of Afro-Mexican slaves sustained this vital colonial industry. During the colonial period there were very few economic areas where slaves were not employed. In protest, they continually resisted the unjust system of slavery. Throughout the colonial period the formation of fugitive slave settle-ments, or *palenques*, and armed insurrections were not uncommon. One of the most famous rebellions occurred in the state of Veracruz, where the mountains of Orizaba created an ideal environment for runaway slaves, or *cimarrones*. It was within this region in the early 1600s that an escaped slave named Yanga established a maroon community and fought against the military campaign of the Spanish. After an intense battle and the loss of many soldiers, Spain sur-rendered to Yanga's demand that "the Spanish Crown establish a free town to be exclusively inhabited by black people who were fugitives before 1608" (Cruz-Carretero 2005, 75). This demand was finally accepted and the free township of San Lorenzo de los Negros was created in 1630, a town that today has changed its name to Yanga in homage to its heroic founder.

Remixing the *Mestizaje* Concept

What happened to the descendants of Mexico's slaves? Following Mexico's in-dependence from Spain in 1821, the country entered a period described by one scholar as "a conscious 'historical forgetting' of the black population" (Vinson 2005b, 67). This period lasted well into the twentieth century, until the work of noted anthropologist Gonzalo Aguirre Beltrán emerged in the 1940s.

When they address issues of blackness in Mexico, some researchers choose a very narrow historical lens (Naveda Chávez-Hita 2001; Martínez Montiel 1995; Thompson 1983); they look for a continuous link that would connect the past with the present and search for pure identifiers of African elements. In contrast to this unilateral approach, other scholars note the multiplicity of black identi-ties that are "defined and redefined, imagined and re-imagined, performed and performed again within the flux of history" (Rahier 1999, xxiv). In order to bet-ter understand how blackness is perceived in Mexico today, it is imperative to recognize the difficulty in identifying "pure" African elements. It is also impor-tant to frame notions of blackness relative to national, state, and local factors; each has a different set of political, cultural, and contextual influences.

Official notions of a national identity, created by elites in Mexico as well as in other Latin American countries, revolve around the process of *mestizaje*, or race mixing. This process involves the racial and cultural whitening of all other groups. The ideology highlights indigenous contributions while negating Afri-can influences.

> The very construction of the notion of the "mestizo" ("mestizaje") as the Mexican racial archetype—an admixture of Spanish ancestry and native ancestry—systematically omits the African origins of the Mexican popu-lation. Indeed, the mestizo narrative also omits the fact that the Spanish population itself, including conquistadores, long had been, literally and figuratively, intimately connected to Africa via the presences of the so-called Moors. (Darity 2005, 47)

Renowned Mexican anthropologist Gonzalo Aguirre Beltrán attributes this lack of interest in Mexico's African diaspora to a fascination with its indigenous roots. He writes, "We only had eyes for what was indigenous and we closed our minds to anything else that represented something other than our romantic understandings of the indigenous" (Aguirre Beltrán 1958, 11). Despite attempts to paint Mexico as a homogenous society, cultural variation does exist within its borders, as is evident in the Veracruz case.

In an effort to illustrate the complexity inherent in the racial discourse sur-rounding the *mestizaje* process in the Americas, colonial governments mobilized images in paintings that attempted to neatly categorize each racial type, or *casta*. In opposition to the classification imposed by *casta* paintings, José Vasconcelos argued in *The Cosmic Race* (1925) for a more pan-mestizo identity that was a spiritual as opposed to biological understanding of the *mestizaje* concept. Marilyn Miller has noted that in effect, "the reference to race as 'cosmic' shifted the semantic weight from the material to the spiritual," thus leaning toward a more unifying interpretation of this concept at the national level (Miller 2004, 29). Indeed, most historical scholarship has looked at *mestizaje* as a nation-building ideology. While this definition of *mestizaje* seems to be inclusive, over the years scholars have criticized this concept because of the everyday implications it has for people:

> The major problem found in the "cosmic race" revolutionary policy is that what was disseminated about non-white people, particularly the darker people, actually introduced, reproduced, and massively perpetuated stereotypes. It turned the members of a mainly dark population against one another, made a whole country and its people ashamed of their African heritage and propagated the whitening mentality that infects a considerable portion of Mexican mestizos up to the present (Hernández Cuevas 2004, 101).

In particular, the so-called inclusivity of the term was critiqued by Ronald Stutzman (1981) who redefined *mestizaje* as an "all-inclusive ideology of exclusion," appropriately making note of the term's exclusion of blacks and indigenous peoples.

Recent scholarship has begun to challenge ideological interpretations of the *mestizaje* concept by focusing on embodied and lived experience. In particular, Peter Wade argues in his work on Afro-Colombian communities that *mestizaje* should be seen as a lived process, focusing on how people deal with this racial-cultural mixture on a daily basis. Wade defines *mestizaje* as

> a mosaic made up of different elements and processes, which can be manifest within the body and the family, as well as the nation. Seen in this way, *mestizaje* has spaces for many different possible elements, including black and indigenous ones, which are more than merely possible candidates for future mixture. (Wade 2005, 254)

Diana Taylor's interpretation of culture as performance is also useful; she defines performance as "a way of knowing, not simply an object of analysis" (2003, xvi). Incorporating notions of performance in our understanding of the *mestizaje* concept helps us identify other types of knowledge. This includes a shift from written to embodied and performed culture. Taylor accurately notes that from its very conception, *mestizaje* dealt more with the body than with texts since "the primary site of *mestizaje* is the body, linked as it is to the *mestizo/a*, the child born of European and indigenous parents" (Taylor 2003, 94). Taylor also posits that even *casta* paintings revolved around issues of performance, noting that "both the indigenous groups and the Spaniards had a highly codified system of identification grounded in visible social markers" (Taylor 2003, 87). The invisible nature of Mexico's African heritage forced Afro-descendants to perform the phenomenon of "collective passing" (Darity 2005, 47) in their search for ways to relate to the larger mestizo national identity.

Today we find the physical presence of *negro, moreno*, Afro-mestizo, Afro-Mexican, Afro-Latin, or Afro-*caribeño* people in the phenotypes associated with African ancestry. Yet the Mexican population has more Afro-descendants than many people realize:

> Based upon long-standing American norms of race classification there are regions of Mexico where people bear a phenotypical resemblance to African Americas. These include Veracruz, Oaxaca, and the Costa Chica zones in particular. But since estimates of modern African ancestry in the Mexican population run as high as 75 percent of the population, persons of African descent are distributed far more widely across Mexico; ancestry often is present where phenotypical traits are not (Darity 2005, 47).

The present situation in Mexico is such that phenotype alone cannot be used as a marker of African roots. As Hernández Cuevas notes in his work on African Mexicans, "when visibly black Mexicans are referred to, it is not a reference to a separate group: it is a reference to a portion of Mexicans that due to their looks alone were singled out by the racist *criollo* thought" (Hernández Cuevas 2004, xiv). The larger questions of cultural identification require an investigation of the multiple agendas inherent in the daily performance of cultural identity.

Two significant issues exist regarding cultural identification with African ancestry in Mexico—a variation in regional interpretations and comparative interpretations, which highlight emic and etic perspectives. The variation in regional perspectives is highlighted by Bobby Vaughn, who argues that two main discourses exist on blackness in Mexico:

> One discourse exists in the Costa Chica, where blackness is ubiquitous, taken for granted, and permeates people's daily lives. The other discourse is what I call a central Mexican discourse on blackness—a discourse . . . where blacks are almost never seen and where most people have no idea that there are blacks in Mexico at all (Vaughn 2005, 49).

My field research in Veracruz suggests a third discourse: blackness is viewed as a mixture of the first two discourses—neither totally absorbed nor ignored. It is within this context that blackness is not a matter of being "seen" but rather a state that is performed and, as Wade would argue, lived as an everyday experience.

These regional interpretations highlight the ways that blackness in Mexico is often framed via comparison with "others." Vaughn notes that "in central Mexico the discussion of blackness tends to shift immediately outside of Mexico's borders; blackness is, as such, displaced from Mexico [to the United States], while in the Costa Chica blackness is almost entirely about local blacks, local Indians and local mestizos" (Vaughn 2005, 52). Blackness is also displaced in Veracruz, where people compare blackness and Cubanness. Charles Rowell notes the characteristics that bind Veracruz communities:

> It is not a mythologized or historicized Africa as homeland but an invented Cuba as their point of origin. Unlike Afro-Brazilians, Haitians, Afro-Cubans, and U.S. African Americans, coastal Afro-mestizos seem to have disremembered Africa, the true origin of their non-Indigenous and non-European ancestors. For a number of these southern Veracruzanos, Cuba, they tell us in their interviews, is their ancestral home. (Rowell 2006, 397)

In my field research, I found it not uncommon for people to be more willing to refer to their Cuban ties and much more reluctant to claim specific African heritage. This interpretation is sharpened by the historical and geographical distance of Africa compared to more contemporary cultural exchanges in Cuba.

In addition to these regional differences, it is also imperative that scholars address the power dynamics of naming by recognizing the differences in emic and etic interpretations inherent in identity formation. Research on issues of African ancestry in Mexico illustrates that many Afro-Mexicans prefer not to acknowledge African ties, favoring instead their ties to Mexico, as Adriana Naveda Chávez-Hita notes:

> Within us there exists populations that could be classified as afro-mestizo; in these communities you find that although people possess characteristics that could be defined as from African origin, these populations are not conscious of having a distinct identity . . . they simply see themselves as Mexicans, despite the fact that they appear to have different characteristics than their neighbors (Naveda Chávez-Hita 2001, 42).

Many times during my field research I asked Veracruzanos questions about Afro-Mexican identity or culture in their community. The answers I heard reflect the ambiguity about identity that Chávez-Hita writes about. For example, when I was interviewing a local man about his family history, he explained his curly hair and dark skin as a result of his great-grandmother's Cuban ancestry.

Laura Lewis associates this phenomenon with different emic and etic interpretations of identity. She explains this analysis in the context of her work on Costa Chica communities:

> The discrepancy between outsider perspectives that anchor the past in "wild" African things and give value to their benign survival in the present, and the perspectives of local people who do not self-identity as "Afro" Mexican or even as black, has become very clear over my years of fieldwork. San Nicoladenses look back on the past with a mixture of nostalgia and shame; they see themselves as modern Mexicans looking toward a future that distances them from the past (Lewis 2006, 804).

What makes this situation particularly complex is the diversity in contemporary understandings of identity in communities of African descent in Mexico. While terms such as Afro-mestizo, Afro-*caribeño*, and Afro-Mexican are used by scholars to refer to members of these Mexican communities, my research seeks to understand how members of these communities refer to and see themselves. It is important, therefore, to consider both insider and outsider perspectives. In doing so, we need to recognize the disconnect that exists for these communities of African descent, "in part because of their migration experiences and global restructuring, and in part because, as they see it, they are 'Mexicans' for whom the past is not only *not* African, but gone" (Lewis 2006, 802).

Given the negative connotations of blackness in Mexico, blackness and Mexican national identity are seen as contradictions: if you are black, you are not Mexican, and if you are Mexican, you are not black. This disconnect is directly linked to the concept of *mestizaje* that constructs the idea of what it means to be Mexican as a racial mixture solely of Spaniards and Indians. The obsession with the concept of *mestizaje* is further illustrated in the use of the term Afro-mestizo by Mexican scholars who prefer this to the more commonly used term Afro-Mexican. This distinction in terminology is further complicated by the use of "Afro" to describe blacks in other Latin American countries; examples include Afro-Cuban, Afro-Colombian, or Afro-Brazilian (Vaughn 2005, 54). The use of the term Afro-mestizo seems to further disassociate blackness from a perceived "pure" racial mixture in Mexico.

Theory and Practice: Ethnography and/as Performance

Today the surge of interest in Afro-Latin populations in Mexico has its roots in the scholarship of renowned Mexican anthropologist Gonzalo Aguirre Beltrán, who beginning in the 1940s conducted key ethnographic studies on Mexico's African-descent population. Charles Rowell notes the significance of Aguirre Beltrán's work:

> The visual in Latin America in general, and in Mexico in particular, does not always tell us who are the people of African descent. To interrogate the "absent-presence" of contemporary people of African descent in Mexico, we need to take as our departure point the invaluable pioneering work of Gonzalo Aguirre Beltrán on Mexico (Rowell 2004, xiii).

In 1946, Aguirre Beltrán published *La población negra de México* (*The Black Population in Mexico*), followed in 1958 by *Cuijla: Esbozo etnográfico de un pueblo negro* (*Ethnographic Outline of a Black People*). Both works began the important work of repositioning the African presence in Mexico. Aguirre Beltrán's ethnographic accounts of Mexico's African-descent population helped shape future academic interest in this area.

In 1989 the Third Root program, or Tercera Raíz, was created by another Mexican anthropologist, Guillermo Bonfil Batalla. As part of the 500th anniversary of the arrival of the Spanish in the Americas, the Mexican government officially acknowledged that the Afro-Latin populations in Mexico represented *la tercera raíz*, or the third root of the national ethnic composition of the country, after Spanish and indigenous populations. Batalla was then president of the General Direction of Popular Cultures, an institution dedicated to preserving and recognizing popular culture in Mexico. He and anthropologist Luz Maria Martinez Montiel coordinated the Third Root program. The project's goal was to support research related to the history of Mexico's population of African descent as well as that group's contemporary culture as part of the activities to celebrate the 500th anniversary of the "Discovery of the Americas" in 1992. However, as Hernández Cuevas aptly notes,

> The problem with this perception [Third Root] is that it creates an artificial division of Mexican mestizos based on the way people look. . . . In some instances it seems more appropriate to call the African element the first root, in others, the second, or the third, or fourth. It should be clear . . . that a considerable part of Mexican mestizos, even many whose appearance would make one believe otherwise, possess black African genes (Hernández Cuevas 2004, xiv).

An appreciation of a broader definition of the *mestizaje* concept lends itself to the performative element of identity formation in Mexico.

In general, performance theory can be divided into two major positions. One approach interprets performance as a means of communication (Bauman 1977), while the other sees performance as offering knowledge of a particular community's "social drama" (Turner 1986). Furthering Bauman's understanding of performance as verbal exchange, Askew notes that "performance constitutes a *conversation*, not one-way speech directed solely from controlling performers to a passive audience" (2002, 22). Thus, a dialogical process between and among performers and audience members is inherent in performance.

In accordance with the shift from a text-based to a performance-based analysis, Victor Turner emphasizes the reflective nature of performance by describing cultural performances as "not simple mirrors but magical mirrors of social reality: they exaggerate, invert, re-form, magnify, minimize, dis-color, re-color, even deliberately falsify, chronicled events" (1986, 42). Adding to our understanding of performance, Barbara Myerhoff writes, "Cultural performances are reflective in the sense of showing ourselves to ourselves. They are also capable of being reflexive, arousing consciousness of ourselves as we see ourselves" (1982, 7).

The link between power and performance is also essential to this study. It stems from the recognition of cultural performances as "sites of social action where identities and relations are continually being reconfigured" (Guss 2000, 12). The performance of culture becomes a source of power when it functions as an agent of change. Kelly Askew examines the relationship between performance and power:

> Performance, like power, is not a product that can be given, exchanged, or recovered. It always necessarily is a process that is subject to on-the-spot improvisation, varying expectations, the vagaries of history and context, multiple associations and connotations, and remembered or projected meanings. Just as power is a diffuse resource accessible—albeit to varying degrees—to everyone, so too is performance engaged in by everyone present (2002, 291).

Utilizing this holistic approach to the analysis of performance culture, my research illustrates how, as Royce notes, performances "provide subtle and multivocalic entryways to cultural understandings and artistic expression, both in the actual embodied performance and in the memory of it" (2004, 4).

As Diana Taylor stresses in *The Archive and the Repertoire* (2003), performances embody knowledge and memory. This is a powerful interpretation that can add new voice to traditional histories, which are often defined by the static existence of the archive. Taylor's work asks us to consider how the repertoire of performance can supplement archival accounts of history and culture in the Americas. An analysis that includes culture as performance is clearly applicable to the experience of Afro-Mexicans, especially where the invisibility of this population in the national discourse forces scholars to go beyond text-based knowledge to include other forms of embodied experiences found in performance.

My research is also grounded in ethnographic methodology. It consists of over a decade of fieldwork conducted in the state of Veracruz. I used participant observation, formal and informal interviews, audio and visual documentation, and the collection of material culture related to the Afro-Caribbean Festival—posters and clothing. I was a participant observer at many formal and informal cultural events and I conducted numerous interviews, both structured and semi-structured. I also documented my research on performance with digital photography and video and audio recordings of daily life in Veracruz in order to support my interpretation of the *mestizaje* concept as it is performed and embodied in Mexico.

Veracruz Case Study

The state of Veracruz encompasses much of Mexico's eastern coast. Veracruz is comprised of breathtaking beaches, lively cities, and a lush landscape dotted by roaming cattle and coffee and sugar plantations. It covers an area of over 45,000 square miles, roughly 3.7 percent of Mexico's national territory (INEGI 2002, 33), and is the eleventh largest state in the republic of Mexico. It is contiguous with seven Mexican states, and its coastline along the Gulf of Mexico extends for 500 miles.

Historically home to such rich civilizations as the Huastec, Totonac, and Olmec, Veracruz also witnessed the arrival of the Spanish and Cortés's first steps on American soil. Its history is overflowing with bouts of foreign intrusion by Spain (1825), France (1839), and the United States (1847 and 1914). Each of these invasions only sparked more strength and independence in the local people while simultaneously exposing them to new cultures, peoples, and ideas that would later shape their own way of seeing the world. Today, Veracruz is still strongly tied to the land, and many of its nearly 7 million residents cultivate tobacco, coffee, and sugar and operate cattle ranches. But the vast majority of the state's income flows from the sea through the fishing industry and from beneath the ground in the form of oil.

El Puerto de Veracruz, more commonly known as just "El Puerto" or simply "Veracruz," is one of the oldest port cities in the Americas. It is located roughly seven hours or 261 miles due east of Mexico City, the nation's capital, and only two hours or 65 miles southeast of the state capital of Xalapa. The strategic location of this port city invited foreign intervention. On April 21, 1519, Hernan Cortés and his Spanish fleet landed on the coast of Veracruz, roughly facing the

Isla de Sacrificios, or Sacrifice Island. The Spanish named their settlement La Villa Rica de la Vera Cruz, or The Rich Village of the True Cross. This original city was actually situated roughly 50 miles north of its present location. The Spanish maintained Veracruz as their main port of entry until 1760.

The arrival of African slaves in Veracruz quickly followed the arrival of Cortés. Two regions of the state are particularly noted for the presence of African slaves—El Puerto de Veracruz and Los Tuxtlas. Africans were found in the first city because it was a port of entrance and exit, and they were located in the second area because its fertile lands required the hard labor of slaves to produce sugar and tobacco. The first slaves to arrive in Veracruz are believed to have come from Angola and the Congo, but over time the practice of bringing slaves directly from Africa decreased. The majority of slaves who later arrived in Veracruz were known as *negros criollos* because they were the first generation of slaves born in the Americas. These individuals came principally from the Caribbean (Naveda Chávez-Hita 2001, 32).

Today this port city of over half a million people assaults the senses. The pungent odor of salt water and fish permeates the air. The heat is often unbearable and the humidity is stifling. The heart of the city is the historical downtown area, which is comprised of several small city blocks with deliciously cool *callejones* or alleys scattered between and behind businesses. Small marimba bands and lone guitarists who jockey for position inside and outside downtown restaurants and bars provide a constant soundtrack. It is within this city space that the performance of Afro-Mexican identity takes place.

Performances in Veracruz redefine the ways *mestizaje* is remixed to incorporate a uniquely Afro cultural element in Mexican national discourse. This process occurs at national, regional, and local levels. On the national level, the unifying *mestizaje* concept is performed with slogans that insist "*todos somos iguales*," or "we are all equal," yet depictions of Afro cultural elements often mobilize stereotypical representations. For example, the National Folkloric Ballet of Mexico, which presents choreographed pieces illustrating the different states and regions of the country, performs a popular section on Veracruz. This piece uses dancers wearing huge heads depicting overly exaggerated African phenotypes such as bulging white eyes and large red lips. These figures of "smiling and dancing negative Others" point to the power of this dance ensemble as a political institution to "reflect the political and social realities and national discourses of the nation" (Shay 2002, 83, 225). The misrepresentation and stereotypical imagery found in this piece further illustrates the disconnect between emic and etic notions of identity. While patrons and governmental agencies traditionally subsidize performances that support conventional mestizo identity categories, in the case of Veracruz, such subsidies support cultural representations that emphasize African influences that challenge historically accepted notions of *mestizaje*.

Festivals are another cultural performance. They provide occasions for community members to reflect upon and define themselves. In 1994 the Veracruz Institute of Culture, or IVEC, a state-sponsored organization, created a festival to educate the public about and celebrate African heritage. The Afro-Caribbean Festival highlighted artistic, academic, and magical/religious elements from Veracruz. The artistic portion of the festival consisted of live performances of music, dance, and theatre, while the academic component included panel presentations and roundtable discussions that brought together academics and diplomats from around the Caribbean. The section of the festival dedicated to religion enabled both local and visiting Caribbean communities to publicly share elements of their religious beliefs in the form of altars, rituals, and consultations. IVEC's Afro-Caribbean Festival, which has become an annual event, is thus a cultural performance where identities are crafted and communicated.

The original goals of this state-sponsored festival were to research, share, and revalorize the rich history and culture of Afro-Caribbean communities. IVEC leaders proposed to "go further than just a mere celebration in itself or a simple event, to a singular act of justice for a culture [that] up until now [has been] marginalized" (Arias Hernández 1997, 12). This festival was a major step in recognizing Mexico's Afro-Latin roots. For example, it located Afro-Mexican identity in Santería presentations. While the festival's original goals stemmed from a desire to rekindle a connection to African influences and the African historical context in Veracruz and in Mexico, these goals have changed over the years. Most recently, the festival's community ties have dwindled in favor of increased ties to businesses. Festival activities that were once geared toward educating and including local community members now seek the approval of domestic and international tourists. An analysis of festival activities illustrates how Afro-Mexican identity is performed in this context.

The festival began to change in 1998 when IVEC administrators eliminated the religious portion of the festival in the wake of public protests in response to the performance of religious rituals. Up until this point, the local presence of Santería was readily apparent in festival activities that included public altars, performances of sacred music, and ritual sacrifices. The performance of Afro-Mexican culture was marked by public Santería rituals, for example celebrations for Yemayá, goddess of the ocean, and divination consultations. Public ritual performances took place on local beaches and at the downtown offices of the Veracruz Institute of Culture. These performances were marked by large crowds consisting of Santería practitioners and non-initiates as well as locals and domestic tourists, both young and old. The removal of this portion of the festival marked an obvious denial of the very important religious roots that permeate daily life in Veracruz and other Afro-Caribbean communities.

In this example, IVEC succumbed to pressure from staunch Catholic religious groups and animal rights organizations. These protests focused on the sacrifice of animals for Santería religious rituals, which some determined to be inhumane and "satanic." Locals recalled that demonstrations were organized at important tourist spaces such as the Acuario de Veracruz (Veracruz Aquarium) and the boardwalk, where protestors handed out flyers that encouraged tourists not to attend any festival activities. Although the number who participated in these protests was small, the group actions were successful because they targeted key tourist zones. The majority of festival events take place in public spaces downtown, on IVEC grounds, and at local beaches, all of which are destinations for tourists.

In addition to the format change that excluded Afro-Caribbean religions, the name of the festival changed temporarily in 1999. The "Afro" portion of the title was omitted and the festival was simply called the "International Caribbean Festival." The name change was reportedly another consequence of the protests against African-influenced religious practices. Locals criticized these changes at the festival, asking, "How are you going to deny a young person the Afro-Caribbean culture from which we come? Hiding what they do in the Caribbean is not a way to teach others about our culture" (Castañeda 2004, 78). Indeed, locals questioned how IVEC could boast that it was sharing Afro-Caribbean culture if it chose which parts of that culture were worthy enough to share. Excluding parts of a culture such as the religious aspects of Santería or links to an African ancestry seemed to negate the original goals of the festival.

Another change to the festival format included the creation of symbols that misrepresent Afro-Caribbean influences in Veracruz. Of particular interest is the design for the 2001 festival, which highlighted coffee as one of the main exports in Veracruz. The image depicted a large cup filled with coffee from which a black man and woman sprang up dancing (see Figure 4.1). Their only accessories were a pair of *maracas* and *rumbero* sleeves on the man and a red bandana with white polka dots on the woman's head. The woman's posture accentuates her breasts and buttocks. A similar design was used in a 1998 poster (see Figure 4.2), which included the same outline of a woman wearing nothing more than the polka-dotted bandana. These symbols both sexualize the female body and relegate her to the domestic sphere, symbolized by the bandana on her head that is reminiscent of a "mammy" role. The woman in these posters becomes an example of Shay's "smiling and dancing negative Others" whose bodies become the main vehicle for the message. The symbols demonstrate how IVEC festival organizers attempted to link local Veracruz identity with romanticized and overly

Figure 4.1. Poster for the Afro-Caribbean Festival, 2001.

Figure 4.2. Poster for the Afro-Caribbean Festival, 1998.

exotic images of African ancestry. They are a negative illustration of Cadaval's observation that "cultural performances manipulate collective symbolic expressive forms to reflect, interpret, and influence society" (1998, 10).

While the festival was apparently "whitened" when the magical/religious portion of the festival was removed, the 2002 festival activities marked a reincorporation of select symbols of Afro-Caribbean Santería religion and culture. Included in the 2002 festival publicity materials was the depiction of a man of African descent standing with his hands flat against a wall that displayed

Figure 4.3. Poster for the Afro-Caribbean Festival, 2002.

the logo and name of the festival (see Figure 4.3). The man is shirtless and is wearing multiple necklaces made from beads of various colors. This is of particular importance; the beads in the photograph are distinctly symbolic of religions of the African diaspora, especially Santería. The beaded necklaces, or *collares*, signify a person's level of participation and initiation into the religion of Santería. Utilizing particular religious symbolism in this way, festival organizers reframed the connection with an African past for their own means; they wanted to use certain Santería symbols to project an image that would spark interest yet would not marginalize their main constituent base of domestic and international tourists.

Ultimately, by highlighting an exotic Afro-Caribbean identity in Veracruz, IVEC was able to market its festival to a wider audience and distinguish it from festivals in other Mexican states. It attempted to use these symbols to construct a local culture that might illustrate how locals embody their understanding of an Afro-Mexican identity. The selectivity of the symbols IVEC mobilized are an illustration of Cadaval's observation that "festival as cultural performance provides a multifaceted camera lens that selects, magnifies, and frames elements of an ongoing historical process of imagination" (1998, 10). IVEC organizers manipulated the message they wanted to convey using symbols that created a new and idealized past. The festival was "whitened" by its exclusion of Santería and other nontraditional religious practices. Yet it would appear that festival organizers used certain symbols of what they associate with "Afro" and "black" culture to represent festival activities. In this way they manipulated the connection with an African past for their own means—especially an increase in tourism.

The fact that the symbols IVEC mobilizes are selective manipulations is an example of how collective memory becomes commodified by the state (Van Young 1994). IVEC festival organizers attempted to use historical links in a mythic and exotic form to construct new relationships with other Caribbean communities. This Afro-Caribbean link was oftentimes imagined or re-created to serve the needs of those in power, who are mostly members of the white and/or mestizo elite. In effect, Veracruz was transformed into a cultural battlefield where popular cultural forms were threatened by appropriation and commodification by a state government in need of unifying symbols (Hall 1981, 237). The fact that Afro-Caribbean religious elements were erased from the festival only later to be reinscribed without any contextual support from the local community illustrates the imbalance of power in the representation of Afro-Mexican identity at the IVEC festival.

It is apparent that Mexico needs its Afro-Mexican citizens to disappear if it is to perpetuate its homogenizing myth of the mestizo. Yet at the same time, the state needs its Afro-Mexican citizens to be visible in specific authorized ways so it can conform to larger global demands for plurality and to bring financial support to the nation in the form of tourist dollars. These citizens are celebrated when they embody an identity that conforms to the script, which devalues the performative power of the repertoire in favor of the archive. Yet in the town of Yanga, Veracruz, we find an example of how blackness is literally performed in the repertoire of carnival.

Carnival in Yanga is celebrated in the month of August, and as the work of Mexican anthropologist Sagrario Cruz-Carretero notes, it has taken on a new meaning that is dedicated to black culture:

> The elements that are distinctive from Mexico's Hispanic-Indigenous tradition come back to life in this carnival. For example, to revive the black skin that no longer exists in many parts of the town of Yanga, the actors paint their skin and put on masks. Yanga the black slave, the man who headed the first historically significant anti-colonial rebellion in the Americas and the founder of the town, appears as the main character. Symbolically they represent the black hero although their knowledge of him is somewhat diffused (Cruz-Carretero 2005, 76).

Community members have transported the historical figure of Yanga from the archive to the repertoire by performing his presence in their annual Carnival celebration, therefore reinforcing their identity and their link to the African diaspora.

Indeed, both the national and regional levels of cultural performance utilize *mestizaje*, but with different intentions. On the one hand, national institutions circulate imagery that promotes national unification with the "*todos somos iguales*," or "we are all equal," ideology. At the same time, a provincial institution such as the Veracruz Institute of Culture reenvisions its own localized version of national culture to include a stronger African element. Ultimately, while the national level seeks to blend any cultural or ethnic differences into one new and united population, the Veracruz state embraces this *mestizaje* ideology by concentrating on the African component that distinguishes this state from others, thereby creating a new and exotic image to increase tourism to the region. Peter Wade addresses this confrontation between racial and national identities in his work on communities of African descent in Colombia. Wade notes, "We need to understand the tensions that exist between sameness and difference and to grasp how difference is a positive as well as a negative resource for representations of nationhood and processes of constructing identities" (2001, 856).

Conclusion

Today, two cultural trends focus on the contemporary lived presence of Africa in Mexico. One trend emphasizes new global exchanges and linkages, while the other is marked by a strong disconnect between insider and outsider views of ancestral roots.

Changes over the past two decades have brought about stronger diasporic connections and coalitions with the Afro-Latin community. These changes have taken place in Mexico as state-sponsored scholarly research has brought attention to the African presence in certain areas of the country. In addition, interactions between international organizations and Afro-Mexican groups have increased. For example, the Costa Chica organization México Negro has collaborated with U.S. African American communities to create museum exhibits in Detroit and San Francisco (Vaughn 2005, 55), and in 1988 the mayor of Yanga in Veracruz established relations with the embassy of the Ivory Coast by inviting dignitaries to participate in Yanga's local carnival festivities, thus further strengthening the town's ties to its African roots (Cruz-Carretero 2005, 76).

The other trend takes place in the context of cultural initiatives marked by a sharp disconnect between insider and outsider interpretations of Afro-Mexican identity. Some people feel the emphasis on "Afro" cultural elements in these initiatives only works to further marginalize Afro-Mexican communities. Anthropologist Laura Lewis comments on this dynamic vis-à-vis the Costa Chica:

> What is happening in Mexico is similar to what has happened in other Latin American locales, where a "black" culture is identified by outsiders and then equated with African survivals depicted as isolated and leftover fragments of a tangible past to which the value of the present is seen to adhere. Within this discourse, the meanings local people give to their "roots" are overlooked in favor of the priorities of outsiders (Lewis 2006, 809).

Instead of uniting Mexican citizens, this trend emphasizes difference by creating a narrative of a group's past that is unfamiliar to members of that group. In Veracruz, where elites craft state-sponsored festivals that translate Veracruz culture through political rather than local notions of identity, cultural events that purport to "re-imagine" links to Africa are a clear example of a "process of the active construction of otherness by national elites" (Wade 2001, 855). This is illustrated by the exclusion of certain sectors of local culture, specifically religious activities, from IVEC festivals. Lewis comments on this dynamic vis-à-vis the Costa Chica:

Cultural promoters and political activists impose identities without addressing the community's experiences or concerns. . . . The interests of the cultural promoters focus on a few local residents, particularly the musicians. . . . Many in the community see themselves giving away their cultural capital without getting anything in return. (Lewis 2006, 811)

This kind of disconnect in dialogue creates both misrepresentation and misinterpretation. And since representation is the power to both describe and define, the festivals sponsored and organized by state institutions exhibit their power over the performances and the people they seek to represent.

Both trends have brought their own set of challenges, but both have also increased awareness of and interest in issues related to the African diaspora in Mexico. In 2005, Mexico hosted public debates on race in the wake of negative comments President Vicente Fox made about the type of work associated with U.S. Latinos and African Americans and the controversy created when a stamp was released with the image of the comic book character Memím Penguin, a character many interpret as celebrating blackface. These examples illustrate the emergence of "new Mexican sensitivities to the topic of black identity. . . . In this sense, a small segment of the Afro-Mexican community is engaging in the project of multi-cultural politics that has been sweeping Latin America since the 1980s" (Vinson 2005a, 6).

Afro-Latin communities in Mexico have undergone tremendous changes in how their cultures are represented. While in the past they have gone through periods of complete erasure from the national archive, now embodied performances of their cultures are featured prominently at cultural events. As Bobby Vaughn notes:

The ways that race is understood by Afro-Mexicans appears to be on the cusp of change. Afro-Mexicans are "no longer invisible." They are no longer invisible to mestizos who until recently have associated ethnicity and culture only to indigeneity. They are no longer invisible to Mexican and non-Mexican outsiders who have taken an interest in Afro-Mexican communities for scholarly or activist reasons. (Vaughn 2005, 56)

My research illustrates the complexity inherent in Afro-Latin communities and advances new interpretations of the process of *mestizaje*, a concept essential for understanding historical and contemporary relations in Latin America. Moreover, it contributes to our understanding of the promise and limitations of the archive by reinforcing the need for a more holistic reinterpretation of Afro-Latin communities in a performative context.

Bibliography

Aguirre Beltrán, Gonzalo. 1958. *Cuijla: Esbozo etnográfico de un pueblo negro*. Mexico City: Fondo de Cultura Económica.

Arias Hernández, Rafael. 1997. *Festival Internacional Afro-Caribeño*. Xalapa, Veracruz: Instituto Veracruzano de Cultura.

Askew, Kelly M. 2002. *Performing the Nation: Swahili Music and Cultural Politics in Tanzania*. Chicago: University of Chicago Press.

Bauman, Richard. 1977. *Verbal Art as Performance*. Prospect Heights, Ill.: Waveland Press.

Cadaval, Olivia. 1998. *Creating a Latino Identity in the Nation's Capital: The Latino Festival*. New York: Garland Publishing.

Castañeda, Angela. 2004. "Veracruz también es Caribe: Power, Politics, and Performance in the Making of an Afro-Caribbean Identity" PhD diss., Indiana University, Bloomington.

Cruz-Carretero, Sagrario. 2005. "Yanga and the Black Origins of Mexico." *Review of Black Political Economy* 33 (1): 73–77.

Darity, William. 2005. "Afro-Mexicano Symposium: An Introduction." *Review of Black Political Economy* 33 (1): 47–48.

Guss, David M. 2000. *The Festive State: Race, Ethnicity, and Nationalism as Cultural Performance*. Berkeley: University of California Press.

Hall, Stuart. 1981. "Notes on Deconstructing 'The Popular.'" In *People's History and Socialist Theory*, ed. Raphael Samuel. Amsterdam: Van Gennep.

Hernández Cuevas, Marco Polo. 2004. *African Mexicans and the Discourse on Modern Nation*. Dallas: University Press of America.

INEGI. 2002. *Cuaderno Estadístico Municipal*. Aguascalientes, México: Instituto Nacional de Estadística, Geografía e Informática.

Lewis, Laura A. 2006. "Home Is Where the Heart Is: Afro-Latino Migration and Cinder-Black Homes on Mexico's Costa Chica." *South Atlantic Quarterly* 105 (4): 801–829.

Martínez Montiel, Luz María. 1995. *Presencia Africana en México*. Mexico City: Consejo Nacional Para la Cultura y las Artes.

Miller, Marilyn Grace. 2004. *Rise and Fall of the Cosmic Race: The Cult of the Mestizaje in Latin America*. Austin: University of Texas Press.

Minority Rights Group, ed. 1995. *No Longer Invisible: Afro-Latin Americans Today*. London: Minority Rights Group Publications.

Myerhoff, Barbara. 1982. "Life History among the Elderly: Performance, Visibility, and Remembering." In *A Crack in The Mirror: Reflexive Perspectives in Anthropology*, ed. Jay Ruby. Philadelphia: University of Pennsylvania Press.

Naveda Chávez-Hita, Adriana. 2001. *Pardos, mulattos y libertos: Sexto encuentro de afromexicanistas*. Xalapa, Veracruz, México: Universidad Veracruzana.

Proctor, Frank T., III. 2003. "Afro-Mexican Slave Labor in the Obrajes de Paños of New Spain, Seventeenth and Eighteenth Centuries." *The Americas* 60 (1): 33–58.

Rahier, Jean Muteba. 1999. "Presence of Blackness and Representations of Jewishness in the Afro-Esmeraldian Celebrations of the Semana Santa (Ecuador)." In *Representations of Blackness and the Performance of Identities*, ed. Jean Muteba Rahier. Westport, Conn.: Bergin & Garvey.

Rowell, Charles Henry. 2004. "'Todos somos primos'/We Are All Cousins: The Editor's Notes." *Callaloo* 27 (1): xi–xiv.

————. 2006. "Africa in Mexico: The Editor's Notes." *Callaloo* 29 (2): 397–400.

Royce, Anya P. 2004. *Anthropology of the Performing Arts: Artistry, Virtuosity, and Interpretation in Cross-Cultural Perspective.* Walnut Creek, Calif.: Altimira Press.

Shay, Anthony. 2002. *Choreographic Politics: State Folk Dance Companies, Representation, and Power.* Middletown, Conn.: Wesleyan University Press.

Stutzman, Ronald. 1981. "El Mestizaje: An All-Inclusive Ideology of Exclusion." In *Cultural Transformation and Ethnicity in Modern Ecuador,* ed. Norman E. Whitten. Urbana: University of Illinois Press.

Taylor, Diana. 2003. *The Archive and the Repertoire: Performing Cultural Memory in the Americas.* Durham, N.C.: Duke University Press.

Thompson, Robert Farris. 1984. *Flash of the Spirit: African & Afro-American Art & Philosophy.* New York: Vintage Books.

Turner, Victor. 1986. *The Anthropology of Performance.* New York: PAJ Publications.

Van Young, Eric. 1994. "Conclusion: The State as Vampire—Hegemonic Projects, Public Ritual, and Popular Culture in Mexico, 1600–1990." In *Rituals of Rule, Rituals of Resistance: Public Celebrations and Popular Culture in Mexico,* ed. William H. Beezley, Cheryl English Martin, and William E. French, 343–374. Wilmington, Del.: Scholarly Resources.

Vasconcelos, José. 1925. *The Cosmic Race (La raza cósmica, mission de la raza iberoamericana).* Paris: Agencia Mundial de Librería.

Vaughn, Bobby. 2005. "The African Diaspora through Ojos Mexicanos: Blackness and Mexicanidad in Southern Mexico." *Review of Black Political Economy* 33 (1): 49–57.

Vincent, Ted. 1994. "The Blacks Who Freed Mexico." *Journal of Negro History* 79 (3): 257–276.

Vinson, Ben, III. 2005a. "Afro-Mexican History: Trends and Directions in Scholarship." *History Compass* 3 (1): 1–14.

————. 2005b. "Fading from Memory: Historiographical Reflections on the Afro-Mexican Presence." *The Review of Black Political Economy* (Summer): 59–72.

Wade, Peter. 2001. "Racial Identity and Nationalism: A Theoretical View from Latin America." *Ethnic and Racial Studies* 24 (5): 845–865.

————. 2005. "Rethinking *Mestizaje:* Ideology and Lived Experience." *Journal of Latin American Studies* 37 (2): 239–257.

5

Visions of a Nineteenth-Century Cuba

Images of Blacks in the Work of Víctor Patricio de Landaluze

ELIZABETH MORÁN

The nineteenth century was significant for the political and economic development of Cuba's African and African-descended population. After Haiti's struggle for independence from Spain ended successfully in 1804, sugar production boomed in the other Spanish colonies nearby, and Cuba had emerged as the largest producer of sugar by the middle of the century. But the sugar economy was also a slave economy, and plantation owners brought in more and more slaves to meet the demand for labor. As a result, early in the century, the majority of the population living on the island was African or of African descent. Spanish authorities responded by passing laws that encouraged Europeans to emigrate to the island.

Although these laws did increase the proportion of nonblacks in Cuba by the middle of the century, the African and Afro-Cuban population had an enormous presence within (and outside) the city of Havana. They were politically active and very involved in planning and executing Cuba's three wars against Spain (which took place over the period 1868 to 1898) as the island fought for its sovereignty. They also worked to end slavery in Cuba. In addition to their political contributions, blacks increased their economic power in the nineteenth century. Many purchased their freedom and established themselves as merchants, artisans, and other craftsmen. Amid all this conflict and change, members of the white Cuban bourgeoisie fought to maintain what they perceived of as their "place."

Artists working on the island during this time produced work that reflected the desires of the aristocracy and the bourgeoisie—idealized and romanticized views that reflected none of the conflicts of the growing Cuban nation. It is ironic that one of the most popular artists during that time, Víctor Patricio de Landaluze, painted scenes that depicted the activities of the African and African-derived associations that had been growing in numbers and strength since the seventeenth century. Landaluze's works are significant because they are often referred to as the source and inspiration for later artists of the twentieth century who worked to define blackness in Cuba and identify the importance of the African presence in Cuban culture. Yet at the time Landaluze's works were produced, his patrons and others interpreted them as satires and parodies of an inferior race. This chapter will explore how Landaluze depicted blacks to meet the needs of the white bourgeoisie and will examine how fear of a growing, economically vital and politically significant black population was "erased" through his work.

Frequent subjects for Landaluze were the performances and individual members of the *cabildo de la naciones*—confraternities of similar African groups. *Cabildo* members forged cultural links that continued and altered African traditions, and many *cabildo* members were also members of the Cuban-founded but African-derived Abakuá Secret Society, which dates back to the colonial period. Initially an exclusively African and Afro-Cuban male association, the Abakuá Secret Society is still active in Cuba today. In discussing *cabildo* performances and festival theory, art historian David H. Brown notes that the symbols of authority used by members and performers (whether they derived from Africa or were borrowed from Europe) were misread, possibly because the white audience could not reconcile their anxiety about blacks using these important signs of power (Brown 2003, 43–47). *Cabildos* themselves were a symbol of authority that could not be reconciled in the Spanish colonial mind. This is evident in the relationship Spanish authorities had (or pretended *not* to have) with these associations. It is clear that Spanish authorities saw these institutions as a threat as early as the late eighteenth century; they are mentioned in Havana's *Bando de Buen Gobierno y Policía de 1792* (Proclamation for Good Government and Policy of 1792). Before the 1792 regulations, *cabildos* were allowed to gather and perform within Old Havana's fortress walls—the area referred to as *intramurros*; after 1792 they were relegated to the areas outside the walls, or *extramuros* (Brown 2003, 28). These regulations removed Africans and Afro-Cubans who had been using public space to demonstrate their presence (and power) from the presence of wealthy merchants, the titled Spanish nobility, and the bourgeois class living within the *intramurros*.

Of course, let us not forget that both the Church and the Spanish government had approved these associations in the first place. Authorities in these two institutions saw *cabildos* as a way to keep the African and Afro-Cuban population under control. But this strategy backfired, and *cabildos* in effect became institutions of empowerment for blacks. The activities members were allowed to participate in—owning land and property, organizing public celebrations and performances—were very significant for blacks under a colonial power

(Castellanos 1996, 44–45). The political and economic power of the Abakuá Secret Society was also a significant outlet for blacks; as an organized workforce, members had great influence on the wharves of Havana for over one hundred years (Miller 2000, 183). Contrary to the wish of Spanish authorities, *cabildos* became places where rebellion was nurtured. Members often participated in independence movements against Spanish authorities; examples include the 1812 Aponte affair and the 1844 Conspiracy of La Escalera (ibid.). Both of these events have often been thought of as isolated and led by single individuals, yet recent scholarship has shown that the Aponte affair was certainly not a conspiracy led by José Antonio Aponte alone but was the work of a group of individuals working from various places (Childs 2006, 150–154). Many historians also recognize La Escalera as an international antislavery conspiracy (Miller 2000, 183). Abakuá members participated in both of these pro-independence movements.

At the same time that *cabildos* were exercising their power and influence, Spanish authorities were tightening control over *cabildo* activities. Historian and anthropologist Israel Moliner Castañeda documents the various policy changes the government made with regard to *cabildos* and carnival performances (Moliner Casteñeda 2002, 22–23). Most of the ordinances were concerned with limiting performances and activities to a specific time and place. But as the nineteenth century progressed, the regulations also refer more and more to the paraphernalia, mostly visual material, that *cabildos* used. African and African-derived artistic expression was seen as a potential threat to Cuban national culture as soon as *cabildos* were sanctioned by the church and state. In Havana, police records from the 1870s provide information about raids on *cabildo* and Abakuá meeting places. In these raids, musical instruments, dance costumes, and other ritual objects were confiscated or destroyed (Moore 1997, 18). Spanish authorities were concerned with controlling the physical space of African and Afro-Cubans, but perhaps even more importantly, they wanted to control their icons of power.

Landaluze came to Havana around 1850, although when he was planning to leave Spain he had originally hoped to settle in Mexico. He had studied with the artist José Madrazo (1781–1859) in Spain, then he studied lithography in Paris. He returned home to continue his studies with the artist Mariano Fortuny (1838–1874). When he arrived in Cuba he established himself as an illustrator and caricaturist for the anti-separatist newspapers *Moro Muza, Juan Palomo,* and other publications. He also funded his own anti-separatist newspaper shortly after his arrival. In addition, he contributed to several books as an illustrator, including *Los cubanos pintados por sí mismos: Colección de tipos cubanos* (1850). In 1881, he illustrated *Tipos y costumbres de la Isla de Cuba.*

Cuban writer José Antonio Portuando points out that it is possible that

Landaluze had not been to Cuba when he collaborated on the 1850 manuscript since the characters depicted in the book are generic and the landscapes almost nonexistent. In fact, there is very little in each image to make it a specifically Cuban character or landscape. It is thus likely that Landaluze did this work while still living in Spain (Portuando 1972, 58–59). Portuando clearly demonstrates a marked difference in the 1850 work and Landaluze's later work in 1881. In particular, he notes the absence of depictions of blacks in the 1850 work, whereas Africans and Afro-Cubans constitute the bulk of the depictions in the 1881 book. Interestingly enough, the racially mixed female, or *mulata*, appears frequently in the 1881 publication.

Some of the images in the 1881 work are especially significant because they appear out of character for a person who was vehemently opposed to the growth of the black population and to Cuban independence from Spain. For example, in the work *Los Mataperros* (The Urchins), Landaluze illustrated what many have interpreted as a vision of the new Cuban identity. His street urchins include three boys—a white, a black, and a racially mixed mulatto—playing a game of marbles. The boys are grouped at the center of the picture, the white and black children on their knees focusing on the marbles that have been thrown on the ground, and the mulatto child standing over them, keenly watching the activity. The boys are rendered almost lovingly, each child showing specific details of facial characteristics and personalities.

Portuando reads this image as positively reflecting the idea of the three cultures of Cuba. It is, however, significant that while the three children portrayed represent diverse racial backgrounds, are all poor. Portuando interprets this as a critical comment on child poverty in Cuba, but other writers have commented that Landaluze appeared to have been almost indifferent to some aspects of social existence in Cuba at that time. Landaluze had to keep the needs and tastes of his patrons in mind, and the trend during this period was a romantic view of the lower classes (Mohammed 1997, 13a). The artist was very popular with the Cuban aristocracy and bourgeois class. These patrons were not eager to purchase scenes that reflected the cruelty and inequality of poverty and slavery; rather, they were looking for work that reflected their idealistic view of the lower classes. This need was met by artists, such as Landaluze, who produced images of blacks that were nonthreatening: children playing, black men behaving comically, or black women completely unaware of their surroundings and their state of dress or undress (and therefore their own sexuality). None of these images reflected the important presence of the black population on the island in an accurate way.

Thus, the sweet but romanticized depiction of the children in *Los Mataperros* is less about the subject matter and more about the style of the painting. A comparison of Landaluze's work in the 1850 and 1881 publications reveals that his style changed significantly over the years. Landaluze's 1881 lithographs are much more mature: the figures are fuller, more contoured, and fleshier. They are not generic and idealized types of social and racial classes and instead demonstrate a keen observation of people in action. In order to read works such as *Los Mataperros* accurately, it is helpful to look at the overall output of the artist.

In some works, Landaluze's anti-separatist and pro-slavery sentiments are clearly apparent. In *En La Ausencia* (When Nobody Is Around; Figure 5.1), a black female slave has forgotten her task of sweeping and has gone into her mistress's wardrobe. She puts on a feathered and ribboned hat over her simple white head wrap and ties a fine blue dress around her waist. She looks back at her reflection in the vanity mirror, smiling approvingly at her new appearance. In *José Francisco* (Figure 5.2), her male counterpart is also standing in the middle of the room and, like the female slave, has forgotten his domestic duties of dusting. He holds his feather duster lifelessly in his hands while he leans into a bust of a Spanish woman, lips pursed into a kiss.

Both paintings, done in 1880, are typical of the ways blacks were represented in Cuba during the colonial period. Black women were often sexualized—as she looks into the mirror to admire her new look, the female slave is unaware that her own simple white dress has dropped down her shoulders and is sliding off her back; her smooth black skin makes a stark contrast with the white dress. Black men are often portrayed playing nonthreatening and even comic roles. In *José Francisco* the male slave leans in to kiss the marble bust, his large lips ridiculously pursed as he prepares for the kiss, his own face uncouth, a sharp contrast to the dignified female rendered in the marble bust. His attention is not focused on the heavy bosom of the woman, but rather, like a child gazing at his first love, he stares into her face and moves toward her lips.

Both works, currently in the Museo Nacional de Bellas Artes, Havana, are identical in size (30.5 × 24 cm.) and medium (oil on cardboard). It is likely that they were done as a pair. In both paintings, the absurd actions of the servants are meant to humor the audience and are typical of the *costumbrismo* genre that was characterized by its picturesque recording of customs and physical types. *Costumbrismo* was a significant trend in Latin America and the Caribbean (especially Cuba). It appeared first in Cuban literature during the early nineteenth century and then began to appear in lithographs and paintings (Moore 1997, 21). By no means a New World invention, this movement had its origins in the artistic trends of eighteenth- and nineteenth-century Europe. Portuando notes that *costumbrismo* first appeared in print in the newspaper *Papel Periódico de La Habana* (The News of Havana, published 1790–1805) and originally reflected various types within the Cuban bourgeois class (Portuando 1972, 52). In the

Figure 5.1. Víctor Patricio de Landaluze, *En la ausencia* (When Nobody Is Around), ca. 1880. Museo Nacional de Bellas Artes, Havana. Photo: Rodolfo Martinez, Havana.

New World, where different racial types were mixing and new social classes were developing, *costumbrismo* eventually became a way of recording these new social and cultural changes.

Satire and parody were a fundamental part of *costumbrismo* representations in both literature and art. Landaluze's newspaper illustrations were often harsh parodies of separatists and antislavery leaders. Portuando documents a case when

Figure 5.2. Víctor Patricio de Landaluze, *José Francisco*, ca. 1880. Museo Nacional de Bellas Artes, Havana. Photo: Rodolfo Martinez, Havana.

Landaluze published an image of Francisco Vicente Aguilera (1821–1877), a pro-independence and antislavery leader who funded a school to teach newly freed slaves how to read and write (Portuando 1972, 61). In the image Aguilera is shown drunk with a bottle hanging from his neck, teaching with small chalkboards that clearly show his anti-Spanish propaganda. This was typical of Landaluze's work, who participated in a trend that was evident in many of the anti-separatist newspapers. Parodies of blacks were especially prevalent in nineteenth-century *costumbrismo* images. Landaluze created images such as *En La Ausencia* and *José Francisco* to poke fun at what was seen as an inferior race, but such jesting is evidence of the growing tensions and fears of the Cuban white bourgeoisie.

The year these two works were made, 1880, marked the culmination of the second of three liberation wars that Cuba fought against Spain (the Little War of 1879–1880). In 1868, Cuba began the Ten Years' War (1868–1878), which ultimately led to the War of Independence (1895–1898). Some of the events that led to these conflicts also facilitated the commercial growth of the island. In August 1791, a slave revolt in one of Saint Dominique's most important sugar plantations marked the official beginning of the Haitian Revolution. After the revolution succeeded in 1804, Haiti was the first free colony in the Caribbean, but it had also lost its dominant position as the world's largest sugar producer (Klein 1986, 90). The decline of production on Saint Dominique created new commercial opportunities for Cuba, which had been producing sugar since the early eighteenth century. By 1810, only four years after the Haitian Revolution, Cuba's production had doubled from what it had been during the eighteenth century. By 1870 Cuba was the world's largest sugar producer.

Slavery, of course, was a component of the Cuban sugar plantation economy. Cuba was a major sugar producer because it exploited the labor of slaves. While African slaves had been a part of the production and economy of Cuba since the sixteenth century, they represented only a small portion of the population. Instead, blacks and mulattos predominated; by 1811, they constituted more than 54 percent of the population (Moore 1997, 16). Slavery was officially prohibited in Cuba by 1853, yet because of the lucrative sugar economy, trafficking in slaves continued for at least another ten years.

Writing about Landaluze's work, Cuban artist Jorge Rigol (1910–1991) has noted:

> At first sight Landaluze's painting appears utterly non-political, but it is [as] reflective of his political sentiments as his cartoons, the only difference being in the mode of expression. The gay and carefree personages of his canvases enjoying life under the sun of "the loyal island of Cuba" seem to suggest that war is undesirable: to disrupt this idyllic existence would be a crime, if not worse. (Gonzalez Jane 1978, 16)

There are no signs of the conflict and turmoil in Cuban society in the two 1880 works Landaluze produced. *En La Ausencia* and *José Francisco* do not depict the tensions between slaves and masters or reflect the increasing discontent of the black population and the real threat that population posed. They do not illustrate the growing fear of the pro-Spanish population in Cuba.

In both paintings, the main character is alone in a room yet not fully out of the presence of his or her white master. Notice that the black female slave is standing to the right of a portrait of her male master (or some other white male authority figure), while José Francisco is standing directly underneath a painting of his female overseer. In the portrait of the female slave, the white male figure portrayed in the image is clearly rendered; the viewer is meant to notice (and perhaps recognize) him, maybe even identify with him. While the black female is oblivious to her master, the audience is not.

In *José Francisco* we have almost the opposite effect. The woman in the portrait is rendered unclearly, her facial characteristics and personalities obscured. In fact, there is a Madonna-like presence in her image; her head is covered by a veil. The effect is one of desexualizing the black man in the image. Not only is he unaware of the sexual presence of the female represented in the marble bust (and therefore his own masculinity) but he is standing in the presence of a woman who has been herself desexualized. The black slave is more like a child than a man. Landaluze has created acceptable images of blacks; a female who can be gazed upon and admired and a black man who is nonthreatening. The satirical depiction of blacks in these two works is not just about establishing an ideology of an inferior race (and class); it is also intended to allay the fears associated with a large African and Afro-Cuban population and growing civil unrest and uncertainty in nineteenth-century Cuba. Landaluze's success as an artist was based on his ability to meet the demands of the Cuban bourgeoisie who needed to see images like these that erased the reality of the changing racial and political climate in Cuba.

The Haitian Revolution had an immense impact on slave laws, and in the Caribbean and the Americas, local governments tightened control over slaves (Klein 1986, 91). As Cuba's sugar economy boomed in the period 1820–1860, authorities instituted severe anti-black policies. These laws strictly regimented the lives of slave laborers, repressed African and Afro-Cuban social and cultural activities, and sought to "whiten" the population of Cuba by importing European and Chinese laborers (Brown 2003, 26). They also decreased the possibility of *coartación*, or self-purchase by slaves. *Coartación*, which had been recognized as early as the eighteenth century in Spanish and Portuguese America, gave slaves the right of owning personal property. Slaves were allowed to keep surpluses from their own gardens; rented slaves had the right to keep their own earnings outside rental contracts. Historian Herbert Klein notes that *coartación* was economically sensible for owners; it provided incentive for slaves to produce more and often allowed owners to reduce their maintenance costs (Klein 1986, 194). Significantly, it also allowed a slave to purchase his or her own freedom and the freedom of other slaves.

In colonial Cuba, this system was fully utilized by African *cabildos*. Initially *cabildos de la nación* were associations formed by Africans from the same ethnic background (or ones that were similar). They first appear in Havana's written record in 1792 (Moliner Castañeda 2002, 12). In the nineteenth century, membership was expanded to include slaves born in Cuba, mulattos, and even whites. They were headed by hereditary or elected rulers: a "king," and a "queen," usually, but sometimes a "president" or a *capataz*, or "boss." These organizations were fully recognized by the Spanish Crown and the Church, and were allowed to collect fees, acquire land and houses, organize celebrations, and participate in carnival festivities. These societies provided a collective identity, allowing Africans and Afro-Cubans to share similar experiences and assist one another (Castellanos 1996, 45; Brown 2003, 27).

The Spanish authorities saw *cabildos* as another way to control the African and Afro-Cuban population. They believed that *cabildos* would decrease the likelihood of mass uprisings or conspiracies and enable recently arrived Africans to adjust to their new environment and learn Spanish or *bozal* (the Spanish of recently arrived slaves). Outwardly, *cabildos* conformed to the customs and laws of the Spanish government, and members were typically baptized, held Catholic-style masses and acknowledged Catholic saints.

Cabildos incorporated the various syncretic religions of Africans and Afro-Cubans in Cuba. Ceremonies from African-derived religions such as Regla de Ocha (*santería*) and Regla de Palo Monte were incorporated into *cabildo* activities and rituals. Significantly, the ideology and rituals of the Abakuá Secret Society were also part of this religious incorporation (Fernández Olmos and Paravisini-Gebert 2003, 87). The society was first established in Cuba at the port of Regla in 1836 by the Carabalí group, a name given to the Cross River peoples of southeastern Nigeria from the section referred to as "Old Calabar" in Cuban colonial records (Fernández Olmos and Paravisini-Gebert 2003, 86). In Cuba, the society originally began as an unofficial guild for African dock workers and other important labor sectors. These associations were principally derived from the male "leopard societies" of Ejagham, Efut, and other related peoples of the Cross River section (Miller 2000, 164).

Abakuá elements are recognizable in Día de Reyes (Epiphany) celebrations organized by African and Afro-Cuban *cabildos*. On January 6 of each year, groups of performers from various *cabildos* would overtake the streets of Havana to perform and collect *aguinaldo*, or monetary "gifts," for their performances. This money would later be used to continue *cabildo* business, which included buying property and buying the freedom of slaves. Figure 5.3 is Landaluze's *Día de Rey en La Habana* (Day of the Magi, Havana), an undated oil on canvas. Like most of the artist's canvases, it is small in scale, measuring only 51 × 61 cm. As one

Figure 5.3. Víctor Patricio de Landaluze, *Día de Rey en la Habana* (Day of the Magi, Havana), n.d., Museo Nacional de Bellas Artes, Havana. Photo: Rodolfo Martinez, Havana.

of the few depictions of the celebration, it is an important documentation of African and African-influenced rituals in Cuba. In it Landaluze has captured the moment when the *cabildo* procession has stopped in front of several houses to continue their performance and ask for money. The houses frame the left and right edges of the canvas, while in the distance, behind the dancers and performers, is a view of a church, and farther back, the Plaza de Armas, or main square of the city. The focus is on the *cabildo* performers; they are in the foreground and at the center of the picture.

While there is a high level of movement in the painting, there is also a structure and order to the various activities of the *cabildo* members. The viewer's eye immediately focuses on the center of the picture, where a male performer stands out because of his elaborate costume and headdress. Wearing a long fiber skirt that reaches his ankles and a large horned and feathered headdress, he extends one arm up in the air. Around his wrists are rattles called *ensani* or *maracas de muñeca*; these were usually worn by drummers and are a Congo-derived element (Brown 2003, 42). He also has his mouth open, probably singing to the accompanying drum-playing of the two male drummers to the left of the group. A small black child, perhaps not part of the official group, has joined the drummers and is swinging his arms to the rhythm of the music. Around the costumed character is a group of finely dressed women and several other male costumed dancers. The painting is a wonderful documentation of the syncretism and transformation of African-derived performances in the Caribbean; for while the women are dressed in European-style dresses, the men are in traditional African or African-derived costumes with palm or fiber skirts and feathered headdresses.

Behind the central character is a group of women proceeding under a large umbrella; one is certainly the queen of the association and the other holds a doll identified as *anaquillé,* an African-derived doll that has been referred to as a fetish or idol in the literature but is a container of power. It probably derived from the Congo. Parallel to the group of women but out of the viewer's sight is a standard bearer; one can make out the flag that he holds erect in the air. Behind this grouping are other dancers and musicians.

Two other characters stand out in Landaluze's image, and both are interacting with the audience. One is to the right of the central character. His costume identifies him as a *ñáñigo*—erroneously but popularly called *el diablito* (little devil). This costumed dancer is an *íreme,* and his checkerboard outfit is a re-embodiment of the Nigerian Ibibio leopard dancer (Thompson 1984, 261–262). The *íreme* stands to the right of the group collecting donations from several onlookers. There are many colonial written references to these performers. Historian David H. Brown has recorded one eyewitness account:"The chief object in the group was an athletic negro, with a fantastic straw helmet, an immensely thick girdle of strips of palm-leaves around the waist, and other uncouth articles of dress. Whenever they stopped . . . this frightful figure would commence a devil's dance, which was the signal for all his court to join in" (Brown 2003, 37). The *íreme* takes center stage in other visual representations of Epiphany celebrations. In *El Día de Reyes* (Day of Kings) by the French artist Pierre Toussaint Frédéric Mialhe (1810–1868), the *íreme* and the horned costume dancer appear in the center of the image; behind them the *cabildo's* flag is held straight in the air, its shape echoed by the tower of the Plaza de Armas (see Figure 5.4).

While references to *ñáñigo* performers are frequent in written accounts of the colonial period, the term was also used generically for other costumed dancers. The horned dancer that appears prominently in the work of both Landaluze and Mialhe has also been identified as a *diablito.* The costumed dancer was derogatively labeled *la culona* (a big-butted woman) by the audience, a butchered rendition of the original word associated with the dancer: *kulona* or *lonna,* an adjective meaning wise or educated (Ortiz 2001, 31). Robert Farris Thompson

Figure 5.4. Frédéric Mialhe, *El Día de Reyes* (Day of Kings),1853. McGill University Library. Photo MBAM, Christine Guest.

suggests that the hoop skirt is derived from the Calabar Aban dancer and that the hoop skirt itself is a sign, a piece of ancient writing worn as a dress (Thompson 1984, 266). The horns of the headdress are a reference to the horned crown of rulers in the Congo area (Ortiz 2001, 26). For the African and Afro-Cuban audience, these visual materials were probably not interpreted or read as they would have been in their place of origin, yet the black audience certainly understood them as both sacred and powerful.

The second *cabildo* character that is differentiated in the group because of his interaction with the audience is the *capataz*, or king, who is also collecting money from a white family at the left of the picture. He is identifiable by his costume: European-style pants and a coat with tails. He wears a red sash across his chest, tied at the waist, and carries a staff in his left hand. His top hat is off and becomes a container to collect money from the white audience. Landaluze's *capataz* carries himself with great dignity; he strolls solemnly to the audience with his top hat in hand. Yet there is undoubtedly an underlying sense that the artist is making fun of the man; he asks for money from women and children, and his European costume, most likely borrowed from a white person, is completely out of balance with his place in society.

The way Landaluze has included and placed his white audience is significant. In the image they only appear in relation to the giving of gifts and are physically separated from the *cabildo* performers—either by height, such as the two women and child close to the stairs on the right; or by another physical barrier, such as the family who watches from their gated window on the ground level. Significantly, in both cases, only white women and children are included. In another work titled *Ñañigo* (Little Devil), Landaluze depicts another *írime* dancer; and like his counterpart in the *Día de Rey en La Habana*, he performs solely for women and children (see Figure 5.5). This is a curious representation since it is clearly not historically accurate. *Cabildo* performances on the Day of Epiphany were watched by many, yet by excluding white men from the audience Landaluze minimizes the significance of these performances. They are entertainment for women and children, two groups that were, in effect, inconsequential in nineteenth-century Cuba. As an interesting contrast, in Mialhe's lithograph, both Spanish (and white) men and women appear as part of the crowd watching

Figure 5.5. Víctor Patricio de Landaluze, *Diablito* (Little Devil), n.d. Museo Nacional de Bellas Artes, Havana. Photo: Rodolfo Martinez, Havana.

the performance. And unlike Landaluze's white audience, they are not physically separated from the crowd but are mixing with blacks and creoles in the audience.

Landaluze's *Día de Rey en la Habana* helps illustrate the tensions inherent in the constant shifts in the balance of power between the *cabildos* and Spanish authorities. Other representations of carnival in the nineteenth century, especially those on cigar labels, are often caricatures of Cuba's black population. Landaluze's work is much more subtle and perhaps much more dangerous. There is nothing overtly demeaning in his representation. With great accuracy he records some of the most significant emblems of power associated with both the *cabildos* and the Abakuá Secret Society; ritual objects such as the flag, drums, and umbrellas and important authority figures such as the *capataz* and the queen. Yet he purposely removes white men from the audience, making the Epiphany performance a mere spectacle that would be of interest only to women and children. By *not* representing the white male, he in effect erases the concerns the Spanish authorities had with the growing power and influence of these associations.

The placement of the characters in the foreground is also worth noting. The *capataz*, the woman in the green dress, the costumed dancer moving on the ground, the two drummers, and the child with his back to us are all on an equal horizontal level. They are visually connected to one another and can be read as an extension of each other. It is here that Landaluze illustrates some of the perceived "silliness" of the carnival for his intellectual patrons. We begin from left to right with a black man who is dressed as a figure of authority yet is asking women for donations. We continue with a *mulata* who is also dressed in European fashion, but with her back to the viewer it is her voluptuous curves that focus our eyes. Facing her is a black man who is crawling on the floor like an animal. And finally we end with two musicians who are consumed by their drumming and finally a dancing black child. Landaluze is presenting the black figures in the foreground as acceptable satirical characters to his audience. As in the case of *José Francisco* and *En La Ausencia*, this image would make the *cabildos*, the Abakuá Secret Society, and blacks in general seem less threatening and more tolerable. Paradoxically, representing the Epiphany carnival as a comic and nonthreatening event, helped whites release their anxieties and tensions about the growing power and influence of these associations. Icons of African and black power, such as the costumed dancer on the ground, who would have been understood by the Afro-Cuban audience to be reflecting the power and authority of "the leopard," can only have been misunderstood by the white audience.

It cannot be said that Landaluze's depiction of blacks is one-dimensional, however. As already noted, he paid particular attention to the representation of the female black, especially the racially mixed *mulata*. She appears quite frequently in his 1881 lithographs as well as in small paintings. The 1881 lithograph

La Mulata de Rumbo (The Mulata on the Road) is a stunning depiction of a beautiful, voluptuous, racially mixed woman. She is dressed in a fine gown that accentuates her full breasts and small waist. Holding a fan in her right hand, she places her left hand on her hip, drawing the viewer's attention to her female curves. She looks to her left, a soft smile playing on her lips. She is unaware that the viewer is looking at her appreciatively; her attention is completely focused on what has caught her eye. The artist has placed her in an empty exterior scene—perhaps she is standing on the street alongside a house—and therefore the viewer is free to look upon her as he wishes.

Surprisingly, there are also beautiful depictions of black men in Landaluze's work. *El Gallero* (The Cock Fighting Owner), also an 1881 lithograph, shows a young mulatto smiling as he kneels down to pick up a rooster. Situated outside a barn, he is framed by a wooden chicken coop on his right and a door on his left. Like the woman in the *Mulata de Rumbo* lithograph, he looks outside of the picture plane, smiling absentmindedly at something that has caught his attention. He is not as well dressed as the *mulata* but his appearance is neat; his clothes are clean and not tattered. It is clear that Landaluze used the same mulatto model for the figures in *La Mulata de Rumbo*, *El Gallero*, and *Los Mataperros*: the *mulata*, the *gallero*, and the mulatto boy playing marbles.

Cuban writer Guillermo de Zendegui notes that another character type that appealed to the artist was the *calesero*, or carriage driver. He writes:

> As far as we know there is no counterpart in the rest of [the] Latin American cast of characters to these very Cuban servants of the Creole aristocracy. . . . Among their own class, the caleseros held high status that was coveted and envied because of both the special treatment they received as slaves and the reputation as Don Juans that attended them, not unreasonably, since they were always chosen from among the most handsome and well proportioned servants. (Mohammed 1997, 24)

El Calesero, which was published in the 1881 book, is one of many examples of this type that Landaluze produced. In this work, the carriage driver is in the center of the image and gazes out of the picture plane to his left. He is on the street, standing in front of his horse and carriage, waiting for his master to come out of the *macen de viveres* (store) in the background. Two black women in shawls and headdresses stand outside the store, talking to one another. But our carriage driver is not distracted; he simply holds his riding whip in his hands and waits patiently. He is smartly dressed in an outfit consisting of riding pants with black riding boots that reach to his knees, a white shirt with a bow, and a cropped jacket. His black top hat finishes the ensemble. Other Landaluze images show the carriage driver character resting while he waits for his master or stopping to give his horse a drink from a fountain and using the time to flirt with a passing black woman.

One of Landaluze's works seems to be a departure from his parodies of blacks; *Black Family* is a small undated work. In it, two women stand outside a basic but clean home and exchange some unidentifiable objects, perhaps plates of food. One woman wears a fine dress; her black patent leather shoes poke out just enough to be noticed. She wears her hair up and has golden hoops in her ears. Obviously she is not part of the black family who is greeting her; more likely she is part of the Creole class and is bringing something for the black family. The woman who greets her is poorly (but neatly) dressed and her hair is hidden under a wrap. Her mouth is open as if she is speaking to the Creole woman. Next to her is a seated older black man, also poorly dressed but clean. He too has his head wrapped and looks at the Creole woman. In the far left corner of the picture is another person who is too unclear to read properly. While at first the image seems to depart from Landaluze's oeuvre, it reflects the tastes of the patrons, as most of his other work did. The painting was most likely either commissioned by a Creole or created with the intent to sell to a Creole; it presents racial categories that are distinctly connected to class—a poor black family and the good-willed upper-class Creole.

Finally, it is Landaluze's representation of the class of blacks referred to as *curros* that is of most interest. Portuando theorizes that the word *curros* is a corruption of the word *horros*, which means free blacks (Portuando 1972, 73). He also connects the word to the term *currutaco*, which refers to an exaggerated dress, style, or personality. The term is probably associated with both notions— freedom and an ostentatious style. Brown notes that *los negros curros*, as they were often referred to, literally translates as "the black showoffs;" their classification was not grounded on a social category but rather on a perceived cultural personality (Brown 2003, 32). While it is not entirely clear who this group of blacks was, they appear frequently in nineteenth-century Cuban literature and art. Usually they are men and women who do not conform to the norms of their particular social and ethnic or racial status—in this case, that of a free black.

In his 1881 lithograph *Los Negros Curros*, Landaluze captures a black couple on the street stopping to chat with one another. The man is dressed in bell-bottomed pants and has a puffy-sleeved white shirt tucked into his waistband. A red belt is tied around his waist and a colorful handkerchief around his neck, and he holds another handkerchief in his right hand. As if this ensemble was not enough, he wears a straw hat at a daring angle. His female companion is also lavishly dressed: her long white dress ends in a pattern of lines and dots in bright red. The color red is again picked up by the handkerchief tied on her head, the shawl thrown over her shoulder, and her striped shoes. Underneath her red head wrap, her hair is dreadlocked. Around her neck is a heavy necklace, large gold hoop earrings adorn each ear, and a thick gold bracelet accents each wrist. The couple is caught in a congenial moment; she gestures with her right hand to embellish her story, and he listens to her with a smile on his lips. Notably, the woman is presented in a straightforward manner, her facial expression detailed without any mockery, while that of the man is characteristic of satirical scenes on cigar labels; a lopsided smile plastered on his face as he awaits the climax of the story. In addition, their outrageous dress adds to the parody of their display.

While some of these representations are merely romantic stereotypes that the Cuban bourgeoisie demanded of nineteenth-century artists, these images are useful visual contrasts to works such as *José Francisco* and other similar depictions of black men and women. The diverse portrayals of Africans and Afro-Cubans in Landaluze's paintings and lithographs reflect the complex and shifting attitudes toward blacks in Cuba and the varied ways in which whites saw or refused to see them. Blacks were an integral part of the Cuban society in the nineteenth century, present both visually and economically in everyday life. Whether or not whites wanted to acknowledge it, Africans and Afro-Cubans were contributing to the process of defining and transforming the island.

Paradoxically, it is the work of Landaluze, and other *costumbristas* that later became the inspiration for writers and artists who are trying to define Cuban nationalism. The Vanguardia artists of the 1920s and 1930s introduced Afro-Cuban themes, developing a style known as *afrocubanismo* (Martínez 1994, 75). Although this term is mostly associated with music and literature, many Vanguardia visual artists explored African and Afro-Cuban elements in their work, most notably scenes of dances and rituals, and of course, the sensual *mulata*. Art and architectural historian Narciso G. Menocal notes that the sensuality that Landaluze brought into his work was shaped by the national character of Cuba (Menocal 1996, 191). Landaluze's *tipos*—whether black or white—were subsequently transformed by other artists into national symbols. Yet the context in which these images were produced is vital to the discourse of blacks in the Caribbean. Landaluze's works were created for an audience that needed to allay their fears of a growing political and economic "other." The fact that later Cuban artists adopted these images as national types is an indication that how blackness is seen in Cuba is still a contested issue.

Bibliography

Brown, David H. 2003. "Black Royalty: New Social Frameworks and Remodeled Iconographies in Nineteenth-Century Havana." In *Santería Enthroned: Art, Ritual, and Innovation in an Afro-Cuban Religion*, ed. David H. Brown, 25–61. Chicago: University of Chicago Press.

Castellanos, Isabel. 1996. "From Ulkumí to Lucumí: A Historical Overview of Religious Acculturation in Cuba." In *Santería Aesthetics in Contemporary Latin American Art*, ed. Arturo Lindsay, 39–50. Washington, D.C.: Smithsonian Institution Press.

Childs, Matt D. 2006. *The 1812 Aponte Rebellion in Cuba and the Struggle against Atlantic Slavery.* Chapel Hill: University of North Carolina Press.

Fernández Olmos, Margarite, and Lizabeth Paravisini-Gebert. 2003. *Creole Religions of the Caribbean: An Introduction from Vodou and Santería to Obeah and Espiritismo.* New York: New York University Press.

Gonzalez Jane, Ricardo, ed. 1978. *National Museum of Cuba: Painting: The Fayum Portrait, Western European Painting, Cuban Painting.* Havana, Letras Cubanas.

Klein, Herbert S. 1986. *African Slavery in Latin America and the Caribbean.* Oxford: Oxford University Press.

Martínez, Juan A. 1994. *Cuban Art and National Identity: The Vanguardia Painters, 1927–1950.* Gainesville: University Press of Florida.

Menocal, Narciso G. 1996. "An Overriding Passion: The Quest for a National Identity in Painting." *Journal of Decorative and Propaganda Arts* 22: 187–219.

Miller, Ivor. 2000. "A Secret Society Goes Public: The Relationship between Abakuá and Cuban Popular Culture." *African Studies Review* 43 (1): 161–188.

Mohamed, Patricia. 1997. *The Visual Grammars of Gender, Race and Class in the Caribbean in the Paintings of Brunias, Bellisario, Landaluze, and Cazabon, Four 18th and 19th Century Painters.* Université Antilles Guyane, Groupe de recherche AIP-CARDH.

Moliner Castañeda, Israel. 2002. *Los cabildos Afrocubanos en Matanzas.* Havana: Ediciones Matanzas.

Moore, Robin. 1997. *Nationalizing Blackness: Afrocubanismo and Artistic Revolution in Havana, 1920–1940.* Pittsburgh, Pa.: University of Pittsburgh Press.

Ortíz, Fernando. 2001. "The Afro-Cuban Festival 'Day of the Kings.'" In *Cuban Festivals: A Century of Afro-Cuban Culture*, ed. Judith Bettelheim, 1–40. Princeton, N.J.: Markus Wiener Publishers.

Portuondo, José Antonio. 1972. "Landaluze y el costumbrismo en Cuba." *Revista de la Biblioteca Nacional José Martí* 63 (1): 51–84.

Thompson, Robert Farris. 1984. *Flash of the Spirit: African and Afro-American Art and Philosophy.* New York: Vintage Books.

PART
2

Afro Social Movements and Mobilization

6

Afro-Colombian Social Movements

PETER WADE

By some estimates, Colombia has the second largest population of Afro-descendants in Latin America, after Brazil (Sanchez and Bryan 2003). It also arguably has the most comprehensive array of legislation aimed at Afro-descendant people, including special land titles for "black communities" (as defined by the law); ethno-education programs in schools; university places reserved for candidates from black communities; representation on committees and decision-making bodies at various levels of the local, regional and national state; a special Directorate of Black Community Affairs; and two seats in the Chamber of Representatives of the Congress reserved for candidates representing black communities.[1] Yet before the 1990s, when these laws came onto the statute books, Afro-Colombian social mobilization was not very well developed and, indeed, many academics and activists bemoaned the fact that Afro-Colombians were "invisible" in the eyes of the state and in the nation more generally. Even academic disciplines, such as history, anthropology and sociology, were said to ignore Afro-Colombians, preferring to concentrate on slavery, indigenous peoples, and the poor (defined in terms of class rather than ethnic identity). In this chapter, I will outline the background and current situation of Afro-Colombians and try to explain how the changes in their "visibility" came about (which will also involve arguing that they were not quite as invisible as is often maintained).

My own experience of Colombia and Afro-Colombian people began informally in 1980, when I spent some time in the city of Cartagena, on the Caribbean coast of Colombia, where there is a substantial Afro-Colombian population. From 1983 to 1998 I carried out a series of projects in rural and urban areas, using techniques of ethnographic enquiry and interviews to explore issues of identity, discrimination, political mobilization, and the intersection of culture and politics. I also used the analysis of documents, especially in a study on the social history of music from the Caribbean coastal region, but my methodology has been mainly anthropological.

Background and Context

Africans were imported into Colombia from the 1520s and concentrated first in and around Cartagena, a port on the Caribbean coast, where they did domestic and agricultural labor. The main occupation of slaves, however, was gold mining and this was focused on the Pacific coastal region and in valley zones of the provinces of Cauca and Antioquia. The Pacific coastal region was particular for having a population composed mainly of slaves, free blacks, and indigenous people with a tiny minority of whites. Interbreeding was limited and the emergence of mestizos (mixed people) was thus also restricted, in contrast to many other areas of Colombia where they became a majority by the end of the eighteenth century. Slavery was abolished in 1851 and the Pacific coastal region remained a poor, underdeveloped area with little infrastructure. This history helped constitute the Pacific region as a particularly "black" region in a regionally diverse country.

Colombia is often represented as a country of regions. Typically, four main regions are said to exist. The central Andean region, with three mountainous cordilleras running north to south separated by two impressive river valleys, encompasses the biggest cities and is the seat of political power and economic wealth. It is predominantly white and mestizo with small groups of indigenous peoples, especially in the higher areas. The Pacific coastal region to the west is damp, poor, heavily forested, and sparsely populated and has rather little infrastructure. It is often seen as the "black region" of the country, with a population that is about 80 percent black and the significant presence of indigenous groups. The hot Caribbean coastal region to the north has some medium-sized cities and a population that includes significant numbers of both Afro-Colombian and indigenous peoples and a majority of mestizos with a lot of African and indigenous heritage. Finally, the plains and jungles to the east of the Andes are famed as the territories of cowboys (on the plains, or *llanos*) and indigenous peoples (in forests). This "racialized" geography, whereby regions have stereotypical associations with certain racial identities, is important in understanding the situation of Afro-Colombians and their processes of political mobilization. It is similar to some other Latin American countries, such as Peru, where the highlands are associated with *indios* and the coastal plains with whites and mestizos, or Ecuador, where the Pacific coastal region is the "black region." Often the regions associated with black and indigenous peoples are marginalized in terms of socioeconomic development and political power. Thus, racial inequality becomes entwined with overall processes of national development and the mechanisms that disadvantage these peoples appear to be matters of "underdevelopment," distance from the centers of wealth, lack of influence in politics, and so on. This masks the fact these mechanisms continue to marginalize not just certain regions but certain categories of people. At the same time, the status of particular regions as the country's "black" territories opens avenues for political mobilization and racial-ethnic identification around issues that affect those areas.

However, it is also important to realize that whatever the broad images associated with particular regions are, the Pacific coastal region is not home to the majority of Afro-Colombians because of its low population density. Counting Afro-descendants in Colombia has been a difficult matter, as it is in Latin America generally, because of the absence of a widespread consensus about who counts as "black" (or Afro-Colombian, or whatever other terms are used). Early in the twentieth century, when enumerators decided who was who, censuses classed about 10 percent of the national population as *negro* (Smith 1966). Later estimates varied from 4 percent to 26 percent—the latter figure produced by the National Planning Department in 1998 (Wade 2002, 21). In 2005, the state carried out a census with a new "ethnic" question that asked people to self-identify as one of a number of ethnic categories (which I discuss in more detail later). On the basis of this, about 4 million people, or 10.5 percent of the national total, were categorized by the census department as *población afrocolombiana* (DANE 2006). What the results of the 2005 census also make clear is only about 20 percent of these Afro-Colombians live in the Pacific coastal region.[2] In fact, nearly 600,000 of the self-identified Afro-Colombians in the census live in the province of Antioquia, generally famed for being one of the whitest in the country.[3] In addition, the 2005 census reinforced what had already been demonstrated (Barbary and Urrea 2004, 77–78): that 29 percent of Afro-Colombians lived in the large cities of the interior of the country, Cali, Medellín, and Bogotá, and the medium cities of the Caribbean coast, Barranquilla and Cartagena (DANE 2006, 20).

There are other important aspects of the geography of blackness in Colombia. The first concerns the so-called *raizales* (a word derived from *raíz*, meaning root), "black" people who live in the Colombian island territories of San Andrés, Providencia, and Santa Catalina, off the Caribbean coast of Nicaragua. These people are of Anglo-Antillean origin, speak a creole English (as well as Spanish), and are mainly Protestant. According to the 2005 census, they form 57 percent of the island population, the rest being mostly mainland Colombians. *Raizales* have participated in Afro-Colombian mobilizations, although their concerns are not necessarily the same as those of mainland Afro-Colombians and tend to concern the defense of their culture in the face of "Colombianization" and the onslaught of tourist development. The second aspect concerns the special character of the village of Palenque de San Basilio, about 50 kilometers from Cartagena. *Palenque* was the name given to colonial settlements formed by runaway slaves or *cimarrones* (maroons), although such villages sometimes became ethnically mixed even in colonial times. They formed in many areas of Colombia and elsewhere (Price 1979) but generally lost their identity as *palenques* after abolition. Palenque de San Basilio, however, retained that identity, along with a unique creole language, and *palenqueros* have been important figures in Afro-Colombian political movements, particularly in the Caribbean coastal region, but also more widely (Cunin 2003). Overall, this uneven distribution of blackness, which nuances the stereotypical image of black coasts versus a white-mestizo interior, is important when it comes to understanding the significance of the legislation about Afro-Colombians and the nature of Afro-Colombian political mobilization.

The socioeconomic conditions of Afro-Colombians present contradictory features. For example, 2005 census data showed that the life expectancy of Afro-Colombian men was lower than the national average by 5.5 years for men and nearly 11 years for women. Infant mortality for Afro-Colombian girls was 44 deaths per thousand births, compared to the national average of 19. Afro-Colombians suffered much higher percentages of major health problems than the overall population, while nearly 6 percent of Afro-Colombians changed residence due to a threat to their life, compared to a national average of 4 percent. The census also revealed that 79 percent of the population of Chocó Department, which occupies the northern half of the Pacific coastal region, had "unsatisfied basic needs," the highest proportion in the country, while 54 percent of all Afro-Colombians had unsatisfied basic needs (compared to 47 percent of non-Afro-Colombians). Unemployment is higher for Afro-Colombians than for non-Afro-Colombians (6 percent versus 3 percent) and poverty is greater (10 percent versus 7 percent). Survey data for 2003 indicate that the provision of secondary and higher educational facilities was also worse for Afro-Colombians. On the other hand, the census showed that literacy rates for Afro-Colombians were only marginally lower than for the nation (86 percent versus 88 percent), and educational levels were not markedly different overall.[4] This suggests that Afro-Colombians work hard to gain an education despite the lack of facilities and services in their communities but that their education does not benefit them as much as it does other people in terms of employment and income.[5]

Early Afro-Colombian Mobilizations

Colombia did not see the kind of early Afro-descendant mobilizations that occurred in Cuba, where the Partido Independiente de Color was formed in 1908 (Helg 1995), or in Brazil with the emergence of a black press (Mitchell 1992) and the formation of the Frente Negra Brasileira in 1931 (Andrews 1991). However,

Colombia did experience its own form of *negrismo*, or aesthetic attention to black creativity and culture: this occurred to a limited extent in literature and painting, but mostly in relation to music. Genres from the Caribbean coastal region generally identified as "black," such as *cumbia*, became popular nationally from the 1940s (Wade 2000), just as Afro-Cuban and Afro-Brazilian music had also become national icons.

Black political mobilization started in the 1970s, with the formation of small urban groups, often led by university students and graduates who had been influenced by indigenous mobilizations and, more powerfully, by overseas black movements. Figures such as Martin Luther King, Malcolm X, and Nelson Mandela were inspirations. For example, one group formed in 1976 in the city of Pereira was called Soweto. In the reading group they formed, they tackled Frantz Fanon and Amílcar Cabral as well as black leaders in the United States. In 1982 Soweto changed its name to Cimarrón (subtitled The National Movement for the Human Rights of Black Communities in Colombia), invoking the figure of the rebellious runaway slave, a name that had already been used in Jamaica, Brazil, and Haiti to signify black resistance (Wade 1995). Such groups produced publications, including books, newsletters, and newspapers; held meetings; and participated in academic conferences (Wade 2009).

At the same time, and linked to such movements, academic interest in Afro-Colombians began to increase, led by anthropologist Nina de Friedemann, who started publishing on Afro-Colombian culture in the Pacific coastal region in the late 1960s, although there had been some predecessors in the field.[6] A key concern of Friedemann and these early groups was with the "invisibility" of black people in Colombia. In fact, Afro-Colombians were not quite so invisible, since school textbooks routinely referred to black people (or rather slaves), a form of stylized blackness had carved out space of a limited kind in music, and the term *negro* was used widely in Colombia to refer to people perceived as black (Wade 2000, 30–52; Wade 2005). But blackness was certainly marginalized, trivialized and folklorized, and it was quite invisible in terms of the mass print media and public representations of the Colombian nation. Friedemann's project was to display the historical and contemporary presence of Africanness in Colombian culture through the notion of *huellas de africanía* (traces of Africanness), which she developed with fellow anthropologist Jaime Arocha. Friedemann's work highlighted the distinctiveness of Afro-Colombian cultural forms in the context of Colombian popular culture. She was also concerned with racism, principally in terms of the denial and marginalization of blackness but also in terms of discrimination against members of Afro-Colombian communities (Friedemann 1976; Friedemann and Arocha 1986).

Afro-Colombian organizations at this time, such as the Centre for the

Investigation and Development of Black Culture, led by Amir Smith Córdoba, and Cimarrón, led by Juan de Dios Mosquera—both men who had migrated from the Pacific coastal region to cities of the interior of the country—shared these concerns and spearheaded a consciousness-raising movement that sought to confront a number of problems.[7] As these leaders saw it, too many "black" people denied their own blackness, perhaps preferring not to identify in relation to ethnicity or race, perhaps trying to avoid the perceived stigma of blackness and of Africa; too many refused to recognize that they were "black," claiming they were mestizos, perhaps brown-skinned, but not "black"; and too many were ignorant of black history and even denied that racism affected Afro-Colombians. These movements thus addressed invisibility and denial by publishing and disseminating information about Afro-Colombians' role in history and society, but they also addressed racism in urban life. In contrast, the academics tended to focus more on Afro-Colombian history and culture that was rooted in the Pacific coastal region and, to a lesser extent, the Caribbean coastal region (where Palenque de San Basilio took pride of place).

The varied nature of the other organizations that existed at this time can be illustrated by two examples. The Corporación de Negritudes in Medellín mainly provided services and education for female domestic service workers from the Pacific coastal region but also aimed to foster black identity by holding classes on black history and culture for the young women. The Chocoano Action Committee, also in Medellín, was an association of more middle-class migrants from Chocó who participated in the party political networks of their home province. They pursued a regionalist project that sought to enhance the political influence of Chocó—the only *departamento* (province) with a majority black population that, since 1947 when it gained departmental status, had been able to elect a senator to Congress—as well as their own political ambitions. Although blackness was a central aspect of Chocoano identity, this committee was only tangentially concerned with promoting something called black identity (Wade 1993, 327–333).

1990s Reform, the Afro-Colombian Movement, and Multiculturalism

In 1991, Colombia, like many other countries in Latin America around this time, underwent a constitutional reform, which included an apparently significant shift toward official multiculturalism (Van Cott 2000; Sieder 2002). The new Constitution declared it would "recognize and protect the ethnic and cultural diversity of the nation" (Article 7). The reasons for this region-wide shift are varied and include a desire by the state to appear more in line with international criteria of modern liberal democracies, the growing power of indigenous and ethnic rights movements worldwide, and, in the Colombian case, an attempt to address issues of violence and dissent by bringing guerrilla forces into the process of reform. Colombia was unusual because of the inclusion in the new Constitution of a Transitory Article that promised land titles for "black communities" in the Pacific coastal region, for reasons I will explore below. This article was followed by Law 70 of 1993 and further decrees and laws that consolidated this opening and provided for the kind of rights and representation outlined at the beginning of this chapter.

This process of change had a key feature. The Constituent Assembly had no Afro-Colombian elected representative, despite the fact that several candidates had stood for election. In the Pacific coastal region, a number of organizations had emerged in the 1980s, often initiated by the Catholic Church and usually directed toward helping peasant farmers, for example, ACIA, the Integral Peasant Association of the Atrato River, formed in 1984. Some of these organizations had allied with local indigenous groups—also supported by the Church, which had much more experience in dealing with indigenous matters—and thus had begun to fit themselves into a mold shaped by the concept of *indígena*. Indigenous people already had land reserves, some of them of colonial antiquity, others a result of more recent negotiations with the state. Indigenous peoples had a particular status vis-à-vis the state, that of a small, vulnerable, and protected ethnic minority whose members lived mainly in rather peripheral zones of the country. In the Constituent Assembly, it was no accident that an Emberá indigenous leader, Francisco Rojas Birry, represented an alliance based on Afro-indigenous interests linked to the Pacific coastal region. Any consideration of Afro-Colombian matters was a struggle in the Assembly; most representatives initially rejected the idea that black people in Colombia could be considered an "ethnic group." Faced with the possibility that petitions to recognize Afro-Colombians might go unheeded, Rojas Birry and a number of academics began a lobbying campaign that was backed by Afro-Colombian mobilizations, including a telegram campaign to Constituent Assembly delegates and the occupation of government offices, the cathedral in Quibdó (Chocó) in May 1991, and the Haitian embassy in Bogotá (see Centro del Pastoral Afrocolombiana 2003). At the last minute, the Transitory Article was included.

Law 70, when it emerged, not surprisingly reflected this regional and ethnic bias. It indigenized, regionalized and ruralized the question of blackness in Colombia. Although it included a host of measures and also defined black communities in Colombia as an ethnic group, the law was essentially about the provision of land titles to rural riverine black communities in the Pacific coastal region, communities defined in terms of their kinship links, their rootedness in the land, and their "traditional production practices." This definition fitted an indigenist mold.

After the 1991 reform, the initial impetus was to make sure that the Transitory Article became law and Afro-Colombian organizations multiplied, particularly in the Pacific region but also elsewhere. Leaders from Palenque de San Basilio, for example, were influential in negotiations leading up to Law 70, but perhaps because of the status of Palenque as an old, well-delimited, and rural community (although community members had migrated to cities all over the Caribbean coastal region), this did not move Law 70 away from the figure of the "black community." The most influential and durable organization to emerge, the Proceso de Comunidades Negras (PCN), was decidedly centered on land titling and was Pacific in its regional orientation. Cimarrón, as an urban organization based in Bogotá, was marginalized and had to work hard to reinvent networks in the rural Pacific region.

By the mid-1990s, the profile of blackness in Colombia privileged the ethnicity and distinctiveness of a specific region. The juridical and conceptual construct of the *comunidad negra* implied "the abandonment of the socio-political specificities" of actual black communities in the Pacific region (Hoffmann 2004, 218); for example, the variety of economic activities—which included fishing, mining, logging, hunting, agriculture, trading, all with more or less use of modern technologies—was hidden in the blanket reference to "traditional production practices." If this was true for the Pacific region, it was even more the case for Colombia generally: the huge variety of contexts in which Afro-Colombians lived was masked in the name of a more singular and homogeneous black ethnic identity.

The emergence of Law 70 and its particular ethnocultural character was the outcome of a complex set of interactions between academics and Afro-Colombian organizations and the state, not to mention the Church and indigenous organizations (Wade 2009). Colombian academics such as Arocha and Friedemann had established Afro-Colombian anthropology and defined it as the study of cultural difference, above all in the Pacific region: they both participated in discussions in the Constituent Assembly. Afro-Colombian organizations were already burgeoning in the Pacific region, fighting for land rights in alliance with indigenous groups and supported by the Church with its liberation theology–inspired concern for oppressed peoples. Meanwhile, urban black organizations of the interior, fired by transnational black movements, struggled for support and resources.

For its part, the state was not necessarily rigidly opposed to either Afro-Colombian or indigenous rights, as long as these could be controlled. A number of authors argue that Law 70, and multiculturalist policies more generally, actually fit with neoliberal projects that seek to create effective governance and the free circulation of goods and people while cutting back on direct state investment. Such policies bring actors in previously marginal areas into a direct relationship with the state (in this case as land-holders) while also making them responsible for their own management (community members have to organize their land claim and then manage the collective title). Meanwhile, capitalist development of the area can continue outside the collectively titled areas and can even access community labor and resources more freely. For example, Oslender (2002) gives the example of a commercial firm that exported *palmitos* (edible palm hearts) to Europe that sponsored a collective land title claim in the southern Pacific region and continued its operations using local community labor.[8] In addition, attention was suddenly paid to the immense biodiversity of the Pacific region: this was a resource to be protected for posterity (but also for future exploitation by a conservationist form of development), and the state, Afro-Colombian communities, and international development agencies agreed on the importance of sustaining biodiversity. Although this apparent consensus did not mean they necessarily understood this agenda in the same way—for example, biodiversity as a development resource versus biodiversity as the basis for a local lifestyle—*comunidades negras* could figure, alongside indigenous communities, as guardians of the environment (Escobar 1997; Escobar 2008).

Thus, the state could see advantages in Law 70 and the recognition of (regional) blackness: it helped open up the resource-rich but isolated Pacific region to development while creating mechanisms that could enhance governance of the region and its communities. The law also reinforced the liberal democratic credentials of the Colombian state in the international arena. The state was, however, predisposed to assimilate the new political presence of blackness to the more familiar figure of ethnic indigenousness when considering matters of governance (Hooker 2005). This meant that small, bounded, rural black communities fitted into an existing mold of state-minority relations and helped keep these relations within controllable bounds (Anderson 2007).

In this overall scenario, the issue of racism, while it by no means disappeared, became more muted. Indeed, the PCN argued that "presenting the situation of Afro-Colombian communities in terms of racial discrimination has little audience" (Pedrosa 1996, 251, my translation). The struggle was to protect a vulnerable poor minority by giving its people land rights that recognized their historical cultural difference (e.g., their collective production practices). The reason for their poverty was neglect and indifference, and, while these could be linked to racism, this did not occupy center stage. Many black people in Colombia—as elsewhere in Latin America—tended to deny that racism was a problem for them, citing poverty as the key issue and avoiding the idea that their blackness might be a stigma (Wade 1993, 253–266; Sheriff 2001, 59–83; Burdick 1998, 5). Phrasing the struggle primarily in terms of racism was thus difficult.

Afro-Colombian organization was not, however, entirely limited to the Pacific coastal region. In 1997, for example, I carried out a study in the city of Cali that focused on the intersection of politics and musical expression. Situated only a couple of hours (on today's roads) from the Pacific coast and located near areas of historically dense Afro-Colombian population such as Puerto Tejada and the towns of the northern Cauca province, Cali has long had a substantial black presence, reinforced in the last two decades by large migrations from the Pacific coastal region. According to 2005 census figures, Afro-Colombians were 26 percent of the city's population.[9] I found that there were a number of different Afro-Colombian organizations in operation (Wade 1999). Some of them were basically groups of dancers and rap musicians, but many of the young people in them showed an awareness of issues of black identity and racism that made it impossible to ignore the political dimensions of these organizations. A local black barbershop, for example, was an enterprise linked to fashion and consumption, but it also acted as a public expression of Afro-Colombian identity—with Rastafarian colors, a map of Africa, and posters of Michael Jordan and Bob Marley on display—and a source of income for young black activists involved in a local community organization and rap crew called Ashanty. Ashanty and other similar groups were explicitly political, even if their practical activities were centered on music and dance. They adopted a discourse of black pride and anti-racism while they worked to promote hip-hop culture as an expression of these ideas and as a set of performance and organizational skills that could be valuable social capital for young black people.

Other organizations were formal NGOs, usually with development and consciousness-raising agendas for Afro-Colombians, that were similar to Cimarrón or PCN, albeit often smaller and more ephemeral. And there also existed a local branch of a national political party called Movimiento Nacional de Comunidades Negras that sought to get Afro-Colombian candidates elected to government office. Complex networks ran through this diversity and into the Church and the local state. For example, Ashanty negotiated for funding from the recently formed "Negritudes" division of Cali's city council, from the Catholic Church, from an international aid NGO, and also from a national beer company, which helped fund a hip-hop event. Another group, focusing more on "folkloric" dance from the Pacific region and calling itself a "cultural youth association," was led by an Afro-Colombian man who had close links to politicians in the Movimiento Nacional de Comunidades Negras and organized Afro-Colombian ethno-education projects, covering everything from Law 70 to black hairstyles. A third group was funded in part by an oil company that was developing a gas pipeline in the region: the funds were used for workshops on Law 70 and citizenship, low-income housing projects, research projects, and so on. This gives some sense of the range of activities and networks that make up a "social movement."

In the Caribbean coastal region, there were also significant processes of organizing that nuanced the association between blackness and the Pacific coast, even if Afro-Colombian organizations centered in Cartagena and to some extent in the Caribbean coastal region as a whole have been dominated by leaders from Palenque de San Basilio—a village that fits well with the image of a *comunidad negra* (Cunin 2003; Cunin 2000). In one case, Cimarrón started a legal campaign to have a "black community," as defined by the law, recognized in the city of Santa Marta, which would allow its representatives to sit on city council committees. After a long judicial battle, in which the presence of a black community was denied, it was recognized by a 1996 decision of the Constitutional Court (Wade 2002, 18). This was significant because it broke with the association between the legal category *comunidad negra* and the Pacific region—a possibility foreseen in Transitory Article 55, which said its provisions could apply to other regions of the country with "similar conditions" to those of the Pacific region.

In short, while the Pacific coastal region and issues of cultural difference associated with Afro-Colombians as an "ethnic group" dominated the panorama of Afro-Colombian social movements in the wake of Law 70, muting questions of racism, by the late 1990s there were already some departures from this scenario that drew both on pre-1991 Afro-Colombian organization and on the fact that Law 70, despite its focus on the Pacific coastal region, had opened up a more public space for blackness than had existed previously.

Violence, Displacement, and Race

The gains of the 1990s, whatever their limits, have been put at severe risk by the waves of violence that have shattered the social fabric of the Pacific coastal region. From the late 1990s, conflicts between guerrilla forces, the army, and right-wing paramilitaries (often colluding with the army) have dominated the area, moving from Chocó province in the north toward the south (Wouters 2001). These complex conflicts, which affect large areas of Colombia, are driven by many forces. A key factor is the relative weakness of the Colombian state, which is unable to control portions of the national territory and has sought to do so in part via the U.S.-funded Plan Colombia, which involves development aid but also military assistance.[10] Another factor is the convenience for the state of the existence of paramilitaries, who carry out state violence by proxy (Sanford 2004). Also vital are the pervasive effects of the drug trade, which helps fund guerrillas, paramilitaries, and, indirectly, the state and sustains the self-propelling character of the violence. Lastly, the violence, especially by paramilitaries, "cleanses" tracts of land of people and communities, leaving them open for further capitalist developments, especially African palm oil plantations but also industrial shrimp farming and mining (Escobar 2003; Oslender 2007; Escobar 2008; Restrepo and Rojas 2004).

Violence has undermined the region's collective land titles, agendas that would sustain biodiversity, and diverse local projects, from women's shellfish-collecting cooperatives to small enterprises for marketing forest products. Huge numbers of Afro-Colombians (and indigenous people) have been displaced into, first, the local cities of Buenaventura, Tumaco, and Quibdó and then into cities of the interior. According to the Colombian NGO CODHES (Consultoría para los Derechos Humanos y el Desplazamiento; Human Rights and Displacement Consultancy), 4.6 million Colombians were forced from their homes from 1985 to 2008, with high points of about 400,000 individuals a year in 2002 and 2008 (see CODHES 2009). Of these people, CODHES estimates that about 23 percent are Afro-Colombians, more than double their proportion in the total population in the 2005 census. About 12 percent of all Afro-Colombians are classified as displaced persons. The state estimates that in 2000–2002, the rate of displacement of Afro-Colombians was nearly twice that of non-Afro-Colombians. CODHES states that in the port of Buenaventura, which has been inundated with Afro-Colombian *desplazados* (displaced people), there is effectively an "ethnocide" of young Afro-Colombians, with 382 murders in 2007, giving a rate of 112 murders per 100,000 population (compared to 38 per 100,000 for Colombia as a whole; see CODHES 2008; Vicepresidencia de la República de Colombia 2009).

Afro-Colombian organization in the Pacific region continues despite these fearful setbacks and much of the emphasis is now on human rights, violence, and displacement, with a corresponding focus on youth (who figure largely among the displaced and those killed by violence). The scenario is diverse and complex, and organizations range from small income-generating cooperatives to the PCN, which continues to be one of the most influential Afro-Colombian organizations. Some of the PCN's leaders have international stature, such as Carlos Rosero, who ran unsuccessfully for the Constituent Assembly in 1991, became a lynchpin for the PCN, and now participates in a number of transnational networks (one such network offered a 2007 tour of the United States that included an opportunity to meet members of Congress). International bodies ranging from the World Bank through the U.S. Congressional Black Caucus to the Catholic Church have an interest in and/or channel funds to the region. Of the multiple branches of the Colombian government, some support a range of local endeavors, including Afro-Colombian organizations, while other branches support mega-development projects, military incursions, and the contracting of international private security companies to assist with the implementation of Plan Colombia projects, such as crop-spraying (Colectivo de Abogados José Alvear Restrepo 2008).

Meanwhile, the horizons of Afro-Colombian movements have broadened a little more since the late 1990s. While the vast majority of the 132 collective land titles handed out to black communities by 2005 were in the Pacific coastal region, a few small territories have been titled in riverine areas of Antioquia province.[11] Land is a major concern for many Afro-Colombians outside the Pacific coastal region: activists from around Cartagena, for example, are concerned about the security of their landownership—which is often not fully legalized, despite a long history of privatization of land—and they face gradual dislocation by tourist and other capitalist ventures. While Afro-Colombian organizations in the area work to promote black consciousness and culture, they also seek to protect human rights for Afro-Colombians, including rights to land. Organizations put varying emphases on issues of identity and matters of material livelihood, but, as in Cali, the two aspects tend to intertwine.

Another example of geographical expansion beyond the Pacific region is education. Provisions heralded in Law 70 were followed up by Decree 1627 of 1996, which created mechanisms that exempted some students from Afro-Colombian communities from paying university fees. The Ministry of the Interior signed agreements with a number of universities that gave about 400 fee-exempt places nationwide to such students during 1997–2001. The government entity that helps Colombian students study abroad reportedly helped 2,550 Afro-Colombian students from 1996 to 2000 (DNP 2002, 6). Such initiatives have been spreading, although they have not approached the quota systems in place in some Brazilian universities (Htun 2004). For example, in 2009, the University of San Buenaventura de Cartagena signed an agreement with the Ministry of the Interior to provide fee discounts to Afro-Colombian students (see Ministerio del Interior y de Justicia n.d.). These small measures indicate an openness to thinking about blackness on a national rather than a purely regional level.

This incipient shift is also evident in the 2005 census. An "ethnic question" was first tried in the 1993 census and was a dismal failure. It asked people to identify as a member of a "black community" and then name the community; the question was based on the very recent concept of the *comunidad negra* as a bounded entity in the Pacific region. Only 1.5 percent of people identified as such. Prior to the 2005 census, there were intensive discussions, some of them in conferences funded by the World Bank, about how to improve the question, with participation from government census officials, academics, and black organizations. The 2005 ethnic question asked people to identify as a) *raizal*, b) *palenquero*, or c) *negro(a)*, *mulato(a)*, *afrocolombiano(a)* o *afrodescendiente* (or indigenous or Rom—or none of the above). Results were reported in a way that lumped the three "black" categories into a single Afro-Colombian one. The figure of 10.5 percent was criticized as an undercount by Afro-Colombian organizations, which had lobbied unsuccessfully for the inclusion in the list of the category *moreno* (brown), a term widely used to describe self and others across a broad range of racialized phenotypes. *Negro* still carries a stigma for some people and may be thought to signify a person who is very African-looking. *Mulato* is not a term commonly heard in Colombia, while *afrocolombiano* and *afrodescendiente*, although increasingly apparent, are still linked to an intellectual and activist discourse. Actual numbers aside, the significant thing was the state's institutionalization of a category of blackness that ran counter to the category of the *comunidad negra*, based in the Pacific coastal region, that the state had worked hard to construct and confine within a region. At this stage, it is difficult to say what impact such an institutional shift has on everyday identifications, but censuses are important tools and the categories they deploy get used extensively in the public domain, where they become more consolidated (Nobles 2000).

Changes are also evident in the arena of electoral politics. There has long been a handful of Afro-Colombian members of Congress—partly because Chocó was granted the status of *departamento* in 1947—and Law 70 provided for two representatives to be elected to the Chamber of Deputies by a special electoral constituency of black communities. In 2007, these two—one a former sporting champion with electoral support from the Pacific coast, the other a career politician elected by voters in the Caribbean coastal province of Bolívar—made up part of a short-lived Bancada Parlamentaria Afrocolombiana (a black caucus) with seven other politicians, including Piedad Córdoba, who is known to support the social inclusion of minorities, including Afro-Colombians.[12] Congress has more Afro-Colombian members than ever (thirteen over the 2006–2010 congressional period), although they vary in their explicit support of Afro-Colombian rights (Bravo 2010). However, several of these politicians have been plagued by charges of corruption and it is difficult to detect a real driver for change from this direction. Afro-Colombian electoral politics is also beset by fragmentation. In the congressional elections held in March 2010, there were a total of 169 candidates who were allied to 67 separate political parties. This group of candidates competed for the two representatives' seats reserved for Afro-Colombian communities in the Chamber of Deputies. In contrast, the total number of candidates for the special electoral constituency seats for indigenous communities in both Senate and Chamber was only twenty, and they were allied to only five parties.[13] Agudelo (2005) argues that electoral politics in the Pacific region may trade on ideas of black identity, but it continues to thrive on old-style clientelism and pork-barrel politics. Meanwhile, President Uribe appointed Afro-Colombian academic Paula Moreno (who had researched biodiversity management in the Pacific coastal region) as Minister of Culture in 2007 (until 2010), in a move that was seen by some as a bid to gain the support of the U.S. Congressional Black Caucus for the U.S.-Colombia Free Trade Agreement.

Finally, there appears to be a (slightly) greater interest in questions of racism, partly in the wake of the 2001 Durban conference on racism. The PCN, which in 1996, saw racism as a theme with little audience now has as one of its aims the struggle against racism and has a link to the Racial Discrimination Observatory, established at a private university in 2007 to monitor racism, mainly by publishing statistical information on racial inequality and publicizing incidents of racism.[14] Hoffmann (2004, 221) also notes "a reorientation of the ethnic debate towards the anti-discrimination struggle." In May 2009, there was the first National Campaign Against Racism, supported by the vice-president, who presented the recommendations of the Inter-Sectoral Commission for the Advancement of the Afro-Colombian, Palenquero, and Raizal Population that he had been heading up: the first recommendation was to combat racism at a national level (see Vicepresidencia de la República de Colombia 2009). One may doubt the efficacy of such government pronouncements, but they do indicate a shift in focus. Interestingly, Meertens (2009) looks at cases of *tutelas* (legal actions brought by citizens in defense of their constitutional rights) that have challenged everyday racial discrimination. For example, a young woman alleged she was denied entry to a music club because she was black: the Constitutional Court found in her favor.

The reasons for this recent shift are linked to various factors: a growing transnational interest in "Afro-Latins" and Afro-descendants—for example, from the World Bank, the United Nations, and the U.S. Congressional Black Caucus; the increasing organization of Afro-Colombians outside the Pacific region, spurred by Law 70; activists' use of judicial instruments, such as Law 70, to push the boundaries of the law itself (for example, by claiming the existence of a "black community" in Santa Marta); the gradual consolidation of legislation that developed aspects of Law 70, such as educational opportunities for Afro-Colombians, in a way that extends beyond the Pacific region; and shifts in academic emphasis toward racism and urban Afro-Colombians (e.g., Barbary and Urrea 2004).

Conclusion

Colombia before 1991 was dominated by the ideology of *mestizaje* that claimed that it was a mestizo country with black and indigenous populations that were supposedly on the road to a mixed, integrated modernity. Black and indigenous people were not invisible—indeed, their presence, especially in underdeveloped areas, was necessary to confirm the supposed superiority and modernity of the central image of the whitened mestizo nation. But they certainly occupied a lowly place in the nation's social and cultural hierarchies, although certain powers were attributed to them with regard to music, dance, magic, healing, and physical prowess. Ideologies and practices of *mestizaje* allowed the simultaneous existence of racism and nonracism. Afro-Colombians could be both excluded and included: interracial unions, for example, could both undo racial hierarchy (by crossing racial difference and producing more mixed children) and express it (through observers' assumptions that the darker partner was motivated by a desire to whiten). This simultaneity of inclusion and exclusion generated ambiguity that masked racism.

Since 1991, black and indigenous peoples have been assigned—and have fought for—a place in legislation. Affirmative action policies of various types have been designed to right previous wrongs. This does not mean that *mestizaje* and all it implies has disappeared—far from it, it is still a powerful force in everyday life. But the differences of race and ethnicity—usually glossed as ethnicity alone by the state, which prefers to avoid reference to "race"—are now much clearer and more public. *Mestizaje* is about the integration and modernization of the nation, but it also relies on a discourse about private, domestic matters—sexual relationships between men and women. Multiculturalist policies place racial and ethnic difference more firmly in the public domain and challenge the ambiguities and masking that *mestizaje* generates.

What we see, however, is that, alongside the inclusions of multiculturalism (some of them more apparent than real), exclusions continue. They persist in familiar ways, but also now in much more violent forms: murder, displacement, terror. It seems that making difference public and inscribing it in the law has brought with it more drastic and violent forms of disciplining difference.

In this light, it is unclear what the implications will be of the incipient shift from the almost exclusive focus on the Pacific coastal region toward a more encompassing notion of Afro-Colombianness, in which blackness begins to have a higher profile in civic life in general. The Pacific coastal region has suffered terrible violence and it continues to be a place where radical forms of cultural difference and alternative notions of development and modernity are being elaborated (Escobar 2008). It is also a place where black and indigenous social movements overlap in ways that challenge the divide (of colonial origin) between "black" and "indigenous" and generate interethnic alliances, which, although not problem-free, have the potential to mount combined challenges to violence and exclusion (Hale, Gurdián, and Gordon 2003; see also French 2009). If the difference of blackness is institutionalized more deeply in Colombian civic society, such violence may subside, but probably at the cost of the alternative life forms (and lives) of the people of the Pacific coastal region.

Notes

1. Representatives of black communities are included in the INCODER (Colombian Institute of Rural Development), the Ministry of Mines, the Ministry of the Environment, and the Ministry of Education, among others. The Dirección de Asuntos para Comunidades Negras, Afrocolombianas, Raizales y Palenqueras (Directorate of Affairs for Black, Afrocolombian, Raizal and Palenque Communities) is a dependency of the Ministry of the Interior and Justice.

2. See the Excel file "Muncipio con Territorios Colectivos de Comunidades Negras," 2007, available at http://www.dane.gov.co/files/etnicos/taller/terri_colectivos_cnegras.xls (accessed September 6, 2010).

3. This is partly because Antioquia has a Caribbean coastline, but even so, there are more "blacks" in Antioquia than in the province of Bolívar, generally considered by Colombians as one of the "blacker" provinces and the capital city of which is Cartagena, which is usually seen as quite a "black" city.

4. Afro-Colombians with no education = 13 percent (compared to 10 percent nationally); with basic secondary = 20 percent (compared to 19 percent nationally); with professional qualifications = 4 percent (compared to 7 percent nationally). Afro-Colombians have 6.7 years of schooling on average (compared to 8.2 years for non-Afro-Colombians). This picture varies a bit if one looks at specific municipalities in the Pacific coastal region. Thus, for Tumaco, Afro-Colombians with no education = 16 percent; with basic secondary = 16 percent; with professional qualifications = 2 percent.

5. For the 2005 census data, see DANE (2005; n.d.) and Vicepresidencia de la República de Colombia (2009). For the 2003 survey data, see DNP (2004). The municipal education data cited in note 4 come from the Excel file "Muncipio con Territorios Colectivos de Comunidades Negras," at http://www.dane.gov.co/files/etnicos/taller/terri_colectivos_cnegras.xls (accessed September 6, 2010). See also the website of the Observatorio de Discriminación Racial, which has useful data on racial inequality: http://odracial.org/index.php (accessed June 12, 2011).

6. A handful of writers, including students of Melville Herskovits and some folklorists, had published studies; see Wade 1993.

7. Cimarrón's full title is now Movimiento Nacional Cimarrón; see http://www.cimarron-racismo.org/.

8. See Gros (1997), Hale (2005), and Speed (2005) for general arguments about what Hale calls "multicultural neoliberalism." See Wade (2002) on the Pacific coastal region.

9. See "Comisión Intersectorial para el Avance de la Población Afrocolombiana Palenquera y Raizal: La Población Afrocolombiana," at http://www.vicepresidencia.gov.co/Es/iniciativas/Afrocolombia/Paginas/PoblacionAfrocolombiana.aspx (accessed June 12, 2011).

10. Plan Colombia was initiated in 1998 with U.S. backing as a broad development package centered on an anti-narcotics project that sought to eliminate and replace the cultivation and production of narcotics, which often took place in areas where state presence was weak. The Pacific coastal region has felt the effects of Plan Colombia, both in terms of the expansion of African palm oil plantations and because both guerrilla and paramilitary forces have imposed the cultivation of coca leaf in the area.

11. See the Excel document "Muncipio con Territorios Colectivos de Comunidades Negras," and the map Resguardos Indígenas y Títulos Colectivos de Comunidades Negras at http://sigotn.igac.gov.co/sigotn/PDF/SIGOT_SocResguardos_Nal.pdf, accessed September 6, 2010. These territories are on the borders of Zaragoza, Anorí and Segovia municipalities on the River Porce, in Yondó municipality near the River Magdalena, and in Sopetrán municipality on the River Cauca—all a long way from the Pacific coastal region. See also DANE (2006, 19–20).

12. Formed in about 2006, the Bancada Afrocolombiana was under investigation for irregularities by 2010.

13. For the list of candidates, see Registraduría Nacional del Estado Civil 2010a. For the voting results, see Registraduría Nacional del Estado Civil 2010b.

14. See the PCN website, http://www.renacientes.org (accessed September 6, 2010). See also the Observatorio de Discriminación Racial website, http://odracial.org/index.php (accessed June 12, 2011).

Bibliography

Agudelo, Carlos E. 2005. *Multiculturalismo en Colombia: Política, inclusión y exclusión de poblaciones Negras*. Medellín: Carreta Editores, Institut de recherche pour le développment, Universidad Nacional de Colombia, Instituto Colombiano de Antropología e Historia.

Anderson, Mark. 2007. "When Afro Becomes (Like) Indigenous: Garifuna and Afro-Indigenous Politics in Honduras." *Journal of Latin American and Caribbean Anthropology* 12 (2): 384–413.

Andrews, George Reid. 1991. *Blacks and Whites in São Paulo, Brazil, 1888–1988*. Madison: University of Wisconsin Press.

Barbary, Olivier, and Fernando Urrea, eds. 2004. *Gente negra en Colombia, dinámicas sociopolíticas en Cali y el Pacífico*. Cali, Paris: CIDSE/Univalle, IRD, Colciencias.

Bravo, Luis. 2010. "Sólo dos congresistas afros son considerados 'Visibles.'" *Semana.com*, January 13. Available at http://www.semana.com/wf_InfoBlog.aspx?IdBlg=51&IdEnt=2295. Accessed September 6, 2010.

Burdick, John. 1998. *Blessed Anastácia: Women, Race, and Popular Christianity in Brazil*. London: Routledge.

Centro de Pastoral Afrocolombiana. 2003. *Historia del pueblo Afrocolombiano: perspectiva pastoral*. Popayán: Centro de Pastoral Afrocolombiana. Available at http://axe-cali.tripod.com/cepac/hispafrocol.

CODHES (Consultoría para los Derechos Humanos y el Desplazamiento). 2008. "Afrocolombianos desplazados, un drama sin tregua." May 8. Available at http://www.codhes.org/index.php?option=com_content&task=view&id=157&Itemid=1. Accessed September 6, 2010.

———. 2009. *Víctimas emergentes*. Bogotá: CODHES. Available at http://www.codhes.org/index.php?option=com_docman&task=cat_view&gid=61&Itemid=50. Accessed September 6, 2010.

Colectivo de Abogados José Alvear Restrepo. 2008. *Private Security Transnational Enterprises in*

Colombia. Case Study: Plan Colombia. Bogotá: Colectivo de Abogados José Alvear Restrepo. Available at http://www.colectivodeabogados.org/IMG/pdf/0802_merc_wisc_eng-2.pdf.

Cunin, Elisabeth. 2000. "Relations interethniques y processus d'identifaction à Carthagène (Colombie)." Cahiers des Amériques Latines 33: 127–153.

———. 2003. Identidades a flor de piel. Lo "negro" entre apariencias y pertenencias: Categorías raciales y mestizaje en Cartagena. Trans. María Carolina Barreto and Guillermo Vargas. Bogotá: Instituto Colombiano de Antropología e Historia, Universidad de los Andes, Instituto Francés de Estudios Andinos, Observatorio del Caribe Colombiano.

DANE. 2005. "Censo General 2005: Necesidades Básicas Insatisfechas." Bogotá: Departamento Administrativo Nacional de Estadística. Available at http://www.dane.gov.co/files/investigaciones/boletines/censo/Bol_nbi_censo_2005.pdf. Accessed September 6, 2010.

———. 2006. Colombia una nación multicultural: Su diversidad étnica. Bogotá: Departamento Administrativo Nacional de Estadística.

———. N.d. "Colombia una nación multicultural: Su diversidad étnica." Slide Presentation. Bogotá: Departamento Administrativo Nacional de Estadística. Available at http://www.dane.gov.co/censo/files/presentaciones/grupos_etnicos.pdf. Accessed September 6, 2010.

DNP (Departamento Nacional de Planeación). 2002. Política para la población Afrocolombiana. Documento Conpes 3169. Bogotá: Departamento Nacional de Planeación, Ministerio del Interior.

———. 2004. Política de acción afirmativa para la población negra o Afrocolombiana. Documento Conpes 3310. Bogotá: Departamento Nacional de Planeación, Ministerio del Interior y de Justicia.

Escobar, Arturo. 1997. "Cultural Politics and Biological Diversity: State, Capital and Social Movements in the Pacific Coast of Colombia." In Between Resistance and Revolution: Cultural Politics and Social Protest, ed. Richard G. Fox and Orin Starn, 40–64. New Brunswick, N.J.: Rutgers University Press.

———. 2003. "Displacement, Development and Modernity in the Colombia Pacific." International Social Science Journal 55 (1): 157–167.

———. 2008. Territories of Difference: Place, Movements, Life, Redes. Durham, N.C.: Duke University Press.

French, Jan Hoffman. 2009. Legalizing Identities: Becoming Black or Indian in Brazil's Northeast. Chapel Hill: University of North Carolina Press.

Friedemann, Nina de. 1976. "Negros, monopolio de la tierra, agricultores y desarrollo de plantaciones de Azúcar en el Valle del Río Cauca." In Tierra, tradición y poder en Colombia: Enfoques antropológicos, ed. Nina de Friedemann, 143–167. Bogotá: Colcultura.

Friedemann, Nina de, and Jaime Arocha. 1986. De sol a sol: Génesis, transformación y presencia de los negros en Colombia. Bogotá: Planeta.

Gros, Christian. 1997. "Indigenismo y etnicidad: El desafío neoliberal." In Antropología en la modernidad: Identidades, etnicidades y movimientos sociales en Colombia, ed. María Victoria Uribe and Eduardo Restrepo, 15–60. Bogotá: Instituto Colombiano de Antropología.

Hale, Charles R. 2005. "Neoliberal Multiculturalism: The Remaking of Cultural Rights and Racial Dominance in Central America." PoLAR: Political and Legal Anthropology Review 28 (1): 10–28.

Hale, Charles R., Galio C. Gurdián, and Edmund T. Gordon. 2003. "Rights, Resources and the Social Memory of Struggle: Reflections on a Study of Indigenous and Black Community Land Rights on Nicaragua's Atlantic Coast." Human Organization 62 (4): 369–381.

Helg, Aline. 1995. *Our Rightful Share: The Afro-Cuban Struggle for Equality, 1886–1912*. Chapel Hill: University of North Carolina Press.

Hoffmann, Odile. 2004. *Communautés noires dans le pacifique Colombien. Innovations et dynamiques ethniques*. Paris: IRD, Karthala.

Hooker, Juliet. 2005. "Indigenous Inclusion/Black Exclusion: Race, Ethnicity and Multicultural Citizenship in Latin America." *Journal of Latin American Studies* 37 (2): 285–310.

Htun, Mala. 2004. "From 'Racial Democracy' to Affirmative Action: Changing State Policy on Race in Brazil." *Latin American Research Review* 39 (1): 60–89.

Meertens, Donny. 2009. "Discriminación racial, desplazamiento y género en las sentencias de la Corte Constitucional. El racismo cotidiano en el banquillo." *Universitas Humanística* 66: 83–106.

Ministerio del Interior y de Justicia. N.d. "Ministerio del Interior firmó convenio con Universidad en Cartagena para favorecer a estudiantes afrocolombianos." Available at http://www.mij.gov.co/eContent/newsdetailmore.asp?id=3670&idcompany=2.

Mitchell, Michael. 1992. "Racial Identity and Political Vision in the Black Press of São Paulo, Brazil, 1930–1947." *Contributions in Black Studies* 9: 17–29.

Nobles, Melissa. 2000. *Shades of Citizenship: Race and the Census in Modern Politics*. Stanford, Calif.: Stanford University Press.

Oslender, Ulrich. 2002. "'The Logic of the River': A Spatial Approach to Ethnic-Territorial Mobilization in the Colombian Pacific Region." *Journal of Latin American Anthropology* 7 (2): 86–117.

———. 2007. "Violence in Development: The Logic of Forced Displacement on Colombia's Pacific Coast." *Development in Practice* 17 (6): 752–764.

Pedrosa, Alvaro et al. 1996. "Movimiento negro, identidad y territorio: Entrevista con la Organización de Comunidades Negras de Buenaventura." In *Pacífico: ¿Desarrollo o Biodiversidad? Estado, Capital y Movimientos Sociales en el Pacífico Colombiano*, ed. Arturo Escobar and Alvaro Pedrosa, 245–265. Bogotá: CEREC.

Price, Richard, ed. 1979. *Maroon Societies: Rebel Slave Communities in the Americas*. 2nd ed. Garden City, N.Y.: Anchor Books.

Registraduría Nacional del Estado Civil. 2010a. "Elecciones 14 de Marzo 2010: Candidatos: Presidencia y Vicepresidencia." Available at http://www.registraduria.gov.co/Informacion/elec_2010_cand.htm. Accessed September 6, 2010.

———. 2010b. "Elecciones 2010: Resumen Nacional." Available at http://www.registraduria.gov.co/elec2010/resultados.htm. Accessed September 6, 2010.

Restrepo, Eduardo, and Axel Rojas, eds. 2004. *Conflicto e (in)visibilidad: Retos de los estudios de la gente negra en Colombia*. Popayán, Colombia: Editorial Universidad del Cauca.

Sanchez, Margarita, and Maurice Bryan. 2003. *Afro-Descendants, Discrimination and Economic Exclusion in Latin America*. London: Minority Rights Group.

Sanford, Victoria. 2004. "Contesting Displacement in Colombia: Citizenship and State Sovereignty at the Margins." In *Anthropology in the Margins of the State*, ed. Veena Das and Deborah Poole, 253–277. Santa Fe, N.M.: School of American Research.

Sheriff, Robin E. 2001. *Dreaming Equality: Color, Race, and Racism in Urban Brazil*. New Brunswick, N.J.: Rutgers University Press.

Sieder, Rachel, ed. 2002. *Multiculturalism in Latin America: Indigenous Rights, Diversity and Democracy*. Houndmills, UK: Palgrave Macmillan.

Smith, T. Lynn. 1966. "The Racial Composition of Colombia." *Journal of Inter-American Studies* 8 (2): 213–35.

Speed, Shannon. 2005. "Dangerous Discourses: Human Rights and Multiculturalism in Neo-liberal Mexico." *PoLAR: Political and Legal Anthropology Review* 28 (1): 29–51.

Van Cott, Donna Lee. 2000. *The Friendly Liquidation of the Past: The Politics of Diversity in Latin America*. Pittsburgh, Pa.: University of Pittsburgh Press.

Vicepresidencia de la República de Colombia. 2009. "ABC de las recomendaciones de la 'Comisión Intersectorial Para el Avance de la Población Afrocolombiana, Palenquera y Raizal.'" Available at http://www.renacientes.org/attachments/257_Comision%20afro.pdf.

Wade, Peter. 1993. *Blackness and Race Mixture: The Dynamics of Racial Identity in Colombia*. Baltimore, Md.: Johns Hopkins University Press.

———. 1995. "The Cultural Politics of Blackness in Colombia." *American Ethnologist* 22 (2): 341–357.

———. 1999. "Working Culture: Making Cultural Identities in Cali, Colombia." *Current Anthropology* 40 (4): 449–472.

———. 2000. *Music, Race, and Nation: Música Tropical in Colombia*. Chicago: University of Chicago Press.

———. 2002. "The Colombian Pacific in Perspective." *Journal of Latin American Anthropology* 7 (2): 2–33.

———. 2005. "Rethinking *Mestizaje*: Ideology and Lived Experience." *Journal of Latin American Studies* 37 (2): 235–257.

———. 2009. "Defining Blackness in Colombia." *Journal de la Société des Américanistes* 95 (1): 165–184.

Wouters, Mieke. 2001. "Ethnic Rights under Threat: The Black Peasant Movement against Armed Groups' Pressure in the Chocó, Colombia." *Bulletin of Latin American Research* 20 (4): 498–519.

7

Beyond Citizenship as We Know It

Race and Ethnicity in Afro-Colombian Struggles for Citizenship Equality

BETTINA NG'WENO

I could see that she was agitated. She did not want us to be here at her front porch asking her questions about land tenure, black communities, and her aspirations for the future. On hearing I was from Africa, she told me in no uncertain terms that she believed I was there to take her land and the community's land and that I would bring people from Africa to do so. As I excused myself, letting her know that participation in our survey was completely voluntary, she said, "The indigenous people here tell us to go back to Africa, but we have nothing to do with Africa." We left without talking to her, feeling the weight of her words. Go back to Africa! What a powerful and terrible comment for those who have never been there. What an effective means of distancing citizens from their citizenship, their nationality, and their land. What histories of restrictions of citizenship and nationality these words frame. Go back to Africa! The depth of discrimination they call up. In these four short words are held slavery and its legacies, the creation of an African diaspora, and finally the exorcism of African culture in the Americas. Go back to Africa! Emplacement and displacement in time and space.

This was the first time I had heard the words "we are told to go back to Africa," but it was definitely not the last during the fourteen months of ethnographic research I conducted in 1999 in the northern part of the department of Cauca in southwestern Colombia. My research focused on claims to ethnic territories by Afro-Colombians in the Andes under the rubric of the 1991 Colombian Constitution as a means of understanding how states are transforming and reorganizing. The words "go back to Africa" are an important indication of the fragile nature of Afro-Colombian efforts to transform what citizenship means through social movements that demand recognition of their presence, difference, rights, and equality.

New descriptions of the national makeup as multicultural and visible social mobilization around citizenship issues are noticeable features of Latin American countries since the 1990s. Older political mobilizations of class have been expanded through discussions about culture and belonging and are creating new ways of thinking about citizenship vis-à-vis the state. Fiscal and administrative decentralization of governments, transnational ethnic organizing that includes indigenous and black groups, environmental movements, and international legislation such as the International Labour Organization's (ILO) Convention 169[1] enables new recognition of indigenous and Afro-Latin Americans as citizens with special status and rights. In their new constitutions, a good number of Latin American countries, including Colombia and Nicaragua, have declared themselves multicultural or pluriethnic (Van Cott 2000; Ng'weno 2007b).

More recently, Bolivia and Ecuador have declared themselves intercultural (Government of Bolivia 2009; Government of Ecuador 2008). "Intercultural" here means negotiating difference in such a way that bridges are built across knowledges, practices, and peoples of equal standing (Walsh 2002; Schroder 2008). These states are using the reorganization of regions as well as new categories of citizens to create governable populations, to demonstrate and acquire legitimacy and authority, to negotiate societal divisions, and to distribute resources: in short, to continue ruling. Communities that mobilized over, fought for, and voted for these changes in their relationship to the state for the most part have conducted their struggles as citizens who were demanding equality and recognition from the state.

While state recognition as a practice and concept has become a sought-after goal in itself, for many communities there is a huge range as to what can be and is being recognized by the state. At the most fundamental level, indigenous and Afro-Latin American communities demand that the state recognize their existence. This would include a recognition that the lands they occupy are not empty and thus free for others to occupy. Second, they demand that their presence as indigenous people or Afro-Latin Americans be recognized—that is, a recognition of difference that plays against a national ideology of *mestizaje* (race and cultural mixing) and sameness. At another level, they are asking for recognition as citizens in spite of this cultural difference—that is, they want recognition as citizens without fitting the cultural description of the Colombian national. They are also demanding that the state (and society more generally) recognize that in order for them to be equal citizens who are culturally different, a space must be provided where they can maintain that difference free from forced assimilation. This is a conceptual and intellectual space as well as a physical one, and it is a space that is often articulated in terms of territory and autonomy. Territory in this context is more than land: it is a political and social space in which life can flourish rather than just an economic space. Autonomy is likewise more than self-governance as a community in terms of things such as educational policy and content, development, and taxation; it is also about the jurisdictional governance over a territory. In addition, it is the freedom and ability to define and create meanings of community, rights, and citizenship within this space. Finally, many Afro-Latin American communities are also demanding recognition as marginalized citizens in need of redress for past marginalization. As such, they are demanding that the state and society recognize the existence of racism and the need to do something about the conditions it has put in place.

Across Latin America even those communities demanding autonomy in how they govern their territories (with the possible exception of the Zapatista movement in Mexico) have done so in the capacity of citizens rather than as separatists. Unlike older mobilizations of the past, the aim was not to overthrow the state or to secede from it but rather to change it to include new and different ways relating to the state that transform citizenship as we know it.

Bolivia is perhaps the best-known example of this transformation. The election of indigenous activist Evo Morales as president of Bolivia in 2005 illustrates the new changes in Latin American states. In an article about the January 2009 referendum that allowed Evo Morales to seek reelection, *The Telegraph* quotes Morales as saying, "Brothers and sisters, the colonial state ends here. . . . Here we begin to reach true equality for all Bolivians" (Rubin 2009). Morales's statement emphasizes two important aspects of the present state: it is no longer colonial, with all the cultural and racial hierarchies that entails, and it is in the process of addressing inequality. Morales's statement about reaching for true equality is important because indigenous Latin Americans and Afro-Latin Americans might be described as having what Holston calls in Brazil "differentiated citizenship." By this he means a citizenship whereby formal membership in a nation-state is combined with an unequal distribution of the "rights, meanings, institutions and practices that membership entails to those deemed citizens" (Holston, 2008, 8). In other words, it is a citizenship by which everyone is a citizen but rights, duties, and resources—what Holston calls the substantive aspects of citizenship—are distributed unevenly. According to Holston, this form of citizenship is inherently unequal and perpetuates inequality. Evo Morales's comment is pointing to the end of this kind of exclusionary citizenship.

Citizenship in this chapter is not only a legal definition conferring a relationship to the state; it is also a practice, a concept of belonging and a context within which other activities are made possible. As Holston points out, these different aspects of citizenship do not necessarily overlap. The formal membership in a nation-state is insufficient to guarantee the same treatments or distribution of the substantive aspects of citizenship. A community's understanding of belonging and their relation to the state sometimes mirrors the formal membership or

signs of inclusion but is sometimes foreshadowed by the attainment of rights—
or the lack thereof. Citizenship (a conceptual relationship) to the state then is
more than just the legal definition but is also how that definition is actualized.
In many countries the new changes in Latin American states are understood to
transform citizenship: *The Telegraph* also quotes Elisa Canqui (a representative
of an Indian community from La Paz) as saying, "A new era is starting now in
which indigenous people will be the citizens of this country" (quoted in Rubin
2009). Where do Afro-Latin Americans fit in the broader process of citizenship
transformation?

Colombia is often cited as an example of the new ways citizenship is being
rearticulated in Latin American constitutions regarding Afro-Latin Americans
because of the way the 1991 Constitution tied resources (in the form of collective territories) to recognition of Afro-Colombians as an ethnic group based on
cultural difference. In 1991, in response to intense public pressure, a new Constitution was created by a national Constituent Assembly that declared Colombia multicultural and pluri-ethnic. Specific recognition of black communities
and their rights to collective territories came in the form of Provisional Article
55 (Artículo Transitorio 55, or AT55) in response to demands from Afro-Colombian communities in the Pacific Basin (Asher 2009). With the backing and
funding of the World Bank in August 1993, AT55 was made into law in the
form of Law 70. The 1991 Constitution and Law 70 stipulate that because of
their cultural distinction from the rest of the nation, Afro-Colombian ethnic
groups have a right to collective territories. These collective territories are in-
alienable, immutable, unmortgageable, and unrentable. In other words, these
collective territories rest with the community in perpetuity. However, they do
not include public use goods such as beaches and mangrove swamps and renew-
able resources such as oil and coal. While so far the granting of title has taken
place only in the Pacific Basin (the focus of Law 70), it is an ongoing process.
Law 70 also protects the right to cultural identity free from discrimination and
racism, including in the realm of education. Law 70 was followed by a number
of decrees over the next five years to implement AT55 and Law 70 regarding the
culture, representation, education, and development of Afro-Colombians.

The 1991 Constitution and Law 70 transformed existing institutions and
built new institutions to govern Afro-Colombian rights. AT55, Law 70, and
subsequent decrees tie recognition of Afro-Colombians as citizens with special
status and rights to ethnicity and to territory. This recognition has resulted in
the transfer of 4.7 million hectares (almost 10 million acres) to Afro-Colombians, or about 4.13 percent of the national territory. This is the largest transfer of territory to peoples of African descent of any country in the Americas
(DANE 2007). These lands were designated Collective Territories of Black

Communities under the 1991 Colombian Constitution and Law 70. The ability of communities to make successful claims to collective territory rests on their ability to be recognized by the state as ethnic groups.

Since 1996, Constitutional Court ruling T-422, an important ruling on the equality of Afro-Colombian citizens, has created the possibility of affirmative action measures for Afro-Colombian populations based on a different type of recognition—that of a marginalized racial group (Ng'weno 2007a). The ruling declares that because of historic marginalization, Afro-Colombians have not been equal citizens and therefore have a right to affirmative action measures. Demands for such measures continued to increase after the World Conference Against Racism, Discrimination, Xenophobia and Related Intolerances held in Durban, South Africa, in 2001 and were incorporated in some national and city development plans in Colombia (Mosquera Rosero-Labbé and León Díaz 2009). Nevertheless, full attainment of these rights and resources and of recognition as citizens marginalized because of their race continues to be a day-to-day struggle for many Afro-Colombian communities (Ng'weno 2007a; Bernard and Audre Rapoport Center for Human Rights and Justice 2007; Mosquera Rosero-Labbé and León Díaz 2009).

Holston argues that in Brazil, poor subaltern populations in urban areas have fought against the unequal distribution of substantive aspects of citizenship through practices that allowed them to gain political rights and to become landowners. Through such practices the urban poor "made law an asset, created new public spheres of participation, achieved rights to the city, and became modern consumers" (2008, 9). Holston describes these practices as "insurgent citizenship" through which citizens have built their own institutions, demanded rights, and made legal new processes that have created access to resources. In so doing, they have rethought citizenship. He sees the city as essential to making these practices possible. In Colombia, rural communities that claim territory have also gained political rights, created new political constituencies, and used the law as an organizing tool. In the process they have created new spheres of participation and achieved broader rights than their original claims would have granted (Ng'weno 2007b; Asher 2009). Because rural Afro-Colombian social movements have also struggled for recognition as citizens, territory, and autonomous governance of their territories, insurgent citizenship has taken place in rural areas as well. Interestingly the combination of rural and urban insurgent citizenship and the newly created space for demanding equality highlights the tension between race and ethnicity: each is used to justify different ideas of equality.

This chapter examines the struggles of Afro-Colombians for citizenship and the ways they have transformed and created new spaces for equality. I suggest that the practices and claims of Afro-Colombians, and Afro-Latin Americans more generally, profoundly challenge what it means to be a citizen in Latin American countries. In the process, race and ethnicity have been mobilized in new ways to broaden spaces of inclusion and demand equal citizenship. However, historical understandings and categorizations of Afro-Colombians and of Afro-Latin Americans more generally limit the degree to which citizenship has been and can be transformed. In particular, the historic categorization of Afro-Latin Americans as members of diasporic racial groups and, as a consequence, as groups of people who are not attached to the national territory and who lack a unique culture has placed both rural and urban Afro-Latin American populations in a fragile position in relation to the law.

Afro-Colombians and Citizenship Equality

According to the 2005 Colombian national census (DANE 2007), the current population of Colombia is 41,468,384 people, of which Afro-Colombians account for an estimated 10.6 percent. Surprisingly, this estimate is well below the Colombian government's 1998 estimate of 26 percent (Departamento Nacional de Planeación 1998). The 1993 Colombian census was the first census to use references to race or ethnicity in seventy-five years. Nevertheless the 1993 census, which estimated the Afro-Colombian population to be 1.5 percent (Bernard and Audre Rapoport Center for Human Rights and Justice 2007), was considered to have severely underestimated the population because of the way the data were collected. The census asked for membership in a "Black Community," a legal category of a kind of ethnic group with a territorial base. The issue in contention was the fact that the census collected ethnic rather than racial data. The Department of Planning used regionally collected local data, information from grassroots organizations, and the 1993 census to arrive at an estimate of 26 percent in 1998.

There has also been a renewed interest in Colombia in disaggregating census data by ethnicity. As with many Latin American countries in the early twentieth century, references to race in the Colombian census were dropped in 1918 in keeping with national ideologies of *mestizaje* (racial and cultural mixing) and the description of the Colombian population as unitary and mestizo. With the 1991 Constitution and the new national definition of Colombia as multicultural, disaggregation of census data became important once more. The push toward disaggregation was also driven by communities that wanted their presence recognized. In addition, from 2000 the disaggregation of census data was simultaneously advocated by the World Bank and the Inter-American Development Bank in technical workshops titled "Todos Contamos" (We All Count) aimed at disaggregating social indicators by race to understand the dynamics of exclusion and inclusion in Latin American societies.

Colombia joined other Latin American countries that were collecting disaggregated census data for the first time in over seventy-five years. Beginning with the 1993 census, Colombia has made an effort to make the data being collected more accurate. Nevertheless, this change has not resulted in any stable idea of the total Afro-Colombian population, and the figures are continuously disputed by activists, policymakers, and communities (Minority Rights Group International 2008). Changes in how statistics were collected did not necessarily produce corresponding changes in how individuals identified themselves or how people understood social categories. Nevertheless, even with the considerable reduction in numbers estimated by the 2005 census, at 4,311,757, the Afro-Colombian population constitutes the third largest African-descendant population in Latin America after Brazil and Cuba. The Afro-Colombian population is dispersed throughout Colombia but resides in larger numbers in the Valle Interandino zone (the Andes and their interlocking valleys) and along the Pacific and Caribbean coasts. They compose the majority in specific regions such as the Pacific Basin (in the departments of Nariño, Cauca, Valle, and Chocó) and in specific municipalities (such as Buenos Aires, where I conducted field research). The largest numbers of Afro-Colombians live in the departments of Valle, Antioquia, and Bolivar and are primarily urban populations. Cali, for instance, has almost one million Afro-Colombian inhabitants, which is about one-third the population of the city. The department of Chocó on the Pacific coast has the highest percentage of blacks among its population (85 percent), followed by Magdalena (72 percent) and Bolivar (66 percent), both on the Caribbean coast (Departamento Nacional de Planeación 1998). Although the Pacific littoral running from Panama to Ecuador is the main region where Afro-Colombians form a majority, in areas such as northern Cauca and southern Valle they constitute regional majorities.

While Colombia has transferred the largest amount of land to black communities of any Latin American country through Law 70, it has been less exemplary in terms of improving disparities in access to substantive rights such as health, education, and employment. The Bernard and Audre Rapoport Center for Human Rights and Justice argues that not only have the promises regarding collective land in Law 70 not been fulfilled but many of the law's "provisions regarding education, economic development (including financial assistance), and local governance have yet to be implemented" (Bernard and Audre Rapoport Center for Human Rights and Justice 2007, 3). In addition the report argues that structural racial discrimination, as evidenced by the poverty and marginalization of Afro-Colombians, has not been addressed in any substantial manner by the Colombian state.

According to the United Nations Development Programme's (UNDP) human poverty index report for Colombia, which looks at a number of social indicators such as health, education, infant mortality, and access to drinkable water to measure economic and social inequalities, the human poverty index for the Afro-Colombian population is almost two times that of the national mean. This is reflected in regional differences among departments. For instance, the department of Bogotá, which is in the Andes, has a poverty index of 7.9 percent, and the department of Chocó, which is located in the Pacific Basin, has a poverty index of 21.9 percent. In addition, UNDP researchers argue that such disparities are found in all of the variables used to calculate the poverty index (Sarmiento Gómez et al. 2003).

People in Colombia's rural areas are about twice as poor as urban residents. They have a low life expectancy, and half as many of their youth go to university. Most rural workers in Colombia make less than two dollars a day. The UNDP report argues that "huge economic and social inequalities between rural and urban areas characterize Colombian development" (Sarmiento Gómez et al. 2003, 5). This is significant because Afro-Colombian populations are concentrated in the regions with the most poverty.

The UNDP report locates the department of the Chocó at the bottom of the human development index, just after Cauca and Nariño. The report argues that the widespread violence and consequent displacement of local communities within these regions adds to the disparities and exacerbates social inequalities. All three departments are found within the Pacific region and in all three a high percentage of the population lives in rural areas. In Chocó, life expectancy is lower today (66.6 years) than the average national life expectancy for Colombia as a nation was ten years ago (68.1 years). Also in Chocó, social expenditure per capita and government investment is the lowest in the country (in 1998, the government spent seven times as much per capita in Bogotá as it did in Chocó). Social indicators of health, education, sanitation, and housing for municipalities of departments in the Andes and along the Atlantic coast, where Afro-Colombians are concentrated, are lower than the national mean (Departamento Nacional de Planeación 1998; Sarmiento Gómez et al. 2003). In light of this varied and extensive evidence, the UNDP report concludes that "inequality in Colombia is extremely high" (Sarmiento Gómez et al. 2003, 7).

In addition to these social indicators, Escobar argues that "the fact that the Pacific has always been connected with a dominant national Euro-Andean modernity has entailed the persistent suppression (often violent exclusion) of black and indigenous knowledges and cultures" (2008, 12). This has also happened in the Andes, where the largest Afro-Colombian populations live.

The municipality of Buenos Aires in Cauca has predominantly (90 percent) Afro-Colombian inhabitants, most of whom work in agriculture (coffee farming) and in gold mining. The inhabitants of this municipality live in rural areas at the lowest economic strata of Colombian society. They have basic houses made of adobe, often with dirt floors and metal roofs. These houses generally have electricity (recently available because of a new hydroelectric dam constructed in the municipality) and running water (which they have had for fifty years); however, they lack basic sanitation services. Campesinos own small farms that cultivate coffee or cassava averaging about one hectare, and some are able to hire day laborers during harvest. Miners have artisanal gold mines that are horizontal tunnels in the mountains. Some have compressors to provide oxygen at certain depths, and one or two have lights, but the average mine and mill is not mechanized. Whether they are miners or farmers, most families live at, below, or just above subsistence.

In 1999 two black communities in the Andean region made claims to territory and autonomy and demanded recognition as ethnic groups. Their claims were based in differing circumstances. One claim, to the hill Cerro Teta, was made on the basis of the fact that Afro-Colombian gold miners living in the hinterland of the hill made their living from the land they claimed. The other claim, in Alsacia, was for a parcel of planted forest, where Afro-Colombian coffee farmers had moved after they had been displaced by a hydroelectric dam from their supplementary economic activity of panning for gold. While the organization that made the claim in the first community had historical roots in a mining cooperative, the organization that mobilized in the second community had historical roots in the evangelical Christian church and in organizing against the construction of the hydroelectric dam.

Neither of these communities is typical of black communities that have been recognized and have received collective territories. Rather than coming from the rural riparian zones of the Pacific Basin (as decreed by AT55), these communities are located in the Andes and were formed through different histories. The claims were also not entirely rural. While each community claimed self-governance of rural territory, many of the community members worked in both rural and urban spaces, depending on the availability of work and income. They are similar to successful claims of communities of the Pacific Basin in that their emplacement (permanence of being) in and connection to the territory has been threatened and continues to be threatened. Extralegal armed groups (in particular the paramilitary) and large-scale extractive industries present a constant threat that the communities will be displaced from their land. To date neither of these communities have been recognized by the Colombian government.

Fragile Suspect Citizens

The words "we are told to go back to Africa" highlight the importance of citizenship as a goal, the centrality of land to that citizenship, and the precariousness of the category of citizen for Afro-Colombians. Why Africa? Why are any group's claims to difference still seen as anti-national or unpatriotic in this day of multiculturalism? I refer to this as the condition of being "suspect citizens" (Ng'weno 2007b). Suspect citizens are those whose tie to the land (and therefore to the nation) is continually questioned. While any claims to difference may be seen as anti-national or unpatriotic, Afro-Colombians' claims to citizenship rights based on difference are seen as more suspect than those of indigenous Colombians because indigenous people's ties to land are rarely questioned. In fact, an indigenous tie to land acquired through *mestizaje* helps legitimate other Colombians' construction of their identity as nationals. It is thus useful to think of Afro-Colombian citizenship as fragile, not something that can be taken for granted.

The continuation of slavery after the formation of the republic meant that membership as citizens was not always extended to Afro-Latin Americans. For those to whom citizenship was extended (the free) it was suspect or fragile because of Afro-Latin American ties to slavery and to Africa and because of the absence of a recognized bond between Afro-Latin Americans and the national territory. In Colombia this process is heightened because of the way ethnicity is tied to territory in the new legal spaces that have been created from which demands for equality are taking place.

Afro-Latin Americans struggled to be included in the category of citizen in various ways as Latin American republics were formed and developed after colonialism ended. Although Latin American countries formed some of the first nation-states (Anderson 1991) after colonialism ended in the early nineteenth century, slave uprisings, indigenous revolts, the mobilization of free Afro-Latin American and indigenous populations, and the recent Haitian Revolution proved to be a problem for the new post-colonial nation-states trying to legitimate and justify rule by creole leaders. In particular, the new republican governments of the early nineteenth century were faced with the difficulty of deciding how people were tied to land. Government leaders found an answer in the idea of the creole—the individual who was born in the Americas—as the legitimate ruler. This idea, that legitimacy was based on birth in the Americas, faced multiple challenges from marginalized populations who were also born in the Americas but were not included in the creole ideal of legitimate rulers. The challenges included the alternative claim of indigenous peoples that they were the true natives of the land and the claim of Afro-Latin Americans that they too were born in the Americas (Ng'weno 2007b). Ideas of national citizenship were developed in opposition to these competing ideas of belonging.

Afro-Latin Americans struggled for inclusion in terms of both formal incorporation as citizens and distribution of the substantive aspects of citizenship in various ways during the development of republican Latin American states.

Freedom from slavery was a promise made to Afro-Latin Americans in almost all Latin American countries during the struggles for independence (Andrews 2004). Across the Americas, all sides told slaves they would give them their freedom (personal or collective) if they would fight alongside them in the wars of independence. Slavery and freedom were thus not separated conceptually in the struggles for independence but in fact were essential to the wars for independence and their outcomes. Nevertheless, instead of ending slavery immediately at independence, most Latin American countries ended slavery gradually through free birth or free womb laws that declared only those born in the new republics "free" regardless of the status of their mothers, thus delaying the full abolition of slavery by thirty to fifty years (Andrews 2004). An additional delay was due to the fact that "free" was a relative term because the moment of emancipation was tied to adulthood (Andrews 2004). During that period, slaves and citizens continued to have clearly different statuses vis-à-vis the state. This made the status of all Afro-Latin Americans as citizens uncertain. During the first half-century of independence in most Latin American nations, the struggle for equality by Afro-Latin Americans centered on the abolition of slavery (Andrews 2004). Sanders (2004) argues that in Colombia this involved continuous negotiations between elites and the popular classes about the formal and substantive aspects of citizenship. Afro-Colombians organized in support of abolition and those groups that could guarantee abolition and fought in the civil wars for the parties that promised abolition, which finally took place in 1851. Sanders (2004) argues that bargaining was an important part of struggles to determine what citizenship would look like until the state grew more powerful and less dependent on popular support and moved away from such negotiations at the end of the nineteenth century.

During the twentieth century, efforts to legitimize rule by restructuring national identity through ideas of *mestizaje* and the development of national races (e.g., the "Colombian" race) meant that claims to difference were seen as anti-national and unpatriotic. Claims to or expressions of a different culture were read as a failure to be properly national. Today in the multicultural environment of current constitutions, new spaces are available that Afro-Latin American populations can use to challenge these older notions of citizenship, and in theory, it should be more difficult for states to tolerate the notion of culturally suspect citizenship. However, as the comment "go back to Africa" indicates, this change is not coming easily.

Because states had already recognized the cultural difference of indigenous groups and the legitimacy of the ties of indigenous groups to land, the new multicultural legal environment of the 1990s and the unstable categorization of Afro-Colombians at times precipitated new types of conflicts between indigenous and Afro-Colombian communities, as illustrated by the example that opens this chapter. At other times, such as during the negotiations for the new constitution in 1991, the prior recognition of indigenous difference and indigenous rights to land produced new types of solidarity based on shared political struggles and goals (Asher 2009). Because recognition of cultural difference in Colombia is linked to ethnicity and territory, Afro-Colombians remain fragile citizens even as they try to claim equal citizenship because governments are less willing to recognize their cultural difference.

In the comment "go back to Africa" the past and the present are brought together in a de-territorializing move. To tell Afro-Colombians to go back to Africa denies both the reality that they have lived on Colombian soil for multiple generations and the existence of Afro-Colombian culture. The person who says this is locating both the land and culture of the people to whom it is being said somewhere other than Colombia. Yet both land and culture are necessary elements of the new legal basis of demands that challenge unequal citizenship.

Demanding Citizenship

In the cloud forest of the Western Cordillera of the Andes in the north of Cauca there is a small two-room community school that was built by the community of Alsacia. This school started with one teacher, whom the community paid until the government was willing to support the school. The community wanted to have a school near where they worked so their children could live with them as they got an education. More important, they wanted to build a school that would teach their children things that were culturally and socially relevant to their lives as Afro-Colombian coffee farmers. Thus, the education was to be relevant to the culture and livelihoods of the local community; the community aimed to have an education where their children could remain within the community instead of an education that would mean that most of their educated members would leave. The first teacher of the school remembers working as a youth as an agricultural laborer planting the trees on the plantation where the school was finally built. She saw the creation of the school as bringing the fruit of her labor full circle and as a symbol of self-sufficiency and autonomy to make decisions and to self govern as a community.

The building of the school was an example of a community's practice of emplacement in a fragile environment in which displacement repeatedly occurred—as the result of a new hydroelectric dam, a coffee blight, and, finally, at the hands of paramilitaries. The community had come to Alsacia after it was displaced by a hydroelectric dam. Community members wanted to rebuild their community in the area they were familiar with instead of dispersing to other locations in Colombia. This concern for cultural and ecological coherence is reflected in their goals for the school. They wanted to maintain not only their cultural practices, including a life based on agriculture but also their residence in the area. They wanted to prevent the breakup and dispersion of the community to multiple locations.

The community of Alsacia also claimed the land they lived on as a collective territory in order to further secure their emplacement. The experience of the community of Alsacia can be thought of as one of fragility in relation to territory. The group had to take possession of the space of Alsacia as a community, build their school, and organize from this territorial base in order to start a dialogue with the state about autonomy to self-govern, recognition (as a community, as a black community, and as citizens), and citizenship. They built their school before they knew the state would support it. In this manner, the community retained autonomy to decide educational content, but they had to build the school and pay the teachers themselves. Services the government usually provides to citizens such as schools were first provided by the community for itself and only later supported by the state. These practices of emplacement can be thought of as rural insurgent citizenship by which rights, institutions, and the meaning and practices of citizenship are produced and demanded through the practices of citizens. In a sense the state is one step behind the community in providing the substantive aspects of citizenship.

The community of Alsacia was making the most of the new political opening in the 1991 constitution that allowed for the state to recognize new ideas of citizenship and equality. Before and after the 1991 Constitution, the community of Alsacia demanded to be recognized as citizens in numerous ways, some more readily accepted than others. In 1989 they organized against their displacement because of the hydroelectric dam. Once they had been displaced, they organized against their dispersal as a community by making a claim to land "at home" as campesinos in the context of agrarian reform. They took over land in Alsacia within the region where they had previously lived and organized to legalize their possession. They argued for this right as citizens who have a social right to land under the Colombian Constitution prior to 1991. After 1991 they organized to secure their presence on this land by claiming it as a collective territory for black communities. They argued for this right as citizens who have special status and rights under the rubric of the 1991 Constitution and Law 70.

The community of Alsacia mobilized two parts of the new legal provision of the 1991 Constitution to claim the land as a collective territory. First they organized for ethno-education, education that was relevant to their community, culture, and location, in their school. And second, they claimed the land on which they lived as a collective territory for black communities, asking for recognition as a black community in Colombia and for the distribution of the rights that accrue with recognition of this new form of citizenship. Through these two activities the community of Alsacia argued for autonomy and territory as a way of obtaining equal citizenship (Ng'weno 2007b). They saw the new Constitution and Law 70 as creating steps they could take toward this equality. However, the new equality was tied to their success in obtaining legal title to collective territories that indicated the recognition of the communities as Afro-Colombian, as autonomous entities, and as citizens.

Recognition as an ethnic group with special rights—and thus equal citizenship as well—is legally tied to a rural land base. This has meant that rural concerns (for instance, territory) have come to dominate the process of recognition and the legal space available for claims to equality as Afro-Colombian ethnic groups. The possession of the territory is thus an important part of demands for equal citizenship. Although they do so in different circumstances than residents of cities, rural Afro-Colombians have engaged in practices that have demanded that their presence as citizens be noticed, as have urban subaltern populations in Brazil (Holston 2008).

Two Forms of Equality

Today in Colombia the legal space available to claim equality enables two separate notions of equality: equal treatment under the same law and equality obtained through separate laws. Together these two approaches to equality include provisions for education, political representation, and collective territories. From the point of view of law, these are citizenship rights that enable Afro-Colombians to equally enjoy citizenship and participate equally as Colombian citizens. In the first idea of equality, the same law applies to all individuals equally. A new space for this form of equality was opened with the 1991 Constitution's stipulation that all Colombians are guaranteed equality of rights without discrimination (Article 13). This space has been used to fight discrimination, including racial discrimination. For Afro-Colombians, this space was expanded by Constitutional Court Ruling T-422 in 1996, whose idea of affirmative action has been incorporated into some national and city development plans (Mosquera Rosero-Labbé and León Díaz 2009). Once it is completed, the Anti-Discrimination Statute will also complement these rulings and the constitution (Mosquera Rosero-Labbé and León Díaz 2009).

Constitutional Court Ruling T-422, "Positive Differentiation for Black Communities," concerns the rights of urban Afro-Colombian inhabitants of the town of Santa Marta on the Atlantic coast of Colombia to representation on district education boards. The case was brought to the Constitutional Court to decide the constitutional rights of Afro-Colombians in relation to education. The court ruled that Afro-Colombians had the right to such representation, basing its ruling on Article 13 of the 1991 Constitution, which guarantees equality of rights, liberties, and opportunities for all Colombians without discrimination, instead of basing the ruling on Law 70, which guarantees the rights of ethnic groups. Importantly and significantly, T-422 stressed that because of segregation and marginalization, Afro-Colombians were not in fact equal and that affirmative action measures were needed to make equality real and effective. T-422 in effect recognized that Colombian citizenship is not equal and argued that this inequality is not in step with the new Constitution. In this regard the position of the Colombian Constitutional Court was not very different from that of regional courts of the State of Rio de Janeiro, Brazil, which have instituted affirmative action measures in the form of quotas at institutions of higher education (Htun 2004).

Ruling T-422 is thus based on the ideal of one law that applies equally to all people. It acknowledges that the law has not been equally applied in the past and that this has created marginalization that must be addressed through affirmative action measures. In the case of T-422, the affirmative action was to allow Afro-Colombian representatives on the district education boards. Although this court case was originally brought to the lower courts under the rubric of Law 70, the Constitutional Court decided that as an urban case brought by displaced Afro-Colombians, ethnicity did not apply and that this case did not fall under Law 70. That is to say, the Afro-Colombians who brought the lawsuit were not members of an ethnic group but were instead raced citizens. In addition, the court decided that race could not be the basis for separate legal status, although ethnicity can. Therefore, the Afro-Colombians who brought the case to court had to do so as ordinary citizens under ordinary laws. However, the court also decided that discrimination based on race could necessitate temporary compensation measures to make citizenship equal. The court decided that Afro-Colombian representation on district education boards was a means to ensure that education in the future would not be a site of discrimination.

Ruling T-422 opens a space for demands based on racial marginalization and allows for claims against discrimination. It also illustrates the difficulty of making claims in urban spaces under the rubric of ethnicity. Nevertheless, comments such as "go back to Africa" remind us that mobilizing the space of ethnicity in rural areas is not always simple. For example, in Alsacia, the displacement of Afro-Colombians by the hydroelectric dam and the fact they were located in the Andes proved obstacles to claiming ethnic status. The Bernard and Audre Rapoport Center for Human Rights and Justice (2007) argues that the government's practice of keeping applications to collective territories in perpetual pending status, legal restrictions against creating bi-ethnic territories, and the government's refusal to recognize urban communities are additional means of denying Afro-Colombians their rights to collective land. While some Alsacian community members argued that they had been marginalized as Afro-Colombians on the basis of their race, and as rural campesinos, they would not be able to claim the territory they occupied or autonomy over governance of that territory through arguments of marginality because marginality because of race is not tied to a rural land base the way cultural distinction is.

The second notion of equality is one that is guaranteed through separate laws. The 1991 Constitution opened this new space in the Colombian legal system for ethnic groups, including Afro-Colombians. Various groups have used this space to fight for territory and autonomy as ethnic groups. This space was expanded for Afro-Colombians in 1993 by Law 70, which acknowledges the separate status of ethnic groups based on cultural distinction that provides for their autonomy over governance within a territory. The law acknowledges if equal citizenship is to be created, different citizens will require different laws based on their cultural distinctiveness.

Colombia is often held up as a model of land distribution to communities of African descent in the Americas. However, under the 1991 Constitution not all Afro-Colombian communities are automatically recognized as ethnic groups. The provision applies mainly to those living in the rural riparian zones of the Pacific Basin. Consequently, none of the land that has been titled to black communities has been located outside that region. Alsacia is a case in point. That community found that its location in the Andes proved an obstacle to getting the state to recognize their claim. Colombia has restricted the process of titling land to black communities to an area where only 20 percent of Afro-Colombians live.

While the success of titling in the Pacific Basin has influenced the process and possibility of titling outside that region, legal and financial constraints have greatly limited the success of groups claiming collective lands in these areas. This difficulty is compounded by the displacement of Afro-Colombian groups from their traditional lands and by the fragile state of Afro-Colombian citizenship. As an African doing fieldwork in Cauca, I posed a particular kind of threat to those who were struggling to claim territory and autonomy. I reminded them of something better forgotten or hidden (Africa), for I made visible the latent contradiction (what Povinelli [2002] would call the "cunning of recognition") of the new laws that recognized black communities as ethnic groups yet made no clear statements about the substantive aspects of citizenship for such communities, leaving them in a fragile and unstable condition as citizens.

To complicate matters further, in 2000 the small school in Alsacia had to be abandoned when a large part of the Alsacian community was displaced by paramilitaries who demanded that that all people vacate the area within a day under threat of violence. Like so many of the black communities recognized in the Pacific Basin, the community became separated from its territory because of violence. The efforts, practices, dreams, and goals of insurgent citizens were cut short by the violent activities of extralegal armed groups. Many of those who are displaced relocate in cities, where they continue to organize around issues of ethnicity, race, territory, autonomy, and return. Thus, members of populations that have been displaced by violence join those who have been displaced by economics, natural disasters, and poor living conditions and mobile individuals and groups who move back and forth between urban and rural spaces. These populations complicate the easy divide between urban and rural spaces.

Conclusion: Transforming Citizenship

In the context of the new multicultural, pluri-ethnic, and intercultural structures of Latin American states, recognition of Afro-Latin Americans as citizens has come in many forms that reflect the differences in thinking about equality. Some states have attempted to redress inequality with one law for all citizens, while others have instituted separate laws for groups based on their difference. In the countries that have formulated new constitutions since the 1990s, Afro-Latin American communities have been recognized and in some cases their demands have been met in constitutional and legal forms (e.g., Colombia, Ecuador, Brazil, Nicaragua, Guatemala, Honduras, and Mexico [Oaxaca]) under rubrics influenced by the World Conference against Racism, Racial Discrimination, Xenophobia and Related Intolerance in Durban, South Africa, in 2001 (e.g., Brazil) and by the ratification of the ILO's Convention 169 (e.g., Colombia, Nicaragua). For instance, in Brazil some states have legislated against discrimination in public spaces, in employment, and in education (Htun 2004). In Nicaragua, Honduras, and Guatemala, Afro-Latin Americans have the same rights to territory and autonomy as indigenous groups (Hooker 2005).

Laws that have attempted to redress inequality in Colombia have approached the issue from two different legal perspectives. They have focused on either race or ethnicity, on civil rights or autonomy, on discrimination or collective territories, and on urban or rural spaces. The two perspectives—focused on race, civil rights, discrimination, and urban space, on the one hand, and on ethnicity, autonomy, collective territories, and rural space on the other—correspond to conceptualizations of the solution to the problem of inequality and difference as a single law or as separate laws. The legal divide between these two perspectives depends on demonstrating cultural distinction that is territorially based.

Ironically, within its legal statutes Colombia has legalized both perspectives, opening diverse spaces for transforming citizenship. However, this two-pronged legal approach has conceptually divided black communities that are recognized as ethnic groups from black communities that are not.

The people in the municipality where I did my research emphasized that they were claiming both autonomy and territory. They also emphasized that the realization of their claims would make them equal citizens as opposed to a nation within a nation. These claims to autonomy were not claims to take over the state or to secede from it, but rather claims to autonomy were framed within the idea of equal citizenship.

The form of claims to autonomy Afro-Colombians have made creates new ideas of citizenship because it transforms older ideas of who could be autonomous (indigenous Colombians and Palenqueros) and how people can be autonomous. In fact these ideas of citizenship are not just new but are rather unique to Latin America because they are made by a rural diasporic population. That is to say, around the world such claims to autonomy and territory are usually made by communities indigenous to the region rather than by populations who arrived from somewhere else, even if in the distant past. Afro-Latin American claims to autonomy are not the same as indigenous claims (that is, they are not based on primordial rights, or the association of people with land) or regional claims to autonomy (because they are based on culture rather than on territorial jurisdiction) or maroon communities (because such claims appeal to the state for autonomous status instead of gaining their status outside state authority). These claims to autonomy force a new understanding of citizenship in the way they challenge and rearrange the categories of belonging and rule.

Colombia is also interesting because it has promoted two different ideas of equality, both of which have been mobilized by Afro-Colombians in efforts to gain a more equal citizenship. Constitutional Court Ruling T-422 and Law 70 operate from different understandings of how to address the problem of unequal citizenship. One deals with equality obtained through one law for all citizens, the other with separate laws for groups of citizens. One deals with race as a legal concept, the other with ethnicity. One deals with an urban population, the other with a rural one.

The engagement of Afro-Colombians with both ways of thinking about equality has the potential to transform citizenship in a far-ranging way. This challenges us to think not just of race or of ethnicity but of both simultaneously. It challenges us to think of both rural and urban at the same time and to think of equality in two ways—obtained by one law for all and obtained through separate laws. This engagement with two different ways of thinking about equality demands that we both build bridges across different worldviews (through the recognition of ethnic difference) and break down structural hierarchies (through fights against racial discrimination).

Afro-Colombians are uniquely placed to realize the potential inherent in these two ideas of equality through insurgent acts of citizenship because of their historical categorization vis-à-vis land and culture and because of their place in the hierarchical structure of Colombian society. In fact, their positioning demands such creative acts, as they do not fit totally within any one legal concept of equality. Communities like Alsacia push what it means to be a citizen and what it means to be equal by insisting—in spite of the many obstacles—that they *are* equal citizens. They are slowly opening up spaces that could eventually lead to claims for territory and autonomy in urban spaces or in the Andes or fights against discrimination in rural areas or demands for basic services that could qualitatively improve life. The insurgent acts of citizenship being waged by Afro-Colombians could lead to all Afro-Colombians being recognized as citizens regardless of where they live.

Notes

The research for this chapter was funded by the Wenner-Gren Foundation.

1. The ILO's Convention 169 concerns indigenous and tribal peoples in independent countries. The convention defines these as peoples who are distinct from the rest of the nation by virtue of their culture, history, institutions, and social conditions. It makes specific stipulations concerning these people's rights of ownership and possession of land they traditionally occupy. In addition, the convention emphasizes the collective aspects of how such peoples relate to land.

Bibliography

Anderson, Benedict. 1991. *Imagined Communities: Reflections on the Origin and Spread of Nationalism.* Rev. ed. New York: Verso.

Andrews, George Reid. 2004. *Afro-Latin America: 1800–2000.* New York: Oxford University Press.

Asher, Kiran. 2009. *Black and Green: Afro-Colombians, Development, and Nature in the Pacific Lowlands.* Durham, N.C.: Duke University Press.

Bernard and Audre Rapoport Center for Human Rights and Justice. 2007. "Unfulfilled Promises and Persistent Obstacles to the Realization of the Rights of Afro-Colombians: Report on the Development of Ley 70 of 1993." Report submitted to the Inter-American Commission on Human Rights, July 18, 2007. Austin: University of Texas at Austin School of Law.

DANE (Departamento Administrativo Nacional de Estadistica). 2007. *Colombia: Una nación multicultural: Su diversidad étnica.* Bogotá: DANE. Available at http://www.dane.gov.co/files/censo2005/etnia/sys/colombia_nacion.pdf.

Departamento Nacional de Planeación. 1998. "Hacia una nación plurietnica y multicultural: *Plan Nacional de Desarrollo de la Población Afrocolombiana, 1998–2002.*" Bogotá: Departamento Nacional de Planeación, Comisión para la Formulación del Plan Nacional de Desarrollo de la Población Afrocolombiana.

Escobar, Arturo. 2008. *Territories of Difference: Place, Movements, Life, Redes*. Durham, N.C.: Duke University Press.

Government of Bolivia. 2009. "República de Bolivia Constitución de 2009." Available at http://pdba.georgetown.edu/Constitutions/Bolivia/bolivia09.html.

Government of Ecuador. 2008. "Constitución de la República de Ecuador." Available at http://issuu.com/elciudadano/docs/proyectodenuevaconstitución.

Holston, James. 2008. *Insurgent Citizenship: Disjunctions of Democracy and Modernity in Brazil*. Princeton, N.J.: Princeton University Press.

Hooker, Juliet. 2005. "Indigenous Inclusion/Black Exclusion: Race, Ethnicity and Multicultural Citizenship in Latin America." *Journal of Latin American Studies* 37 (2): 285–310.

Htun, Mala. 2004. "From 'Racial Democracy' to Affirmative Action: Changing State Policy on Race in Brazil." *Latin Research Review* 39 (1): 60–89.

Minority Rights Group International. 2008. "World Directory of Minorities and Indigenous Peoples-Colombia: Afro-Colombians." Available at http://www.unhcr.org/refworld/docid/49749d3cc.html.

Mosquera Rosero-Labbé, Cladia, and Ruby Esther León Díaz. 2009. *Acciones afirmativas y Ciudadaniía diferenciada étnico-racial negra, Afrocolombiana, Palenquera y Raizal: Entre bicentanarios de las independencias y Constitución de 1991*. Bogotá: Universidad Nacional de Colombia.

Ng'weno, Bettina. 2007a. "Can Ethnicity Replace Race? Afro-Colombians, Indigeneity and the Colombian Multicultural State." *Journal of Latin American and Caribbean Anthropology* 12 (2): 414–440.

———. 2007b. *Turf Wars: Territory and Citizenship in the Contemporary State*. Stanford, Calif.: Stanford University Press.

Povinelli, Elizabeth A. 2002. *The Cunning of Recognition: Indigenous Alterities and the Making of Australian Multiculturalism*. Durham, N.C.: Duke University Press.

Rubin, Gareth. 2009. "Bolivia Faces Crisis as Evo Morales Wins Referendum." *The Telegraph* January 27, 2009. Available at http://www.telegraph.co.uk/news/worldnews/southamerica/bolivia/4346584/Bolivia-faces-crisis-as-Evo-Morales-wins-referendum.html.

Sanders, James E. 2004. *Contentious Republicans: Popular Politics, Race and Class in Nineteenth-Century Colombia*. Durham, N.C.: Duke University Press.

Sarmiento Gómez, Alfredo, Lucía Mina Rosero, Carlos Alonso Malavar, and Sandra Alvarez Toro. 2003. "Colombia: Human Development Progress Towards the Millennium Development Goals." Human Development Occasional Papers 1992–2007, HDOCPA-2003-08. Human Development Report Office, United Nations Development Programme.

Schroder, Barbara. 2008. "Developing Intercultural Science Education in Ecuador." *Diaspora, Indigenous, and Minority Education* 2 (1): 25–43.

Van Cott, Donna Lee. 2000. *The Friendly Liquidation of the Past: The Politics of Diversity in Latin America*. Pittsburgh, Pa.: University of Pittsburgh Press.

Walsh, Catherine. 2002. "Interculturalidad, reformas constitucionales y pluralismo jurídico." *Boletin ICCI-RIMAI* 4 (36). Available at http://icci.nativeweb.org/boletin/36/walsh.html.

8

Black Activism in Ecuador, 1979–2009

OLLIE A. JOHNSON III

Blacks have lived in Ecuador for more than 400 years.[1] Yet this demographic reality is not currently reflected in the country's scholarly studies of history and politics. The Afro-Ecuadorian experience under slavery and in the postslavery period remains largely unexplored in elementary, secondary, and university educational institutions. In mainstream media, if they are mentioned at all, blacks are often presented as criminals, athletes, or entertainers. Newspapers, magazines, and journals rarely cover Afro-Ecuadorian life.[2]

According to the census of 2001, Afro-Ecuadorians are 5 percent (more than 600,000 citizens) of the national population and live in each of the country's twenty-two provinces. Blacks are concentrated in four main areas: the provinces of Esmeraldas, Guayas, and Pichincha and in the Chota Valley, which runs through the provinces of Imbabura and Carchi. The provincial capital cities of Esmeraldas, Guayaquil, and Quito are the centers of urban political organization and activism among blacks. As a result of decades of internal migration from Esmeraldas and the Chota Valley, Guayaquil and Quito have emerged as cities with large numbers of blacks, even though blacks constitute less than 10 percent of these municipal populations (Whitten [1974] 1986; Whitten and Quiroga with Savoia 1995; Pabón Chalá 2007; Antón Sánchez 2009).

Ecuador's political and economic structures are dominated by whites and mestizos (Roitman 2009; Cervone and Rivera 1999; Dixon 1997; Minda Batallas 2002; Stutzman 1981). Since the 1990s, the rise in indigenous organization, mobilization, and protest has challenged these arrangements and contributed a new and dynamic element to the country's politics. During the last two decades, indigenous groups have condemned the poverty, marginalization, and discrimination they face as well as the inequality, corruption, and elite rule rampant throughout the country. The indigenous uprising of June 1990 demonstrated that indigenous groups had developed the organizational capacity to paralyze the country. Since then, the Confederation of Indigenous Nationalities of

Ecuador (Confederación de Nacionalidades Indígenas del Ecuador; CONAIE) and other groups have organized impressive uprisings, marches, and protests. The Ecuadorian state has been forced to recognize and negotiate with major Indian organizations (Selverston-Scher 2001; Yashar 2005, 85–151; Van Cott 2005). Blacks share some of the goals of the indigenous movement, especially the importance of respecting cultural diversity and promoting social and political change. Blacks have allied with indigenous organizations and movements and other social movement groups. At the same time, there have been some tensions between Indians and blacks because indigenous groups have increased their political visibility and influence while Afro-Ecuadorians have remained more marginal.

This chapter examines the evolution of black political activity since 1979. During the last three decades, blacks have formed local, provincial, and national groups to affirm their racial identity, strengthen their cultural legacy, fight for their rights as citizens, and connect with international campaigns for human rights. They have participated in the struggle against poverty, racism, and invisibility. This history of activism shows that black political activists have worked to organize fellow Afro-Ecuadorians and to expand their role in Ecuadorian politics and society. However, black leaders have not been successful in creating a strong national social movement or in mobilizing adequate resources (material and human) to give themselves substantial organizational autonomy or political power.

Recent scholarship has described Afro-Ecuadorian activism as an emerging social movement in recognition of the creation of new organizations and the modest protests these organizations have mounted (Medina Vallejo and Castro Torres 2006). In the last few decades, Afro-Ecuadorians have devoted time and resources to making their presence felt as citizens with constitutional and human rights. They have condemned various manifestations of racial prejudice and discrimination. Afro-Ecuadorian leaders have raised critical questions. How long will black women be stereotyped as undeserving of dignity and respect? Why are black men seen as prone to violence when they regularly suffer police brutality? When will the country's leadership take action to improve the unjust living conditions of most black children? Afro-Ecuadorian organizations are demanding changes to the status quo.

This chapter analyzes the challenges that hinder black progress and the opportunities that facilitate it. Black poverty is at the core of the difficult socioeconomic situation of Afro-Ecuadorians. Limited material resources in urban and rural areas require inordinate time and attention to basic survival. Participation in the political process has yielded limited results. Important self-proclaimed allies such as President Abdalá Bucaram have been disappointments. (It is too early to evaluate President Rafael Correa's relationship with Afro-Ecuadorians.) This chapter also discusses select black groups and their activities. What role has the Catholic Church, especially the Comboni missionaries, played in supporting black organization? Black activists often complain that white and mestizo political elites rarely embrace their concerns and fight for the passage and implementation of public policies that will benefit the Afro-Ecuadorian masses. The conclusion notes the new visibility of famous black athletes and the serious challenges that black Ecuadorians continue to face.

Most of the research for this chapter was conducted from August 2001 to August 2003 while I was a professor of political science at Universidad San Francisco de Quito (USFQ). While living in Quito, I regularly attended, observed, and participated in black political and cultural events, including celebrations, religious ceremonies, lectures, workshops, marches, and protests in various parts of the municipality. I also traveled throughout the country; visited black communities and organizations in Guayaquil, Esmeraldas, and the Chota Valley; experienced Afro-Ecuadorian hospitality; and witnessed firsthand the poverty and lack of basic social services and infrastructure of many urban and rural neighborhoods. In addition to many informal conversations with Afro-Ecuadorians (activists and non-activists), I interviewed more than twenty black activists and politicians about their personal backgrounds, their work with organizations, their political activities, and their perspectives on the socioeconomic and political realities of Afro-Ecuadorians and the country. In sum, I used a multifaceted qualitative research strategy to explore various dimensions of black political activism.

As an African American born and raised in the United States with no previous experience in Ecuador, I had the privilege of meeting Patricio Congo, a basketball coach and professor of physical education at USFQ in August 2001. As two of the few full-time black professors at the university, Patricio and I quickly became friends. I explained my research interests in Afro-Ecuadorian politics, and Patricio agreed to introduce me to black activists. In general, these activists appreciated my interest in and respect for their work. They allowed me to attend meetings and events and invited me to lecture on African American history and the black experience in the United States. In exchange, I brought them to USFQ to discuss the Afro-Ecuadorian movement with my students. In March 2009, I returned to Quito to participate in an international conference on affirmative action. This conference was organized in part by black activist Alexandra Ocles, then a member of the National Assembly, to explore the possibility of implementing affirmative action policies for Afro-Ecuadorians.

Poverty, Inequality, and Exclusion

Throughout Latin America, black and indigenous groups tend to constitute the poorest and most excluded sectors of their countries. Three centuries of European colonialism and slavery have had a devastating impact. Indigenous peoples suffered extreme population loss and marginalization while blacks experienced brutal violence and racial oppression. From the 1500s through the 1800s, a social and racial hierarchy of wealth, income, status, privilege, and prestige developed in Latin America. At the top of this pyramid were whites, and at the bottom were indigenous peoples and blacks. In the middle were mestizos, mulattos, and the other mixed groups. This hierarchy was perpetuated during the twentieth century, during which there were few massive, sustained, or effective government educational and social policies to improve living conditions of blacks, Indians, and the poor. As a result, Latin America currently has the highest level of inequality in the world (De Ferranti et al. 2004; Andrews 2004).

Ecuador is representative of Latin America in that it is a racially and culturally diverse country where black and indigenous people remain at the bottom in socioeconomic terms. Poverty is the ever-present reality of Afro-Ecuadorian life. Afro-Ecuadorians face major difficulties in obtaining employment, education, housing, and health care. In general, blacks have the highest unemployment rate and work in the most physically demanding and least prestigious occupations. Blacks work for subsistence or low wages in agriculture, service, and commerce as sharecroppers, domestic servants, security guards, street vendors, and movers. After the indigenous population, blacks have the highest illiteracy rate and the fewest years of formal education. Similarly, after indigenous groups, blacks live in the most hazardous housing situations and experience the worst health conditions. When I visited Esmeraldas in 2002, I observed a scenario of blacks washing clothes, bathing, relieving themselves, swimming, and playing in a shallow river basin. The community largely lacked the infrastructure of indoor plumbing, sewage drainage, and paved roads. Contemporary black and indigenous living conditions are the consequence of colonialism, slavery, ethnoracial discrimination, and a lack of government intervention to reduce or eliminate structural and institutional disadvantages (Secretaría Técnica del Frente Social 2004; Ponce 2006; Whitten and Quiroga 1995).

One of the challenges of documenting the role of Afro-descendants in Latin American society and politics relates to the exclusion of race from most national censuses. This reality has delayed a more informed scholarly discussion of racial inequality, black poverty, and racial discrimination. Latin American political and social elites have tended to embrace the ideologies of racial democracy and racial harmony. These ideologies accentuate an allegedly high degree of racial

miscegenation and interracial cordiality and the alleged absence of racial segregation and discrimination against blacks. Afro-Latin American activists and intellectuals have often experienced racial discrimination and therefore have been more
critical of notions of racial democracy. One of their demands has been for racial
censuses to increase understanding of national and regional race relations (Johnson 2007).

In 2001, the Ecuadorian government conducted a census that for first time
included a question regarding the population's racial identity. The relevant census question was: "What do you consider yourself: Indigenous, Black (Afro-
Ecuadorian), Mestizo, Mulatto, White, or Other?" This census is the first official
and comprehensive description of Ecuadorian life that includes socioeconomic
and demographic data disaggregated by ethnicity and race. According to this
census, Ecuador had a population of more than 12 million inhabitants and the
vast majority (77.6 percent) identified as mestizos. Whites were 10.5 percent
and indigenous people were 6.1 percent. Government officials and scholars have
generally combined the black (2.3 percent) and mulatto (2.7 percent) categories
to form a black, Afro-Ecuadorian, or Afro-descendant group for descriptive and
analytical purposes (Secretaría Técnica del Frente Social 2004, 127).[3]

The 2001 census confirmed what previous studies had found (World Bank
1996). Ecuador faces many serious social and economic challenges. Using a definition of poverty based on the concept of unsatisfied basic needs (Necesidades
Basicas Insatisfechas; NBI), a majority (61.3 percent) of Ecuadorians are poor.
Blacks and Indians are poorer than whites and mestizos throughout the coastal
and highland regions as well as in the urban and rural areas of the country. Approximately 70 percent of blacks are poor, and 38 percent of poor blacks are
extremely poor. More recent government research from 2003 that defined the
poverty line as $60 per month found that 34.5 percent of Ecuadorians earn less
than that amount. Similarly, blacks (of whom 41 percent live below the poverty
line) and indigenous peoples (of whom 55 percent live below the poverty line)
are poorer than whites (of whom 25 percent live below the poverty line) and
mestizos (of whom 33 percent live below the poverty line). This racial hierarchy
of income is visible in other spheres of social life (Secretaría Técnica del Frente
Social 2004, 43–52; Ponce 2006).

Ecuadorian Politics and Black Activism

Ecuador has been characterized by political instability and party fragmentation
since independence in 1830. The citizenry has lived under more than twenty
constitutions, and presidents have regularly failed to complete their terms in
office. Regionalism continues to characterize the diverse political cultures of the
coast, highland, and Amazon regions. Strong national political parties have not

developed. The traditional political parties have tended to be vehicles for Ecuador's oligarchy. The poor and marginalized mestizo, black, and indigenous masses have historically been excluded from elite politics. Populism and personalism were personified in the figure of José María Velasco Ibarra, who was president five times between 1934 and 1972 (Conaghan 1995; Jiménez 1998; Mejía Acosta 2002; de la Torre Espinosa 1997).

From 1972 to 1979, the country was governed by a military dictatorship that ruled with an authoritarian developmentalist model. The country has had thirteen presidents from 1979 to 2009. All of them have faced serious political or economic crises. Since 1997, three presidents (Abdalá Bucaram, Jamil Mahuad, and Lucio Gutiérrez) have been forced from office before completing their terms. The party system has been characterized by extreme multipartism and only limited attachment of citizens to specific political parties. Ambitious politicians have changed parties or created their own party as a result of permissive electoral legislation. The military has not formally returned to power, but some sectors of it have allied with other political actors to remove presidents from office (Conaghan 1995; Sánchez 2008).

Within this political context, Afro-Ecuadorians have rarely attained highly visible roles as individuals or collectively. Blacks are underrepresented in the national legislature and in practically all political parties. The only Afro-Ecuadorian in the National Assembly currently is Zobeida Gudiño, a Movimiento País deputy from the province of Zamora Chinchipe. The most important parties on the coast are the Social Christian Party (PSC), the Roldosista Ecuadorian Party (PRE), and the Party of National Action and Institutional Renovation (PRIAN). In the highlands, the strongest parties are the Democratic Left (ID) and Popular Democracy (DP). The Popular Democratic Movement (MPD) is a far leftist party that includes among its members highly visible black politicians such as Ernesto Estupiñán Quintero, the mayor of Esmeraldas. Ecuadorian parties are usually identified with a few strong leaders rather than a highly organized and disciplined cadre of members and activists. New political parties include Pachakutik, led by the indigenous movement, and Movimiento País, of which the current president Rafael Correa is a leader (Freidenberg and Sáez 2001; Peñaherrera Solah 2002).

Before the 1970s, most black activism was manifested primarily in peasant and worker struggles for land, respect, jobs, and justice. The discourse and the organizations of such activists centered on the rights of blacks as farmers, rural laborers, and urban workers. Scholar Jhon Antón Sánchez highlights how four individuals played key roles in laying the foundation for explicitly black and Afro-Ecuadorian identification and organization. Saloman Chala Acosta and Alonso Tadeo from the Chota Valley and Nelson Estupiñán Bass and Juan Garcia from Esmeraldas worked as intellectuals, teachers, and activists to emphasize the ethnic and racial dimensions of the discrimination, marginalization, and oppression suffered by Afro-Ecuadorians. These grassroots leaders had more formal education than most blacks but were deeply rooted in the rural struggles of their communities. As blacks migrated in increasingly large numbers to the urban centers of Guayaquil and Quito, the influence of these leaders spread through their children, family members, friends, students, and fellow activists (Antón Sánchez 2009: 60–69, 125–143; Saloman Acosta interview; Juan Carlos interview; Oswaldo Espinoza interview; Jacqueline Pavon interview).

One of the most important examples of black activism in recent Ecuadorian history occurred in Quito in 1979. The Afro-Ecuadorian Studies Center (Centro de Estudios Afroecuatorianos; CEA) was started by black university students frustrated by their isolation at the Universidad Central; the lack of information on black history, culture, society; and the subordinate socioeconomic and political situation of blacks. These students came from various parts of the country and realized that they knew relatively little about other blacks in their own country. Some of the participants at the center later became well-known black activists, including its first president, historian Andrés Jurado; popular scholar Juan Garcia; anthropologist Oscar Chalá; economist Renán Tadeo; cultural worker Luzmilla Bolanos; and politician Victor Junior Leon (Tadeo 1999; Bolanos interview; Antón Sánchez 2007, 237).

The main objectives of the center were to organize blacks, research Afro-Ecuadorian history, and raise consciousness about the unjust circumstances of overwhelming black poverty. The group met every two weeks at their headquarters in Quito. At these meetings, the participants discussed the situation of their home communities, the situation of blacks in Quito, and the situations of the places where they studied. By the early 1980s, the center was a legally recognized group with officers and special work committees. Tadeo argues that the center had the positive effect of improving understanding between blacks from the highlands and the coast. Because they had shared their life, work, and study experiences with each other, members were better able to confront racial discrimination (Tadeo 1999; Bolanos interview).

Founders of the CEA explored the city of Quito, interviewed Afro-Ecuadorian elders, and began to document the experiences and traditions of black people. The group created an archive of interviews and materials and wrote short, accessible essays and pamphlets on Afro-Ecuadorian history and culture. CEA members reached out to black youth, especially high school students, and encouraged them to work to improve their communities and to take their education seriously. Juan Garcia was one of the leaders in recognizing the beauty and originality of Afro-Ecuadorian culture. He later became a respected advocate, scholar, and defender of black cultural manifestations and traditions, including the poetic storytelling art form of *la décima* (Bolanos interview; Garcia 1988; Sánchez 2002).

Passionate about what they were doing, many CEA members were influenced by socialist and leftist views popular in Ecuador and Latin America in the 1970s and 1980s. These were decades when students, workers, activists, and some armed insurgents were fighting against military dictatorships and authoritarian regimes in South and Central America. But by the mid-1980s, the center began to decline as members returned to their provinces and communities after their university studies. At home, they often formed new organizations that continued the work of the center in new settings (Tadeo 1999; Bolanos interview). Tadeo suggests that the CEA was a seminal experience in the history of black activism in Ecuador. It confirmed the importance of organizing around and affirming black identity and culture.

The major institution that followed the Afro-Ecuadorian Studies Center was the Afro-Ecuadorian Cultural Center (Centro Cultural Afroecuatoriano; CCA). The CCA was founded by Father Rafael Savoia, an Italian Comboni missionary, in Guayaquil in 1981 and moved to Quito in 1983. The CCA still exists and is one of the country's most important spaces for black scholarship and activism. The CCA's founding was controversial for some CEA founders. Father Rafael visited the CEA, borrowed its materials, and spoke with members about their activities and work. He then founded the CCA to do essentially what the CEA was already doing. Juan Garcia and Father Rafael had a major argument on this point. Garcia argued that Father Rafael should support black student activists instead of stealing their ideas and building a competing institution in the name of black Ecuadorians (anonymous interviews 2003).

This example and the later activities of Father Rafael and the Comboni missionaries led some black activists to maintain a critical perspective about the CCA. According to them, the CCA and other institutions of the Catholic Church often have a paternalistic structure in which white Europeans have ultimate power while black Ecuadorians are simply employees in projects and programs that operate in the name of uplifting black Ecuadorians. When I responded to that view by highlighting the sincerity and commitment of the Comboni missionaries in general and Father Rafael in particular, some black activists noted that the missionaries get paid for what they do. Furthermore, the activists emphasized that the missionaries raised money for their projects. According to this view, in the name of helping Afro-Ecuadorians, the missionaries were in reality maintaining blacks in a subordinate position in a dependent relationship (anonymous interviews 2003). This early disagreement between black activists and the CCA was a harbinger of future difficulties with creating and sustaining independent black institutions.

In the last thirty years, Afro-Ecuadorians have formed hundreds of groups throughout the country, especially in Quito, Guayaquil, Esmeraldas, and the Chota Valley. These groups represent a broad range of social, cultural, political, and economic interests. Afro-Ecuadorian leaders have created an unprecedented informal and decentralized organizational structure and network. The work, activities, and demands of these organizations have increased the visibility of blacks nationally and internationally (Antón Sánchez 2009, 57–124). At the same time, scholars still lack critical information about many of these organizations. How many members do they have? How often do they meet? How effective have they been in achieving their goals?

Since the 1980s and 1990s, black groups have emerged to demand land rights, ethno-education, and an end to discrimination. In the province of Esmeraldas, blacks organized to fight against corporations taking their land for commercial development in the areas where Afro-Ecuadorians made their livelihoods in mining, and shrimp farming, harvesting timber, and growing African palm. Although these economic enterprises received state concessions, local groups formed the Process of the Black Communities of North Esmeraldas (Proceso de Comunidades Negras del Norte de Esmeraldas) and argued that blacks had ancestral rights to the land. Other groups such as the Union of Black Organizations of North Esmeraldas (Union de Organizaciones Negras de Norte Esmeraldas—La UONNE) and the Afro-Ecuadorian Confederation of North Esmeraldas (Confederación Afroecuatoriana del Norte de Esmeraldas—La CANE) also demanded that black communities be given formal and official title to their historically occupied lands. These groups worked with the Chachis, an indigenous group facing removal, to demand the creation of the Gran Comarca (Great Black and Indian Territory) (Halpern and Twine 2000; Medina Vallejo and Castro Torres 2006, 41–50, 54–59).

Juan Garcia was one of the Esmeraldas leaders in the struggle for land rights and ethno-education. Although he refused to take official leadership positions, Garcia was often called upon to articulate the demands of the movement. He emphasized the sacred bonds between blacks and the land, tracing this connection to the blacks who escaped from slavery into the forest and established their *palenques*, or communities free from white control. From this perspective, blacks and Chachis had lived in harmony with the land and natural resources and had become the guardians of the territory (Pallares 1999; Sánchez 2002). In 2006, the national legislature passed the Law of Collective Rights of Afro-Ecuadorians (Ley de Derechos Colectivos del Pueblo Afroecuatoriano), giving blacks another constitutional mechanism to use to strengthen their rights to their ancestral lands (Antón Sánchez 2007, 237, 239).

For decades, Juan Garcia has listened to his Afro-Ecuadorian elders, collected their stories, and applied their wisdom to contemporary realities. He, perhaps more than any other person, is linked to the movement for Afro-Ecuadorian ethno-education. In the last ten years, he has donated his massive archive of materials to the Universidad Andina Simón Bolívar (UASB) in Quito. Under the direction of Garcia and cultural studies professor Catherine Walsh, UASB has created the Afro-Andean Documentary Fund as a way to preserve, catalog, and share Afro-Ecuadorian historical, cultural, and educational experiences. The books, documents, teaching guides, and other materials the fund has produced are creating the foundation for what they hope will be the eventual full inclusion of the black experience into all levels of Ecuadorian education (Sánchez 2002; Walsh with Garcia 2002).

Black Activists and the Comboni Missionaries

The Comboni Mission is an order of the Catholic Church named after Italian priest Daniel Comboni (1831–1881), who dedicated his life to missionary work in Central Africa. Since Comboni's death in Khartoum, Sudan, his followers have expanded their founder's mission to include working with African descendants in the diaspora and with the marginalized and excluded of all races and ethnic groups throughout the world. Comboni missionaries arrived in Ecuador in 1955 and have had a continuous presence since then. They have focused their work in the provinces with the largest black populations, Esmeraldas, Guayas, and Pichincha. Sociologist Carlos de la Torre argues that the Comboni missionaries have played a fundamental role in promoting black identity and black organization among Afro-Ecuadorians, especially in the national capital of Quito. He adds that through their various activities, institutions, and publications, they have shaped a generation of black leaders (de la Torre 2002, 111; Doneda 2000).

The most important institutions of the Comboni missionaries are the Afro-Ecuadorian Cultural Center (CCA) and the Afro-Ecuadorian Pastoral Department (Departamento de Pastoral Afroecuatoriana; DPA), founded in 1981 and 1983, respectively. The founding director of both institutions was Father Rafael Savoia, an Italian, who remained as formal leader until he left Ecuador in the late 1990s. Father Rafael was replaced as director of both institutions by Father Martín Balda, a priest from Spain, who remains in Ecuador. The other Comboni missionaries who worked most closely with black activists, especially in Quito, were Father Franco Nascimbene and Father Aldo, both priests from Italy. The work of the Comboni missionaries in reaching out to and supporting the Afro-Ecuadorian population cannot be denied. Black activism in the last three decades is clearly intertwined with the Comboni missionaries (de la Torre 2002, 111; Doneda 2000, 160–161; Alexandra Ocles interview; Catherine Chalá interview), but this activism cannot be reduced to the influence of the Comboni representatives.

For example, Father Rafael was inspired and influenced by black activist groups in Ecuador, Latin America, and around the globe to take the initiative to found the CCA. Under his leadership, the CCA has focused on document-ing the history of blacks in Ecuador and providing educational inspiration and opportunities to Afro-Ecuadorians. Father Rafael organized four congresses on black history that resulted in the following books: *El Negro en La Historia de Ecuador y del Sur de Colombia* (Blacks in the History of Ecuador and Southern Colombia; Savoia 1988), *El Negro en la Historia: Aportes para el Conocimiento de las Raíces en América Latina* (Blacks in History: Contributions to Understand-ing the Roots of Latin America; Savoia 1990), *El Negro en la Historia: Raíces Africanas en la Nacionalidad Ecuatoriana* (Blacks in History: African Roots of Ecuadorian Nationality; Savoia 1992), and *El Negro en la Historia del Ecuador: Esclavitud en las Regiones Andina y Amazónica* (Blacks in the History of Ecua-dor: Slavery in the Andean and Amazon Regions; Savoia and Gómezjurado 1999). These meetings were opportunities to bring together research on Afro-Ecuadorians and share this scholarship with black students and activists in par-ticular and the Ecuadorian public in general. CCA has an impressive library of books, audio and videotapes, and primary source materials on Afro-Ecuador-ians and blacks from around the world. CCA has also published a quarterly newsletter, *Palenque*, since 1982 with news and commentary on Afro-Ecuador-ians, Afro-Latin Americans, and blacks around the world. Father Rafael traveled widely throughout Ecuador and outside the country collecting much of the early material for the library and for *Palenque* (Alexandra Ocles interview; Catherine Chalá interview).

Father Rafael and the CCA's focus on education paralleled that of black activ-ists such as those in the CEA. All the black activists interviewed for this study reported that there was practically no discussion of Afro-Ecuadorians in their elementary, secondary, and university courses. At best, teachers mentioned that blacks had been enslaved. In contrast, the activists reported that they learned much more about indigenous history and culture in school. Indigenous resis-tance to oppression and the names and details of indigenous leaders such as Atahualpa and Rumiñahui were part of the educational curriculum. The formal invisibility of Afro-Ecuadorians in education is matched by the widespread neg-ative images of Afro-Ecuadorians in the mainstream media. In a content analysis of a leading national magazine, *Vistazo*, from 1957 to 1991, anthropologist Jean Rahier has shown that Afro-Ecuadorians are often presented in a stereotypical and racist way. Rahier believes that through these distorted and repulsive images, Afro-Ecuadorians are placed outside the country's narrative of itself as a white-mestizo nation (Rahier 1999; Rahier 1998).

One of the most powerful strategies of black groups and the CCA over the last thirty years was the development of a more positive, inclusive, and active Afro-Ecuadorian identity. In the 1980s, the Afro-Ecuadorian Consciousness Movement (MAEC), Sociedad Afroecuatoriana, Familia Negra, Angara Chimeo, and other groups worked in Quito and around the country to counter the poverty blacks lived in, the absence of the black experience in the classroom, and the negative images of blacks in the mass media. MAEC met every two weeks or whenever possible to raise black consciousness and promote constructive activity. In this sense, MAEC was both influenced by Father Rafael and the CCA and continued the work of the CEA. By meeting in their homes and neighborhoods, members of MAEC were able to listen to community grievances and complaints and dialogue about possible specific responses (Tadeo 1999; de la Torre 2002; Alexandra Ocles interviews).

During the 1980s, 1990s, and continuing after 2000, the CCA has served as a meeting place and resource for Afro-Ecuadorians. As noted earlier, some critics resented CCA as a white-controlled space. But others appreciated the opportunity to meet, study, and learn at the CCA. Over the years, the CCA has employed blacks who were talented, smart, and active. The staff in the 1980s included Pilar Morales, Ana Rosa Menedez, Patricio Flores, and Cecilia Sánchez. In the 1990s, Alexandra Ocles and Catherine Chalá joined the staff. Since 2000, Afro-Ecuadorians Ximena Chalá and Gabriela Viveros have worked there. Most of these staff members engaged in CCA and Afro-Ecuadorian Pastoral Department activities and were members of other black organizations (Alexandra Ocles interviews; Catherine Chalá interview; Balda interview; Gabriela Viveros interview; Ximena Chalá interview).

The CCA was more active in the 1980s and 1990s than it is currently. Since its inception, it has been located in a large house in a middle-class neighborhood two blocks from the busy commercial district of 12 de Octubre street. The CCA is walking distance from two important Catholic universities (Universidad Salesiana and Pontificia Universidad Catolica del Ecuador), convenient public transportation, and many restaurants and commercial establishments. Under Father Rafael's leadership the CCA had a larger budget and staff than it does now. The Comboni missionaries also had another house in Quito called Casa Palenque. This home was an important meeting place for black groups and a place where visiting missionaries could stay. The Casa Palenque was sold to raise funds for a new larger structure, Centro Juvenil Daniel Comboni, in the neighborhood of Carcelan in the northern part of Quito (Alexandra Ocles interview; Catherine Chalá interview; Balda interview).

The new center was created shortly before Father Rafael was called back to Italy. Most Comboni missionaries are rotated from one place to another after a few years. Father Rafael had spent over twenty-five years in Ecuador. His leaving created a crisis for the CCA and black activists because senior Comboni missionaries in Ecuador wanted to transfer the CCA to the new building. Father Rafael and the CCA staff were strongly opposed to this proposed move. They reasoned that since some missionaries did not share Father Rafael's goals and others were actively opposed to them, the move would likely result in a further decline and marginalization, if not the eventual elimination, of the CCA. Father Rafael delayed his departure from Ecuador to ensure that the move did not occur and that his replacement was someone who shared his commitment to education and to the organization. Father Rafael was happy when it was decided that the CCA would remain in its location and Father Martín had been selected to be the new director of the CCA and the Afro-Ecuadorian Pastoral Department (Alexandra Ocles interviews; Catherine Chalá interview; Balda interview).

During this period of crisis and transition in the late 1990s, the CCA was closed for over a year. Worried about what would happen to the CCA, the employees proposed that they be allowed to continue to run it. This proposal of black control was not given a response. Apparently, it was not an option (Alexandra Ocles interview; Catherine Chalá interview; Balda interview). This experience confirmed who owned the CCA: the Comboni missionaries. They were the only decision-makers regarding where the CCA would be located and who would direct it. The process also highlighted the dependence of some black activists on the Comboni missionaries and the inability of activists to raise sufficient funds to rent or purchase their own meeting space. This lack of money and material resources is an ongoing dilemma for black activists.

In the late 1980s and 1990s, Afro-Ecuadorians continued to organize at the local level, but there were also unprecedented attempts to build provincial and even national groups. Two national groups, the National Coordination of Black Groups of Ecuador (Coordinadora Nacional de Grupos Negros del Ecuador) and the Association of Black Organizations of Ecuador (Asociación de Organizaciones Negras del Ecuador; ASONE) were created during this period. The former was an attempt to develop a mechanism for black groups to communicate with each other, share information, and develop a national black presence. ASONE, which was founded in Esmeraldas, was a more militant group committed to protesting racism and racial discrimination and promoting joint economic development projects. ASONE had a strong political voice and many activists thought that it could become a major national voice for blacks and even evolve into a political party. However, the leadership of the organization was associated with Victor Leon and his son Victor Junior Leon, black activists and politicians in Esmeraldas. They became associated with the PRE and its most important leader, Abdalá Bucaram. Bucaram, a politician of Lebanese ancestry from Guayaquil, was popular among blacks along the coast. After becoming president in August 1996, Bucaram presided over a period of major economic and political crisis, and he was removed from office in February 1997. In supporting Bucaram and the PRE, ASONE's leaders exhibited poor decision making that led to a sharp decline in popularity and support outside their home province (Alexandre Ocles interviews; Alexandra Ocles lecture at Universidad San Francisco de Quito in 2003; Bolanos interview; Caicedo interview; Whitten and Quiroga 1995).

Black women formed their own new groups in the 1990s that put the issues of gender and sexism on the agenda of black civil society. In Esmeraldas, Guayaquil, and Quito, black women organized themselves to address the economic, health, and social problems that challenged black communities and families. In addition to poverty, employment, and racial discrimination, these women addressed the difficult problems of alcoholism, domestic violence, and sexual abuse. They demanded that local, provincial, and national governments develop public policies to reduce these problems and support activist groups searching for solutions. The Black Women's Movement of Quito (MOMUNE-YEMANYA) was created in 1997, and the Black Women's National Coordinating Committee was founded in 1999. Both groups were based in Quito and were led by Sonia Viveros, Vanthy Chalá, Catherine Chalá, Alexandra Ocles, Celeste Arboleda, and Maria Soledad. Just as black activists felt the need to begin organizing around their black and Afro-Ecuadorian identity in the late 1970s, black women activists embraced the same organizational imperative in the 1990s. They held an unprecedented national congress of black women in the Chota Valley in September 1999 and approved a formal organizational structure in Quito in February 2000. Black women have continued organizing and meeting regularly in Quito and around the country (Medina Vallejo and Castro Torres 2006, 68–71, 145–154; Coordinadora Nacional de Mujeres Negras 2000; Alexandra Ocles interview; Catherine Chalá interview).

Black women activists are committed to offering positive images of black women to Afro-Ecuadorian communities and Ecuadorian society and to countering negative ones. In this spirit, MOMUNE-YEMANYA produced the first African fashion show, "En Cuerpos de Ebano," in Quito on April 5, 2002. The event, at which black women and men modeled African clothes and presented aspects of Afro-Ecuadorian culture, was a great success. News of the show spread throughout Ecuador and black women's groups were soon inviting the show to their cities. This show was developed in part to challenge the negative image of black women as sexual objects. The first Afro-Ecuadorian Miss Ecuador, Monica Chalá, assisted MOMUNE-YEMANYA with the production (Sonia Viveros interview; Alexandra Ocles interview; Catherine Chalá interview; Vanthy Chalá interview; Celeste Arboleda interview; Maria Soledad interview; Natahly Salazar interview).

Despite the success of the fashion show and other activities, black women's groups suffered from problems that plagued other black groups. MOMUNE-YEMANYA was able to get only a small number of women (five to ten) to attend regular meetings. This placed a great burden on each woman to work harder to carry out their group's program or to do less than they hoped to do because of the small number of participating volunteers. In addition, there was a division of labor based on the education and diverse backgrounds of members. In 2003, some members were graduate students in the social sciences and some were women who had not completed high school and worked as maids and cooks in the homes of middle-class whites. This led to a situation in which the most highly educated members dealt with formal correspondence, presentations, and other activities that called for their skill set. They also had more opportunities to travel nationally and internationally, including to the United States. These two or three leaders were also single mothers working full-time jobs to support themselves and their families (Sonia Viveros interview; Alexandra Ocles interview; Catherine Chalá interview; Vanthy Chalá interview; Celeste Arboleda interview; Maria Soledad interview; Natahly Salazar interview). This situation placed a strain on the organization and reduced its effectiveness. The same leaders tended to be the public face of the organization, which created a heavy burden for them and resentment from other members.

Black Political Participation in Government

Given the socioeconomic difficulties and organizational challenges that Afro-Ecuadorians face, it is not surprising that there are very few blacks at the highest levels of politics and government. The most successful black politician in the postmilitary period was the lawyer Jaime Hurtado. In 1979, Hurtado was elected to Congress as the national representative of the leftist MPD. From 1979 to 1984, he served as the only elected MPD member in Congress. A dynamic and eloquent speaker, Hurtado was his party's presidential candidate in 1984 and 1988, receiving 161,810 votes (7.33 percent) and 152,970 votes (5.03 percent), respectively (Peñaherrera Solah 2002, 37, 54–59, 84–89). Because of his political commitment and leadership position, Hurtado traveled and campaigned throughout the country to present a revolutionary class analysis of Ecuador's problems and defend socialism as the fundamental solution. Despite the indigenous uprising of 1990, Hurtado consistently subordinated race and ethnicity to class in his discussion of the country's political situation. Hurtado sincerely believed that the fundamental social and political division in the country was between the dominant and popular classes, between the oppressors and the oppressed (Frank, Patino, and Rodriguez 1992, 71, 81–82). For this reason, he did not prioritize organizing black or indigenous groups. Some Afro-Ecuadorians viewed Hurtado as an outstanding black leader and role model given his black identity, strong educational background, and long struggle for radical social change (Congo interview). Others argued that he never presented himself as a black leader. They emphasized that he did not speak to blacks about race-specific issues and did not use his extraordinary skills to denounce racism, organize blacks, and build strong black institutions. He focused his discourse and work on all poor people, the exploited classes, and the masses (Bolanos interview). Tragically, Hurtado and an aide were assassinated on February 17, 1999, in Quito. Several black activists have stated that during the last year of his life, Hurtado was becoming increasingly interested in working with black movement groups (Alexandra Ocles interview; Catherine Chalá interview).

Other black members of Congress were much less prominent than Jaime Hurtado. In 1998, Victor Junior Leon was elected from the PRE as provincial deputy from Esmeraldas. Junior Leon was unable to complete his term because he was arrested and imprisoned for killing a man, Eduardo Reina Jimenez, in a bar fight in Quito (*El Comercio* 2001). Junior Leon had been a member of CEA and ASONE in the 1980s and 1990s. The majority of interviewees felt that despite great potential, he had become an embarrassing figure. Junior Leon argued self-defense and blamed racism for his plight.

From 2003 to 2007, Rafael Erazo, another black lawyer from the MPD, served in Congress. Erazo was also a provincial deputy from Esmeraldas. He supported his party's emphasis on class, revolution, and socialism but was open to learning more about what black activists were doing and how he could assist them. In this spirit, he hired activist Alexandra Ocles as a consultant and they worked on a piece of legislation titled "Collective Rights of Black Peoples" (Derechos Colectivos de los Pueblos Negros). As the only black representative in Congress and a member of a small political party, Erazo had great difficulty getting his colleagues to address his legislative concerns (Erazo interview). Alexandra Ocles herself served in Congress (National Assembly) from 2007 to 2009 as a supporter of President Rafael Correa. She worked in the Correa administration as minister of the Secretariat of Peoples, Social Movements, and Citizen Participation (Secretaría de Pueblos, Movimientos Sociales y Participación Ciudadana) from January 2010 to January 2011. In that capacity, she led the government's efforts to eliminate racial discrimination and ethnic exclusion in Ecuador.

In 2001, the municipality of Quito, under Mayor Paco Moncayo, created the Metropolitan Development Unit of the Afro-Quiteño People (Unidad Metropolitana de Desarrollo del Pueblo Afroquiteño). Led by black attorney and activist Juan Carlos Ocles, this government initiative was a response to the demands of activists for participation in government. Attorney Ocles was the former president of the Federation of Black Organizations and Groups of Pichincha (Federacion de Organizaciones y Grupos Negros de Pichincha; FOG-NEP). Ocles and FOGNEP worked to build unity among more than twenty local black political and cultural groups. In his government position, Ocles was charged with getting the municipal government to respond to the demands and address the needs of the local black population. Underfunded and understaffed, this unit began and continues in a difficult situation (Juan Carlos Ocles interview; Vasquez S. 2002; Torres 2002; Medina Vallejo and Castro Torres 2006, 138–144, 184–185).

Conclusion

The activities of black leaders and organizations discussed in this chapter are a small part of the largely unwritten history of Afro-Ecuadorian politics. Since 1979, blacks have created their own organizations and participated in diverse political coalitions to challenge elite and oligarchic rule. Many black groups share characteristics of Ecuadorian politics in general such as regionalism, personalism, and instability. These groups often have a similar life cycle: great interest, participation, and enthusiasm in the beginning followed by a dramatic decline in involvement. Many activists point to organizations such as MAEC and ASONE that were at one time vibrant but later basically existed as paper organizations. These types of organizations rarely had abrupt endings. They simply faded away to be overshadowed by new organizations.

Organizing blacks in a country where informal racism is widespread and blacks are not fully recognized members of the nation remains a challenge. Maria de los Angeles, a young activist in Quito, described the responses of black youth she meets in the poorest communities and housing complexes in Quito. First, the youth did not share her enthusiasm for organizing, mobilizing, and encouraging black students to take advantage of real and potential educational and job opportunities. Second, young people told her that it was a waste of time, that things would not change, and that racism would always be there. CCA staffer Gabriela Viveros argued that some blacks are still brainwashed to reject their blackness and thereby avoid recognizing and fighting against the brutal daily reality of racial discrimination (Maria de los Angeles interview; Gabriela Viveros interview).

Some middle-class black professionals avoid political involvement and activism because they are burdened with economic survival, work, family life, and are often supporting members of their extended family. Other black professionals do a cost-benefit analysis and choose to avoid the burdens of confronting racism. That was the case with Afro-Ecuadorian government economist Jose Caicedo. In 2003, Caicedo was in a government car going to an appointment when he was stopped by the police, beaten, and imprisoned for five days. His crime: being black in a nice car. The police officer made racist comments to him and refused to accept his explanation that he was in the car because he was a government official on government business. Despite the clear violation of his rights, Caicedo decided not to pursue charges against the law enforcement official because of the extended time, financial resources, and uncertain outcome of such a case given the widespread racial discrimination against blacks in the country (Jose Caicedo interview; Robinson 2002; Medina Vallejo and Castro Torres 2006, 179).

One of the most interesting developments for Afro-Ecuadorians in the last decade relates to the prominence and recognition of black soccer players on the national team. Players such as Augustin Delgado, Ulises de la Cruz, and Iván Hurtado led Ecuador to the 2002 and 2006 World Cups and became national heroes. They have also become wealthy through playing for top national and international teams. Many of these players come from extremely poor backgrounds in the Chota Valley and Esmeraldas. Some black activists were hopeful that these newly wealthy Afro-Ecuadorians would use some of their resources to help their home communities and support the causes of black groups. The results so far have been less than inspiring. Several players have created foundations in their home communities, but the new schools, recreation centers, and investments have been slow in coming. More critically, most of these players are surrounded by white advisors and do not seem to be committed to changing the situation facing Afro-Ecuadorians (Ximena Chalá interview).

Despite the challenges of organizing in Ecuador, black activists continue to denounce widespread poverty, inequality, and political underrepresentation. They have marched against and continue to condemn racist police brutality, violence, and murder. In this way, they join other Afro-Latin Americans in fighting for national citizenship rights and human rights. They acknowledge that racism in Latin America (especially notions of racial democracy, racial harmony, and miscegenation) have made the struggle for black political autonomy and advancement extremely difficult. Blacks in Ecuador and other Latin American countries continue to pursue their struggle in two ways. On one hand, they emphasize that their group heritage, identity, community, and organization are vital to their cultural affirmation and political advancement. On the other hand, they recognize that they must work with other forces such as political parties, the church, indigenous groups, government agencies, and nongovernmental organizations to achieve group progress and the broader national goals of a more prosperous, egalitarian, democratic, and inclusive Ecuador.

Acknowledgments

Scholars Lori Robinson, Kelli Morgan, and Mary C. Vergowven provided important research assistance. For constructive critical comments on this chapter, I thank Stanley Bailey, Todd Burroughs, Kwame Dixon, Rosalind Fielder, Pamela Martin, and Lori Robinson. My colleagues at USFQ, especially Alvaro Alemán, Fernando Bustamante, Claudio Creamer, José Julio Cisneros, Diego Quiroga, Cornell and Mona Menking, improved my understanding of Ecuadorian society and politics.

Notes

1. In this chapter, the term "blacks" will refer to the census categories of black and mulatto. "Blacks," "Afro-Ecuadorians," and "Afro-descendants" will be used interchangeably.

2. Magazine articles that discuss the Afro-Ecuadorian experience and racism include Larrea and Trujillo (2001), *Vistazo* (2001), and Pallares (1999).

3. Black and indigenous leaders believe that their groups were undercounted in the 2001 census.

Bibliography

Andrews, George Reid. 2004. *Afro-Latin America, 1800–2000*. New York: Oxford University Press.

Antón Sánchez, Jhon. 2007. "Afrodescendientes: Sociedad civil y movilización social en el Ecuador." *Journal of Latin American and Caribbean Anthropology* 12 (1): 233–245.

———. 2009. "El proceso Organizativo Afroecuatoriano: 1979–2009." PhD diss., Facultad Latinoamericana de Ciencias Sociales (FLACSO-Ecuador), Quito, Ecuador.

Cervone, Emma, and Fredy Rivera, eds. 1999. *Ecuador racista: Imágenes e identidades*. Quito: FLACSO, Sede Ecuador.

Conaghan, Catherine M. 1995. "Politicians against Parties: Discord and Disconnection in Ecuador's Party System." In *Building Democratic Institutions: Party Systems in Latin America*, ed. Scott Mainwaring and Timothy R. Scully. Stanford, Calif.: Stanford University Press.

Coordinadora Nacional de Mujeres Negras. 2000. *Agenda política de Mujeres Negras del Ecuador*. Quito: UNIFEM, Coordinadora Politica de Mujeres Ecuatorianas, CONAMU.

De Ferranti, David, Guillermo E. Perry, Francisco H. G. Ferreira, and Michael Walton. 2004. *Inequality in Latin America: Breaking with History?* Washington, D.C.: World Bank.

De la Torre, Carlos. 2002. *Afroquiteños: Ciudanía y racismo*. Quito: Centro Andino de Acción Popular—CAAP.

De la Torre Espinosa, Carlos. 1997. *La seducción Velasquista*. Quito: Ediciones Libri Mundi, Enrique Grosse-Luemern, FLACSO, Sede Ecuador.

Dixon, David L. 1997. "Race, Class and National Identity in Black Ecuador: Afro-Ecuadorians and the Struggle for Human Rights." PhD diss., Clark Atlanta University, Atlanta, Georgia.

Doneda, P. A. 2000. *Los Primeros 45 años de los Misioneros Combonianos en Ecuador y Colombia*. Quito: Editorial Sin Fronteras.

El Comercio. 2001. "J. León fue condenado a seis años." September 26.

Fernandez-Rasines, Paloma. 2001. *Afrodescendencia en el Ecuador: Raza y genero desde los tiempos de la Colonia*. Quito: Ediciones Abya-Yala.

Frank, Erwin, Ninfa Patino, and Marta Rodriguez, eds. 2002. *Los politicos y los indigenas: Diez entrevistas a candidatos presidenciales y máximos representantes de partidos políticos del Ecuador sobre la cuestión indígena*. Quito: Ediciones Abya-Yala.

Freidenberg, Flavia, and Manuel Alcántara Sáez. 2001. *Los duenos del poder: Los partidos políticos en Ecuador (1978–2000)*. Quito: FLACSO, Sede Ecuador.

Garcia, Juan. 1988. *Cuentos y decimas Afro-Esmeraldeñas*. Quito: Ediciones Abya-Yala.

Halpern, Adam, and France Winddance Twine. 2000. "Antiracist Activism in Ecuador: Black-Indian Community Alliances." *Race & Class* 42 (2): 19–31.

Jiménez, Agustín Grijalva. 1998. *Elecciones y representación política*. Quito: Corporacion Editora Nacional.

Johnson, Ollie A., III. 2007. "Black Politics in Latin America: An Analysis of National and Transnational Politics." In *African American Perspectives on Political Science*, ed. Wilber Rich. Philadelphia, Pa.: Temple University Press.

Larrea, Silvana, and Ernesto Trujillo. 2001. "¿Es usted racista? El Ecuador es un país multirracial, con graves problemas de intolerancia." *Diners* 21 (235): 18–27.

Medina Vallejo, Henry, and Mary Castro Torres. 2006. *Afroecuatorianos: Un movimiento social emergente*. Quito: Ediciones Afroamerica, Centro Cultural Afroecuatoriano.

Mejía Acosta, Andrés. 2002. *Gobernabilidad democrática: Sistema electoral, partidos políticos y pugna de poderes en Ecuador*. Quito: Fundacion Konrad Adenauer.

Minda Batallas, Pablo Aníbal. 2002. *Identidad y conflicto: La lucha por la tierra en la zona norte de la provinica de Esmeraldas*. Quito: Ediciones Abya-Yala.

Pabón Chalá, Ivón. 2007. *Identidad Afro: Procesos de construction en las comunidades negras de la Cuenca Chota-Mira*. Quito: Ediciones Abya Yala.

Pallares, Martin. 1999. "Negros: Odisea y Lucha de Una Raza." *La Revista*, November 14, 11–13.

Peñaherrera Solah, Blasco. 2002. *Trazos de democracia: 22 años de elecciones—1978–2000*. Quito.

Ponce, Juan. 2006. *Los Afroecuatorianos*. Washington, D.C.: International Bank for Reconstruction and Development/World Bank.

Rahier, Jean. 1999. "Mami, ¿que será lo que quiere el negro?: representaciones racistas en la revista Vistazo, 1957–1991." In *Ecuador racista: Imágenes e identidades*, eds. Emma Cervone and Fredy Fivera, 73–109. Quito: FLACSO, Sede Ecuador.

Rahier, Jean Muteba. 1998. "Blackness, the Racial/Spatial Order, Migrations, and Miss Ecuador 1995–96." *American Anthropologist* 100 (2): 421–430.

———. 2008. "Race, *Fútbol*, and the Ecuadorian Nation: Ideological Biology of (Non-)Citizenship." *E-misférica* 5 (2): *Race and Its Others*. Available at http://www.hemisphericinstitute. org/eng/publications/emisferica/5.2/en52_rahier.html.

Robinson, Lori S. 2002. "A New Day for Blacks in Ecuador." *The New Crisis* November/December: 32–35.

Roitman, Karem. 2009. *Race, Ethnicity, and Power in Ecuador: The Manipulation of Mestizaje.* Boulder, Colo.: First Forum Press.

Sánchez, Francisco. 2008. *Democracia no lograda o democracia malograda? Un análise del sistema político del Ecuador: 1979–2002.* Quito: FLACSO, Sede Ecuador.

Sánchez, Ninfa Patiño. 2002. "El proceso de comunidades negras del Ecuador desde el testimonio de Juan Garcia." Master's thesis, Universidad Andina Simon Bolivar, Quito, Ecuador.

Savoia, P. Rafael, ed. 1988. *Actas del primer congreso de Historia del Negro en el Ecuador y Sur de Colombia.* Quito: Centro Cultural Afro-Ecuatoriano.

———. 1990. *El negro en la historia: Aportes para el conocimiento de las raíces en America Latina.* Quito: Centro Cultural Afro-Ecuatoriano.

———. 1992. *El negro en la historia: Raíces africanas en la nacionalidad Ecuatoriana.* Quito: Centro Cultural Afro-Ecuatoriano.

Savoia, P. Rafael, and Javier Gómezjurado, eds. 1999. *El negro en la historia del Ecuador: Esclavitud en las regiones Andina y Amazónica.* Quito: Centro Cultural Afro-Ecuatoriano.

Secretaría Técnica del Frente Social. 2004. *Los Afroecuatorianos en Cifras: Desigualdad, discriminacion y exclusion segun las estadisticas sociales del Ecuador.* Quito: Secretaria Tecnica del Frente Social, Sistema Integrado de Indicadores Sociales del Ecuador, Republica del Ecuador.

Selverston-Scher, Melina. 2001. *Ethnopolitics in Ecuador: Indigenous Rights and the Strengthening of Democracy.* Coral Gables, Fla.: North-South Center Press, University of Miami.

Stutzman, Ronald. 1981. "El Mestizaje: An All-Inclusive Ideology of Exclusion." In *Cultural Transformations and Ethnicity in Modern Ecuador,* ed. Norman E. Whitten Jr. Urbana: University of Illinois Press.

Tadeo, Renan. 1999. "Movimiento negro en Quito." In *El negro en la historia del Ecuador: Esclavitud en las Regiones Andina y Amazonica,* ed. P. Rafael Savoia and Javier Gomezjurado, 67–76. Quito: Centro Cultural Afroecuatoriano, Conferencia Episcopal Ecuatoriana.

Torres, Victor Hugo, ed. 2002. *La participación en Quito: Miradas plurales.* Quito: Ediciones Abya Yala.

Van Cott, Donna Lee. 2005. *From Movements to Parties in Latin America: The Evolution of Ethnic Politics.* New York: Cambridge University Press.

Vazquez S., Lola. 2002. "La Participación desde la diversidad: presencia de los pueblos indígena y negro en Quito." In *La participación en Quito: Miradas plurales,* ed. Victor Hugo Torres, 85–118. Quito: Ediciones Abya Yala.

Vistazo. 2001. "Orgullo Negro." September 13, 54–65.

Walsh, Catherine, with Juan Garcia. 2002. "El pensar del emergente movimiento afroecuatoriano: Reflexiones (des)de un proceso." In *Praticas intelectuales en cultura y poder,* ed. Daniel Mato, 1–15. Buenos Aires: CLASCO.

Whitten, Norman E., Jr. (1974) 1986. *Black Frontiersmen: Afro-Hispanic Culture of Ecuador and Colombia.* Prospect Heights, Ill.: Waveland Press.

Whitten, Norman E., Jr., and Diego Quiroga. 1998. "'To Rescue National Dignity': Blackness as a Quality of Nationalist Creativity in Ecuador." In *Blackness in Latin America and the Caribbean: Social Dynamics and Cultural Transformations,* vol. 1, *Central America and Northern and Western South America,* ed. Norman E. Whitten Jr. and Arlene Torres, 75–99. Bloomington: Indiana University Press.

Whitten, Norman E., Jr., and Diego Quiroga with the assistance of P. Rafael Savoia. 1995. "Ecuador." In *No Longer Invisible: Afro-Latin Americans Today,* ed. Minority Rights Group, 287–317. London: Minority Rights Publications.

World Bank. 1996. *Ecuador Poverty Report*. Washington, D.C.: The International Bank for Reconstruction and Development/The World Bank.

Yashar, Deborah J. 2005. *Contesting Citizenship in Latin America: The Rise of Indigenous Movements and the Postliberal Challenge*. New York: Cambridge University Press.

Interviews conducted by Ollie Johnson

Name	Location	Date	Organization
Saloman Acosta	Ibarra	July 20, 2003	Federacion de Comunidades y Organizaciones Negras de Imbabura y Carchi (FECONIC)
Maria de los Angeles	Quito	July 16, 2003	Palenque Yowa
Celeste Arboleda	Quito	June 28, 2003	Black Women
Father Martín Balda	Quito	June 5, 2003	CCA director
Luzmilla Bolanos	Quito	July 16, 2003	Cultural worker
Jose Caicedo	Quito	July 17, 2003	Government economist
Juan Carlos	Ibarra	July 18, 2003	Guayas activist
Catherine Chalá	Quito	May 28, 2003	DPA staff
Vanthy Chalá	Quito	May 21, 2003	Black Women
Ximena Chalá	Quito	May 23, 2003	CCA staff
Patricio Congo	Quito	May 20, 2003	Sports coach
Rafael Erazo	Brasília, Brazil	November 23, 2003	MPD
Oswaldo Espinoza	Ibarra	July 19, 2003	Chota leader
Alexandra Ocles	Quito	June 3 and July 23, 2003	DPA staff
Juan Carlos Ocles	Quito	July 29, 2003	FOGNEP
Jacqueline Pavon	Quito	June 16, 2003	Fundo Afro
Natahly Salazar	Quito	July 27, 2003	Student
Maria Soledad	Quito	July 27, 2003	Black Dance
Gabriela Viveros	Quito	May 19, 2003	CCA staff
Sonia Viveros	Quito	May 20, 2003	Azucar Foundation

9

Afro-Ecuadorian Community Organizing and Political Struggle

Influences on and Participation in Constitutional Processes

JEAN MUTEBA RAHIER

Over the last two decades, following the adoption of "multicultural" policies targeting indigenous and African diasporic populations by institutions of international development and global governance such as the United Nations and the World Health Organization (Hale 2002, 2004, 2005, 2006) and as a result of the political activism of indigenous and African diasporic communities, many Latin American nation-states revised their constitutions and passed special laws that express a concern about greater inclusion of African diasporic and indigenous populations. In this context what Charles Hale (2004) has called *el indio permitido* (the "permitted Indian") emerged and Latin American African diasporic populations gained relatively greater agency compared to the exclusion (Rahier 1998, 1999) they suffered during the era of "monocultural mestizaje" (Silva 1995; Polo 2002; Espinosa Apolo 2003; Ibarra Dávila 2002; Rahier 2003a). In Ecuador, that era lasted from the early twentieth century until the indigenous uprisings of the early 1990s (Whitten, Whitten, and Chango 2003; Clark and Becker 2007), culminating in the adoption of a multicultural Constitution in 1998 by a National Constituent Assembly.

In this chapter, I analyze two major moments in recent Ecuadorian history. First I examine the process that led to the first Ecuadorian Constitution to adopt multiculturalism, which gave collective rights to indigenous peoples and (in a less obvious way) to Afro-Ecuadorians. I then discuss the process by which the second multicultural Constitution was adopted in 2008, with a special focus on the role of Afro-Ecuadorian activists.

According to Ecuador's 2001 census, 2.2 percent of the population self-identified as *negros* (Afroecuatorianos), 4.9 percent self-identified as either *negros* or *mulatos*, and 7 percent identified as *indígenas*, out of a national population of 12,156,608. The overwhelming majority of the national population (77.4 percent) self-identified or were counted by census takers as mestizos. It is clear that the number of indigenous peoples and Afro-Ecuadorians were underreported

(Izquierdo 2007); it is well known that the Ecuadorian state—which is controlled by various sectors of the white and white-mestizo national elite—tends to underreport the size of both indigenous and black populations. This tendency has continued despite the "multicultural turn" officially celebrated with the passing of the 1998 Constitution.

Ecuador's two "traditional" Afro-Ecuadorian communities (see Figure 9.1) emerged during the colonial period as the result of the importation of slaves. One community is located in the coastal province of Esmeraldas (West 1952, 1957), and the other is found in the Andean Chota-Mira Valley, located in the highlands (Coronel 1987a, 1987b, 1988). A small *zambo* (black-indigenous) community also formed in Esmeraldas Province in the sixteenth century by escaped slaves (Rueda Novoa 2001; Lane 2002). Over the past three decades, Afro-Ecuadorians have migrated from Esmeraldas and the Chota-Mira Valley to Quito, Guayaquil, and the Amazonian region. This movement of Afro-Ecuadorians has changed the urban landscape, and now the city of Guayaquil is said to have the biggest Afro-Ecuadorian concentration in the country (Figure 9.1).

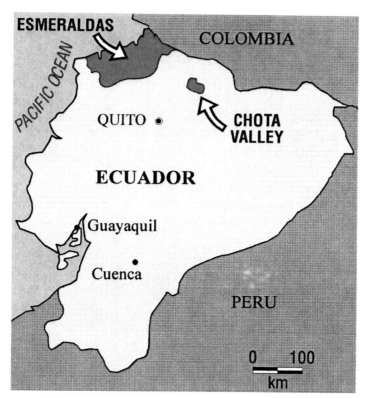

Figure 9.1. Map of Ecuador's traditional Afro-Ecuadorian communities, Esmeraldas and Chota Valley. Map by Jean Muteba Rahier.

The 1998 Constitution: *Una Constitución de la Derecha?*

There is considerable irony in the fact that the first Ecuadorian Constitution with a multiculturalist orientation was adopted by a Constituent Assembly that was mainly comprised of political parties from the right. On February 6, 1997, the president of Ecuador, Abdalá Bucaram Ortiz, was declared unfit to serve because of "mental incapacity" by the Ecuadorian Congress less than six months after he had assumed the presidency (Báez et al. 1997; Córdova del Alcázar 2003). This decision followed massive protests against Bucaram's neoliberal economic policies, which led to an increase in the price of domestic gas by 245 percent, of electricity by 300 percent, of public transportation by 60 percent, and of telephone service by 1,000 percent (de la Torre n.d., 13). The protests were staged by indigenous, Afro-Ecuadorian, women's, student, and other grassroots movements and organizations. Student rallies began on January 10th, and by February 2nd the indigenous movement had blocked all roads in the countryside, paralyzing the economy. The Frente Patriótico, the Frente Popular, and the Coordinadora de Movimientos Sociales called for a general strike on February 5, 1997, demanding the resignation of Bucaram and the end of his neoliberal policies.

With the fall of Bucaram, which many saw as a victory for grassroots social movements, and his replacement by Fabián Alarcón—then the president of the National Congress—the focus turned to constitutional reforms that the political left hoped would redefine the nation's social contract by articulating a vision of "communal life for the entire society. A project that we all feel as ours, and from which we could derive our rights and our obligations, and which we could only reach if we actively participate in its elaboration process" (Acosta quoted in de la Torre n.d., 14).[1]

The seventy members of the Constituent Assembly were elected following a relatively short electoral campaign, in which the political parties that came out on top were those that attracted votes through clientelism and the support of local political bosses (*caciques*). The Social Christians won 30 percent of the seats, the Christian Democrats (Democracia Popular) won 17 percent, Pachakutik (a political party close to the Confederación de Nacionalidades Indígenas del Ecuador, CONAIE) won 10 percent, and the Populist Partido Roldosista Ecuatoriano (PRE), the party of the outgoing president, won 10 percent. What is quite remarkable is that the demands of the social movements, and particularly those from the indigenous and Afro-Ecuadorian movements, were adopted by *asambleistas* (members of the assembly) who belonged to the political right and to populist parties, with the exception of Pachakutik. This led to the adoption of a Constitution that has been seen by many as politically ambivalent. For some social scientists, the new Constitution was progressive because of its inclusion of collective rights. But numerous observers were concerned that along with this inclusion came a neoliberal agenda. Nina Pacari, an indigenous *asambleista* for Pachakutik, indicated, for example, "that if this Constitution was very advanced because it recognizes the collective rights of indigenous people, women and Afro-descendants, it was otherwise missing a great deal if we consider the proposals from sectors on the left for political and economic reforms, areas for which the political parties of the right imposed their agendas. . . . Many on the left and in indigenous organizations have read that Constitution as neoliberal"(de la Torre n.d., 16–17).

A critical reading of the Constitution reveals that the project of multiculturalism reinforces the difference between Afro-Ecuadorian and indigenous peoples and that these groups are not treated equally (Hooker 2005; Rahier 2008a, 2008b). Chapter Five, Article 83 of the Constitution, on Collective Rights, reads: "The indigenous peoples, who self-identify as nationalities of ancestral roots, and the black or Afro-Ecuadorian peoples, are part of the Ecuadorian state, unique and indivisible" (República de Ecuador, 1998). Some have praised this article because it is the first time that the state officially recognized the existence of indigenous and Afro-Ecuadorian peoples instead of proclaiming the national population to be exclusively composed of mestizos (Walsh and García Salazar 2002, 5; Antón Sánchez n.d., 5–6). However, it is immediately followed by Article 84, which reads: "The State will recognize and guarantee to indigenous peoples, in conformity with this Constitution and the law, the respect of public order and of human rights, the following collective rights." The article then lists fifteen collective rights, among which are the right to keep communal land; to use, administer, and conserve the natural resources found on their land; to keep and to promote traditional land use practices that foster biodiversity, and so forth. While this is all quite progressive, it is noteworthy that there is no mention of Afro-Ecuadorians in this article. Article 85 seeks to qualify this absence as follows: "The State will recognize and guarantee to black or Afro-Ecuadorian peoples the rights listed in the previous article, every time that they are applicable [to their specific situation(s)]." The fact that the collective rights of blacks or Afro-Ecuadorians were not dealt with in Article 84 in the same breath as those of indigenous peoples reflects the belief of most Ecuadorian whites, white-mestizos, and indigenous peoples that blacks do not fit the notion of indigeneity that informs Latin American multiculturalist thought. Shane Greene argues that most black communities are not recognized as "peoples," or *pueblos*, because their situations do not fit the "holy trinity of multicultural peoplehood." Instead, they are looked at as having been historically more incorporated—unlike indigenous peoples—within the national polity:

Often implied in state campaigns of Afro-Indigenous recognition is what
I have come to think of as the "holy trinity" of multicultural "peoplehood."
Culture + language + territory = *un pueblo*. To have "legitimate" claims
to all three is, it seems, necessary to be considered a recognizable, even
if not fully recognized, collective. . . . To be perceived as missing one or
more of these key ingredients . . . is to be considered already absorbed by
another, fully recognized collective: the formally sovereign polity of the
nation-state itself. (Greene 2007b, 345)

Afro-Ecuadorian Community Organizing and Political Struggle

Afro-Ecuadorian community organizing has been very different from comparable indigenous processes. Indigenous peoples' political activism at the national
level followed the 1964 agrarian reform, when they began demanding a more
just distribution of cultivable land and developed an ethnocultural political discourse linking them, as "authentic owners" of the land, to what they argued were
their *territorios ancestrales* (ancestral territories). Demands for landownership
progressively served as a catalyst, bringing together the different indigenous ethnic groups from the three regions of the country: the coast, the Andes (Sierra),
and the Amazonian forest (Oriente). In 1986, indigenous regional organizations
founded a national confederation (Confederación de Nacionalidades Indígenas
del Ecuador, CONAIE) that sought to become an interlocutor with the national government and to represent and defend indigenous interests nationally.
In the early 1990s, the indigenous movement led a series of national uprisings
that were followed by others through the 1990s and early 2000s. CONAIE established international linkages and received support from international actors.
The preparation of the celebrations for the 500th anniversary of the "Discovery
of the Americas" provided a boost to CONAIE, which proposed instead to celebrate "500 years of resistance." European guilt toward Latin American indigenous peoples explains why millions of dollars were channeled to their organizations either directly from the coffers of European national governments or
from the budgets of multilateral institutions such as UNESCO and other UN
agencies. But international actors and donors did not look at African diasporic
organizations in the same way as they looked at indigenous organizations, and
those organizations did not benefit from European guilt to the same extent that
indigenous organizations did, at least at the beginning of the 1990s.

Organizing for land did not play the same role for Afro-Ecuadorians as it
did for indigenous activists. While the agrarian reform of 1964 had an impact
on the political action of Afro-Ecuadorians in the Chota-Mira Valley (the lands
of many haciendas were distributed among cooperatives of small Afro-Choteño

farmers [Agencia Latinoamericana de Información n.d.; Medina Vallejo 1996]), the reform had little impact on the daily realities of Afro-Ecuadorians living in the forested sector of Esmeraldas or among urban Afro-Ecuadorians living in Esmeraldas, Ibarra, Quito, or Guayaquil. Additionally, unlike indigenous peoples, Afro-Ecuadorians received little benefit from the opening up of white-mestizo society in Ecuador (de la Torre 1996; Cervone and Rivera 1999). As I have discussed elsewhere, Afro-Ecuadorians have not been part of official *mestizaje*, or what I call "the ideological biology of national identity," the ideology of racial mixture that blends European and indigenous ancestries and proclaims the mestizo to be the prototypical Ecuadorian identity (Rahier 2008a, 2008b). As a result, Afro-Ecuadorian claims to ancestral landownership have not been received by Ecuadorian white-mestizo elites in the same way as indigenous claims for land have been. The historical trajectory of Afro-Ecuadorians—as imagined by white-mestizos and indigenous people—has been narrated by officials as being rather similar to Europeans' as they also came from elsewhere, continental Africa, and are not seen as "indigenous to the land." This point is at the heart of the difference between indigenous peoples and Afro-Ecuadorians that informs the 1998 Constitution.

In the remainder of this section, I wish to complicate the conventional claim that Afro-Ecuadorian activism had its origins in the work of Catholic missionaries (de la Torre n.d., 8, see also 2006a and 2002, 105–134). I lived in Ecuador from June 1985 through May 1991 and was close to what was then called the Grupo Afroecuatoriano led by Juan García Salazar. In 1997, I recorded an extensive interview about the process of Afro-Ecuadorian organizing with Oscar Chalá.[2]

For many Afro-Ecuadorian political activists who are in their forties or fifties today, the first attempt to organize nationally dates to August 1977, when an Afro-Ecuadorian delegation went to Cali, Colombia, to participate in the Primer Congreso de la Cultura Negra de las Américas (First Congress for the Black Culture of the Americas), organized by the Fundación Colombiana de Investigaciones Folclóricas (FCIF), the Asociación Cultural de la Juventud Negra Peruana, and the Centro de Estudios Afro-Colombianos.[3] Delegations from Brazil, Colombia, Ecuador, the United States, Honduras, Nigeria, Panama, Peru, and Venezuela participated. At the first session of the congress, Afro-Colombian writer Manuel Zapata Olivella was elected president and Afro-Panamanian Roy Simón Bryce-Laporte was elected secretary. The Ecuadorian delegation was composed of four people: Justino Cornejo, Salomón Chalá, Oscar Chalá, and Esmeraldian writer Nelson Estupiñán Bass (Fundación Colombiana de Investigaciones Folclóricas 1988, 14). The congress focused on collecting data about the social realities and cultural traditions of the African diaspora of the

Americas. The idea was that the results of this research would help consolidate political action based on ethnoracial identity and would suggest specific policies that would defend the cultural traditions and improve the socioeconomic conditions of members of the African diaspora (ibid., 3).

Upon their return home, members of the Afro-Ecuadorian delegation met with Afro-Ecuadorians who were students in postsecondary education in Esmeraldas, Ibarra, Quito, and Guayaquil. They decided to create the Centro de Estudios Afro-Ecuatorianos, members of which collected oral histories with elders in both the Chota-Mira Valley and Esmeraldas Province on the topic of oral traditions. At some point, some of the members of the Centro de Estudios began to disagree with what they increasingly saw as the "romantic orientation" of the *centro*, which focused exclusively on cultural traditions without paying attention to the politics related to efforts to obtain a greater share of local, regional, and national resources. The group split at the beginning of the 1980s, an event that brought an end to the Centro de Estudios. Some, led by Juan García, were satisfied with the cultural traditions approach, while those who wanted to pay greater attention to political issues, such as Oscar Chalá, became active in leftist parties. Juan García obtained funding from the Inter-American Foundation to continue collecting oral histories about Afro-Ecuadorian traditions. He created the Grupo Afroecuatoriano with those who agreed to continue to do fieldwork to record interviews of elders in the Chota-Mira Valley and in Esmeraldas Province. Those who did this work filled hundreds of audio cassettes.[4] They published excerpts of their recordings—mostly *cuentos* ("tales") and oral poetry—in the *Cuadernos Afroecuatorianos* (Afro-Ecuadorian Notebooks; see García Salazar 2002). Part of the disagreement between advocates of the two approaches was that the recipient of the Inter-American Foundation grant was not the Centro de Estudios but Juan García himself, which put him in a privileged position vis-à-vis the other members of the Centro.

Oscar Chalá provides a good illustration of what has happened to those who became active in political parties of the left in the 1980s and thereafter. At the end of the 1990s, Chalá was very close to Pachakutik, which has been operating as the arm of the CONAIE on the national political scene. During the deliberations of the 1998 National Constituent Assembly, he was in fact the *diputado alterno* (alternate representative) to the *asambleísta* for Pachakutik Nina Pacari. In this position, he actively relayed Afro-Ecuadorian demands during debates.

In the 1980s, Afro-Ecuadorian activists were mostly divided and dispersed, and they generated only one major project which combined with the actions of the Catholic Church through the Combonianos Order. Comboniano Catholic leaders developed a *pastoral afro* for Ecuador and created the Centro Cultural Afroecuatoriano. It attracted some nuns and priests to religious and missionary service and helped others who were already active in urban and rural areas in the Chota-Mira Valley and Esmeraldas Province. The Italian priest Padre Rafael Savoia, who led the founding of the Centro Cultural, was proud to help form a group of Afro-Ecuadorian priests. The Centro Cultural has supported small projects in black communities aimed at increasing the quality of life. While radical Afro-Ecuadorian activists complain about the Combonianos' paternalism, no one can deny that they have played an important role in cultivating black identities in Quito, the Chota-Mira Valley, and Esmeraldas Province (see de la Torre 2002, 111–134).

In the 1990s, events that took place in Colombia had a major influence on Afro-Ecuadorian organizing nationally, through the Proceso de Comunidades Negras (PCN). Peter Wade (1997) has explained why blacks in Colombia had to Indianize their claims to be successful: that is, they had to present their demands to the state as if they were an indigenous people, making sure that how they represented their situation approximated as much as possible what is taken to be the case of indigenous peoples. The result was that Colombia's 1991 Constitution recognized the black communities of the Pacific coast as *comunidades negras* (Wade 1995; Restrepo 2002). Recently, building on the work of Wade and Eduardo Restrepo, Bettina Ng'weno has shown how global discourses of indigeneity relate to Afro-Colombian claims to land (Ng'weno 2007). She points out that a traditional relationship to the land contributes a great deal to definitions of indigenous communities in Colombia and elsewhere in Latin America, and it is this claim that gives an ethnocultural (quasi-indigenous) status to Afro-Colombian communities of the Pacific (for Ecuador, see Walsh and García Salazar 2002; Antón Sánchez 2007a, 2007b). The perception that Afro-Colombians living on the Caribbean coast and in urban areas of the interior lack such a relationship to the land explains why they have not been recognized as *comunidades negras*.

The PCN, which was also referred to as the Proyecto de la Gran Comarca del Pacífico (the Project of the Vast Region of the Pacific), involved Afro-Ecuadorian organizations from the northern sector of Esmeraldas Province. To correct the ambiguous wording of the 1998 Constitution regarding Afro-Ecuadorian collective rights, Afro-Ecuadorian organizations and individuals began a political process that culminated in writing, proposing, and debating in the National Congress a special law inspired by Colombia's Law 70 (see Wade 1995; Restrepo 2002). It was called Law 46, or "Law of Collective Rights of the Black or Afro-Ecuadorian Peoples" (Ley de Derechos Colectivos de los Pueblos Negros o Afroecuatorianos), and was approved by Congress on May 9, 2006, and later published in the Registro Oficial no. 275 of May 22, 2006. It used very specific language about the notion of Afro-Ecuadorian collective rights.

Later, on July 5, 2007, thanks to the activism of the Federación de Organizaciones y Grupos Negros de Pichincha (FOGNEP), which was led by Juan Ocles, the Metropolitan Council of Quito (Consejo Metropolitano) approved municipal ordinance no. 0216 *para la inclusión social con enfoque étnico cultural* (for social inclusion with an ethnocultural focus) that seeks to protect Afro-Ecuadorians from anti-black racism (*El Comercio* 2007a, 2007b). Despite the use of the expression "ethno-cultural focus," the language of the ordinance is clearly about Afro-Ecuadorians as racial "others" or as people who suffer more from racism than from the denial of special "cultural rights."

Afro-Ecuadorian Organizing, Corporatism, and the 2008 Constitution

Other Afro-Ecuadorian attempts to organize nationally that took place in the 1990s and in the 2000s (see Walsh and García Salazar 2002; Antón Sánchez 2007a, 2007b) had only fleeting success. From conversations I have had with Afro-Ecuadorian activists over the years, it appears that one of the major problems in forming a single and solid national Afro-Ecuadorian organization has been the egotism of some leaders or *caudillitos* (small dictators)—this is the term they used—who perceive the organizations they lead and/or have created as means to satisfy their individual projects of self-aggrandizement. The opening of a space for Afro-Ecuadorians in multiculturalist Ecuador has meant that some resources (sometimes in the form of salaries) have become available and are reserved for that specific population's representatives. The contest for access to state resources that ensues has had the negative consequence of causing Afro-Ecuadorians in both rural and urban areas to lose trust in black organizations and their leaders.

In this section, I discuss Afro-Ecuadorian participation in corporatism, which has mostly developed since the end of the 1990s in tandem with the corporatist integration of other sectors of Ecuadorian society, including indigenous groups and workers' unions. I show that Afro-Ecuadorian influences on and participation in the process that led to the adoption of the 2008 Constitution was in fact corporatist. According to Carlos de la Torre, in corporatism, the state co-opts or "creates interest groups, intends to regulate their number and gives them the appearance of having a quasi-representational monopoly with special prerogatives. In exchange for these prerogatives and monopolies the State demands the right to monitor the groups represented" (2002, 80–81).

Scholarly work about Latin American and Ecuadorian corporatism abounds (see Malloy 1977; Oxhorn and Ducatenzeiler 1998; Wiarda 2001; León 1991, 1994, 1997). In corporatism, the state channels demands for reform into institutionalized spaces of negotiation in order to defuse and manage social protest. States define acceptable protests as those that can be dealt with in the institutionalized space and repress what it considers to be unacceptable protest, sometimes violently. The leader of the movement eventually becomes an employee of the state. Although the Ecuadorian state played an important role in promoting certain black organizations (de la Torre 2002, 86–94), it did so because it was subjected to international pressure and because Afro-Ecuadorians had already begun to occupy a more visible space on the national political scene. During the government of Fabián Alarcón (February 1997–August 1998), the foreign affairs minister (who was white-mestizo) promoted the promulgation of the Plan Nacional de Derechos Humanos del Ecuador that included specific proposals about the collective rights of Afro-Ecuadorians and sought to consolidate the Afro-Ecuadorian movement. During Alarcón's administration, the Consejo para el Desarollo de los Pueblos Indios y Negros (CONPLADEIN; Council for the Development of Indian and Black Populations) was created. CONPLADEIN fragmented after blacks and Indians couldn't agree on how to use the resources provided by the Programa de Desarollo de los Pueblos Indígenas y Negros del Ecuador (PRODEPINE; Development Program for Indigenous and Black Peoples of Ecuador), which was financed by the World Bank. Indians created the Consejo de Desarrollo de las Nacionalidades y Pueblos del Ecuador (CODENPE; Council for the Development of the Nationalities and Peoples of Ecuador), and blacks created the Corporación de Desarrollo Afroecuatoriano (CODAE; Corporation for the Afro-Ecuadorian Development: both have the objective of channeling the resources provided by PRODEPINE. During the government of Jamil Mahuad (August 1998–January 2000) the state sponsored the first national congress of Afro-Ecuadorians in the Chota-Mira Valley, during which the Confederación Nacional Afroecuatoriana (CNA; National Afro-Ecuadorian Confederation) was founded (see also Antón Sánchez 2007b).

CODAE is one—if not the most important—of the state's institutions through which Afro-Ecuadorian corporatism takes place. It was created through Executive Decree no. 244 and published in the Official Register no. 48 on June 28, 2004 to be "an organism subjected to public law that is decentralized and integrated by representatives of the central government and by delegates from the Afro-Ecuadorian peoples constituted legally, so that it can contribute to the planning of public policies for the Afro-Ecuadorian people." CODAE's early history sheds light on the dangers of corporatism. During the government of Lucio Gutiérrez (2003–2005), Vidal Alberto Leones Rodríguez was appointed as the representative of the central government in CODAE. As such, he was also its leader. In April 2005, the National Congress put an end to what was supposed to be a four-year term and replaced Gutiérrez, after a week of street disturbances, with his vice-president, Alfredo Palacios. The majority in Congress argued that Gutiérrez had abandoned his office even though he was still in the presidential palace and refused to leave. As the political situation became progressively more complicated for Lucio Gutiérrez in the last months of his presidency, Vidal Alberto Leones Rodríguez drew CODAE into a desperate partisan battle to support the president. It is hard to know if Leones Rodríguez decided to express his and CODAE's support spontaneously or if he had been asked to do so by the president's office. By November 2004, he had been at the helm of the CODAE for a bit more than a month. Around three weeks after Alfredo Palacios assumed the presidency (in April 2005), Leones Rodríguez was replaced by Nercis Leandra Quiñónez Rodríguez as the representative of the president in CODAE and José Libio Arce Arboleda was appointed as CODAE's executive secretary (see Executive Decrees 106 and 107 of May 30, 2005). On November 14, 2005, the executive director of the Comisión de Control Cívico de la Corrupción (CCCC)—a state agency in charge of fighting against corruption—issued a press release in which he charged the leadership of CODAE with corruption. This is but one example of the risks inherent in Afro-Ecuadorian corporatism, especially during its earlier stages, when leaders of the CODAE might have illegally distributed funds acquired from development agencies such as the World Bank to Afro-Ecuadorian organizations without keeping records. It is not surprising to find corrupt bureaucrats and state agents in Ecuador, regardless of racial and ethnic background.[5]

Following the widespread practice of appointing political friends and sympathizers to state offices, the current executive secretary of CODAE, José Franklin Chalá Cruz, was appointed in May 2007, during the first administration of President Rafael Correa. This suggests that he is at least sympathetic to Alianza País, the president's party. Since Chalá Cruz is determined to do the best job he can, he has hired quite capable collaborators from among the educated leaders and activists of the Afro-Ecuadorian movement. One of the first actions of his CODAE administration involved cleaning up and organizing the rudimentary archives inherited from previous executive secretaries. In reports published on CODAE's website and on paper in 2006 and following years, Chalá Cruz and his team reported what they had accomplished during the year, presented the plans they had for the future, and shared how deplorable the state of CODAE's archives were when they inherited them from the previous team.

A few leaders of Afro-Ecuadorian organizations criticized Chalá Cruz and his team after they issued such reports:

While the Afro-Ecuadorian people are suffering from an injurious poverty, CODAE feasts with the state's resources, which were supposed to be used to deal with the needs of black people, Domingo Valencia said emphatically. He is a representative of the organized civil society of that social group who is also a former legal advisor of CODAE who came to Congress to reveal these abuses.

Valencia denounced the fact that although the budget had earmarked $600,000.00 for developing the infrastructure of the agriculture and livestock sectors and for designing residential projects, these resources have been diverted and don't reach the beneficiaries, leaving them without any opportunity to develop. (*El Mercurio* 2009)

One of the groups that question the activities of CODAE is the Confederación Nacional Afroecuatoriana (CNA). Its leader, Mary Quiñónez, says that the organization she represents decided to not participate in the session during which CODAE's report was presented because CODAE has not dealt with fundamental aspects of the lives of Afro-descended peoples. "The current administration [of CODAE] has conducted many studies, and we don't need any more of these because we already know what the problems are: we need housing and better health care. There have been a lot of technical concerns which have not resolved any problem," complains Quiñónez. The CNA leader is unsatisfied because Afro-Ecuadorian groups "were not consulted about the various things they need" (*El Telégrafo* 2009).

One does wonder if this criticism is a direct consequence of the unavoidable jealousy provoked by corporatism, a process by which one or a select few are chosen among many civil society leaders, or if it is the result of the fact that Chalá Cruz put an end to past practices of corruption and abuses of state funds, a change that frustrates past beneficiaries of CODAE's clientelism.

In February 2008, at the invitation of Jhon Antón Sánchez, an advisor to CODAE, I accompanied an Afro-Ecuadorian delegation to the Constituent Assembly in Montecristi for a full day. This delegation was formed as an initiative of CODAE, and Chalá Cruz had asked Antón Sánchez to put together a series of PowerPoint presentations to explain Afro-Ecuadorian aspirations to the various tables (or *mesas*) in charge of discussing the future constitution. Another objective of the delegation was to give to each *asambleista* a copy of the "Propuesta del Pueblo Afroecuatoriano a la Asamblea Nacional Constituyente" ("Proposal from the Afro-Ecuadorian People to the National Constituent Assembly"; Corporación de Desarrollo Afroecuatoriano 2007). I accompanied the delegation when they met with the president of the assembly, Alberto Acosta, and when Chalá Cruz gave him the "Propuesta del Pueblo Afroecuatoriano." Alejandra Ocles, the only *asambleísta* who was openly associated with the Afro-Ecuadorian movement, was part of the group that met with Acosta (see Figure 9.2). While Chalá Cruz explained the concern of the delegation that collective rights for Afro-Ecuadorians be renewed and be established more firmly than they had been in the 1998 Constitution, Acosta responded that he understood their concern perfectly but looked forward to a time when specific ethnic groups would look beyond their immediate interests to embrace a larger perspective that would express a concern for the entire pluricultural nation. Chalá Cruz agreed that it was necessary for leaders of ethnic groups to not limit their concerns to their specific groups but to also think about the entire nation. He added that in fact the document he was giving Acosta showed that Afro-Ecuadorians were interested in the greater good of the country as a whole.

One could read some paternalism in Acosta's statement, in the way he so easily brushed aside the delegation's aspirations as Chalá Cruz presented them. Chalá Cruz's reaction, on the other hand, was also illuminating since he chose not to engage in an open confrontation with a high government official. This moment clearly reveals a corporatist ethos. After the brief exchanges, the entire group stood outside Acosta's office for pictures (see Figure 9.3).

Figure 9.2. Afro-Ecuadorian delegation meeting with Alberto Acosta. Photo by Jean Muteba Rahier.

Figure 9.3. Outside the president's office at the Constituent Assembly in Montecristi. Photo by Jean Muteba Rahier.

All of the members of the delegation shared the feeling that they were participating in a historical process that was in fact refounding and reinventing the country. Their contagious enthusiasm moved me to reflect on the history of the Afro-Ecuadorian movement since the end of the 1970s, when everyone was talking of "invisibility," and to note that the state had played a part in producing and reproducing this invisibility. The constituent process that Afro-Ecuadorians were engaged in in 2008 as full participants, even if in a corporatist way, provided a significant contrast.[6]

The 2008 Constitution refers to Afro-Ecuadorian collective rights mostly in its Chapter Four, "Rights of Communities, Peoples, and Nationalities." Four articles in that chapter are relevant here. Article 56 indicates that "the Indigenous communities, peoples, and nationalities, the Afro-Ecuadorian people, the Montubio people and the communes form part of the Ecuadorian State, unique and indivisible." This is the first departure from the language of Article 83 of the 1998 Constitution, with the exception of the inclusion of the Montubios (rural mestizo people from the southern coastal area of the country) and "communes"

(see below). Article 57 adds: "The following collective rights will be acknowledged and guaranteed to Indigenous communes, communities, peoples and
nationalities, in conformity with the Constitution and with pacts, agreements,
declarations and other international instruments of human rights." The article
then lists twenty-one collective rights that are not that different from the fifteen
rights listed in the 1998 Constitution. Again, just as in Article 84 of the 1998
Constitution, there is no mention of Afro-Ecuadorians in Article 57. That group
is not mentioned until Article 58: "The collective rights of the Afro-Ecuadorian
people established in the Constitution, law and pacts, agreements, declarations
and other international instruments of human rights law will be recognized so
that they may strengthen their identity, culture, traditions and rights." The relationship between Article 57 and Article 58 reproduces the distinction between
indigenous peoples and Afro-Ecuadorians found in the 1998 Constitution. It
was the clear intention of most of the *asambleistas* involved to list the specific
collective rights granted to indigenous peoples in a separate article. Article 60 of
the 2008 Constitution, however, introduces something new: "The ancestral indigenous, Afro-Ecuadorian and Montubio people may delineate territorial cir-
cumscriptions for the preservation of their cultures. The law will regulate their
formation. The collective landownership of the Communes will be recognized
as a form of ancestral territorial organization." The wording of that additional
article adds a definitive and unambiguous character to the collective rights of
Afro-Ecuadorians to their cultural traditions and their lands. Indeed, the use of
the word *comuna(s)* ("communes") refers to the Afro-Ecuadorian communes of
the northern sector of Esmeraldas Province, located on the banks of the Santiago and Onzole rivers.

Asambleista Alexandra Ocles kept a short diary of the progress made during
the various debates that led to the adoption of the text of Articles 56, 57, 58, and
60. It is instructive to read in her record that although the Afro-Ecuadorians
close to the process did not succeed in preventing the kind of distinction that
continues to be established between the collective rights of indigenous and Afro-
Ecuadorian peoples (see Articles 57 and 58), they were nevertheless able to con-
vince the *asambleistas* of Table 1 (where these articles on collective rights were
discussed) to do two things: use the unambiguous wording that clearly recognizes Afro-Ecuadorians as a "people" or *pueblo* in Articles 56, 58, and 60; and ban
the use of the term *negro(s)* from the Constitution because of its significance in
the repertoire of racial terms and its recalling of the colonial past and replace it
with *afroecuatoriano(s)*, which—they felt—emphasizes the ethnic and cultural
dimensions of their identity and contributes to identifying them as a *pueblo* (see
Ocles 2008).

Conclusion

This examination of Afro-Ecuadorian influences on and participation in the constitutional processes of 1998 and 2008 in light of the history of their organizing and political struggles helps us appreciate how quickly Afro-Ecuadorians have progressed over the past thirty years. They have moved from a situation of "invisibility" that was reproduced in both civil society and state institutions to a situation in which their existence as a people with acknowledged cultural traditions and collective rights is enshrined in the country's political Constitution, which many in Ecuador characterize as one of the most progressive in Latin America.

In addition to the activism of Afro-Ecuadorians, other factors have played a major role in bringing about these changes. Indeed, support from international and multilateral actors was at first nonexistent for most African diasporic peoples in Latin America, in contrast to the financial boost indigenous peoples received at the time of the celebrations for the "500 years." In the 2000s—mostly as a result of the activism of African diasporic peoples in Latin America, which made "invisibility" unsustainable—some financial aid that came to Ecuador from international sources was earmarked for Afro-Ecuadorian peoples.

As de la Torre emphasized, the corporatist Ecuadorian state played an important role in establishing an Ecuadorian version of multiculturalism. Its adoption of multiculturalism as a fundamental principle in the 1998 Constitution by a Constituent Assembly dominated by political parties from the right is not surprising if we consider that many donor countries and multilateral organizations pressured receiving countries to be democratic and multiculturalist. In any case, as Charles Hale argues, neoliberal governance is not necessarily opposed to multiculturalism, since in the 1990s in Latin America it has included "limited recognition of cultural rights, the strengthening of civil society, and [the] endorsement of the principle of intercultural equality. When combined with neoliberal economic policies, these progressive measures have unexpected effects, including a deepened state capacity to shape and neutralize political opposition, and a remaking of racial hierarchies across the region" (Hale 2005, 10).

Although notable changes have occurred since the 1998 "multicultural turn," profound ideological continuities can be observed in everyday life (Rahier 2008a, 2008b). It is true that in this time of Ecuador's participation in the *socialismo del siglo* XXI (socialism of the twenty-first century) through the reforms adopted by the government of Rafael Correa, current corporatist practices and the existence of CODAE make it more difficult to represent and theorize Afro-Ecuadorians as the country's "ultimate Others." But it is also the case that Ecuadorian civil society still has a long way to go to end its long history of anti-black racism. The progress made in the new Constitution and other laws is mostly the result of activism by Afro-Ecuadorians and indigenous peoples and of state and international interventions. In many ways, Afro-Ecuadorians continue to suffer interpellation as noncitizens or ambiguous citizens, despite the multicultural turn (see Rahier 2008a, 2008b). Felipe Caicedo, an Afro-Ecuadorian soccer hero who plays in the British club Manchester United and has been selected to play in the Ecuadorian national team, was recently the victim of an act of racism in Guayaquil when he and some friends attempted to eat in a restaurant that was considered too "chic" for his skin color. *Asambleista* Alexandra Ocles supported Caicedo's formal complaint and indicated that there is now a law against hate crimes in the country (the Código de procedimiento penal). In light of the racist treatment of Felipe Caicedo, I cannot help but ask how many times these laws and the Constitution have been used to rectify a wrong and punish a racist. How many times have they been used to protect the collective rights of Afro-Ecuadorians? How many times have they been invoked to jail someone found guilty of a hate crime? A great deal of research clearly remains to be done if one has the objective to evaluate the concrete impact of these progressive legal texts on social attitudes.

Notes

All translations are mine.

1. It is important to note that Alberto Acosta was the first president of the National Constitutional Assembly that adopted the new Constitution in 2008.

2. Oscar and José Chalá are brothers. They have been involved in politics since the late 1970s (see Roque 2009). They are not directly related to Liliana and Monica Chalá, two sisters who are rather well known in Ecuador. The first was a famous athlete in the late 1980s and early 1990s, and the second became the first black Miss Ecuador in 1995 (see Rahier 1998). Oscar and José are also not directly related to Catherine Chalá, who has been involved with the Centro Cultural Afroecuatoriano. The last name Chalá is indeed quite common among black people of the Chota-Mira Valley in the northern Ecuadorian Andes.

3. Resistance in Ecuador on the part of members of the African diaspora is as old as their presence is. Afro-Ecuadorian organizing prior to the 1970s was mainly focused on specific local issues rather than on national ones.

4. A copy of these cassettes is housed in the Esmeraldas branch of the Centro de Investigación y Cultura del Banco Central del Ecuador. Another set is at the Fondo Afro of the Universidad Andina Simón Bolivar in Quito.

5. In 2010, Ecuador had a corruption perception index score of 2.5 on a scale from 0 to 10, where 0 means "very corrupt" and 10 indicates "squeaky clean" (see Transparency International 2010).

6. At this point, it might be useful to indicate that some of my colleagues and friends residing in Ecuador who have a strong sympathy for Alianza País' government of Rafael Correa and

some of CODAE's leaders do not agree with my analysis of this process as corporatist, following Carlos de la Torre's (2002) definition. They prefer to conceptualize the state as an institution that is no longer dominated by the elites and has instead become an institution that belongs to "all." With all due respect to these friends and colleagues, I find this view rather simplistic and naively optimistic.

Bibliography

Agencia Latinoamericana de Información. N.d. "Movimiento afroecuatoriano." Electronic source. Available at http://alainet.org/publica/diversidad/movafro.html. Accessed July 5, 2009.

Anderson, Mark. 2007. "When Afro Becomes (Like) Indigenous: Garifuna and Afro-Indigenous Politics in Honduras." *Journal of Latin American and Caribbean Anthropology* 12 (2): 384–413.

Antón Sánchez, Jhon. 2007a. *El estado de los derechos colectivos del pueblo Afroecuatoriano: Una mirada desde las organizaciones sobre el derecho al territorio ancestral.* Quito: Ministerio de Coordinación de Desarrollo Social.

———. 2007b. "Afrodescendientes: Sociedad civil y movilización social en el Ecuador." *Journal of Latin American and Caribbean Anthropology* 12 (1): 233–245.

———. N.d. Racismo y política en los debates sobre la ley de los derechos colectivos de los afroecuatorianos. Unpublished manuscript. 21 pages.

Báez, René, Edmundo Ribadeneira, Alberto Acosta, Francisco Muñoz, Andrés Carrión, Willington Paredes, César Verduga, Milton Luna, Simón Pachano, Miguel Donoso Pareja, and Rocío Rosero-Jácome. 1997. *¿Y ahora qué . . . ? Una contribución al análisis político-histórico actual.* Quito: Eskeletra Editorial.

Cervone, Emma, and Fredy Rivera, eds. 1999. *Ecuador racista: Imágenes e identidades.* Quito: FLACSO-Sede Ecuador.

Clark, Kim, and Marc Becker, eds. 2007. *Highland Indians and the State in Modern Ecuador.* Pittsburgh, Pa.: University of Pittsburgh Press.

Corporación de Desarrollo Afroecuatoriano (CODAE). 2007. *Propuesta del Pueblo Afroecuatoriano a la Asamblea Nacional Constituyente.* Quito: CODAE.

Córdova del Alcázar, Gabriela. 2003. *Anatomía de los golpes de estado: La prensa en la caída de Mahuad y Bucaram.* Quito: Universidad Andina Simon Bolivar, Abya Yala, Corporación Editora Nacional.

Coronel, Rosario. 1987a. *El Valle Sangriento 1580–1700, de los Señorios de la Coca y del Algodón a la Hacienda Cañera Jesuita.* Quito: Facultad Latino-Americana de Ciencias Sociales (FLACSO) Maestría en Historia Andina.

———. 1987b. "Riego Colonial: de la Coca a la Caña en el Valle del Chota." *Ecuador Debate* 14: 47–68.

———. 1988. "Indios y esclavos negros en el Valle del Chota colonial." In *El negro en la historia del Ecuador y del sur de Colombia*, ed. Rafael Savoia, 171–188. Quito: Abya-Yala.

de la Torre, Carlos. 1992. "The Ambiguous Meanings of Latin American Populisms." *Social Research* 59 (2): 385–414.

———. 1996. *El racismo en el Ecuador: Experiencias de los indios de clase media.* Quito: Centro Andino de Acción Popular (CAAP).

———. 2002. *Afroquiteños, ciudadanía y racismo.* Quito: Centro Andino de Acción Popular.

————. 2006a. "Ethnic Movements and Citizenship in Ecuador." *Latin American Research Review* 41 (2): 247–259.

————. N.d. "Movimientos sociales y procesos constituyentes en Ecuador." Unpublished manuscript. 38 pages.

El Comercio. 2007a. "El racismo se prohibió por Ordenanza." July 17.

————. 2007b. "Los negros somos parte de Quito porque también la fundamos." June 27.

El Mercurio. 2009. "Se festinan dineros destinados a los afroecuatorianos." May 1.

El Telégrafo. 2009. "CODAE rindió cuentas a pueblo afro del país." January 3. Available at http:// www.eltelegrafo.com.ec/diversidad/noticia/archive/diversidad/2009/01/03/Codae-rindi_ F300_-cuentas-a-pueblo-afro-del-pa_ED00_s.aspx.

Espinosa Apolo, Manuel. 2003. *Mestizaje, cholificación y blanqueamiento en Quito: Primera mitad del siglo XX.* Quito: Universidad Andina Simón Bolivar, Ediciones Abya-Yala, Corporación Editora nacional.

Fundación Colombiana de Investigaciones Folclóricas (FCIF). 1988. *Primer Congreso de la Cultura Negra de las Americas, Cali-Colombia.* Bogotá, Colombia: Editores ECOE, Fundación Colombiana de Investigaciones Folclóricas, UNESCO.

García Salazar, Juan, comp. 2002. *Los guardianes de la tradición: Compositores y decimeros.* Quito: Génesis Ediciones.

Greene, Shane. 2007b. "Introduction: On Race, Roots/Routes, and Sovereignty in Latin America's Afro-Indigenous Multiculturalisms." *Journal of Latin American and Caribbean Anthropology* 12 (2): 329–355.

Hale, Charles. 2002. "Does Multiculturalism Menace? Governance, Cultural Rights, and the Politics of Identity in Guatemala." *Journal of Latin American Studies* 34 (3): 485–524.

————. 2004. "Rethinking Indigenous Politics in the Era of the 'Indio Permitido.'" *NACLA Report on the Americas* 38 (2): 16–20.

————. 2005. "Neoliberal Multiculturalism: The Remaking of Cultural Rights and Racial Dominance in Central America." *PoLAR: Political and Legal Anthropology Review* 28 (1): 10–28.

————. 2006. *Más Que un Indio: Racial Ambivalence and Neoliberal Multiculturalism in Guatemala.* Santa Fe, N.M.: School of American Research.

Hooker, Juliet. 2005. "Indigenous Inclusion/Black Exclusion: Race, Ethnicity and Multicultural Citizenship in Latin America." *Journal of Latin American Studies* 37 (2): 285–310.

Ibarra Dávila, Alexia. 2002. *Estrategias del mestizaje: Quito a finales del siglo XVIII.* Quito, Ecuador: Abya-Yala.

Izquierdo, Santiago, ed. 2007. *Etnicidad, desigualdad y racismo.* Quito: Secretaría Técnica del Ministerio de Coordinación de Desarrollo Social, Unidad de Información y Análisis, Sistema Integrado de Indicadores Sociales del Ecuador (SIISE).

Lane, Kris. 2002. *Quito 1599: City and Colony in Transition.* Albuquerque: University of New Mexico.

León, Jorge. 1991. "Las organizaciones indígenas: igualdad y diferencia." In *Indios,* ed. José Vinueza, Ileana Almeida, and Diego Cornejo Menacho, 373–419. Quito: ILDIS, Duende, and Abya Yala.

————. 1994. *De campesinos a ciudadanos diferentes.* Quito: CEDIME-Abya-Yala.

————. 1997. "Entre la propuesta y el corporatismo." *Íconos, Revista de FLACSO-Ecuador* 2 (mayo–julio): 29–40.

Malloy, James M. 1977. *Authoritarianism and Corporatism in Latin America*. Pittsburgh, Pa.: University of Pittsburgh Press.

Medina Vallejo, Henry. 1996. *Comunidad Negra y Cambio Cultural: El caso de Concepción en la sierra ecuatoriana*. Quito: Centro Cultural Afroecuatoriano, Ediciones Afroamérica.

Ng'weno, Bettina. 2007. "Can Ethnicity Replace Race? Afro-Colombians, Indigeneity and the Colombian Multicultural State." *Journal of Latin American and Caribbean Anthropology* 12 (2): 414–440.

Ocles, Alexandra. 2008. "Como se consagraron los derechos colectivos de los afroecuatorianos en la Nueva Constitución." Unpublished paper.

Oxhorn, Philip, and Graciela Ducatenzeiler. 1998. *What Kind of Democracy? What Kind of Market? Latin America in the Age of Neoliberalism*. University Park, Pa.: Pennsylvania State University Press.

Polo, Rafael. 2002. *Los intelectuales y la narrativa mestiza en el Ecuador*. Quito: Universidad Andina Simón Bolivar, Ediciones Abya-Yala, Corporación Editora nacional.

Rahier, Jean Muteba. 1998. "Blackness, the Racial/Spacial Order, Migrations, and Miss Ecuador 1995–96." *American Anthropologist* 100 (2): 421–430.

———. 1999. "Mami, ¿qué será lo que quiere el negro?: representaciones racistas en la revista *Vistazo*, 1957–1991." In *Ecuador racista: Imágenes e identidades*, ed. Emma Cervone and Fredy Rivera, 73–109. Quito: FLACSO-Sede Ecuador.

———. 2003a. "*Mestizaje, mulataje, mestiçagem* in Latin American Ideologies of National Identities." *Journal of Latin American Anthropology* 8 (1): 40–50.

———. 2003b. "Racist Stereotypes and the Embodiment of Blackness: Some Narratives of Female Sexuality in Quito." In *Millennial Ecuador: Critical Essays on Cultural Transformations and Social Dynamics*, ed. N. Whitten, 296–324. Iowa City: University of Iowa Press.

———. 2008a. "*Fútbol* and the (*Tri-*)Color of the Ecuadorian Nation: Ideological and Visual (Dis-)Continuities of Black Otherness from Monocultural *Mestizaje* to Multiculturalism." *Visual Anthropology Review* 24 (2): 148–182.

———. 2008b. "Race, *Fútbol*, and the Ecuadorian Nation: *El Mundial 2006* and the Ideological Biology of (Non-)Citizenship." *E-misférica* 5 (2): 1–20. Available at http://www.hemisphericinstitute.org/eng/publications/emisferica/index.html.

República de Ecuador. 1998. Constituciones de 1998. Available at http://pdba.georgetown.edu/Constitutions/Ecuador/ecuador98.html.

Restrepo, Eduardo. 2002. "Políticas de la alteridad: Etnización de 'comunidad negra' en el Pacífico sur colombiano." *Journal of Latin American and Caribbean Anthropology* 7 (2): 34–58.

———. 2007. "Políticas de la alteridad: Etnización de 'comunidad negra' en el Pacífico sur colombiano." *Journal of Latin American Anthropology* 7 (2): 34–58.

Roque, Juan Carlos. 2009. "Oscar Chalá: Leccion la vidá." Radio Nederland website, January 9. Available at http://static.rnw.nl/migratie/www.informarn.nl/sociedad/act090109-oscar-chala-redirected. Accessed March 18, 2011.

Rueda Novoa, Rocío. 2001. *Zambaje y autonomía: Historia de la gente negra de la Provincia de Esmeraldas*. Esmeraldas, Ecuador: Municipalidad de Esmeraldas; Quito: Taller de Estudios Históricos.

Silva, Erika. 1995. *Los mitos de la ecuatorianidad. Ensayo sobre la identidad nacional*. Quito: Abya-Yala.

Transparency International. 2010. "Corruption Perceptions Index 2010 Results." Available at http://www.transparency.org/policy_research/surveys_indices/cpi/2010/results. Accessed March 18, 2011.

Wade, Peter. 1995. "The Cultural Politics of Blackness in Colombia." *American Ethnologist* 22 (2): 341–357.

———. 1997. *Race and Ethnicity in Latin America*. London: Pluto Press.

Walsh, Catherine, and Juan García. 2002. "El pensar del emergente movimiento afroecuatoriano: Reflexiones (des)de un proceso." In *Prácticas intelectuales en cultura y poder*, ed. D. Mato, 1–14. Buenos Aires: CLACSO.

West, Robert. 1952. *Colonial Placer Mining in Colombia*. Baton Rouge: Louisiana State University Press.

———. 1957. *The Pacific Lowlands of Colombia: A Negroid Area of the American Tropics*. Baton Rouge: Louisiana State University Press.

Whitten, Norman, Dorothea Scott Whitten, and Alfonso Chango. 2003. "Return of the Yumbo: The Caminata from Amazonia to Andean Quito." In *Millennial Ecuador: Critical Essays on Cultural Transformations and Social Dynamics*, ed. N. Whitten, 184–215. Iowa City: University of Iowa Press.

Wiarda, Howard J. 2001. *The Soul of Latin America: The Cultural and Political Tradition*. New Haven, Conn.: Yale University Press.

10

The Black Movement's Foot Soldiers

Black Women and Neighborhood Struggles for Land Rights in Brazil

KEISHA-KHAN Y. PERRY

Eu quero ter o direito a meu quintal (I want to have the right to my own backyard).

Dona Selma, activist in the homeless movement

The only activity that has ever altered oppression and transformed disenfranchised people's powerlessness is collective grassroots organizing.

Barbara Smith, *The Truth That Never Hurts* (2000)

Our greatest asset in Kenya is our land. This is the heritage we received from our forefathers. In land lies our salvation and survival. It was in this knowledge that we fought for the freedom of our country.

Jomo Kenyatta, 1964 speech

On Saturday, May 3, 2003, the front cover of the Bahian newspaper *A Tarde* showed the picture of 53-year-old Amilton dos Santos sitting on top of a yellow bulldozer. His left hand was on his face, which was hidden by a blue Firestone baseball cap that matched his uniform, and Senhor Amilton was crying. The headline read, "Um Homem" (One Man), and the accompanying caption described the dramatic scene as follows: "The screams of revolt and pain were stronger than the 20 policemen armed even with rifles" (*A Tarde*, March 23, 2003).

The day before, in Palestina, a predominantly poor black neighborhood located on the periphery of Brazil's northeastern city of Salvador, six police cars with more than twenty fully armed military policemen, some with machine guns and rifles, arrived at house number 123, the home of 40-year-old Telma Sena. Accompanying a bulldozer and a moving truck, the military police had arrived in Palestina to complete orders to demolish the home and clear the land where Dona Telma lived with her husband, seven children, two grandchildren, and a daughter-in-law. The family was home when the police and demolition squad arrived and the family and their neighbors immediately reacted with alarm. Upon seeing the family inside the house, the three men who were in charge of removing the furniture refused to follow through with the job. The police told the movers that if they did not carry out their duties, they would be arrested. The men then worked reluctantly to put the family's belongings in the truck parked in front of the house, where a crowd of neighborhood residents, primarily women, had begun to gather and vocalize their indignation. Dona Telma cried uncontrollably as she pleaded with the police and the driver of the bulldozer. Dona Antônia, Telma's aunt, showed the police officers legal documents certifying that the land had passed from the original owner, already deceased, to Telma's grandmother almost two decades earlier.

By late afternoon, the protesting crowd in front of the house had grown. Senhor Amilton, the bulldozer operator, turned the key in the ignition. Dona Telma, with her hands on her head and kneeling in the dirt road, led the crowd in pleading with him to stop: *"Pare, pare, pare."* The screams to save the house became louder. Overwhelmed by the pressure of the crowd, Senhor Amilton froze and sat paralyzed in the bulldozer, unable to put the machine in gear. *"Pelo amor de Deus!"* ("For the love of God!") pleaded the women who stood in front of the bulldozer. The police threatened to arrest the driver if he did not carry out the demolition. The pressure from the police intensified, and the journalists focused their cameras on the face of the conflicted man. "I can't do this, I am a family man and I have nine children," said Senhor Amilton, refusing to move the bulldozer and climbing down (*A Tarde*, March 23, 2003). Applauded by those at the scene, Senhor Amilton later became known as a local and national hero for standing up to the police and for refusing to fulfill the order to demolish the home. Dona Telma's house was safe, at least for the moment.

The media focus on Senhor Amilton's decision to spare Dona Telma's house, while it was admittedly an act of good conscience that merited public recognition, speaks to the general invisibility of black women who work arduously to mobilize urban communities in defiance of the state-sponsored violence of house demolition and land usurpation. The realization of this invisibility leads us to recognize the general lack of knowledge about black women's lives, the brutality of their experiences with interlocking systems of oppression, and their painful political trajectories. While black women occupy the heart of the struggle for urban housing and land rights, they are virtually ignored. From the news media, we learned of one *man's* courage, a notoriety that led to national and international invitations to Senhor Amilton to give lectures and mass support for a political post for him in the municipal government. Yet we heard very little about Dona Telma, her neighbors in Palestina, and the numerous other poor black families and peripheral neighborhoods facing similar land disputes.

The northeastern Brazilian city of Salvador is structurally unequal and operates socially and economically to the detriment of poor black men and women. The city's urban redevelopment process, involving the demolition of poor neighborhoods, is one public manifestation of the power differentials that have defined social relations between blacks and whites, rich and poor, men and women. The Brazilian state represents black people as the "undeserving poor" who should be excluded from the blossoming urban center of Salvador. This logic of exclusion led to the expulsion of residents from the historic city center (known as the Pelourinho) in the mid-1990s and the ongoing threat of displacement of families in the Gamboa de Baixo neighborhood. In the popular imagination, these poor black communities are undeserving of the new, modern spaces they occupy, which have been developed in recent decades, and they are perceived as a violent and criminal threat to the future of the tourism economy. However, the vibrant realities of neighborhoods such as Gamboa de Baixo, all of which have a unique and vivacious culture and a long history in the city center, challenge the position of state-supported land speculators and urban developers. The Gamboa de Baixo neighborhood movement against forced relocation and for land and housing rights expresses collective grassroots organizing for the primary purpose of legitimating their presence in the city center.

I had the opportunity to meet Dona Telma during a forum on housing and land rights organized by a collective of neighborhood associations, the Articulação de Comunidades em Luta pela Moradia (Articulation of Communities in Struggle for Housing Rights), a few months after the government's attempt to forcibly remove her family. Black community activists from around Salvador, the majority of whom were black women, expressed their solidarity with Dona Telma and Palestina and the greater need to highlight black women's central political role in urban communities. Like these activists, I was intrigued by the story of one woman who represented the collective experience of black Brazilian women's violent reality and their long history of resistance. The forum's main purpose was to discuss a dossier the activists of the Articulação had prepared on state actions in their neighborhoods, which included unequal urbanization practices, evictions, and displacement. Though the leaders were from geographically dispersed neighborhoods, they wanted to bring their similar and particular experiences to the attention of local politicians and representatives of civil society organizations, who were also invited to attend the forum, and encourage them to interact with poor black communities struggling for adequate housing and landownership on a more permanent and consistent basis.

At the time Dona Telma delivered her speech, the struggle to keep her home and land had not yet been resolved, and she urgently called for collective action across the city to support her legal claims as well as those of families unable to formally legalize their ownership of land. She identified the ongoing fight against displacement and the anger and anguish she felt as part of the structural violence black women endure in their efforts to claim rights to land throughout Brazil. She told a brief history of the Palestina neighborhood, named aptly after Palestine to symbolize the global connection between black urban settlements in Salvador that are fighting for territorial rights and the settlements of the Palestinians. Dona Telma also recounted that on the day of the scheduled demolition of her home, she had used peaceful tactics to organize family members and neighbors to defend her. For instance, the decision to gather her family, including elderly relatives and children, inside her home was a strategic technique used by neighborhood activists throughout the city. Media coverage of the event had told the public little of her ongoing conflict with the wealthy white businessmen who claimed to own her land, which had begun several years before the demolition squad appeared on her doorstep. Instead, the political organization of her neighborhood appeared to be spontaneous, when in fact the female-led grassroots movement had long been preparing for the violent confrontation. While journalists focused on the *one* man and the *one* moment of the bulldozer driver's individual gutsy decision to stop demolition, not much was said of this calculated, female-led strategic resistance and a politically savvy local population that fought collectively to prevent the demolition of the house, the clearance of the land, and police violence.

After Dona Telma spoke, Ana Cristina, an activist from the Gamboa de Baixo neighborhood association, boldly asked the audience at the forum, "What kind of city do we live in that prepares architects and engineers to demolish homes and expel local populations in order to implement their urban development projects?" They nodded in agreement and applauded when she firmly asserted that "*a terra é do povo*" (the land belongs to the people). The affirmation of collective ownership alludes to a serious question of why the *povo*, or the masses of blacks who occupy Salvador's poorest neighborhoods, have no legal right to the land they have lived on for generations. In the broadest sense, what does it mean for Dona Telma and Ana Cristina, black women who occupy the racial, gender, and sociospatial margins of the city, to make claims to it? This question forces us to examine black women activists in Salvador who are located at the center of political opposition to the urban social order. It also encourages us to look critically at pedagogies and practices that bring ideologies of exclusion into urban planning and land distribution processes. Within a city "structured in dominance," to borrow from Stuart Hall's (1980) formulation of the inevitable relationship between racial domination and economic and political processes, black women carve out a geographic, social, and political space for themselves while expanding definitions of rights, citizenship, and national belonging. It is true that, as Afro-Canadian geographer Katherine McKittrick suggests, "black matters are spatial matters" (McKittrick 2006, xiv). Black urban spaces are racialized, gendered "terrains of domination" where black women's politics are deeply connected to resistance against what McKittrick calls "geographic domination" as practiced in land evictions and displacement in Brazilian cities.

Black Politics "Below the Asphalt"

The story of Dona Telma and Palestina illustrates the pervasiveness of the violent expulsion of black families from land and the resulting displacement they experience as well as the various methods black women use to resist these events. I initially became aware of her story and those of numerous others in Salvador while conducting ethnographic research on the female-led grassroots movement in Gamboa de Baixo, a black coastal community and fishing colony located in Salvador's city center that has been the primary focus of my work over the past decade. During recent processes of urban revitalization, the government's plans to transform Gamboa de Baixo into a historical and cultural site for tourism and leisure have posed a threat of mass land eviction. The local population would be relocated to the distant periphery of Salvador in this plan. Gamboa de Baixo women residents such as Ana Cristina are among the key leaders in the Articulação who have fought to bring attention to how state-sponsored reurbanization practices in Salvador have fostered a culture of demolition and removal that has negatively impacted black communities on a mass scale, including neighborhoods located on the coast and in the city center. Poor blacks throughout Salvador suffer the consequences of the racial, class, and gender biases that underlie eviction and violent displacement. As Ana Cristina regularly recounts the root of their frustration by institutional roadblocks to legalization of landownership, "urban planners, engineers and architects have stated 'Gamboa é a cara da Bahia (Gamboa is the face of Bahia),' but it's not a place for blacks and poor people to live" (personal communication 2007). While Gamboa de Baixo occupies coastal lands in the urban center—areas where black people have lived since slavery times that were traditionally perceived as "undesirable" spaces before the urban revitalization plans—the neighborhood is located on the geographic and socio-economic margins of the city. I call the unique sociospatial location of the poor black urban neighborhood the "periphery in the center."

To further understand the link between the gendered racial stratification of cities and the emergence of social movements against sociospatial exclusion, an understanding of the phrase "below the asphalt" is necessary. "Below the asphalt" is used to describe the location of black politics in the city and refers to the geographic location of the Gamboa de Baixo neighborhood *underneath* Contorno Avenue along the Bay of All Saints. The construction of the avenue in the 1960s dramatically shaped the identity of the neighborhood within the city and solidified sociospatial hierarchies. Contorno Avenue spatially and socially displaced the neighborhood and the poor blacks who live there, especially the black women residents, most of whom work as domestic workers in white elite households above the street. In the literal sense, Gamboa de Baixo refers to a neighborhood located below the asphalt avenue, but the term "below the asphalt" also reflects the popular view of the neighborhood as a separate urban subworld marked by immoral and illegal sexual activities (specifically female prostitution) that are hidden from public view by the avenue. Thus, in the public imaginary, Gamboa de Baixo is both visible and invisible, in plain view and out of view, a critical sociospatial relationship that complicates the categories of periphery and center and has political meaning for the black women activists who lead the community movement there.

Describing political organization as "below the asphalt" focuses critical attention on black women's social location on the periphery of Bahian and Brazilian society. Like in Gamboa de Baixo, the majority of black women in Salvador work as domestic workers for middle- and upper-class white families throughout the city (McCallum 2007). The Articulação's decision to invite Dona Telma to speak at the forum was a deliberate attempt to focus attention on black women's leadership in sustaining the grassroots struggles that have emerged in reaction to spatial displacement in urban environments. The usurpation of land in the Palestina neighborhood was not an arbitrary act by a few elite white businessmen and urban developers but was part of the systemic destruction of black settlements and the pervasive negation of black citizenship that marks Brazilian cities. The fact that neighborhoods across the city have mobilized as the Gamboa de Baixo neighborhood illustrates how widespread efforts are to displace black residents in Salvador. Within this context of widespread violence, Gamboa de Baixo has managed to remain intact as a community and continues to fight attempts to remove and relocate residents. As a female activist in the homeless movement affirmed during an Articulação planning meeting, *"Eu quero ter direito a meu quintal"* (I want to have the right to my backyard). In this spirit, black women in Gamboa de Baixo and throughout the city fight to preserve the land where they have built their homes, forged social networks, and generated the material resources necessary to sustain their families. From "below the asphalt," black women community leaders mobilize for a racially equitable and just future. As local activist Dona Nice recounted, when the government initially threatened to relocate the community in the mid-1990s, "There were women, a dozen or so women, that began to cause alarm, to shout, 'Look what's happening.'" The participation of women in the community-based struggle has always been greater than that of men. Indeed, women were often the *only* organizers. Maria, another activist, claims, "Our association fought without fear." In response to the typical questions about the relative absence of men in their organization, she states that "it is our women who are going to fight and achieve these greater objectives" for the entire community. Women claim that this is because they were more conscious of the short- and long-term impact that land expulsion and relocation to the periphery would have on their families. The centrality of women's participation and their gender consciousness fuel the community movement. Former president of the neighborhood association, Ana Cristina, states:

The women believed more, women have *this thing*. . . . The woman has a mother's spirit, and a mother dies for her child, you know. So we women just believed that this place was right for our children. And it was as if this is my home, and no one invades it, no one enters to take anything, to take me out of it, to take my children. So I think that the women, they had this thing. They believed that they would remove us.

And the men, I think they didn't, because the men thought, and some still think that no, living outside is simple. That they were going to be able to return, to come, the boat stays here, to fish, but the women had a broader vision, [were] more clear about what it was to leave Gamboa to live in whatever other part of Salvador. So, like that, it is as if the women were defending their territory, you know, the woman has more of this thing. So the participation was more of women. It is not because, as they say, there are men who say, "Meeting is a woman's little thing [*coisinha de mulher*]," but we did not see it that way. We see it like this, that women are able to reach a lot farther than the men. . . .

Look, this broader preoccupation of the women was just this preoccupation with the future. Why? It's like I was saying, Gamboa has its own culture, its way of life. Gamboa is one family, and we know, and we think, leaving Gamboa to go somewhere else means being in another environment with another family, being in a place where we don't, people don't know each other, then, new relationships. . . . To see that in Gamboa we had and we have to survive. We have the sea that when we don't have bread in the house, you go there to the beach and you throw your line, you fish your little fish for your child to eat, to go to school walking because you don't have money for transport. And your child wouldn't be able to go? Or drop out of school, or stay hungry midday, you know, or turn into a marginal of some kind, you know? I think that the women got to see Gamboa

and the environment as a way of surviving. It is the natural environment
of Gamboeiros. We need this here. (Ana Cristina, interview with author,
2000)

Ana Cristina also stated, "It's as if we were born to fight." Like her, several of
the women with whom I spoke in Gamboa de Baixo associate their political
awareness in this situation with the recognition of their own different knowledge as women and, for some, as mothers. From this perspective, *this thing* that
empowers black women in grassroots movements around issues of survival is
exactly what they know about life and their position in the world. For instance,
what women in Gamboa de Baixo describe as a broader preoccupation with
"their territory" is a complex understanding of the depth of the everyday social
and economic conditions that define their existence in a poor neighborhood in
the center of Salvador. As stated above, they claim territorial rights and "know"
the essentials of living and surviving in difficult conditions, including disease
and land expulsion. The *thing* that black women have is the will and wisdom to
survive the racially determined socioeconomic inequality of urban spaces.

It is from this perspective that I understand the political lives of black women
in Salvador and cities throughout the black diaspora. Many of these women are
mothers and workers as well as community leaders and organizers of grassroots
movements. Urban housing and land rights are key issues in black women's collective resistance. Carole Boyce Davies asks, "What happens when members of
a subordinated group rise to power within an oppressive system?" (Davies 2006,
67). What happens, especially, when poor black women, who are socially and
geographically invisible in Brazilian cities, located on the "periphery of the center," occupy positions of political power in community movements that protest
state practices of spatial exclusion?

The political organization of black urban neighborhoods has largely depended on the leadership and mass participation of women residents who use
their local wisdom and community networks to galvanize political support when
their home spaces and lands come under siege by the police, development agencies, and private companies. My focus on neighborhood organizing in Salvador brings a heightened understanding of the ways that urban land conflicts
affect the collective formation of black women's political consciousness. From
that consciousness a resiliency and rebelliousness emerges that contests, if not
subverts, the ignorance and hostility that shape their racialized social conditions.
A gendered analysis of these social movements for racial and class claims to urban space and land rights illuminates black women's power to organize, change
policy, and transform the lives of "ordinary" people: blacks, women, and the poor.

A key theoretical assertion of this chapter, then, is that neighborhood movements are at the heart of the black movement in Brazil, a political space in which black women's leadership and mass participation is key. Neighborhood activists constitute the foot soldiers of the national and global movement for social change for black people. Organized community movements for land rights, led by women, constitute an important facet of the historical struggle of black citizens in Brazil for social and territorial belonging. Women are at the forefront of black social movements, as in the case of Salvador, where their political leadership and participation in neighborhood associations wage a struggle for collective access to material resources, such as land, basic sanitation, and health care.

Rarely in the literature on the black movement in Brazil are these kinds of social struggles considered to constitute important grassroots elements. Some scholars, such as Michael Hanchard (1994) and France Winddance Twine (1998), have argued that the black movement in Brazil has not reached the masses of black people who face race-based social inequalities. Twine claims that Afro-Brazilian movements have been unsuccessful because most Afro-Brazilians tend to reject a bipolar racial model and continue to accept the ideology of racial democracy. Hanchard asserts that, because of their focus on the politics of Afro-Brazilian cultural practices, black activists have been unable to organize a mass political movement aimed at transforming institutionalized forms of racial inequality. Because Hanchard and Twine have not explored black women's activism, gender identity politics, and grassroots organizing, they fail to recognize the central role of community-based movements in black identity politics. Thus, for these scholars, the Brazilian "black movement" consists of mainstream organizations such as the Movimento Negro Unificado (MNU) and the União por Igualdade Racial (UNegro). Nonetheless, neighborhood associations led by black women in Salvador have been able to mobilize in pursuit of concrete political objectives centered on their citizenship rights.

Urban Land in Black Diaspora Politics

In black urban communities in Brazil, urban land and territorial rights are the local idioms of black and women's resistance. Claiming the right to land means challenging gendered, racial, and class dominance rooted in colonialism and the legacy of the unequal distribution of the country's resources. In her book *Terra de Pretos, Terra de Mulheres: Terra, Mulher e Raça num Bairro Rural Negro* (Black Women's Land: Land, Women and Race in a Rural Black Neighborhood; 1995), Brazilian anthropologist Neusa Maria Mendes de Gusmão noted that more studies on black struggles for land rights were urgently needed. Her claim that black women must be the central focus in these discussions—since to speak of *terra de preto* (black land) is necessarily to speak of *terra de mulheres negras* (black women's land)—remains relevant today. In Brazil, black women are uniquely positioned, in many cases, because they have collective memory of residence, and in some cases, legal documentation of ownership of ancestral land. They also serve as the primary mediators of familial and social relations within their communities, influencing political decisions and how important resources such as land are distributed. Gusmão's work focuses on black women in rural Brazil, as do most analyses of land rights movements. However, the idea that land has been perceived historically as *o lugar da mulher* (a woman's place) (Gusmão 1995, 109) proves useful for understanding black women's political force in similar land struggles in urban areas. As blacks migrate to Brazilian cities in increasing numbers and from neighborhoods, they rearticulate their sense of belonging to urban spaces. The women who lead local social networks also mobilize politically to make demands for access to urban resources such as adequate housing, education, and employment.

Signifying more than just the physical space where families live, work, and build social and political networks, urban land represents the ability of black women to pass resources from one generation to the next. Black women activists work hard to dismiss representations of black urban residents as "squatters" or "invaders" who occupy the city's social and geographic periphery without any rights to ownership. It is necessary for me to clarify that the discourse of land rights should neither determine nor limit what constitutes black women's *rightful place* within Brazilian society. On the contrary, the social and political place of black women in land rights conflicts and resistance movements debunks the popular notion that men are the natural leaders of communities and that they control the distribution of community resources. An approach to the study of black land rights in urban areas that focuses on women necessitates an examination of how race, gender, and class are central to group recognition and collective claims to citizenship in Brazil. Political organization around land rights constitutes part of a larger fight for racial, gender, and class justice at the local and national levels. This larger fight for justice is what is at stake when black women such as Dona Telma and Ana Cristina use the class-based, racialized discourse of land rights. They do so as a way to broaden the practice of social democracy to include poor blacks and women living in structurally unequal cities. The residents of neighborhoods that are being expelled from the city center are black and poor and work in the nearby formal and informal economies. In this sense, black women's leadership in land rights movements reaffirms that grassroots participation in urban politics necessitates a deeper examination of how these gendered claims to space are negotiated in Brazil. Black women have been able to understand how urgently they need land rights, mobilize the resources necessary to fight the racist/classist storms of evictions, and demand participatory urbanization policies to improve the living conditions of poor black people.

It is in this historical and sociopolitical context that black women's struggle for urban land in Salvador continues. These female-led grassroots struggles in Brazil form part of the black diasporic radical tradition. Throughout the African diaspora, to paraphrase the powerful words of former Kenyan leader Jomo Kenyatta quoted at the top of this chapter, the greatest asset of black people is their land. Blacks in post-abolition North America and the Caribbean and in post-independence Africa saw land acquisition as a necessary conduit to freedom and the alleviation of poverty. W. E. B. Du Bois's seminal text *Black Reconstruction in America* ([1935] 1998) examined free blacks' equation of emancipation with land, employment, and education. Similarly, Angela Y. Davis writes in her essay "Education and Liberation: Black Women's Perspective" that blacks' cries of "freedom" in the postslavery era meant that "they knew exactly what they wanted: the women and the men alike wanted land, they wanted the ballot and 'they were consumed with desires for schools'" (Davis 1981, 70). She also writes, "Black people learned that emancipation's 'forty acres and a mule' was a malicious rumor. They would have to fight for land; they would have to fight for political power" (ibid.). Today's reparations movement in the United States, led by black women activists such as Deadria Farmer-Paellmann, continues to use the discourse of "forty acres and a mule" to demand restorative justice. Post-apartheid South Africa also has had to grapple with the redistribution of land as a crucial mechanism for the social and economic inclusion of the majority black population. In Brazil, black women are the invisible landowners and the often-overlooked defenders of the right of black Brazilians to live in the city.

One of the central reasons for the focus on land in urban communities and the surge in social movements devoted to land rights is the place of the *quilombo* (community of escaped enslaved peoples) in the historical consciousness of Brazilian blacks. *Quilombos* were places where freedom for blacks was practiced and political ideologies of transformation were transmitted (Ratts 2007; Nascimento 1980). The *quilombo* should be understood as a spatial location of freedom for the black women who were crucial in forming and sustaining these communities on vast tracts in Brazil's hinterland. Enslaved peoples imagined and practiced freedom on land that was not given to them but that they claimed as their own. Today, as rural *quilombos* gain territorial rights through the constitutional reform of 1988, the black people who live in urban areas (who constitute the majority of Brazil's black population) see the possibility of obtaining land rights as a key means of securing socioeconomic freedom in a racially unjust society. It is possible to consider these urban communities as modern-day *quilombos* without the land titles necessary to guarantee their survival, particularly the permanent residence of the people who live there. A gendered understanding of this *quilombo* consciousness, as Afro-Brazilian feminist Lélia Gonzalez (in Bairros 1996) suggests, proves fundamental in understanding poor black women's collective claims for formal equality through collective land rights in Brazil.

The political organization of black women in Salvador is as much about the quest for freedom in diaspora communities worldwide as it is about black women's search for citizenship in Brazil. My understanding of Brazil has been informed by a global perspective on urban policies and urban social movements focused on housing and land. Black communities in the United States and the Caribbean are all too familiar with "slash and burn" approaches to revitalizing modern cities. Blacks have also been expelled from land in post-apartheid South African cities. In Zimbabwe, Robert Mugabe's urban renewal program featured a "slum blitz." As Arlene Dávila writes in her account of urban renewal processes in New York, "Gentrification—whether called renewal, revitalization, upgrading, or uplifting—always involves the expansion and transformation of neighborhoods through rapid economic investment and population shifts, and yet it is equally implicated with social inequalities" (Dávila 2004, 3).

Mass demolition projects that feature clearing urban neighborhoods have also been popularly characterized as "slum clearance," a term that corresponds with the official language of international development agencies, such as the World Bank and the International Monetary Fund, that provide financial resources for urban revitalization projects in Salvador and other Latin American cities (World Bank 2009). Moreover, while this analysis of black politics in urban communities departs from what Salvador residents consider to be the pejorative discourse of "*favelas*" or "slums" to describe their communal lands and *bairros* (neighborhoods), Mike Davis's *Planet of Slums* describes the racist thinking behind the demolition that characterizes revitalization efforts as a "war" against mass urban occupation by the poor. He writes that "in response to the burgeoning of shantytowns, authorities in several countries, ardently supported by the urban middle classes, launched massive crackdowns on informal settlement. Since many of the new urban immigrants were *indigenistas* or descendants of slaves, there was often a racial dimension to this 'war on squatting'" (Davis 2007, 54). In Latin American countries such as Venezuela, the "government's solution to the barrios was the bulldozer. On a given morning, policemen and trucks would arrive at the barrio; an official would direct the loading of the residents' belongings onto the truck; policemen would deal with any objections; when the belongings and the residents had been removed to the new apartments, the houses were demolished" (ibid., quoting Karst, Schwartz, and Schwartz 1973, 7). In Brazilian cities, where the vast majority of the nation's black population and poor occupy these settlements, equating "slum clearance" with "black clearance" reflects how black people experience the interconnectedness of class-based racial and gender inequality and spatial displacement. In recent decades in Salvador, black neighborhoods in the city center and on the coast have been partly or completely demolished.

A focus on the black women who play central roles in the social networks of their neighborhoods reveals the gendered meaning of urban revitalization. Women have led the opposition to urban renewal projects in Salvador that result in the destruction of livelihoods, the reduction of access to vital material resources, violent demolition of homes, and mass expulsion and displacement of black communities from urban land that residents have known and cultivated for generations. The neighborhood movements they lead focus on access to citizenship rights and resources such as adequate housing and land. The activism of these black women expands our understanding of the racial politics of urban spaces, collective gender resistance, and racial solidarity. As Thomas Sugrue (1996, 229) argues, urban space is a "metaphor for perceived racial difference." Urban revitalization is a racial project, which in the city center of Salvador is a prime example of the discursive and material effects of institutional racism in Brazilian society. The Brazil case highlights the commonalities as well as the differences among black urban conditions throughout the diaspora. Observing black Brazilian women's conditions in the context of a global practice enables us to identify broad connections between ideas and practices of blackness, black womanhood, the black diaspora, and radical black politics in urban spaces.

Black Women as Community Leaders in Salvador

The political organization of black urban neighborhoods such as Gamboa de Baixo has depended on the mass participation of women residents. From the formation of the Women's Association in the 1980s to the ongoing militancy of the neighborhood association in the 1990s and 2000s, women in Gamboa de Baixo lead everyday social networks as well as the grassroots struggle for land rights, participatory urbanization policies, and the overall socioeconomic improvement of the neighborhood. Women's leadership of this type is rarely visible in Salvador. We are more accustomed to seeing women participating with the masses in street protests and tend not to see them as community leaders. The example of neighborhood movements may change ideas about what constitutes leadership.

Furthermore, the leadership practices of black women political leaders in Gamboa de Baixo differ dramatically from those of male political actors. Their approaches to leadership shape the organizational tactics Gamboa de Baixo activists have used and frame the analytical relationship between gender consciousness, solidarity, and the struggle for collective rights to urban land. In other words, it is possible to understand political consciousness that stems from women's wisdom and, in this case, black women's strong sense of themselves as women, black, poor, and the rightful owners of the Bahian urban landscape.

In the case of Gamboa de Baixo, because of its geographic location and the nature of the political struggle, it is necessary to consider black women's relationship to their neighborhood and how it shapes their political consciousness and approach to social protest. Social movement theorist Cristiani Bereta da Silva (2004) writes that in the well-known Movimento Sem Terra, the "political place" of women activists has yet to be resolved. Specific neighborhood factors such as the everyday social networks that organize birthday parties, funerals, and religious festivals have determined that the "rightful place" of women is in leadership roles of political organizations that confront the state. But black women's leadership has not gone unchallenged by local residents, activists from other neighborhoods, social movement organizations acting in solidarity, and government officials. In essence, the struggle for political recognition as a community rests on the collective struggle of black women to challenge and transform what France Winddance Twine (1998) calls "racist commonsense" or a "taken for granted" attitude about black people and, I would add, about black womanhood in Brazil. African American feminist Patricia Hill Collins has characterized these forms of naturalized representations as "controlling images" that are "designed to make racism, sexism, and poverty appear to be natural, normal, and an inevitable part of everyday life" (Collins 1990, 68).

From this perspective, the struggle for land rights becomes necessarily linked with the struggle to counter public images of black women, particularly those who live in poor neighborhoods, as lacking the political knowledge needed to organize social movements. Even though black women street vendors and religious leaders have been widely celebrated and respected for their role in maintaining Afro-Brazilian religious traditions and communities, the vast majority of black women in Salvador are domestic workers whose work is greatly undervalued. Ninety-five percent of domestic workers in Salvador are black women, and most of the black women activists in Gamboa de Baixo do domestic work. Moreover, most of the government officials that Gamboa de Baixo activists confront have interacted with black women only as babysitters, housekeepers, and washerwomen in their homes or as janitors in their workplaces. As Cecilia McCallum writes, "Some five million women worked as *empregadas domesticas* (domestic employees) in Brazil in 2001. Their symbolic place is in the kitchen, a stereotype reinforced on a daily basis in the mass media. . . . Many women spend much of their lives in these spaces, thereby reinforcing the symbolic ties of black female gender and domestic work" (2007, 56).

As they challenge the fixed notions of black women that limit perceptions of their political potential, Gamboa de Baixo activists must deal with government officials' unwillingness to acknowledge the seriousness of their work. In fact, in the initial years of the organization, government officials often received them by asking, "*Quem é o homem responsavel?*" (Who is the man in charge?). While it seemed to local activists almost natural that they would be the leaders of the community organization because of the social and political networks they lead within the neighborhood, government officials expected men to be the leaders of women as well as of entire communities. The women's claims that residents of Gamboa de Baixo have rights to the land because it had been a fishing community for a century fueled expectations that only men who were fishermen would lead the local economy and make political decisions. Government officials saw the previous Women's Association, which focused on milk and food programs, reproductive health, and social programs in the neighborhood with the support of a female politician, as the rightful political place of poor black women in city politics. Those issues were seen as "*coisinha de mulher*" (a woman's thing), and women were perceived to be defending their rights as women and not necessarily the collective interests of the entire community. The issues of land, urban planning, and public policy in general were seen as men's political terrain, a place where poor black women had neither the knowledge nor the experience to participate. In other words, Gamboa de Baixo activists were not dealing with so-called women's politics. As Gamboa de Baixo activists explain, they have had to remake their position in Bahian society by physically and ideologically inserting themselves in certain political spaces, such as meetings with policymakers and urban planning technicians.

Black Women as Foot Soldiers in Brazil's Black Movement

The Gamboa de Baixo neighborhood movement has been relatively successful in making questions of gender central to the community's struggle for racial and class equality in Salvador. For the Women's Association and the subsequent neighborhood association, new conceptualizations of gender and sexuality that transform personal relationships go hand in hand with the everyday and institutional fight for collective recognition as black political actors and urban citizens with the right to land and the right to participate in urbanization programs. Moreover, the individual and collective empowerment of poor people, blacks, and women in Gamboa de Baixo has been important for mobilizing and sustaining the political movement. Local activists have proven that gender solidarity can be a major force in mobilizing mass support for social justice movements.

However, many black women activists have not formed separate organizations and continue to wage the struggle for women's rights within existing organizations such as neighborhood associations. In Gamboa de Baixo, black women have drawn upon their experiences with various forms of discrimination to forge a political identity and build a political movement aimed at transforming the state's relationship to urban communities. They argue that state practices of land distribution and urbanization must be compatible with local culture and insist that urbanization practices must address the needs of black women simultaneously with the needs of entire black communities. Women in these communities are largely the ones who make decisions about housing design, and more importantly, central location issues for women who are the main ones responsible for taking their children to school and to health care centers. This stance supports the ideas of black Brazilian feminist activist Sueli Carneiro, who writes that black women's struggle includes the transformation of social conditions that determine their everyday existence and that "we must continue to fight for housing, health, sanitation, and antiracist and anti-sexist education—basic conditions to break the vicious cycle that confines the black population, and black women in particular, to the subterranean levels of Brazilian society" (Carneiro 1999, 228).

For black women political leaders in Gamboa de Baixo, this profound ideological understanding of how Brazilian society operates influences their concrete demands for social change. State officials often challenge activists' conceptual and political claims to rights as blacks, women, and poor people occupying urban lands. Black women grassroots leaders face challenges in their engagement with the state that their male counterparts do not. Officials use political co-optation such as offering jobs as a way to undermine black women's leadership and dismiss their critiques of urbanization policies.

The attempt to co-opt community leaders is pervasive and negatively impacts the political outcomes of struggles for urban land rights. Black women experience co-optation differently, usually through the form of sexual seduction. Many male officials believe that all black women, especially poor ones, are sexually available and are willing to sell their bodies in exchange for money and goods. Ultimately, these forms of exchanges are aimed at destroying the leadership base of the movement by focusing on individual women. However, this form of co-optation has not been successful in Gamboa de Baixo, where black women activists are unwilling to negotiate on an individual basis. Their solidarity proves beneficial to the overall community struggle for resources.

This is not the case in the neighboring coastal community of Solar do Unhao, where the government has plans to evict the residents, who, like the residents of Gamboa de Baixo, consider themselves to be a traditional century-old fishing colony. Family ties between the neighborhoods go back for generations. In fact, the urbanization plans considered the two neighborhoods to be one, and residents claim that only in recent decades have they had separate identities. However, Gamboa de Baixo is the poorer of the two neighborhoods because of the construction of Contorno Avenue and the increasing number of immigrants from rural regions of Bahia and other neighborhoods who have settled there. While Gamboa de Baixo residents tend to embrace newcomers, who often must build improvised housing out of wood, Solar do Unhao residents have resisted settlement and have protested the construction of such poor structures. In general, the income levels and the quality of housing have been better in Solar do Unhao, but both communities face the threat of expulsion and displacement and struggle to obtain basic sanitation and other resources.

At the onset of the movement in the mid-1990s, the major difference in the political organization of the two neighborhoods was that a predominantly poor black women's leadership emerged in Gamboa de Baixo, while men assumed leadership in Solar do Unhao. Some of the male leaders in Solar do Unhao worked as civil servants and were formally educated. Some Gamboa de Baixo activists recall that the sexist leadership of men in Solar do Unhao undermined the possibility that the two neighborhoods could join forces. They assert that the survival of both communities is the direct result of women activists' determination to protect the collective interests of both communities. They also remember that the male activists were unwilling to take the women of Gamboa de Baixo seriously and work with them to strategize politically. To further compound the problems, state officials offered benefits such as government posts to individual male leaders that led some of them to abandon the movement or act in ways that were detrimental to the overall political project of both communities. As the movement in Gamboa de Baixo strengthened, the movement in Solar do Unhao steadily lost its political relevance as several residents began to side with government officials. This culminated in the government's false representation of incomplete urbanization projects in the area as a "success," though Gamboa de Baixo activists refused to participate in any government-sponsored celebrations. Also, Solar do Unhao has suffered from land speculation, and the number of outsiders (primarily non-Brazilians) who have come to settle on the Bahian coast has increased.

In contrast, Gamboa de Baixo activists pushed forward collective claims for improvements in local social conditions and the regularization of land rights that have benefited Solar do Unhao residents as well. Today, a new group of male leaders has emerged in Solar do Unhao that has tried to take advantage of the political gains neighboring women activists have made by making attempts to open dialogues with these women, who now have more than a decade of political experience and knowledge as well as the respect of state officials. Gamboa de Baixo activists say that these leaders have much to learn about how the government operates and how it has changed since initial conflicts over land expulsion arose. The challenge for these male activists is how to reverse previous co-optation practices in ways that will allow them to dialogue with the state for collective rights similar to the state recognition and political credibility Gamboa de Baixo activists have been able to achieve as a result of years of hard work.

Black women in the Gamboa de Baixo political movement identify grassroots contributions of the black movement as one of the primary reasons they have not been so easily co-opted and have been able to focus on collective social change to benefit entire black communities. They define the black movement broadly but focus on organizations such as the MNU, UNegro, and Ceafro, three organizations that have worked arduously in political solidarity with Gamboa de Baixo. Black movement organizations have emphasized the affirmation of black identity, racial consciousness, and the historical relationship between present-day struggles for citizenship rights and past movements against colonialism and slavery. The black movement in Brazil has been able to reach the masses of black people contending with race-based social inequalities and the transformation of Brazilian institutions. Social activism in Gamboa de Baixo illustrates how the black movement has been key in the process of racializing the discourses and practices of urban institutions that impact black communities on a mass scale. Most of the discussions led by black movement activists in the neighborhood highlighted the systemic nature of Brazilian racism and emphasized where blacks and black women are socially and economically located in Bahian and Brazilian society. This knowledge fueled black women's interest in claiming political rights that would transform their social conditions and form a new, equal society.

Furthermore, work around black identity and Afro-Brazilian culture has been fundamental to how black women understand their political potential in the context of widespread racism, sexism, classism, and homophobia. The black movement played a crucial role in encouraging local black women activists, who identified themselves as rescuing *"nossa posição enquanto mulheres negras"* (our social position as black women), by empowering them to feel capable of waging struggle against the state. Some said that before their participation in the neighborhood movement they had been unaware of their power as black women and that they learned that they did not need to depend on white leaders, which they have taken to mean that they do not need to give in to attempts by male politicians and other government agents to co-opt them. Rita (Ritinha), a former social worker at the Center for Social Action Studies (Centro de Estudos e Ação Social) in Salvador, has been fundamental in bridging the relationship between the black movement and the grassroots neighborhood movement for land rights. In meetings and street protests with neighborhood activists in the citywide housing and land struggle, she foregrounds the valorization of black-ness and black womanhood; these points help solidify black women's politi-cal identity. Ritinha has also linked Gamboa de Baixo activists with activists in other neighborhoods, not only through her work as a social worker at CEAS but also as an activist in the Alto das Pombas black neighborhood. One example of the bridges between the two neighborhoods is the attendance and participation of Gamboa de Baixo women in the annual black women's dinner in Alto das Pombas, which pays homage to black women past and present. Some activists told me that the idea of an *"homenagem a mulheres negras"* (homage to black women) was a novelty that proved important for countering the racist stigma against poor black women (Ana Cristina, interview with author, 2008).

Social activism in Gamboa de Baixo illustrates how grassroots black move-ment organizations have been significant in the process of racializing the dis-courses and practices of urban institutions that impact black communities on a mass scale. I am calling for a broadening of the concept of the Brazilian black movement to include social movements that have significant participation by black women, such as domestic workers' unions and neighborhood associations (Bairros 1996). The president of the Domestic Workers' Union of Bahia, Creuza Oliveira, related this concern in a statement on black women's struggles in 1999:

> And the struggle for our liberation, the struggle for our dignity, the strug-gle for our survival, continues to today: Princess Izabel signed the Law [of Abolition] but forgot to sign our worker's card![1] And today we still live in a situation of inequality and exploitation, because it is not just signing the card, but giving dignified housing, giving decent work conditions. I make up part of this category that today still continues to be semi-enslaved, where the people continue fighting for our rights, for the law, for the re-spect of the worker's card and other social rights, for public policies. Our struggle began as a category from the times when our ancestors fought for liberation, formed *quilombos,* we, as enslaved domestics, we were there, going to the *quilombos* and all. (Oliveira 1999, 10, my translation)

Most of the discussions led by neighborhood activists highlight the systemic nature of Brazilian racism and illuminate where blacks and black women have been socially, politically, and economically located in Bahian and Brazilian soci-ety throughout history. Black women's knowledge of themselves as a racialized, gendered, and classed category has fueled black women's individual and collec-tive interest in claiming political rights. As Oliveira points out, the struggle for freedom and dignity encompasses the historical fight of free blacks who inhab-ited the *quilombos* as well as domestic workers who today fight for fair wages and adequate housing to support their families. The political development of

Gamboa de Baixo illustrates how complex understandings of race in Bahian and Brazilian society emerge from black urban communities, making race very apparent in these movements. Community and religious leader Makota Valdina Pinto[2] asserts, "I always knew myself as black, I didn't discover myself as black nor did I begin to act in the community from the Black Movement. I discovered, yes, that I had a way, a group, to express all the [racial] experiences that I had accumulated. I learned to do social work in the community of Engelho Velho da Federação. I remember that I could not be part of the neighborhood association because of my age, but I remember that I worked for it since early on" (Castro 1999, 82).

Conclusion

The opening of the Iraci Isabel da Silva Health Center of Gamboa de Baixo on November 22, 2006, was fraught with tension between government officials and local residents. The ceremony took place in a restored building in the Ladeira dos Aflitos neighborhood, situated above Gamboa de Baixo and Solar do Unhao. For decades, black women activists had demanded that a health center be built in Gamboa de Baixo. The long staircases that extend from the Gamboa waterfront to the street make the journey to medical facilities in the city extremely difficult, and the Gamboa needed its own facility to accommodate neighborhood residents, especially those with impaired mobility. As a result of an organized struggle for social services in the area, activists were able to obtain a guarantee that a health center would be constructed, but they were excluded from the planning process that decided where it would be located. Residents immediately questioned how a clinic located outside Gamboa de Baixo would adequately serve their needs and why it should bear the community's name if it was not located in the neighborhood. In several meetings with government officials, neighborhood association leaders criticized the fact that community members had been excluded from the process of deciding where the health center would be located. They also pointed out that a community-based center would better meet the specific challenges of the hilly terrain and contribute to the overall social improvement of the neighborhood. However, to their dismay, by the time they had these meetings, the construction of the center was already well under way. Gamboa de Baixo residents accepted the partial benefits of the new center but demanded that a future clinic be constructed in the neighborhood. As a result of these negotiations, a few local residents received jobs and the health center carries the name of Iracema da Silva (Dona Iraci), a former activist in the neighborhood association who died suddenly in 2002 from a stroke during a violent confrontation with police.

As in the case of land and housing rights, black women's struggle for adequate health care within the Gamboa de Baixo neighborhood is ongoing. Black women in Salvador have been active in black liberation struggles during various periods of Brazilian history, and their participation and leadership in the Gamboa de Baixo neighborhood association constitutes part of this tradition of radical politics. Gamboa de Baixo activists claim land rights not just as women's rights but as collective community rights that will guarantee a lasting black presence in the city center of Salvador. Moreover, this transformation in how the state allocates land in urban spaces will benefit other black neighborhoods facing similar threats of land expulsion and displacement. Within the various forms of organizing that make up the black movement, women recognize their past and present potential to change Brazilian politics.

Notes

Epigraph source: An excerpt from his "Back to Land" speech on September 11, 1964, given while he was president of Kenya (1964–1978), quoted in Mutongi (2007, 163).

1. Princess Isabel was the daughter of Emperor Pedro II and became the Princess Imperial in 1850, after his death. Princess Isabel is often cited for two key historical moments: the signing of the 1871 law freeing all children born to slave mothers and the law abolishing slavery, or the Golden Law, on May 13, 1888. While this date symbolizes the official end of slavery in Brazil, black movement activists often claim that it did not mark the end of slavery in Brazil or the socioeconomic exploitation of blacks more generally.

2. Makota Valdina Pinto is a black environmental rights activist and community and Candomblé leader in Salvador, Bahia. This excerpt is from an interview conducted by Ubiratan Castro, the Afro-Brazilian historian and director of the Palmares Foundation, published in *Revista Palmares* 2 (1999): 82.

Bibliography

Bairros, Luiza. 1996. "Orfeu e poder: Uma perspectiva Afro-Americana sobre a politica racial no Brasil." *Afro-Asiáticos* 17:173–186.

Carneiro, Sueli. 1999. "Black Women's Identity in Brazil." In *Race in Contemporary Brazil: From Indifference to Inequality*, ed. Rebecca Reichmann, 217–228. University Park: Pennsylvania University Press.

Castro, Ubiratan. 1999. Interview with Makota Valdina Pinto. *Revista Palmares* 2.

Collins, Patricia Hill. 1990. *Black Feminist Thought: Knowledge, Consciousness, and the Politics of Empowerment*. New York: Routledge.

Covin, David. 2006. *The Unified Black Movement of Brazil: 1978–2002*. Jefferson, N.C.: McFarland.

Davies, Carole Boyce. 2006. "'Con-di-fi-cation' Black Women, Leadership and Political Power." *Feminist Africa* 7. Available at http://www.feministafrica.org/index.php/con-di-fi-cation-black-women-leadership-and-political-power.

Dávila, Arlene. 2004. *Barrio Dreams: Puerto Ricans, Latinos, and the Neoliberal City*. Berkeley: University of California Press.

Davis, Angela Y. 1981. "Education and Liberation: Black Women's Perspective." In Davis, *Women, Race, and Class*, 99–109. New York: Random House.

Davis, Mike. 2007. *Planet of Slums*. New York: Verso.

Du Bois, W. E. B. (1935) 1998. *Black Reconstruction in America: 1860–1880*. New York: The Free Press.

Gregory, Steven. 1998. *Black Corona: Race and the Politics of Place in an Urban Community*. Princeton, N.J.: Princeton University Press.

Gusmão, Neusa M. Mendes de. 1995. *Terra de Pretos, Terra de Mulheres: Terra, Mulher e Raça num Bairro Rural Negro*. Brasília: Fundação Cultural Palmares.

Hall, Stuart. 1980. "Race, Articulation, and Societies Structured in Dominance." In UNESCO, *Sociological Theories: Race and Colonialism*, 305–345. Paris: UNESCO.

Hanchard, Michael. 1994. *Orpheus and Power: The Movimento Negro of Rio de Janeiro and São Paulo, Brazil, 1945–1988*. Princeton, N.J.: Princeton University Press.

Karst, Kenneth L., Murray L. Schwartz, and Audrey J. Schwartz, 1973. *The Evolution of Law in the Barrios of Caracas*. Los Angeles: Latin American Center, University of California.

McCallum, Cecilia. 2007. "Women out of Place?: A Micro-Historical Perspective on the Black Feminist Movement in Salvador da Bahia, Brazil." *Journal of Latin American Studies* 39: 55–58.

McKittrick, Katherine. 2006. *Demonic Grounds: Black Women and the Cartographies of Struggle*. Minneapolis: University of Minnesota Press.

Mutongi, Kenda Beatrice. 2007. *Worries of the Heart: Widows, Family, and Community in Kenya*. Chicago: University of Chicago Press.

Nascimento, Abdias do. 1980. *O quilombismo*. Rio/Petropolis: Editora Vozes.

Oliveira, Creuza. 1999. Flyer in possession of the author.

Ratts, Alex. 2007. *Eu Sou Atlântica: Sobre a trajetória de vida de Beatriz Nascimento*. São Paulo: Imprensa Oficial.

Silva, Cristiani Bereta da. 2004. "Relacoes de genero e subjetividades no Devir MST." *Estudos Feministas* 12: 269–287.

Smith, Barbara. 2000. *The Truth That Never Hurts: Writings on Race, Gender, and Freedom*. New Brunswick, N.J.: Rutgers University Press.

Sugrue, Thomas. 1996. *Origins of the Urban Crisis*. Princeton, N.J.: Princeton University Press.

Twine, France Winddance. 1998. *Racism in a Racial Democracy: The Maintenance of White Supremacy in Brazil*. New Brunswick, N.J.: Rutgers University Press.

World Bank. 2009. *World Development Report: Reshaping Economic Geography*. Washington, D.C.: International Bank for Reconstruction and Development/World Bank.

PART
3

State Responses

11

Social Movements in Latin America

The Power of Regional and National Networks

JUDITH A. MORRISON

African descendants have organized to resist racial discrimination since they arrived in the Americas. The process of Afro-Latin Americans mobilizing regionally to promote policy reforms is a relatively new phenomenon that gained momentum in the early 1990s and is a direct product of the rich history of organized black civil society groups throughout the hemisphere in places as diverse as Brazil, Colombia, Uruguay and in coastal regions throughout Central America. This chapter explores how African descendants have established national and regional networks, effectively promoted policies of inclusion, and combated discrimination in the region.

Conditions of African Descendants: The Significance of African-Descendant Populations

African-descendant citizens account for 30 percent or more of Latin America's population and number up to 150 million. Ending racial discrimination and finding ways to fully incorporate these citizens into national life are among the most pressing tasks facing Latin America. The health of democracies in Brazil, Colombia, Nicaragua, and many other countries depends on the full extension of rights and opportunities to populations of African descent. African-descendant populations virtually everywhere in Latin America are the target of racial discrimination and exclusion and suffer high levels of economic and social exclusion compared with other racial and ethnic groups in the Americas (Morrison 2007, 39; World Bank 2006, 1–5).

Over the past two decades, several Latin American governments have begun to pay greater attention to their African-descendant populations in response to pressure from civil society organizations. Although the record is still spotty in most places, governments are increasingly collecting and analyzing data on

African descendants. Countries such as Brazil and Colombia have taken policy and legal measures to respond to race-based exclusion, including implementing targeted programs to address the historic discrimination against African descendants. It is also encouraging that a growing (albeit still small) number of African descendants are winning elections, gaining government appointments, and securing leadership positions.

There are persistent gaps between African descendants and whites throughout the region. An Inter-American Development Bank report has calculated that some Latin American economies could expand by up to one-third if people of African descent or indigenous background were fully included in the labor markets of their nations (Zoninsein 2001, 2). The overall impact of racial gaps has clear economic consequences for societies as a whole in the hemisphere.

Socioeconomic Gaps

Brazil has the largest African-descendant population in Latin America and has tracked data by race for over two decades. The findings in these data illustrate the challenges facing African descendants throughout the region as a whole. For example, we know that if Brazil's white and black populations were classified separately, the Human Development Index (HDI) of a hypothetical Afro-Brazilian nation would rank 101 among the world's 165 nations, while that of an all-white nation would rank 46.[1] The official HDI ranking for Brazil is 69, which is roughly the average of the hypothetical rankings for an all-white Brazil and a racially mixed Brazil (Morrison 2007, 41; Instituto Brasileiro de Geografia e Estatistica 2002, 1).

The overall impact of African descendants on Brazilian society can be seen when one considers that they constitute about half the population (or a conservatively estimated 90 million), but their economic participation accounts for only about 20 percent of the gross domestic product. Despite significant improvements in earnings in Brazil and aggressive income distribution programs such as the widely recognized conditional cash transfer programs Bolsa Familia and Bolsa Escola, labor market gaps by race remain. African descendants as a whole were able to improve their earnings by 18 percent from 2003 to 2006, compared to 11 percent for whites, but we see that despite these improvements, white men in Brazil earn 98.5 percent more than African-descendant men (who are defined in the study as individuals who self-identify as *pardo* or *preto*), and white Brazilian men earn 200 percent more than African-descendant women (Paixão 2009b, 20–22).

Unemployment is 50 percent higher among Afro-Brazilians than among whites. The majority of Afro-Brazilians, or 78 percent, live below the poverty line, compared to 40 percent of whites, and the life expectancy of African descendants is only 66 years, compared to 72 years for European descendants (Morrison 2007, 41; United Nations Refugee Agency 2008). Half of all blacks are functionally illiterate, while less than 20 percent of whites are unable to read. Only 4 percent of Afro-Brazilians between the ages of 18 and 24 have attended a university, compared to 12 percent of whites (Instituto Brasileiro de Geografia e Estatistica 2008, 210–211).

Affirmative action in higher education affects only 25 percent of the current African-descendant population because three-fourths of all Afro-Brazilians have less than eleven years of formal schooling. Forty percent of blacks have completed less than seven years of schooling (Paixão 2009b, 3–8). The widely available disaggregated statistics by race throughout Brazil demonstrate a tremendous and consistent socioeconomic gap between blacks and whites, and these data from nations such as Brazil, which has taken a leadership role in compiling statistics, suggest that a gap between black and white populations is present in other countries throughout the region.

Colombia has the second largest African-descendant population in Latin America and faces similar inequality. Estimates suggest that there are 10 million to 17 million African descendants in Colombia, between 20 and 30 percent of the total population. Coastal regions of Colombia may have Afro-Colombian populations as high as 90 percent, as in the case of the Pacific coast, or 60 percent on the Atlantic coast. Chocó is the most African-descendant state (or *departamento*), followed by Magdalena (72 percent), Bolivar (66 percent), and Sucre (65 percent). Southern Valle, northern Cauca, and Urabá have black populations that are as high as 65 percent. African descendants are present in every major city in the country, and with the impact of increasing levels of displacement, large groups of African descendants are moving to urban areas to escape violence.

African descendants in Colombia face significant challenges. Although Afro-Colombians make up about 26 percent of the entire population, they represent well over 75 percent of the poor. Blacks have the lowest per capita income in the country, and 98 percent of Afro-Colombian municipalities are unable to provide basic services such as water, sanitation, education, and electricity to their citizens (Fitts 2002, 5–7).

Afro-Colombians earn 34 percent less than their nonblack counterparts and are overrepresented in the lowest two quintiles of wage earners—blacks are 49 percent of these low wage earners, compared to 40 percent for the nation as a whole. The lack of economic opportunities for blacks is paradoxical because Afro-Colombians, unlike Afro-Brazilians, have participation levels in education that are equal to or greater than other racial groups in the country (U.S. Department of State 2008; Morrison 2007, 41). According to recent

World Bank reports, Afro-Colombians attend primary schools at a level higher than the national average; 42 percent of black children attend school compared to 32 percent of all Colombian children, but black students are less likely to attend high school, because secondary education is available to only 62 percent of Afro-Colombians compared to 75 percent of all Colombians. Further, the quality of secondary schools available to blacks is extremely low; according to ICFES, the national college entrance exam board, 65 percent of schools in Afro-Colombian communities are identified as poor quality or very poor quality. Only 14 percent of blacks pursue higher education compared to 26 percent of all adults in the nation, although blacks and whites have roughly the same high literacy rates (89 percent for blacks and 94 percent for the country as a whole) (World Bank 2006, 39).

Afro-Colombians have historically identified with their geographical communities and have only recently formally identified as an African-descendant racial category. More Afro-Colombians are self-identifying as they migrate to new areas of the country, and because of social movements and the work of prominent academics in the country, there is a growing awareness of the contribution of African descendants to the country. In the 1993 census, only 500,000 people identified as Afro-Colombian, or about 1.5 percent of the total population, while in the 2005 census just under half of the African-descendant population self-identified as African descendant (Contreras 2008, 1–2) In the 2005 population, the percentage of Colombians who self-identified as Afro-Colombian increased to about 10 percent. This is a great improvement, but it is still a significant undercount. In the reports of the national planning office, Consejo Nacional de Política Económica y Social (CONPES; National Council on Economic and Social Policy), the Afro-Colombian population is conservatively estimated at 18 percent, although some official government documents report that Afro-Colombians could be as much as one-third of the total population.

Data from Brazil and Colombia illustrate that racial discrimination continues to be one of the most persistent predictors of poverty in the Americas, yet quantifying the extent of the problem continues to be a challenge in most countries because disaggregated data by race are often unreliable or unavailable. With the exception of Brazil, a longtime front-runner on racial statistics, and a handful of other nations that are making progress with statistics such as Colombia, Costa Rica, Belize, and Bolivia, most countries still do not have an adequate basic count of their African-descendant populations. Civil society groups continue to prioritize data collection by taking on local census projects such as FEDEAFRO in Colombia through a joint initiative of Afro-America XXI and the Universidad Federal del Valle, which is led by Fernando Urrea, a prominent academic researcher. Such programs are a way of providing local resources to support national census bureaus using local community knowledge to improve data collection. The project also serves as a mechanism that encourages governments to take data collection more seriously.

The History of African-Descendant Social Movements

African-descendant social movements have existed since the arrival of African descendants in the Americas in the 1600s (Ribando Seekles 2008, 4). These movements have been an important symbol of resistance, but they have also pushed for significant policy reforms to benefit African-descendant communities throughout the Americas in the modern era.

Much of the long-standing African-descendant resistance has taken place in rural communities within the context of traditional leadership structures. Some activists have argued that secret societies that needed to be hidden in order to be effective have made it difficult for scholars and researchers to document the contributions of some of the most important societies and trace their impact on contemporary political movements. Despite these challenges, there are strong indications that self-help networks and closed societies served as significant cultural and religious influences in black social movements during the period of slavery. The ability of African descendants to lead national policy reforms in Latin America is a relatively new phenomenon that gained momentum in the 1990s and is a product of these historic struggles and leadership structures. Although academics and researchers have studied the cultural aspects of these movements, they have paid little attention to the role of Afro-Latin American movements, and organizations that have focused on issues of justice, equality, and democracy (Johnson 2007, 65). Similarly, most of the research has focused on Brazil and Colombia, and more work is needed on other Latin American countries.

This chapter focuses on social movements, which I define as groups of individuals with a collective ideology working together to create social change. Throughout this chapter we will see examples of how African-descendant social movements illustrate key elements of social movements, including engaging in political action by forming specific organizations, mounting campaigns, and coordinating events designed to increase public visibility. This definition of social movements derives from the work of Tilly (2004, 3–4). In the first half of the twentieth century, the African-descendant social movement consisted primarily of grassroots organizations that were originally formed as informal clubs or societies. In the 1980s and early 1990s, many of these groups received official recognition as nongovernmental organizations or civil society organizations.

The Movement in Stages

Despite the challenges involved in documenting the role of African-descendant organizations over time, four major periods can be identified as fundamental to the development of black social movements and the impact of such movements on policy reform. The first is the birth of black resistance throughout the Americas in maroon communities (1600s–1900). The second is the period of political turmoil, which includes the dictatorships, and the integration of African descendants in progressive social movements throughout Latin America (1900–1960). In the third period, activists recognized the need to defend blackness as an alternative to racial democracy (1960–1995). In the fourth period, which is the present, activists have focused on meeting the expectations of a growing self-identified African-descendant population that has started to receive greater visibility and is recognized as a critical mass that warrants policy measures (1995–present).

The Birth of Black Resistance in the Americas (1600s–1900): Maroon Communities and Their Impact

African descendants have always created mechanisms to try to overcome their condition of oppression in Latin America. Self-help networks and closed societies served as significant cultural and religious influence in black social movements during the period of slavery. A rich body of literature documents the phenomenon of *cabildos* (councils) and similar African societies in Cuba and other places during the colonial period (see Howard 1998; Andrews 2004). Despite the pervasive myth that slavery was somehow more flexible or humane in Latin America, African descendants struggled to free themselves from bondage and established maroon communities in every region of the Americas. These maroon communities, called *quilombos* (or *terras de preto*) in Portuguese or *palenques* in Spanish served as places of refuge for Africans escaping slavery. Maroon communities were often governed by familial or religious structures. The Brazilian *quilombo* model gives us several examples of how land was held and controlled throughout the Americas.[2] Hereditary communities (*herdeiros*) are areas where a leader and her or his heirs control the title to the land. A significant number of hereditary communities pass land titles from one relative to another through matriarchal or patriarchal lineage systems. These traditional structures determine how individuals can use collective land. For example, a newcomer to a community would consult the hereditary leader to determine if he or she could obtain rights to an area to build a home and establish a farming plot.[3] Religious communities (*amocambado*) are based on African religious structures, and title may transfer from one religious leader (often the saint mother/father, or *mãe/pai de santo* in Portuguese) to another. The leader is responsible for assuring that the land is used and preserved in accordance with religious practices and norms (Morrison 2004, 33–35).

These lands, which served and continue to serve as important symbols of resistance, were controlled by a small group of leaders and were located in carefully selected remote geographic areas that often have natural barriers (such as rivers, forests, and mountains) that limited entry and provided opportunities to establish lookout points. The success of maroon communities can be seen throughout the coastal regions of Central America and the Caribbean, where there are large Garifuna populations that have a multifaceted history that developed from marronage. The strength of these structures can still be seen today with the Garifuna that continue to retain their distinct language and culture in diverse countries in the Spanish- and English-speaking Caribbean. The residents of African maroon communities forged intricate political networks that enabled them to retain their freedom, and these communities serve as an important geographical reference for black activists to this day. The great African-descendant resistance leaders such as Zumbi dos Palmares in Brazil and Benkos Biohó in Colombia became black heroes as a result of their leadership of maroon communities. In addition, *quilombos* such as Conceição das Criolas in Pernambuco, which was founded in 1802 by African-descendant women during the time of slavery, serve as a reference point for black women's organizations throughout Brazil, as an example of African-descendant women's leadership.

As refuges from slavery, maroon communities needed to be highly structured and politically astute in order to retain their independence in environments where they were surrounded by hostile slaveholders.[4] Sanchez and Bryan observe that "one of the most important elements in helping to safeguard the human rights and economic survival of Afro-descendant communities in Latin America has been their access to land" (Sanchez and Bryan 2003, 10). Land has profound worth as a symbol of resistance for African descendants. This notion of land and geographical space has enabled communities to continue their leadership across the generations and has provided a foundation for organizing the African-descendant social movement. Protecting the land continues to be relevant, and not unlike the past, some of the most important policy battles facing black communities in Latin America revolve around retaining and restoring their historic land titles (particularly in Colombia and the coastal regions of Central America such as Honduras and Nicaragua).

Political Turmoil and Integration: African Descendants and Integrated Social Movements throughout Latin America (1900–1960)

From the early to late 1900s, African descendants throughout Latin America were engaged in various social movements through their work with political parties, labor unions, community groups, and professional associations (Johnson 2007, 62). At times leaders felt that unifying these more general movements with broader struggles on behalf of the poor would help blacks transcend race. This approach to race was relatively common and coincided with the rise of dictatorships in Latin America. Blacks in Latin America played an important role in the labor movement (Conniff and Davis 1994, 269–291), and blacks actively participated in universal struggles for the working class. However, African descendants working in collective class struggles criticized these movements as not doing enough to address the issues of racial discrimination. This disconnect between movements can been seen in Larkin and Nascimento's analysis of solidarity between the black movement and other progressive social movements: "In the 1970s, Afro-Brazilian organizations proliferated across the country. Yet only very recently, in the 1980s and 1990s, have they found solid support among allies in other social movements" (Nascimento and Larkin Nascimento 2000, 18).

In the early 1900s, African descendants established social clubs and organizations in places such as Brazil and Colombia and began to create a social space for discussing their needs and concerns. The Frente Negra Brasileira (FNB) was established in Brazil in 1931 and is an important point of reference for the black movement in Latin America in part because in 1936 it became the first African-descendant political party in Brazil. Black women actively participated in these organizations, and as early as 1931 (the founding year of FNB), Afro-Brazilian women established the Frente Negrinhas to campaign against all forms of discrimination, including discrimination by gender. This movement of "assertive working class [Afro-Brazilian] women" had an influence over the black movement as a whole (Vieira 1995, 27–28) and changed the discourse on race and class. In 1950, the first national council for black women was established in Brazil, known as the I Conselho Nacional da Mulher Negra. This council, which promoted voting rights and advocated for policies and programs within black communities, was a highly successful mechanism for unifying the black movement as a whole. The unique position of black women at the intersection of race and gender has given black women leaders the unique ability to negotiate space within both the black movement and the labor movement. Afro-Brazilian women fought for recognition very early on in the black movement and promoted a more inclusive race- and gender-based agenda (Nascimento and Larkin Nascimento 2000, 19; Vieira 1995, 27–28). We will see echoes of this history later on when Afro-descendant women transfer their skills and experiences from the Beijing World Conference (1995) to international policy forums on race.

Recognizing and Defending Blackness, Creating Alternatives to Racial Democracy (1960–1995)

The creation of formal registered nongovernmental organizations in Latin American countries to combat racial discrimination and promote racial consciousness began in the late 1980s. They built on African descendants' growing recognition that more formal organizations that focused on combating discrimination could lead to improvements in the quality of their lives. Several leaders point to the civil rights movement in the United States as a model for them to follow in the Latin American context (Morrison 2007, 17). For example, a group of students from the federal university in Aracajú created the Sociedade Afrosergipana de Estudos e Cidadania (SACI; Afrosergipania Society Studies and Citizenship).[5] The name of the organization is an attempt to reclaim a mythical black gnome-like character from Brazilian popular culture. The leaders of this organization were tapped for positions in the federal government in Brasilia during the first term of Lula's presidency. The leaders of many of the most well-known civil society organizations in Latin America that focused on race were student activists or were African studies scholars. They included Brazilian Sueli Carneiro, who founded Geledés; Colombian scholar Juan de Dios Mosquera, who founded Cimarrón; Peruvian lawyer Jorge Ramirez Reyna, who founded ASONDEH; and Uruguayan pan-Africanist scholar Romero Rodriguez, who founded Mundo Afro.

Forming civil society organizations was an important way for communities to interact with the state; without formal civil society organizations African descendants had few options that would enable them to influence policy. Once they were officially registered and recognized by their governments, these organizations were able to access funding from international donors. These funds supported their work to promote equality and limit the discrimination of African-descendant individuals. Before this time, the activities of black social movements were largely financed through fund-raising efforts by black individuals through clubs or societies.

Their exposure to African American popular culture in the United States and the writings of prominent black leaders across the globe helped many Afro-Latin Americans consider the impact of historically inscribed forms of racial discrimination on their lives. The task of forming individual and collective identities was more difficult in Latin America than in the United States; in Latin America, overt racial segregation was less obvious and definitions of race were less rigid. Furthermore, many Latin American countries were undergoing a period of racial democracy and embracing an ideal of collective national identity as a way of discouraging political fragmentation. Many governments promoted a notion of racial democracy that asserted that there was no racism in Latin America because there were no races. In addition, the idea of *mestizaje* implied that there was no division based on race in the region. During this period, Latin American governments promoted *blanqueamiento* (whitening) through policies that encouraged the population to identify as European, bestowed privileges on individuals who looked more European, and established liberal immigration policies to encourage migration from Europe (Wade 1997, 32).[6] Latin American governments pointed to the absence of segregation as evidence of racial democracy and a lack of discrimination.

Some African-descendant activists point to the promotion of *blanqueamiento* as one of the most important challenges of establishing a black social movement, because the state discouraged self-recognition of an African identity. The reluctance of many members of the black community to self-identify as a person of African descent is one of the most important issues the movement has faced; collective action can take place only if individuals identify with others who face similar forms of discrimination. Those who discriminated on the basis of race in Latin America took advantage of the flexibility of racial identification and the historic lack of segregation to create incentives for individuals to self-identify as white or European, even if they clearly were not. This was a form of control because it prevented black populations from coming together for common action and encouraged African descendants to discriminate against other African descendants. Despite these challenges the black movement has made significant advances in the area of self-identification.

The modern black movement has encouraged blacks to identify with their African ancestry. Notions of race are simultaneously ambiguous and clear in Latin America, so members of the same family can self-identify differently based on their own individual concepts of what race means within specific contexts. Yet despite the flexibility of the concept of race, we see that society's concept of how an individual is classified racially has significant consequences. Recent research by Telles demonstrates that members of the same family often live race in different ways depending on how they are classified even though they share the same socioeconomic background (Telles 2007, 149–151). In Brazil alone, there are close to 150 words to describe racial mixtures and combinations. Vieira notes the complications of race in Brazil as she describes a survey with a question about race: "when interviewees spontaneously classified themselves, the result was citation of 136 different color categories, reflecting the effort of the lighter-skinned not to be classed in the same categories as those any darker in hue"

(Vieira 1995, 27). It is not surprising that almost all of the terms used to describe race in Brazil are used to describe people of color and that most are used to describe persons of African descent.[7]

African descendants throughout Latin American history have been encouraged to downplay their African heritage and deny their racial classification as black in order to be more socially acceptable to whites or to obtain greater economic or political status. This dynamic placed a burden on the black movement as it began spreading its consciousness-raising process. The early effort to organize meetings to share experiences about black culture in the hemisphere in the cities of Cali (1977), Panama City (1980), São Paulo (1982), and Quito (1984) were some of the important first steps in raising consciousness about black identity. These historic congresses of Black Culture in the Americas were important catalysts for African-descendant organizations and laid the foundation for future grassroots activism across the Americas. These sessions were led by prominent national leaders such as Manuel Zapata Olivella in Colombia and Abdias do Nascimento in Brazil (Johnson 2007, 65).

Civil society campaigns in Brazil and Colombia have emphasized the importance of labeling identities as African descendant. During the 1991 census in Brazil, the slogan of one civil society group was "*Não deixe sua cor passar em branco: Responda con bom C/senso*" ("Don't Let Your Color Pass in White: Respond with Good Sense"), a statement that urged Brazilians to check a darker color on their census schedules (Nobles 2000, 1744).[8] The challenge of self-identity continues to be a major obstacle in a place such as the Dominican Republic, where the vast majority of the population continues to identify itself as a variation of indigenous or "Indio" (*claro, oscuro*, etc.), although it is clear that the nation's population has deep African roots.

African-descendant organizations have organized extensively to encourage individuals to self-identify as African descendant by reclaiming the roles African descendants have played in the formation of national identity and history. The rise of Mundo Afro in Uruguay is an excellent example of using such a reclaimed identity to plant the seeds for policy change in a country with a small African-descendant population (it is estimated to be 12 percent in the capital city of Montevideo). When it was founded in 1989, Mundo Afro focused on three clear goals: 1) establishing an educational exhibit to explain the origin of enslaved Africans in Uruguay; 2) counting the number of descendants of enslaved Africans still living in Montevideo; and 3) supporting the revival of Candomblé, an Afro-Uruguayan form of cultural expression with strong African roots that is similar to Carnival traditions in neighboring Brazil. At first glance these activities all seem focused on cultural identity or cultural preservation, but ultimately they served as a basis for international advocacy. (I describe this in more detail below.)

Mundo Afro is seen as a prominent African-descendant organization because of its leadership of a regional network of organizations named the Alianza (Alliance). Some other early Afro-descendant organizations with an international reach include the Organización Fraternal Negra Hondureña (OFRANEH) of Honduras, established in 1977; Movimento Negro Unificado (MNU) of Brazil, founded in 1978; Cimarrón (the National Movement for Afro-Colombian Rights) of Colombia, founded in 1982; Geledés of Brazil, founded in 1988; Mundo Afro of Uruguay, founded in 1988; Asociacion Negra de Defensa y Promocion de los Derechos Humanos of Peru, founded in 1991; Criola of Brazil, founded in 1992; Organización de Desarrollo Étnico Comunitario (ODECO) of Honduras, founded in 1992; Proceso de Comunidades Negras de Colombia (PCN) of Colombia, founded in 1993; Asociación para el Desarrollo de la Mujer Negra Costarricense of Costa Rica, founded in 1995; Fala Preta of Brazil, founded in 1997; Asociacion de Afrocolombianos Desplazados (AFRODES) of Colombia, founded in 1999; and La Fundación de Desarrollo Social y Cultural Afroecuatoriana "Azúcar" of Ecuador, founded in 2000.

As more African-descendant organizations formally registered their work in the 1990s through the emerging regional NGO movement they were able to begin to seek funding through international organizations. International donor agencies such as the Ford Foundation and the Inter-American Foundation made significant initial investments in the late 1970s and early 1980s (Lennox 2009, 26). The Inter-American Development Bank (1996) and the World Bank (2000) funded research projects that began to shed light on the disparities black communities faced. These activities all set the stage for a more in-depth analysis of national and international policies by the black movement and the formation of a strategy for the empowerment of African descendants.

The 1990s were an opportunity to capitalize on the consciousness-raising meetings of African descendants that had begun decades earlier. In 1994, Mundo Afro created a hemispheric meeting of African descendants that focused on blacks living in the Southern Cone, a region whose residents take pride in their European heritage and lack of racial and ethnic diversity. This meeting led to the formation of a permanent network of leaders and organizations called the Alianza Afro-Latina y Caribeña, which was led by Romero Rodriguez, president of Mundo Afro, and included several leading scholar-activists in the region. Dr. Sheila Walker held a meeting at the University of Texas-Austin around the same time that brought together African descendants from diverse countries to discuss their experiences and culture. This meeting is highlighted in the film *Scattered Africa: Faces and Voices of the African Diaspora* (2002). Other networks established during this time including ONECA (Organización Negra Centro-Americana—Organization of Black Central Americans), which was founded in 1995 with twenty-one members from seven countries and is closely affiliated with ODECO. Afro-America XXI, which was established in the United States in 1995, had a presence in thirteen countries at one time. Although the formal network no longer exists, active chapters remain in Colombia, Ecuador and Venezuela (Lennox 2009, 22).

The black movement used advances with civil society to begin to occupy more and more political space in the 1990s. Benedita da Silva, a *favela* (Brazilian slum) leader and later the first Afro-Brazilian woman to serve as state lieutenant governor, governor, and member of Congress, emphasized the importance of race and poverty to the movement in her campaigns by prioritizing the economic needs of African descendants over cultural identity and consciousness. Her straightforward analysis of basic needs was very appealing and generated widespread support in the 1980s and 1990s. She used an analysis of race, class, and gender discrimination as a way of gaining political support and combating the pervasive racial democracy theories in Brazil. In the early 1990s, Benedita da Silva participated in an important leadership exchange with African-descendant women in Brazil and the United States led by the nonprofit organization Global Exchange. The program focused on language learning at Howard University, and da Silva's experience of meeting individuals in the United States led to the production of a book and video about her life. Black organizations played a strong role early in her career by lobbying to secure her nomination as a legislative candidate within the workers' party, Partido dos Trabalhadores (Vieira 1995, 23; see also Benjamin and Mendonça 1997).

In the 1990s, women in the black movement were able to consolidate their important role and build upon the lessons they had learned from the UN's Fourth World Conference on Women in Beijing (1995). Independent black women's organizations from Latin America embraced the opportunity to develop "a new and richer encounter ... between organized Black women's groups and the feminist movement" at Beijing (Nascimento and Larkin Nascimento 2000, 18–19), and they won important battles to put race on the agenda within the global women's movement. These encounters were unique opportunities for the leaders of black women's organizations to dialogue with a completely new set of actors using gender as a platform for creating broader racial policies within the women's movement. Black women's groups put themselves and their inclusive black agendas on the front burner at international meetings. Afro-Brazilian women's organizations (such as Geledés and Criola) in particular took the lead on this initiative (Morrison 2003, 10–14). The Beijing conference in 1995 is one of the best examples of the influence of Afro-Brazilian women's organizations in setting comprehensive global agendas.

Because of the flexible definitions of race in Latin America, groups focused on reclaiming identity and consciousness in the 1980s. The activities of black NGOs often involved cultural preservation or advocacy as ways of making African identity more visible within black communities and in the larger society. As a result of this work, the majority of countries in Latin America have at least one African-descendant organization dedicated to protecting or promoting the human rights of black people. Human rights organizing has been instrumental in promoting legislative changes. Although the need to protect African descendants from specific forms of discrimination placed NGO leaders in a position where they were confronting individuals who discriminated against African descendants, these organizations seldom took a strong position of direct confrontation of the state. Instead, in the 1980s and 1990s, the movement focused on culture and the roots of traditional forms of expression; this focus was valuable in establishing community identity and changing impressions of African descendants in the larger society.

National Advances

African-descendant movement leaders have been able to significantly increase their participation in the public sector and the government in their home countries. Because of the earlier focus of African-descendant organizations on culture and visibility, they now represent a broad range of the political spectrum and have not taken an overtly oppositional stand against their national governments. In fact, African-descendant civil society organizations have been able to secure policy reforms in places such as Brazil through government channels and are often looked to by the government as key partners for implementing these new policies.

In 2003, Luiz Ignacio da Silva's administration established the Secretaria Especial de Políticas de Promoção da Igualdade Racial (SEPPIR; Special Secretariat for Policies to Promote Social Inclusion) in conjunction with several key leaders from African-descendant civil society organizations. Matilde Ribeiro was the first to head this agency, which has the status of a ministry. Matilde Ribeiro was a former researcher at the CEERT in São Paulo, an NGO that focuses on labor issues and is led by Cida Bento, a highly regarded Afro-Brazilian scholar. In 2008, Ribeiro was replaced at SEPPIR by Edson Santos, a longtime member of the workers' party (Partido dos Trabalhadores) and a Brazilian senator on leave from his political position. Santos, who has political expertise in the legislative branch, signed an agreement with U.S. Secretary of State Condoleezza Rice to promote exchanges between the United States and Brazil through the U.S.-Brazil Joint Action Plan to Eliminate Racial Discrimination (JAPER) in March 2008. SEPPIR has over 150 staff members and has been given the complex task of coordinating racial inclusion with all of the other Brazilian ministries. SEPPIR also has an international section that focuses on promoting inclusion policies in Latin America and policies related to Africa in Brazil. SEPPIR has developed innovative new policies and programs with an impressive number of ministries in Brazil, including several of the most traditional and conservative agencies in the Brazilian government, such as the prestigious foreign affairs ministry.

Peru and Ecuador have established similar cabinet-level ministries, and special government councils have been established in Honduras, Peru, and Uruguay to address the needs of African descendants and other racial minority groups. The formation of government mechanisms such as SEPPIR represents an important step forward.

Civil society leaders have formed informal partnerships with national governments over the last decade to shape agendas and development programs on a volunteer basis. For example, in Brazil, the founding member of Geledés, Sueli Carneiro, is a leader of the national Council of Economic and Social Development (Conselho de Desenvolvimento Econômico e Social; CDES), and her delegate, Jurema Werneck, is a leader of the Afro-Brazilian women's organization Criola. CDES, which was established in 2003, includes the president of Brazil and ten members of the national government. These two women leaders represent all NGOs in Brazil and have expanded the role of Afro-Brazilian NGOs in Brazilian policymaking. Members of civil society have also worked closely with the government on over thirty new laws specifically related to social inclusion in the public schools, and the African-descendant movement is key to ensuring that the law that makes the teaching of African and Afro-Brazilian history mandatory in all public schools is being implemented by the education ministry (Law no. 10.639/2003, ratified on January 9, 2003). Affirmative action measures have been enacted at select public universities, tax breaks have been enacted for private universities that pursue diversity, and the traditional Brazilian foreign service universities have implemented race-based quota systems for incoming foreign service officers. Brazil, which has the largest African-descendant population in the hemisphere and the second largest black population in the world, has made tremendous advances in social inclusion policies and relies heavily on members of civil society to provide political and technical support for these programs.

Legislators and Leadership

National leaders and congressional members Epsy Campbell in Costa Rica and Luiz Alberto in Brazil both come from African-descendant civil society organizations and are strengthening NGO-government partnerships by promoting conferences of black parliamentarians to bring together the highest-level policymakers throughout the region. These two Congress members organized the first parliamentarian conference in Brazil in 2003, a second conference in Colombia in 2004, and a third conference in Costa Rica in 2005. There was a subsequent follow-up meeting in Colombia in 2007, led by María Isabel Urrutia, an Afro-Colombian congressional representative.

These meetings of African-descendant legislators were designed specifically to address the lack of access to decision-making power facing African descendants. The African-descendant community in the region is represented by fewer than 100 black legislators. A UNDP study concluded that only 2.8 percent of all seats in the Brazilian Congress are occupied by Afro-Brazilians, even where African descendants make up the majority. The Lula administration launched six prominent Afro-Brazilians into leadership positions, but several of these have since left their positions and blacks are still largely absent from national, state, and local government. Indeed, there are only 17 Afro-Brazilians in the 594-member Congress (Ribando Seekles 2008, 9). African descendants are only 11 percent of the state legislative assembly in Bahia, which has an African-descendant population of 79 percent, the largest in the country. In Salvador, the largest black city in the hemisphere, where blacks are over 85 percent of the population, they are the minority (46 percent) of municipal council members. The situation is even grimmer in Rio de Janeiro and São Paulo, where Afro-Brazilians are 44 percent and 32 percent of the population, respectively, but hold only 7 and 3 percent, respectively, of the municipal council seats. Blacks do not seem to fare better in the Brazilian public sector—only 4 percent of public sector employees in Brazil are black, while 66 percent are white.

According to the Black Legislators Network, there are fewer than ten black representatives in the entire Colombian Congress. This statistic is even more troubling when one considers that two of the seats in the 165-member Congress are specifically designated for Afro-Colombian representatives. The first to occupy this seat twelve years ago was Zulia Mena, a civil society leader who continues to work as an educator and social worker in the Pacific coast and is no longer actively involved in electoral politics. In 2006, only one Afro-Ecuadorian was serving in the 100-member Congress (Ribando Seekles 2008, 9).

Interestingly, some countries with smaller African-descendant populations have made notable electoral progress in recent years. Costa Rica, which has an African-descendant population of only 2 percent, elected Epsy Campbell to the Congress after she had served as president of her political party and then vice-presidential and presidential candidate. Uruguay, which has a black population of only 4 percent, elected Edgardo Ortuño as the first Afro-Uruguayan member of Congress. In Honduras, Dayana Martínez Burke, Rubén García, Jerry Dave Hynds Julio, Aurelio Martínez, and Maribel López Solórzano have all been elected to the Congress since 2006. These African descendants, who have been actively involved in civil society activities, are the largest group of Afro-Hondurans to serve in a nation where blacks make up only about 2 percent of the population. The Honduran NGO ODECO, an organization that serves Garifuna, has increased access to the president and high-level decision makers. Such access translates into greater influence in national policymaking and greater visibility for African descendants as a whole in the country.

Impact of International Policies on Social Movements

The Inter-American Convention against Discrimination under consideration by the Inter-American Court of Human Rights at the Organization of American States provides African descendants with a regional body to redress human rights violations throughout the Americas that might be absent from their own nations. Brazil continues to lead the effort to support this convention. In countries where national courts have been reluctant to address racial inequities, African descendants continue to use the Court as a way to pressure governments. Currently every Spanish- or Portuguese-speaking country in the Americas (with the exception of Cuba) has officially yielded jurisdiction to the Court over basic human rights matters. African-descendant communities must continue to use the Court as an instrument for asserting legal rights, as indigenous communities have successfully used the Court to influence their governments to make concessions they would not have otherwise been offered. African descendants are continuing to derive benefits from filing racial discrimination lawsuits with the Court because the act of filing a lawsuit creates a public record that African descendants consider themselves to be the victims of racism in their society, thereby negating claims that blacks do not face discrimination. To date the specifics of how this charter would work are still being debated, and there is strong interest from some quarters in narrowly defining the scope.

Conclusion: Effective New Policies

Clearly African-descendant nongovernmental organizations have significantly contributed to social inclusion policies throughout Latin America. There are indications that several of these NGOs have utilized opportunities that arose after the UN World Conference on Racism in 2001 to position African descendants as a strategic policy priority for governments, making black-movement NGOs a point of reference. The role of key NGOs is particularly clear in the case of Brazil, Uruguay, and Honduras. In countries such as Colombia, African-descendant civil society and political leaders have increased their access to national governments through strategic lobbying campaigns on specific issues.

Examples of social inclusion policy initiatives are varied, but they all represent an increase in government attention to the condition of blacks. Brazil has made tremendous advances in social inclusion policy since Durban. Preparing for the Durban conference taught black leaders in Brazil key lessons, and NGOs mobilized the national government to send the largest civil society delegation of any country. The experience gained through organizing for Durban helps explain part of Brazil's success after the conference. African-descendant NGO leaders have been incorporated in all levels of SEPPIR and they have strategic positions in the Ministry of Education and serve in advisory roles to the president. Afro-Brazilian NGOs are a main distributor of government services in rural *quilombo* communities through cash transfer programs.

The city of Montevideo, with the highest concentration of Afro-Uruguayans in the country (12 percent of the population), has a special ministry of African-descendant affairs to examine the specific policy needs of this community, and several experts are being employed at the national level to explore options for improving policy. Colombia and Honduras are aggressively incorporating African descendants in their requests for foreign assistance, often challenging international donors to focus more attention on how African descendants are disproportionately impacted by underdevelopment. Colombia promotes regional programs that are specifically designed to address problems that disproportionately impact Afro-Colombians, such as international displacement, and pressures USAID and other Plan Colombia actors to incorporate race into their policies. Colombia has also established a national commission on race that includes prominent international members and representatives from civil society. This commission is based on a series of civil society meetings that the vice-president of the nation conducted throughout the country.

Nongovernmental organizations frequently work in partnership with the public sector to improve the quality of services provided to African-descendant citizens. This link has been extremely important to assure that civil society groups are not replacing existing government services in an unsustainable manner. There are several strong examples of civil society groups with access to local and national government resources and decision making processes. In Uruguay, for example, Mundo Afro is implementing a cross-border transnational program with governments in various Southern Cone municipalities that significantly increases community access to municipal services.

Several trends suggest that African-descendant organizations are gaining strength in their policymaking efforts. Afro-Latin organizations are beginning to work on new thematic areas such as local and economic development through existing structures, and new organizations are emerging that focus on specific topics such as economic opportunity. Youth issues may also continue to be a promising area for expansion because many organizations led by youth are working across the traditional boundaries of African-descendant networks and are less concerned about historical divisions between networks and philosophical differences in approaches to black empowerment. Youth leaders have contributed to several important shifts at the level of community groups and are promising actors in the establishment of new policy programs.

African-descendant organizations have astutely prioritized concrete national actions. The decentralization of international donor organizations and donor government programs has led to increased opportunities to exercise influence at the country and subregional level. We can expect that these advances in local and national policymaking will provide an opportunity for African-descendant NGOs to increase their presence in the policymaking processes.

Notes

1. The Human Development Index ranks countries based on quality of life based on indicators such as life expectancy, savings rates, educational levels, employment, and unemployment.

2. These historic land structures have survived into the modern era, and many rural Afro-Brazilian communities are still organized in *quilombos* that have received formal recognition through land titling by the government.

3. Communities with these collective land structures often have a concentrated group of homes in the center of the territory and farmlands on the periphery or in nearby rural zones.

4. Even today many African-descendant leaders have borrowed terminology from these diverse types of maroon communities. For example, in Brazil, Geledés, the name of a black women's organization, is a reference to a religious community of African-descendant women; while in Colombia, Cimarron, the name of a prominent social movement, reclaims a term that was first used to refer to escaped bulls and was used disparagingly to refer to *palenques*. It is not uncommon for social movements to employ the names of maroon heroes to describe their organizations, such as Instituto Palmares (Palmares Institute, the first Afro-Brazilian university), named after Zumbi dos Palmares, the famous Brazilian hero and the founder of the most famous *quilombo*. In 1995, Zumbi dos Palmares' name was used for national and international events, including the Zumbi Third Centennial and the Zumbi dos Palmares March on Brasília Against Racism, in Favor of Citizenship and Life. During this event Zumbi dos Palmares' name was added on the national Pantheon of Freedom, a national shrine, with that of independence hero Tiradentes (Nascimento and Larkin Nascimento 2000, 20).

5. Sergipe is a state in northeastern Brazil.

6. "Closely associated are two corollaries: 1) that slavery [in Brazil] was a more benevolent institution and 2) that the absence of legalized racial segregation and a constitutional provision of equality before the law were sufficient to evidence a nonracist society" (Nascimento and Larkin Nascimento 2000, 16).

7. Interestingly, many of these terms are also gendered and are more commonly used to describe women than men, which suggests that the origins of these descriptors may lie in the exploitation of women of color during slavery.

8. At the time it was common for African-descendant individuals to label themselves as whites on the census because of the pervasive philosophy of racial democracy that was widely promoted throughout Brazil. In 2005 Colombia had a process that was similar to the civil society campaigns in Brazil in 1991. Civil society groups in Colombia launched a media campaign to inform African descendants that the different terms they use to describe themselves privately have a link to the African-descendant category used by the census, such as *raizal* for descendants of the English-speaking Caribbean living on the San Andres and Providencia islands, *niche* for individuals from the coast, *chocano* for individuals from the predominantly African-descendant state of Choco, *palenquero* to describe residents of historic *palenque* communities, *sambo* to describe an African descendant with some indigenous ancestry. Despite the campaign, less than half of Afro-Colombians identified themselves as African descendants in the 2005 census (Contreras 2008, 2).

Bibliography

Andrews, George Reid. 2004. *Afro-Latin America, 1800–2000: Black History in Spanish America and Brazil.* Oxford: Oxford University Press.

Benjamin, Medea, and Maisa Mendonça. 1997. *Benedita da Silva: An Afro-Brazilian Woman's Story of Politics and Love.* Washington, D.C.: Global Exchange.

Carneiro, Sueli. 2000. "Raça e etnia no contexto da Conferencia de Beijing." In *O livro da saúde das Mulheres Negras: Nossos passos vem de longe,* ed. Jurema Werneck, Maisa Mendonça, and Evelyn C. White, 247–256. Rio de Janeiro: Pallas.

Conniff, Michael L., and Thomas J. Davis. 2002. *Africans in the Americas: A History of Black Diaspora.* Caldwell, New Jersey: Blackburn Press.

Contreras, Joe. 2008. "Rise of the Latin Africans: A New Black-Power Movement in Central and South America." *Newsweek,* June 9.

Fitts, Milam. 2002. "The Mundo Afro Project." In *Economic Development in Latin American Communities of African Descent: Presentations from the XXIII International Congress of the Latin American Studies Association, Washington, D.C., September 6–8, 2001,* 29–38. Arlington, Virginia: Inter-American Foundation.

Howard, Philip A. 1998. *Changing History: Afro Cuban Cabildos and Societies of Color in the Nineteenth Century.* Baton Rouge: Louisiana State University.

Instituto Brasileiro de Geografia e Estatistica. 2002. In *Brasil negro e 101 em qualidade de vida,* ed. Fernanda de Escossia. Rio de Janeiro: IBGE Press.

———. 2008. *Sintese de indicadores sociais uma analise das condicoes de vida da populacao Brasileira.* Rio de Janeiro: IBGE.

Instituto Ethos. 2000. *Como as empresas podem e devem valorizar a diversidade.* Sao Paulo: Ethos.

———. 2006. *O compromisso das Empresas com a Promoção da Igualdade Racial.* Sao Paulo: Ethos.

Inter-Agency Consultation on Race in Latin America. 2004. *Afro-Descendants: Development with Participation.* Washington, D.C.: Inter-American Dialogue.

Johnson, Ollie A., III. 2007. "Black Politics in Latin America: An Analysis of National and

Transnational Politics." In *African American Perspectives on Political Science*, ed. Wilber Rich. Philadelphia, Pa.: Temple University Press.

Lennox, Corinne. 2009. "Mobilising for Group-Specific Norms: Reshaping the International Protection Regime for Minorities." PhD diss., London School of Economics.

Morrison, Judith. 2003. "Afro-Brazilian Women's Organizations and Their Influence: Leadership from the Grassroots." Paper presented at meeting of the Latin American Studies Association, March 27–29, 2003, Dallas, Texas.

———. 2004. "Terras de preto in maranhão: Urbanized Afro-Brazilian Clusters in the Northeast." *Delnet News, International Training Center of the ILO* 4 (January–February): 33–35.

———. 2007. "Race and Poverty in Latin America: Addressing the Development Needs of African Descendents." *UN Chronicle* 44 (3): 44–46.

Nascimento, Abdias do, and Elisa Larkin Nascimento. 2000. "Brazil: Dance of Deception: A Reading of Race Relations in Brazil." In *Beyond Racism: Embracing an Interdependent Future*, 7–32. Atlanta, Ga.: Southern Education Foundation.

Nobles, Melissa. 2000. "History Counts: A Comparative Analysis of Racial/Color Categorization in US and Brazilian Censuses." *American Journal of Public Health* 90 (11): 1738–1745.

Paixão, Marcelo. 2009a. "Desiguladades na dinâmica do mercado de trabalho Brasileiro no período 1995–2006: Evidências Empíricas Baseadas na PNAD/IBGE." Paper presented at the Latin American Studies Association conference, Rio de Janeiro, June 11–14, 2009.

———. 2009b. *Paradox of the Good Student*. Washington: Inter-American Dialogue.

Ribando Seekles, Clare. 2008. *CRS Report for Congress: Afro-Latinos in Latin America and Considerations for U.S. Policy*. Washington, D.C.: Congressional Research Service.

Sanchez, Margarita, and Maurice Bryan. 2003. *Macro Study: Afro-Descendents, Discrimination and Economic Exclusion in Latin America*. London: Minority Rights Group International. Available at http://www.minorityrights.org/?lid=933.

Telles, Edward. 2007. *Incorporating Race and Ethnicity into the UN Millennium Development Goals*. Washington: Inter-American Dialogue. Available at http://www.thedialogue.org/page.cfm?pageID=32&pubID=304.

Tilly, Charles. 2004. *Social Movements: 1768–2004*. Boulder, Colo.: Paradigm Publishers.

U.S. Department of State. 2007. "Colombia: Country Report on Human Rights Practices, 2007." Available at http://www.state.gov/g/drl/rls/hrrpt/2007/100633.htm.

Vieira, Rosângela Maria. 1995. "Brazil." In *No Longer Invisible: Afro-Latin Americans Today*, ed. Minority Rights Group, 19–46. London: Minority Rights Group.

Wade, Peter. 1997. *Race and Ethnicity in Latin America*. London: Pluto Press.

World Bank. 2006. *Mas alla de los promedios: Afrodescendientes en America Latina, Los Afrocolombianos*. Ed. Josefina Stubbs and Hiska N. Reyes. Washington: World Bank Publications. Available at http://siteresources.worldbank.org/INTLACAFROLATINSINSPA/Resources/Colombia.pdf.

Zoninsein, Jonas. 2001. "The Economic Case for Combating Racial and Ethnic Exclusion in Latin American and Caribbean Countries." In *Towards a Shared Vision of Development: High Level Dialogue on Race, Ethnicity and Inclusion in Latin America and the Caribbean*, ed. Inter-American Development Bank, 2. Washington: Inter-American Development Bank.

12

Negotiating Blackness within the Multicultural State

Creole Politics and Identity in Nicaragua

JULIET HOOKER

How are Afro-descendant Creoles currently reimagining their collective identities in Nicaragua in the context of multicultural policies that guarantee collective rights to land and culture to both the indigenous and Afro-descendant inhabitants of the country's Atlantic coast? In the context of a Nicaraguan nation that is portrayed as overwhelmingly mestizo or Indo-Hispanic, English-speaking Creoles have imagined and represented their collective identities in shifting and multiple ways over the course of the twentieth century (Gordon 1998). Currently, many Creoles are asserting a strong "black" racial group identity imagined in terms of transnational connections to the African diaspora, including to an African past and Afro-Caribbean ancestry. I am especially interested in analyzing the connections between the current emphasis on blackness in conceptions of Creole identity and changes to Nicaragua's model of multiculturalism that begin to recognize the existence of racial hierarchy and to implement specific policies to combat racism and racial discrimination. In particular, I seek to illustrate the dialectical relationship between rights and identities evidenced by the impact of multicultural policies on the self-making strategies of Nicaraguan Creoles and by how such policies are shaped by the forms of activism emerging from current imaginings of Creole collective identity.

My analysis of the way Afro-descendant Creoles in Nicaragua are currently imagining their collective identity and negotiating blackness in the context of official multiculturalism is framed by two seemingly unrelated events. The first was a special series about Afro-Latin Americans that was published in the *Miami Herald* during 2007, specifically an article focused on the "emergent black cultural and civil rights movement" among Creoles in Nicaragua. The article was notable both because the comments of those interviewed illustrate how Creole racial identity is currently being imagined, and because of the reactions it provoked among other sectors of the Creole community. Interestingly, what was most striking about the article was the quote and accompanying photograph of ⌐ontestant in a Miss Black Pride beauty pageant being held in the Creole community of Pearl Lagoon. When describing her dress to the reporter the young Creole woman said: "It reminds me of Africa. I'm so proud of my heritage and my ancestry" (Burch 2007). This seemingly innocuous statement of pride in one's racial ancestry was noteworthy for a number of reasons. One was that (at least to this observer) there was nothing about the pink sequined dress pictured in the accompanying photograph that would immediately signal a connection to Africa. Another reason was because of the mere fact of the reference to Africa itself, given that it seems more temporally and geographically feasible for Nicaraguan Creoles to establish connections to people of African descent in the diaspora than to Africa.

The second event that frames my analysis occurred at a conference on the black presence in Mesoamerica, where I presented a paper on Creole politics and history and the construction of Nicaraguan citizenship in the nineteenth and twentieth centuries. At the end of my presentation, a prominent historian of Africa asked: "Where is Africa?" In other words, he wanted to know what role a connection to an African past played in Creole self-making practices. When confronted with this question, I realized that it was not one I could readily answer, in large part because a connection to Africa seemed rather absent from Creole accounts of their historical development as a group, which tended to emphasize links to people of African descent in the Caribbean. This question coupled with the young black beauty pageant contestant's comment about Africa led to another set of questions: What does it means to be Creole, and/or black or Afro-descendant in Nicaragua today in the context of a self-proclaimed multicultural state? What does it mean to be Creole and/or black in multicultural Nicaragua? How is blackness negotiated and lived today in a state where multiculturalism has become official state policy, but where, historically, racial hierarchy and racism have not been recognized? How are these identities negotiated and remade in the context of struggles for justice and equality?

In order to examine these questions it is necessary to understand the historical context in which these different self-conceptions of Creole identity are unfolding in Nicaragua. Creoles are not the only Afro-descendants in Nicaragua, but they are the group generally most associated with blackness. In Nicaragua there are two primary types of people of African descent: the descendants of slaves brought by Spaniards during the colonial period; and descendants of free and enslaved blacks and mulattos who formed maroon communities on the Atlantic coast. Creoles and Garifunas on Nicaragua's Atlantic coast are groups of the latter type, while the remaining population of African descent in the rest of the country (which has not developed a group identity separate from the national mestizo majority) is of the former type.

In Nicaragua as a whole, as in other Latin American countries, there is a close connection between skin color and social class. But the racialization of space (i.e., the designation of some regions of the country as the only ones where racial "others" who were viewed as "inferior" and "savage" resided) has also served to legitimize semi-colonial state practices within the country. Historically, the identification of the Atlantic coast with blackness functioned to justify the political exclusion of *costeños* (as the region's inhabitants are known), especially Creoles (Hooker 2010).

The Afro-descendant population in Nicaragua is relatively small, and as a group it faces difficult conditions. According to the latest census carried out in 2005, Nicaragua's total population is 5,142,098, of which only 19,890 persons, or less than 1 percent, self-identified as Creole. The vast majority of Creoles live on the Atlantic coast, where they represent 5.4 percent of the region's total population of 620,640 inhabitants (INEC 2006, 15, 52, 54, 184, 188).[1] According to a 2006 report on racism and ethnic discrimination, "In Nicaragua, there exists an underlying racism, whose most evident expression is the unequal human development of the country. The majority of the territories occupied by Indigenous peoples [and Afro-descendants] are among the poorest with the least access to basic social services" (Kain 2006, 35). The report identifies the variety of ways that racism manifests itself in Nicaragua today, including prejudice based on skin color in hiring, invisibility in daily public life, discrimination against use of non-Spanish mother tongues (such as Creole English), devaluation of local knowledge, and so forth. The disparities from which Afro-descendants on the Atlantic coast suffer are evident when one compares socioeconomic, health, and literacy indicators for the region with those for the rest of the country. For example, of the 5,398 schools in the country, only 361 are on the Atlantic coast, and the illiteracy rate in that region exceeds 50 percent (Kain 2006, 56). In the region, only 20 to 30 percent of the population has access to potable water, compared to 70 percent for the nation as a whole. The maternal mortality rate on the Atlantic coast is two to three times higher than the rate for the rest of the country, and the infant mortality rate is significantly higher in the region (PNUD 2005, 77, 80–81). Despite recent gains in collective rights for Creoles and other Afro-descendant *costeños*, these have not translated into concrete improvements in the general socio-economic conditions of or access to basic services for these populations.

The aim of this chapter is to analyze and explain the interplay between state multicultural policy and the kinds of collective identities and types of rights demands being advanced by Nicaraguan Creoles and other Afro-descendants in

Latin America. In order to do this, I first place the Nicaraguan case in comparative perspective, situating it against wider trends in Afro-descendant political
mobilization in the region. I then discuss the evolution of racial politics in Nicaragua and the features of the model of multiculturalism that was adopted there
in the 1980s. Finally, I analyze Creole self-making strategies in light of these
transformations. This is a qualitative study that draws on a variety of sources,
including archival materials, secondary historical works, government laws and
reports, contemporary accounts of Creole identity in popular media (such as
newspapers), official reports produced by *costeño* nongovernmental organizations, and ethnographic field research on the Atlantic coast.

Afro-Descendant Political Mobilization and the Latin American State

In recent decades, Afro-descendants in Latin America have waged increasingly
visible and successful struggles for various kinds of collective rights to overcome
the racial discrimination and social exclusion to which they have historically
been subjected. In response, Latin American states and national publics have
begun to acknowledge the persistence of racism in their respective societies, and
Afro-descendants have won important collective rights from the state in many
countries in the region.[2]

The collective rights won by Afro-descendants in Latin America can generally be grouped within two broad categories—rights that enable Afro-descendants to preserve land and culture and rights to remedy the effects of racial
discrimination. These two broad rubrics correspond to the different kinds of
philosophical justifications for collective rights for minority groups that theorists of multiculturalism have put forward. Rights to land and culture are viewed
as legitimate for minority cultures in multinational states because the languages,
cultures, and identities of these groups in such states will always be disadvan-
taged compared to those of the majority group. As a result, justice requires the
adoption of permanent collective rights that allow minorities to preserve their
cultures, such as language rights, communal land rights, and self-government
rights in the territories in which they live. Indigenous people in many Latin
American countries and some Afro-descendants have gained these kinds of collective rights (for example, in Guatemala, Honduras, Nicaragua, Bolivia, and
Ecuador). Meanwhile, in states that historically were structured on the basis
of racial hierarchies that determined access to political power and educational
and economic resources, beyond universal negative protections against racism,
racial minority groups are viewed as entitled to positive rights to help redress
racialized inequality. These temporary collective rights include measures such

as affirmative action in education and employment (Brazil) or political representation rights (Colombia). These two broad rubrics of rights have combined in various ways to produce different regimes of multicultural recognition for Afro-descendants in Latin America.[3]

Based on different configurations of rights to land and culture and rights to redress racial discrimination, we can identify three models of multiculturalism in Latin America. In the first model, Afro-descendants and indigenous peoples have achieved fairly similar levels of collective rights to preserve land and culture and have been included in the same legal categories. This is the model that has been implemented in much of Central America, particularly Guatemala, Honduras, and Nicaragua. In the second model, indigenous groups have gained collective rights to land and culture but have not been viewed as either cultural minorities or subordinated racial groups and have failed to gain any collective rights. So far this has been the case in Mexico and Venezuela. In the third model, indigenous and Afro-descendant groups have gained different levels of collective rights to land and culture but Afro-descendants have also won positive rights to remedy racial discrimination. This is the model of multiculturalism that has emerged in Brazil, Colombia, Ecuador, and Peru.

Some of the differences in the models of multiculturalism Latin American states have implemented can be attributed to the types of Afro-descendants present in each country. For analytical purposes it is possible to develop a typology of Latin American Afro-descendants consisting of four principal types or groups that can help us understand the kinds of organizations these groups have developed and the types of collective rights they have struggled for. The first group is what we might call Afro-mestizo people, who are the descendants of slaves brought during the colonial period who over time integrated into the lower socioeconomic levels of colonial society and later into the dominant mestizo cultures and national identities of most Latin American countries. While their phenotypical differences from the national population suggest that they are subject to racial discrimination (given the close association between social class and skin color in Latin America), in most cases they have not developed a separate racial/cultural group identity or made demands for collective rights. Afro-mestizos can be either urban or rural, and they probably represent the largest proportion of Afro-descendants in the region. We can find Afro-mestizos in practically every country in Latin America with an Afro-descendant population, but some notable examples would be Mexico, Brazil, Peru, and Panama. A second group of Afro-Latin Americans is comprised of the descendants of slaves brought during the colonial period who have developed a strong racial-group identity and have struggled for collective rights against racial discrimination. They tend to live in urban settings. The various urban black movements located in many of Brazil's major cities are an example of this type of group (see Hanchard 1994).

A third group of Afro-Latin Americans are the descendants of maroon communities; their ancestors managed to escape from (or otherwise avoid) slavery to establish settlements outside colonial society. These Afro-descendants developed separate racial/cultural collective identities distinct from those of the dominant mestizo majority and forged a relationship to land or territory in the colonial period before the establishment of state sovereignty over the areas they occupied. They have historically struggled for collective rights, in particular in defense of communal lands or territory. Creoles in Nicaragua and Garifuna in Honduras, Nicaragua, and Guatemala are examples of this type of Afro-descendant group. Finally, throughout Central America, we find a fourth group of Afro-Latin Americans who are the descendants of West Indian immigrants who arrived as laborers in the enclave economies that existed in the late nineteenth and twentieth centuries along the Caribbean coasts of the isthmus. They have organized as a racial/cultural group and have struggled for equal civil rights and positive rights to remedy racial discrimination. The black movements in Panama and Costa Rica are examples of this kind of Afro-descendant group.

It is important to keep in mind, however, that these are broad conceptual categories intended to help us understand the kinds of social movements and forms of political organization Afro-Latin Americans have developed. In practice the boundaries between the different categories are quite fluid and they may often overlap. In many countries, multiple types of these Afro-descendant groups live alongside one another, as in Colombia and Brazil, for example, where we find Afro-mestizos, urban black movements, and the descendants of maroon communities.

In general, Afro-descendants who have organized as racial groups have struggled for equal civil rights and rights to combat racial discrimination, while those who have mobilized primarily in terms of an ethnic group identity that is different from the majority mestizo national identity have sought collective rights to land and culture. There also seems to be a strong spatial logic—rural versus urban—that may determine the kinds of rights that Afro-descendants have struggled for (and the kinds of organizations they have formed). Rural Afro-descendants, for example, often conceive of their collective identities in ethnic terms and emphasize the need for collective rights to land and culture. Urban Afro-descendants have generally organized in terms of a racial group identity and have focused more on struggles for equal rights and positive rights to redress racial discrimination. As a result, in many countries in Latin America the struggles of urban and rural Afro-descendants have been somewhat disconnected from each other. This is not always the case, however; in Brazil, urban black movements appear to have championed the struggles for communal land rights of rural Afro-Brazilians, particularly *quilombo* communities (see Linhares 2004). It is also true that in a number of countries (especially, it seems, those where there are descendants of maroon communities), Latin American Afro-descendants have organized as both ethnic and racial groups and have formed organizations that struggle for both kinds of collective rights, although they may emphasize one philosophical justification for collective rights more than another. This, for example, is the case with the Garifuna in Honduras (see Anderson 2007).

The issue of how they fit into the dominant categories of minority group rights has thus been a pressing question for many Latin American Afro-descendants. The different types of collective rights accorded to Afro-descendants and the changing forms of Afro-descendant identity are in a dialectical relationship to each other.[4] Identities are not static, and in Nicaragua in particular the relevant question is how to understand changes in Creole collective identity in light of the various features of the model of multiculturalism adopted in the country since the 1980s.

The model of multiculturalism adopted in Nicaragua has generally been much more successful in recognizing the collective rights to land and culture of Afro-descendant *costeños* but has been far less successful in addressing continuing racialized inequalities and racial hierarchies that reproduce the political and social exclusion and impoverishment that continue to make Afro-descendants one of the most marginalized and vulnerable sectors of the population. The absence of positive rights to remedy racial discrimination in Nicaragua's multicultural model is emblematic of the general absence of an approach to how to overcome racial hierarchies that deny Afro-descendants their fair share of political power and equal access to educational and economic empowerment. For example, while Afro-descendant *costeños* in Nicaragua have gained some of the most extensive rights to protect their land and culture in the region, including regional autonomy, communal land rights, and bilingual education, they continue to be marginalized in the political structures of the country, including regional governments, and they continue to suffer from racial discrimination and racism. Moreover, because collective rights are confined to a specific region in Nicaragua, Afro-descendants outside the Atlantic coast have not had access to the two types of collective rights described here (other than general anti-discrimination guarantees in the Constitution that apply to all citizens) until recently.

Creole Identity and Racial Politics in Nicaragua

Historically, the dominant way that Creoles have understood and portrayed their group identity has not necessarily been in terms of blackness. While their self-representations have changed over time, it is safe to say that while Creoles are the group most closely associated with African descent in Nicaragua, this is not the only or even the dominant way they have understood and described their own identity.

Creoles live on the Atlantic coast of Nicaragua, where they are the largest Afro-descendant group. The Atlantic coast is very different from the rest of Nicaragua, which is generally portrayed (in historiography and nationalist ideology) as a uniformly mestizo nation (Gould 1998). Yet this self-understanding bears little, if any, resemblance to the reality on the Atlantic coast, a region that accounts for approximately 50 percent of the national territory and 10 percent of the country's population. The Mosquito Coast (as it was then known) did not officially become a part of the Nicaraguan republic until 1894; prior to that it was a British protectorate. Today the region is inhabited by six distinct ethnoracial groups, including three indigenous groups, the Miskitus, Mayangnas, and Ramas; two groups of African descent, Creoles and Garifuna; and mestizos, who began migrating to the region after 1894. The region was never fully integrated into Nicaraguan political, economic, or sociocultural life, and its indigenous and Afro-descendant inhabitants thus possess languages, cultures, and collective identities that are quite different from the dominant indo-Hispanic culture and mestizo identity of the rest of Nicaragua.

Creoles (not to be confused with *criollos,* the term used to describe Spaniards born in the Americas during the colonial era) were a group of free people of color that emerged in the late eighteenth century in the southern Mosquito Coast. They were of mixed African, Amerindian, and European descent, predominantly mulattos descended from free and enslaved Africans who had arrived on the Mosquito Coast in the seventeenth century and formed maroon communities in Bluefields and other sites of British settlement after the British left at the end of the eighteenth century. They developed a creolized English language and hybrid culture. By the nineteenth century Creoles were identified primarily as a group of African descent. Creoles became increasingly socially and politically dominant on the Mosquito Coast over the course of the nineteenth century, to the extent that by mid-century, they were vying for political power in the region with the Miskitu. By the end of the nineteenth century, Creoles played a central role in the politics and society of the Mosquito Coast. Beginning in the late nineteenth century but particularly during the first half of the twentieth century, when banana companies and other North American business interests were dominant on the Atlantic coast, the region had a high rate of immigration of West Indian (especially Jamaican) laborers who came to work on banana plantations and for mining and logging companies. While some of these workers returned to their home countries, many stayed on the Atlantic coast and were absorbed into the Creole group (Gordon 1998, 66–67).

According to Edmund T. Gordon, over time Creoles developed multiple strands of what he calls "Creole common sense" to describe their collective identity, and they deployed different identities at different times. These included a black racial identity conceived as linked to transnational African diaspora communities elsewhere in the Americas and an "ethnic" identity defined in terms of the group's ties to Anglo-Saxon cultures and societies such as Britain and the United States. Gordon argues that there was a shift in Creole political activism and sensibilities throughout the twentieth century, from an initial rejection of the Nicaraguan state in the period immediately after the region was annexed to Nicaragua in 1894 to greater acceptance from the 1930s through the 1960s. Creoles embraced racial politics at various periods of the twentieth century. Gordon notes that Creole activism associated with Garveyism reached its height in the 1920s, while in the 1960s, as the civil rights movement was unfolding in the United States, Creoles developed a cultural movement that explicitly contested racial discrimination in Nicaragua (Gordon 1998, 51–85). This movement dissipated with the triumph of the Sandinista revolution in 1979 but has arguably reemerged in recent years among Creoles since the implementation of multicultural policies.

During the 1980s, Creoles were in open conflict with the Nicaraguan state. They, like most other *costeños*, were not involved in the struggle of the FSLN (the Frente Sandinista de Liberación Nacional, or Sandinista National Liberation Front) to overthrow the authoritarian regime of the Somoza family, which had dominated Nicaraguan politics from the 1930s until 1979. By the early 1980s, *costeños* had become disenchanted with the Sandinista government.[5] Indeed, many *costeños*, including some Creoles but especially the Miskitu, joined the *contras* (the counterrevolutionary guerrilla forces that were trying to overthrow the FSLN with the aid of the United States) at this time. In an attempt to resolve the armed conflict on the Atlantic coast and end international condemnation, the Sandinistas adopted a number of multicultural policies in 1986. At that time the Nicaraguan state adopted constitutional language that enshrined a multiethnic, regional model of autonomy for *costeños*, in which all groups shared equally in self-government.

The Nicaraguan Constitution that was approved in 1986 recognized the "multiethnic nature" of the Nicaraguan nation and enshrined the following collective rights for all the "communities of the Atlantic coast": the right to preserve and develop their distinct cultures, languages, and religions; the right to establish their own forms of social organization and administer their local affairs according to their historical traditions; the right to have ownership of their communal lands; the right to use and benefit from the region's natural resources; and the right to regional autonomy (or self-government) (Asamblea Nacional de Nicaragua 1987a). Additionally, the Autonomy Law approved the same year established an autonomy regime for the Atlantic coast, within which "the members of the communities of the Atlantic coast" are guaranteed "absolute equality of rights and responsibilities, regardless of population size and level of development" (Asamblea Nacional de Nicaragua 1987b). Creoles thus have the same rights as other *costeños* in Nicaragua's model of multiculturalism, which grants the same levels of rights to Afro-descendants and indigenous peoples on the Atlantic coast.

Nicaragua's model of multiculturalism created heterogeneous multiracial and multiethnic self-governing regions. The Autonomy Law divides the Atlantic coast into two administrative units: the North Atlantic Autonomous Region (Región Autónoma del Atlántico Norte; RAAN) and the South Atlantic Autonomous Region (Región Autónoma del Atlántico Sur; RAAS). Two indigenous groups (Miskitus and Mayangnas), one Afro-descendant group (Creoles), and mestizos inhabit the northern autonomous region. Three indigenous groups (Miskitus, Mayangnas, and Ramas), two Afro-descendant groups (Creoles and Garifunas), and mestizos inhabit the southern autonomous region. Currently, mestizos constitute a demographic majority in both regions. The Miskitus are the second-largest group in the RAAN, where they are concentrated, followed by the Mayangnas and small numbers of Creoles. In the RAAS, where they have historically settled, Creoles are the second-largest group, followed by small numbers of Miskitus, Mayangnas, Ramas, and Garifunas.

Because of the decision to create heterogeneous autonomous regions rather than spatially segregated units controlled by each group, Creoles did not gain a national homeland over which they could exercise exclusive control. The multicultural policies adopted in Nicaragua in the 1980s instead set up a context in which Creoles find themselves sometimes collaborating but also sometimes competing with two other powerful groups on the Atlantic coast: mestizos, who have continued to play an important role in the region's politics since the adoption of regional autonomy, and indigenous *costeños*, who have often been allies of Creoles in struggles for justice and equality but have also historically been rivals for power.

Demographic changes on the Atlantic coast have played an important role in shaping the shifting context of Creole politics and identity today. For example, while the Atlantic coast continues to be identified with its original Afro-descendant and indigenous inhabitants, who controlled the region before the arrival of mestizos, as a result of intensifying migration mestizos are now the majority of the population in the region.[6] This shift has taken place against the backdrop of rivalries between Afro-descendant and indigenous *costeños*. As the two dominant groups on the Atlantic coast before it became a part of Nicaragua, Creoles and Miskitus have traditionally seen each other as rivals for political power, and tensions between them date back to the colonial period. Since the adoption of multicultural rights in the 1980s, indigenous political movements have been much more visible and powerful on the Atlantic coast than those of Afro-descendants. It is against this backdrop that current shifts in Creole identity and political mobilization are taking place.

Creole Politics and Identity in the Multicultural State

Creole politics and identity have not remained static since the adoption of multicultural rights in Nicaragua. Instead, there have been important changes in the way Afro-descendant Creoles are currently imagining the collective identities on which they base their political mobilization. Indeed, it is in the context of official multiculturalism that the current emphasis on a black racial group identity among Creoles is taking place. This shift in Creole identity can be seen in the changing terms or labels some of the group's members use. For example, recently it has become more common for younger Creole intellectuals to make a distinction between "black" and "white" Creoles when referring to darker- and lighter-skinned members of the group, a distinction that often, though not always, also corresponds to social class position, with the latter being more educated and wealthier than the former. The use of the "black" and "white" Creole labels suggests that currently some Creoles see themselves as a cultural group of which those who identify with a black racial identity are a subset. In this sense, the use of the terms black and white is not simply descriptive of skin color or phenotype, it is also indicative of patterns of self-identification with blackness among Creoles and of political mobilization on the basis of this racial group identity.[7]

Among Nicaraguan Creoles, the emphasis on (or reassertion of) a black identity conceived in terms of transnational connections to the African diaspora has manifested itself in various forms in recent years. This change can be observed in three areas: 1) political mobilization, including the creation of Creole political parties that emphasize a black racial group identity; 2) struggles for communal land rights; and 3) civil society activism around racism and in favor of positive rights to redress racial discrimination.

Since the 1990s there have been tangible changes in Creole political activism. For most of the 1990s, Creoles helped found and participated in multiethnic political parties that tended to be rather short lived, such as Alianza Costeña (Coast Alliance) and the Partido Indígena Multiétnico (Indigenous Multiethnic Party). More recently, however, a political party has emerged called Coast Power (also known as the Coast People Political Movement) that was founded in 2005 by prominent Creole political leaders. Its aim is to achieve greater Creole/black representation in the regional governments on the Atlantic coast. Publicly, Coast Power's stated goal is the promotion of "costeñismo" (a concept it defines rather vaguely), but it is widely perceived as a Creole political movement that emphasizes a strong "black" group identity among Creoles. For the 2006 regional elections in the RAAS, for example, Coast Power entered into an electoral alliance with YATAMA (Yapti Tasba Masraka Nani, or Descendants of Mother Earth in Miskitu), the main indigenous political organization in Nicaragua, which is an almost exclusively Miskitu party in its leadership, membership, and voting base. As a result of this alliance, 40 percent of YATAMA/Coast Power candidates for the RAAS Regional Council were Creole, the largest percentage ever put forward by a regional or national political party.[8] Similarly, in the Miskitu-dominated RAAN, where Creoles are feeling a growing sense of social and political marginalization, particularly in the capital of city of Bilwi, where a thriving Creole community used to exist, the first decade of the twenty-first ` century has seen the emergence of a small but vocal black movement (see Rigby 2007). Creoles' feeling of marginalization in Bilwi and the RAAN is exacerbated by the view of some Miskitus that land rights are "indigenous rights" and therefore do not apply to Creoles because Afro-descendants do not have the same spiritual connection to the land as indigenous peoples.

The struggle for the demarcation and titling of communal lands is also an area where we can observe changes in Creole self-making strategies and political activism. As noted above, struggles for communal land rights pose important challenges for Afro-descendants because they have generally been seen as preeminently indigenous rights. For Nicaraguan Creoles this has been a complicated arena as well. On the one hand, the legal categories adopted in Nicaragua with regard to communal land rights included Afro-descendant costeños, yet they seemed to privilege static understandings of collective identity that weakened the legitimacy of Creole land claims (see Goett 2007). In the 1990s, this political-institutional context appears to have led communities with mixed ancestry that were engaged in struggles for communal lands to privilege indigenous rather than Afro-descendant identifications (see Hale, Gurdián, and Gordon 2003). On the other hand, there have also been instances of collaboration, when indigenous peoples and Afro-descendant communities made joint land claims on the Atlantic coast, as in the case of the Rama-Creole Territory in the RAAS, which encompasses both indigenous Rama and Afro-descendant Garifuna-Creole communities. In fact, in recent years organizing around struggles for communal land rights appears to have become a means of strengthening Creole identity.

It is thus possible to observe the emergence of a strong black racial identity among many Creoles involved in struggles for communal land rights, an identity they conceive in terms of transnational links to other people of African descent in the diaspora. For urban Afro-descendant Creole communities in the RAAS, for example, the adoption of a new Communal Property Law in 2002 that established the mechanisms for the demarcation and titling of *costeño* communal lands was a galvanizing moment that led them to organize and elect communal boards to carry out land claims. The requirements of Law 445 (as it is known) call for detailed ethnohistorical mapping that included 1) an account of the community's historical antecedents; 2) the demographic, social, economic, and cultural characteristics of the community; 3) the traditional forms of land and resource use practiced in the community; 4) an account of overlapping claims and conflicts over boundaries with other communities or *terceros* (third parties) and of communities, entities, or persons occupying adjacent lands to those being claimed (Asamblea Nacional de Nicaragua 2003, article 46). Creole mobilization in Bluefields to fulfill these requirements and to constitute the communal authorities recognized by Law 445 seems to have spurred political organizing that was explicitly linked to a black racial identity and to the idea of regaining Creole communal lands. In a call for Creoles to attend a meeting to elect representatives to the communal boards in 2003, for example, a prominent longtime Creole politician, Pentecostal church leader, and past president of the RAAS Regional Council exhorted listeners of his popular radio program to attend in order to decide "who is going to represent you as *black*, [who] is going to represent you before the central government and the region" (Rayfield Hodgson, quoted in Goett 2007, 367, italics in Goett).

Another area where shifts in Creole identity and politics can be observed is the increasing activism against racism and in favor of rights to address racial discrimination by Creole civil society organizations. Afro-descendant *costeños* have formed a National Commission of Afro-Descendant Peoples (Comisión Nacional de Pueblos Afro-descendientes) composed of Garifuna and (mostly) Creole civil society organizations. In 2009, among other resolutions, the commission "demanded the visibilization of the Kriol [Creole][9] and Garifuna populations as '*Afro-descendant Peoples*' in national legislation, public policy and any other national documentation regarding these historically invisibilized peoples, deprived of their political, economic and social rights and excluded from the processes of decision-making and communal, regional and national development" (Comisión Nacional de Pueblos Afro-descendientes 2009, 4, emphasis in the original). As a result of their mobilization, in 2008 Creole NGOs successfully persuaded the National Assembly to declare the International Day against Racism a national holiday and to formulate and include penalties for crimes of racial discrimination in the penal code for the first time in Nicaragua's history.

Creole NGOs and civil society organizations have also forcefully protested examples of racist treatment of Afro-descendants in national life. The 2008 shadow report to the Committee on the Elimination of Racial Discrimination (CERD) produced by Creole civil society organizations, for example, noted that racist depictions of the Atlantic coast are routine—especially depictions of its Afro-descendant inhabitants—and that such depictions continue to appear in the national media in Nicaragua, particularly the two largest newspapers in the country, *La Prensa* and *El Nuevo Diario*. This is despite the fact that as a result of pressure from *costeño* civil society organizations, these news outlets have been forced to apologize in the past for their racist depictions of the region and of black people. According to the report, "The media tend to ridicule the cultural celebrations of indigenous and Afro-descendant peoples, making them appear degenerate or perverted. . . . They promote the use of racist popular sayings [*refranes*], as well as the caricaturing of indigenous [people] and Afro-descendants in the national newspapers" (JENH-CEDEHCA 2008, 17). The report also noted the virtual absence of Afro-descendants in national government posts during the center-right administrations of Arnoldo Alemán (1997–2001) and Enrique Bolaños (2002–2006). This situation has changed significantly since the FSLN's victory in the presidential elections of 2006, as the FSLN has appointed a number of Afro-descendant (and indigenous) *costeños* to prominent government posts as a result of its electoral alliance with YATAMA (for a list of these appointments, see JENH-CEDEHCA 2008, 24).

One of the most visible examples of the upsurge in Creole civil society activism against racism and the effect of such activism in spurring national discussions about racial discrimination in Nicaragua has been the so-called Chamán case, in which a Creole legislator in the Central American Parliament (PARLA-CEN), Brigette Budier, was denied entrance to a popular nightclub in Managua. As the lead paragraph of an article about the case explains, "It's happened countless times before, in establishments all across the country: a black person denied entrance because of racial discrimination" (Rogers 2009). Budier brought her case before the national media and the Human Rights Ombudsman's office and filed a legal complaint, which led government prosecutors to open the first racial discrimination investigation in Nicaragua's history. This was possible due to the new penalties for racist conduct that Creole activists had succeeded in inserting in the penal code. The investigation of the admission policies of various upscale nightclubs in Managua garnered significant public attention and led to a heated debate about whether the investigation had been politically motivated, as some argued, or if the Chamán case had indeed been an instance of racism. According to the article quoted above, the case "has forced the country to confront its long-ignored culture of racism" in a very public way. The current emphasis among

Creoles on asserting a black racial identity and the consequent focus on political activism around racial discrimination is thus forcing the Nicaraguan state to begin to recognize the persistence of racial hierarchy in the country despite the existence of official multiculturalism and to implement specific policies to combat racism and racial discrimination.

It is important to understand why Creoles have begun to emphasize a black racial identity conceived in terms of transnational links to people of African descent in the diaspora. I would suggest that for Creoles, who as a group have long been culturally distinct from the rest of Nicaragua, this shift has enabled them to find a language that describes the kinds of racialized oppression they are subject to; this is especially important because it suggests that the concept of respecting and accommodating cultural difference is insufficient for this purpose. In trying to make visible the continued operation of racism in Nicaragua despite the existence of official multiculturalism, Creoles seem to be drawing on links to other people of African descent whose struggles can serve as models for their own.

The implications of this analysis of contemporary Creole politics in Nicaragua for broader studies of Afro-Latin American political mobilization is that such changes in the way Afro-descendants conceive and represent their collective identities should not be seen as foreign, imperial impositions or as inauthentic, cynical attempts to gain rights from the state. Rather, they are creative, organic responses to changing circumstances. In other words, they should be viewed as *self-generated* strategies for negotiating official multicultural models whose categories do not always readily recognize Afro-descendants and that may continue to conceal persistent racial hierarchies. As scholars of African Diaspora Studies have noted, the identities of black diasporic subjects are always constituted on multiple levels, and it is important to pay close attention to the specific ways Afro-descendants in Latin America are reimagining identity to meet the different political contexts in which their struggles for justice and equality are taking place.

In conclusion, multicultural policies have had an impact on the self-making strategies of Nicaraguan Creoles and have in turn been shaped by the forms of activism that are emerging from current imaginings of Creole identity. Such changes are not always welcomed and may sometimes be viewed as threatening. For instance, in a recent discussion on *costeño* communal land rights and political empowerment, a long-standing Miskitu political leader observed that the younger generation of Creole leaders (those who are now in their thirties and forties) are much more confrontational and difficult to deal with than the older generation (those in their sixties and seventies). Setting aside questions of personal relationships and generational divides, it seems clear that this perception is related to the ways Creoles are currently conceiving and representing their collective identity and the kinds of political mobilization they are undertaking as a result. In Nicaragua today, Creoles are finding new ways to struggle for justice and equality in a changing political-institutional context. Creoles' changing self-representations correspond to the salience and relevance of particular forms of identity in different circumstances—in this case a strong racial group identity articulated in terms of blackness that seems to better meet the terrain of struggle in which they find themselves, one in which an official multiculturalism recognizes that cultural or "ethnic" identity exists but has still not fully grappled with racism. Moreover, the assertion of a strong black racial identity among Creoles has not precluded their collaboration and alliance with indigenous *costeños*. What we may be seeing in Nicaragua is the emergence of a strong black racial identity among Creoles that parallels the existing strength of indigenous, especially Miskitu, collective identity and political activism. This shift in Creole identity and politics is beginning to force the Nicaraguan state and public to grapple with the continued existence of racial hierarchy in the country, a persistent feature of national life that has not been fully recognized despite the adoption of multicultural rights more than two decades ago.

Notes

1. The population of the Atlantic coast as a whole is the sum of the 306,510 inhabitants of the South Atlantic Autonomous Region (RAAS), where most Creoles live, and the 314,130 inhabitants of the North Atlantic Autonomous Region (RAAN). According to the census there are also 3,271 self-identified Garifuna in the country as a whole (INEC, 2006: p. 52, 54, 184). The 2005 census did not include categories for non-Creole or non-Garifuna Afro-descendants. The figures for the total Creole population provided by the 2005 census are quite low, significantly lower than previous estimates of the size of this group. This may be due to high levels of migration outside the country, particularly to the United States and Caribbean countries such as the Cayman Islands that began in the 1970s as the Sandinista struggles against the Somoza regime intensified. This outmigration has continued in recent decades with the phenomenon of "ship-out" (by which Creoles, especially men, leave to perform relatively well-paid menial labor on cruise ships) or other forms of temporary labor migration.

2. This discussion of the kinds of collective rights Latin American Afro-descendants have gained and their relationship to the kinds of collective identities they have formulated and the forms of political organization they have developed is a refined version of the analysis that originally appeared in Hooker 2008.

3. For an elaboration of the philosophical justifications for different types of minority group rights, see Kymlicka 1995. For a critique of this bifurcation in conceptions of collective rights for minority groups in theories of multiculturalism and a discussion of how this fails to address the complex situation of Latin American Afro-descendants in particular, see Hooker 2009.

4. For instance, according to Eduardo Restrepo, following constitutional changes in Colombia in the 1990s, there was a shift in Afro-Colombian identity from an emphasis on a racial group

identity focused on struggles against racial discrimination to an identity that is understood in explicitly ethnic terms and that privileges cultural and ethnic difference as the basis of black political projects (Restrepo 1997).

5. The conflict stemmed from the Sandinista government's initial hostility to the demands of Creoles and other *costeños* for self-government. Creoles initially welcomed the Sandinista triumph because they believed it would allow them to realize their demands for self-government, but these goals were not easily reconciled with the FSLN's brand of mestizo nationalism. As a result, their initial support for the revolution turned into active resistance by 1981. By 1984 the Atlantic coast was a war zone and the FSLN's international image had been damaged by accusations that it had committed human rights violations against indigenous groups.

6. The growing size of the mestizo population in the region has had serious consequences for the distribution of political power on the Atlantic coast, particularly the composition of regional governments. The net effect has been mestizo preponderance in both regional councils. Between 1990 and 2010, for example, 52 percent of Regional Council members in the RAAS have been mestizos, while only 25 percent have been Creole (see González Pérez 2008, 226–228).

7. The case of the Garifuna in Nicaragua appears to be different, as they have always emphasized their black identity and participated in transnational Garifuna associations and networks of black organizations such as ONECA (Organización Negra Centroamericana).

8. The regional councils are the legislative bodies of the autonomous regions. Together with the regional coordinator or governor, who is elected from the ranks of the council and who can also be the representative of the central government in the region, they form the regional government for each autonomous region. The members of the Regional Council are elected in regional elections in which only inhabitants of the Atlantic coast or their descendants are allowed to vote and run for office. Each Regional Council has forty-five members.

9. Due to its phonetic spelling in Spanish, Creole and Kriol are used interchangeably or jointly in Nicaragua. The census category, for example, is "Creole (Kriol)."

Bibliography

Anderson, Mark. 2007. "When Afro Becomes (Like) Indigenous: Garifuna and Afro-Indigenous Politics in Honduras." *Journal of Latin American and Caribbean Anthropology* 12 (2): 384–413.

Asamblea Nacional de Nicaragua. 1987a. *Constitución política de Nicaragua*. Managua: Editorial el Amanecer.

———. 1987b. *Estatuto de autonomía de las regiones de la costa Atlántica de Nicaragua*. Managua: Editorial Jurídica.

———. 2003. *Ley del régimen de propiedad comunal de los pueblos indígenas y comunidades étnicas de las regiones autonómas de la costa Atlántica de Nicaragua y de los Ríos Bocay, Coco, Indio y Maíz*. Managua: Editorial Jurídica.

Burch, Audra S. 2007. "Afro-Latin Americans, A Rising Voice: Nicaragua." *Miami Herald*, June 10.

Comisión Nacional de Pueblos Afro-descendientes. 2009. "Resolución 21 de Marzo: Día internacional para la eliminación de la discriminación racial." Nicaragua. Available at http://www.unic.org.ar/pag_esp/esp_discriminacion/discriminacion.html. Accessed September 15, 2010.

Goett, Jennifer. 2007. "Diasporic Identities, Autochthonous Rights: Race, Gender, and the Cultural Politics of Creole Land Rights in Nicaragua." PhD diss., University of Texas at Austin.

González Pérez, Miguel. 2008. "Governing Multi-Ethnic Societies in Latin America: Regional Autonomy, Democracy, and the State in Nicaragua, 1987–2007." PhD diss., York University.

Gordon, Edmund T. 1998. *Disparate Diasporas: Identity and Politics in an African Nicaraguan Community.* Austin: University of Texas Press.

Gould, Jeffrey L. 1998. *To Die in This Way: Nicaraguan Indians and the Myth of Mestizaje, 1880–1965.* Durham, N.C.: Duke University Press.

Hale, Charles R., Galio C. Gurdián, and Edmund T. Gordon. 2003. "Rights, Resources and the Social Memory of Struggle: Reflections on a Study of Indigenous and Black Community Land Rights on Nicaragua's Atlantic coast." *Human Organization* 62 (4): 369–381.

Hanchard, Michael. 1994. *Orpheus and Power: The Movimento Negro of Rio de Janeiro and São Paulo, Brazil, 1945–1988.* Princeton, N.J.: Princeton University Press.

Hooker, Juliet. 2008. "Afro-Descendant Struggles for Collective Rights in Latin America." *Souls: A Critical Journal of Black Politics, Culture and Society* 10 (3): 279–291.

———. 2009. *Race and the Politics of Solidarity.* New York: Oxford University Press.

———. 2010. "Race and the Space of Citizenship: The Mosquito Coast and the Place of Blackness and Indigeneity in Nicaragua." In *Blacks and Blackness in Central America: Between Race and Place*, ed. Lowell Gudmundson and Justin Wolfe, 246–277. Durham, N.C.: Duke University Press,

INEC. 2006. *VIII censo de población y IV de vivienda.* Vol. I. *Población, características generales."* Managua: Instituto Nacional de Estadísticas y Censos. Available at http://www.inide.gob. ni/censos2005/censo2005.htm.

JENH-CEDEHCA. 2008. *Informe alternativo: Implementación de la Convención Internacional Para la Eliminación de la Discriminación Racial (CEDR).* Regiones Autónomas de la Costa Caribe: Centro de Derechos Humanos, Ciudadanos y Autónomicos y el Movimiento Jóvenes Estableciendo Nuevos Horizontes.

Kain, Myrna Cunningham. 2006. *Racism and Ethnic Discrimination in Nicaragua.* Bilwi, Puerto Cabezas: Centro para la Autonomía y Desarrollo de los Pueblos Indígenas.

Kymlicka, Will. 1995. *Multicultural Citizenship: A Liberal Theory of Minority Rights.* Oxford: Oxford University Press.

Linhares, Luiz Fernando do Rosário. 2004. "Kilombos of Brazil: Identity and Land Entitlement." *Journal of Black Studies* 34 (6): 817–837.

PNUD. 2005. *Informe de Desarrollo Humano 2005. Las Regiones Autonómas de la Costa Caribe: Nicaragua Asume su Diversidad?* Managua, Nicaragua: Programa de Naciones Unidas para el Desarrollo.

Restrepo, Eduardo. 1997. "Afro-Colombianos, antropología y proyecto de modernidad en Colombia." In *Antropología en la modernidad: Identidades, etnicidades y movimientos sociales en Colombia*, ed. María Victoria Uribe and Eduardo Restrepo, 279–319. Bogotá, Colombia: Instituto Colombiano de Antropología.

Rigby, Betty. 2007. "Vida sociocultural de los Creoles de Bilwi." MA Thesis, URACCAN.

Rogers, Tim. 2009. "Disco's Door Policy Sparks Race Debate: Brigette Budier Has Become the Nicaraguan Rosa Parks." *Nica Times*, February 27–March 5.

13

Todos Somos Iguales, Todos Somos Incas

Dilemmas of Afro-Peruvian Citizenship and Inca Whiteness in Peru

SHANE GREENE

On December 7, 2008, a day known as Popular Leaders Day in Peru, Peruvian president Alan García provided radio talk-show hosts with an incredibly juicy newsbyte. In the midst of a long diatribe against pesky NGO emissaries, he revealed his color-coded, classist vision of Peru's civil society: "I don't like all the white yuppies involved in leftist politics. I like the copper-colored men who are the real Peruvians that fight for justice" (*El Comercio* 2008). Multiple members of the press blasted him for the overtly racialized remarks. His use of a term such as *pituco* (the closest translation I can come up with is "white yuppie") in reference to the leaders of large NGOs involves multiple registers.[1] The term connotes simultaneously class, race, style, language, and urban geographic districts (particularly within metropolitan Lima). And his reference to men with *cobrizo*-colored skin is a clear historical reference to indigenous Andeans.

Garcia's comment apparently constructs whiteness and Andeanness as a contrast. Indeed they often do contrast in the Peruvian context. But upon further reflection about the history of race and power in Peru, this simple white/Andean dichotomy breaks down and Garcia's comment could in fact be read differently. Garcia clearly speaks of an abstract Andean subject: one who is color-coded in racial terms but who is also a "real Peruvian" and thus is at the center of his nationalist discourse. In other words, he speaks of an abstract Andean actor who is central to Peru's current liberal democratic operations and neoliberal economic policies: an actor thought to somehow be involved in some way at the very centers of power and prestige that define "real" Peruvianness. In short, he speaks of an Andean subject who in at least one of many discursive and contradictory manifestations is a representation of the Peruvian nation.

As such, Garcia's copper-colored man is not nearly as distant from the discourse on whiteness as one might believe. Indeed, I will argue that in one particular representation, Andeanness and whiteness are deeply connected in Peru's national history and the convoluted discourses of race and power found there. The central idea rests on an abstraction of Andeans as the inheritors of Peru's coveted Inca past: the past that serves as the core narrative of what Peru as a nation is and who Peruvians as a people are. The Inca legacy, in other words, is central to discourses of power, nation, and citizenship in Peru and in some measure always has been (see Greene 2007a). Following the work of thinkers such as Alberto Flores Galindo (1988), and my earlier work on this topic (Greene 2007a, 2009), I argue that the abstract representation of "the Inca" in Peru serves as a central discourse of nation, civilization, and citizenship. It is thus necessarily conflated with discourses of whiteness, modernity, democracy, and liberalism in contemporary Peru. It also serves to make invisible multiple other forms of postcolonial ethnic difference and the subaltern forms of citizenship that certain members of Peruvian civil society are currently using as they make claims on the state. This includes everyday Andeans (i.e., those envisioned by the Peruvian elite as the downtrodden, impure leftovers of a glorious Inca past) and native Amazonians, who are often written out of Peru's Andean-centric history altogether. It also includes Afro-Peruvians, whose different historical trajectory leads them to be largely invisible in the Peruvian imagination. The status of Afro-Peruvians is particularly difficult to visualize from the point of view of Peru's national narrative because they are represented as both not Inca and not Indian: neither as contributors to Peru's national "civilization" nor indigenous to Peruvian soil.

This historical invisibility of Peru's various racialized groups has become the subject of greater debate in recent years. This has resulted in a fair amount of political discussion and a few relatively superficial legal changes. Peru's current context, like that of many other countries in the Latin American region, is now being shaped by the widespread adoption of a global discourse on multiculturalism and anti-racism. Originally inspired in large part by the mobilization of various social movements and civil society actors, Latin American states throughout the region now seek to respond. They are doing so by adopting in greater or lesser degree multicultural and in a few cases affirmative action–type legislation, particularly with regard to indigenous and Afro-descendant rights (see Greene 2007b; Hale 2006; Hooker 2005; Htun 2004). In previous work I focused on how Afro-Peruvian activists narrate their historical invisibility as a function of something more complex than their blackness and its difference from global whiteness. I demonstrated that Afro-Peruvians' struggle is centrally defined by their non-Andeanness within a country that idealizes the Inca past (see Greene 2007a). In this chapter I build on that work by focusing on how the Peruvian state responds to Afro-Peruvian struggles and the largely race-based claims through which they seek social justice. I do so primarily by examining the work of a congressional committee set up in 2004 to debate indigenous Andean, Amazonian, and Afro-Peruvian issues. I argue that the articulation of complex state discourses on Incanness and democratic liberalism in this congressional committee serve not only to further whiten the Inca but also to continue ignoring the legitimacy of Afro-Peruvian claims.

Theories of Race and Class through the Lens of Inca Whiteness

In the last half of the nineteenth century, Karl Marx elaborated an important theory about the relation between capital and citizens. He argued that bourgeois discourses of liberal citizenship are the perfect disguise for what is really happening in that "hidden abode of production" that is the main focus of his critique of capitalism (Marx 1977). This famous metaphor refers to the sphere where capitalists appropriate the products of other people's labor. They are able to do this "legitimately" because of the liberal state's defense of private property and its faith in contractual arrangements between "freely" acting laborers and their employers. Liberalism constructs an image of a world in which everything is free and equal: my dollar is as good as yours; your labor is worth exactly the amount of your wage on the free market; you have the same rights I have in front of the judge, and so forth. Such liberal discourses serve as a curtain, making it difficult for the oppressed to see the material structures of inequality in the sphere of production that underpin the liberal and ideologically "free" and "equal" society in which they live.

One of the major critiques of Marx, however, was that he saw almost everything in terms of class and very little in terms of race (see Gilroy 1993). He developed his theory in the context of Europe's industrialization, when the transformations in class relations were particularly visible. But the nineteenth century was also the pinnacle of colonial processes of racialization. The second wave of European imperialism led by the British and French was ideologically supported by the development of an emerging scientific discourse on the superiority of the white race. Race scientists in European and U.S. universities worked to justify colonization and defend the threatened institution of slavery, both of which were intimately tied to industrialization and global commerce. In short, Marx's political-economic dichotomies meant nothing without the racialized dichotomies to which they were attached. Country to city, peasant to laborer, proletariat to bourgeoisie, subject to citizen meant nothing without savage to civilized, colonized to colonizer, slave to master, black to white.

While one could point to a number of thinkers who contributed to making these connections between political economy, liberalism, and race explicit, one of the most important is W.E.B. Du Bois. By the early part of the twentieth century Du Bois had begun to explicitly delineate the connections between European imperialism, racialized relations, and the emerging global political-economic and democratic order. He identified whiteness as an ideological weapon used to exclude racialized nonwhites from civil society and as fundamental to the mechanisms the self-proclaimed white elite of the world used to dominate nonwhites. Indeed, Du Bois's view of a world divided by the "color line" translated into multiple demands for inclusion into a modern liberal order and equal access to material resources by those who had been historically excluded from it.

While both Marx and Du Bois launched all-encompassing global visions of the contradictions in an emerging liberal democratic capitalist system, they were also influenced by the contexts in which they lived. Neither vision is fully adequate to describe how global discourses of liberalism, race, and political economy took specific forms in places such as Peru. During the first wave of European imperialism led by the Spanish and Portuguese, the encounter between Europeans and Andeans was never conceptualized in terms of a simple dichotomy of colonizer and colonized or white and nonwhite. Indeed, while the history of conquest in South America is a tale of blood, manipulation, and violence, like colonial adventures everywhere, it is also a tale of complex negotiations among different rulers. It was not simply a confrontation of losers and winners but also an encounter between two imperial states comparing notes about what it meant to be "civilized" among "savages" and what it meant to wield sovereign power over subjects in need of subjection to that power.[2]

Throughout the colonial period an indigenous noble class, made up of members of Inca lineages and regional *kuraka* (chief) intermediaries, continued to enjoy rights and privileges that set them apart from other indigenous and Afro-descendant inhabitants. These groups of "noble Indians," formally recognized as such by the Spanish crown, played the role of local aristocratic intermediaries between indigenous commoners (or *indios del común*) and the Spanish government. This history of recognizing an indigenous ruling class, which would later turn against the Spanish during the massive uprising led by Tupac Amaru in the early 1780s, kept the idea of the Inca sovereign's power and historical vitality alive. Indeed, although the uprising resulted in an immediate ban on Inca imagery and a prohibition of texts such as Garcilaso de la Vega's *Comentarios Reales* (2004), it also ultimately fueled one of Peru's long-standing national narratives: the promise of the eventual creation of an Andean utopia to be led by an Inca returning to claim a soil that is rightfully his.

Peruvian political actors and national ideologues have sought to appropriate the Inca patrimony as central to the national project a number of times in the nation's history. Although we are most familiar with this phenomenon in the context of Andean resistance movements like that led by Tupac Amaru (Sinclair

2003), from colonial times to the present other actors have vied to control the Inca idea and utopian Andean project as their own. And they often did so in an effort to claim a privileged place in Peru's social and political hierarchy, in the context of the nation's claim that it is the birthplace of an autochthonous and admirable Andean "civilization" comparable to the best Europe has to offer. Those who have sought to imagine themselves as inheritors of Peru's Inca image range from colonial *encomenderos* and *criollo* independence leaders to twentieth-century *indigenistas* and military leaders during the 1970s agrarian reforms (see Greene 2007a; Earle 2007; Flores Galindo 1988).[3] Thus, historically members of the country's elite have often sought to imagine themselves as part of the Inca imaginary and thus define discourses of national pride and republican power as derivative of Inca civilization's accomplishments or, in my term, Inca whiteness.

I use the term "whiteness" here as it is used by critical race theorists such as Lipsitz (1998). In such theoretical work whiteness is essentially a representation of power, prestige, and privilege that is ideologically associated with a particular narrative of world history that is deeply Eurocentric. Most important, such work suggests that the key to the power of Europe's whiteness is its ability to constitute itself as the universal standard. Whiteness is that which refuses to mark itself as different and in so doing constitutes other non-Europeans or nonwhites as different and whiteness itself as the implicit norm. This dimension is central in some measure to whiteness almost everywhere it is found, although there are important exceptions. These are made obvious by the long-standing discourses on rural whites (i.e., "white trash") or ethnic/immigrant whites (for example, the Irish and Italians in the United States). And such exceptions result in wonderfully creative book titles like Jim Goad's *Redneck Manifesto* (1997).

Notably, in Peru there is no discourse of rural whiteness or white trashiness. Thus, whiteness is inevitably used as the equivalent of economic and political power and social prestige. However, whiteness in Peru is exceptional in ways that make it different from the discourses of white supremacy found in Europe and the United States. Historically, Peruvian ideologues and national leaders have struggled to establish an equivalence between whiteness and Incanness, or Europeanness and Andeanness in their abstract ideological forms. In part, this struggle is related to the long-term project of comparing Incan "civilizational" achievements with all that is presumed to be universally good and superior in the white civilization that Europeans claimed to have built. Such discourses stretch back to the earliest of colonial writings such as that of the *mestizo* Inca Garcilaso de la Vega, who was also a product of aristocratic negotiation as the child of a conquistador and an Inca princess. Garcilaso de la Vega's *Comentarios reales de los Incas* (2004) explicitly compared Inca society to Rome, one of the key mythical sources of Europe's claim to civilization, and set a precedent that

Peruvian ideologues continue to draw on when trying to define the importance of Peruvian identity in both national and global context.

This colonial discourse of Inca civilization was eventually conflated with an explicit discourse on Inca whiteness during the heyday of race science in the nineteenth century. Various Peruvian and other South American intellectuals as well as a few Europeans explicitly sought to whiten the Inca by incorporating them into the Aryan race or in some cases even by "Incanizing" white Europeans. This kind of Inca-centric thinking, typically rooted in linguistic comparisons between Quechua, Aymara, Sanskrit, and Greek or archaeological analysis of large Inca monuments, was particularly strong in the nineteenth and early twentieth centuries. Writers such as the Uruguayan philologist Vicente López (1871) argued that the Inca were in fact a New World offshoot of the early expansion of the Aryan race. Others such as the Bolivian Emeterio Villamil de Rada (1939) took such Andean-centric thinking to entirely new levels. He combined his Bolivian nationalism, which he pitted against Peru's claim to be the keeper of ancient Andean civilization, with a complexly Judeo-Christian and scientific critique of Vicente López's work. Villamil de Rada suggests that Aymara, which is found primarily in Bolivia (as opposed to Quechua, which is found primarily in Peru), is the language that should be analyzed because it is more ancient. He goes further to imply that Vicente Lopez has pointed the arrows that direct us to world history and civilizational influence in the wrong direction. The point is not that ancient Andeans, who ostensibly were like ancient Egyptians in the older traditions of Aryanist Egyptology, are the descendants of an invading Aryan race, a history that would clearly link them to the expansion of Europe's white civilization. Rather, Villamil de Rada claims, it is the ancient Aymara who are the world's original inhabitants and original creators of the world's languages and standards of civilization. Not only did they give birth to the eventual greatness of the Inca, they gave birth to all great civilizations of the world, including those of the Aryan race. In short, according to Villamil de Rada, the Old World did not discover the New World; instead, the New World is the Old World: hence the title of his work, *La Lengua de Adan y el Hombre de Tiaguanaco* (The Language of Adam and Tiaguanaco Man).

Such debates about the greatness of Andean civilization became so prominent in the nineteenth century that they effectively bridged the culture versus race and religion versus science divides. Hence, a Peruvian writer such as Clemente Palma, the son of the influential intellectual Ricardo Palma, could take the logical step of assuming that the Inca were white not only on cultural and linguistic grounds but also on biological grounds. In his infamous bachelor's thesis, written at the turn of the twentieth century, his scathing pessimism about Peru's racial predicament was obvious. Yet in the middle of a long diatribe against the various Indian, black, Chinese, and mixed races that make up Peru he made room for an important, if inherently contradictory, exception. The Inca lineage, whose civilized state was mythically founded by Manco Capac, a legendary leader from a legendary foreign land, was partially white because Manco Capac had a "few drops of Aryan blood." Or, as Palma puts it:

> It wasn't those old, miserable, Indians that created that relatively prosperous Empire; it was the spirit of a mysterious man, of a wise legislator, who perhaps had a few drops of Aryan blood, who was perhaps a stranger, who perhaps emerged out of that same disgraced [Indian] race like an exotic flower, like one of those unexplainable anomalies of nature that allow an intellectual to be born among a generation of idiots and an idiot among a generation of intellectuals. That's how since the ninth century, according to some, and since the eleventh century, according to others, Manco Capac appeared and until the beginnings of the sixteenth century with the Conquest there was a period of well-defined living, of organized living, of nationality among the Indian race due to the rising spirit of a civilizing lineage. (Palma 1897, 13)

Even "full-blooded" white Europeans of the era were occasionally in dialogue with such ideas. And at times they were clearly convinced of these racial connections between imperial Indians and the inherent superiority of their invented whiteness, which at the time was also explicitly imperial. Vicente Lopez's book *Les Races Aryennes du Perou* was written in French rather than Spanish and was published in Paris rather than Montevideo because he explicitly sought a scientific European (i.e., white) audience. And according to the book's preface, this publication venue was made possible by intellectual and logistical support from Gaston Maspero, not coincidentally a leading French Egyptologist at the time.

In a parenthetical remark in his famous critique of early race science, Stephen Jay Gould (1981, 64) notes how the nineteenth-century Philadelphia physician Samuel Morton was completely baffled by one particular detail in the racial data he collected. It had to do with an apparent anomaly in his measurements of Inca heads. Morton is now infamous for his contrived methodology for measuring cranial capacity and his scientific endeavor to prove the existence of superior and inferior races based on false assumptions about a relation between intelligence and cranial size. When he measured Inca heads, he found that ancient Peruvian crania were actually very small, in fact, way, way too small. Not only was the Peruvian average skull size smaller than the averages for Europeans (which he no doubt expected) and Asians (who he had fewer concerns about), it was also smaller than the average skull size for "negroes," who were by all accounts at the very bottom of his list, since his argument about white superiority was ultimately a justification for the continuation of black enslavement. Furthermore, Morton found that the Inca average was the smallest of all crania in his collection from Native American groups, including many who were by his standard clearly still in a savage state compared to the highly civilized Inca. It simply made no sense: how was it that an advanced civilization that Morton appreciated in his more ethnological descriptions of ancient Peru as something comparable to ancient Greece or Egypt would be run by humans with such small heads? This was a question for which Morton had no answer.

In fact it made so little sense that other European intellectuals interpreting Morton's studies simply ignored his data on the Inca and put them back in their rightfully racially superior place, right alongside white Europeans. Explicitly footnoting and yet completely misreading Morton's work, the eminent British historian William Prescott published this remark in his oft-cited *History of the Conquest of Peru* in 1847:

> It was the Inca nobility, indeed, who constituted the real strength of the Peruvian monarchy. Attached to their prince by ties of consanguinity, they had common sympathies and, to a considerable extent, common interests with him. Distinguished by a peculiar dress and insignia, as well as by language and blood, from the rest of the community, they were never confounded with the other tribes and nations who were incorporated into the great Peruvian monarchy. After the lapse of centuries, they still retained their individuality as a peculiar people. They were to the conquered races of the country what the Romans were to the barbarous hordes of the Empire, or the Normans to the ancient inhabitants of the British Isles. . . . They possessed, moreover, an intellectual preeminence, which, no less than their station, gave them authority with the people. Indeed, it may be said to have been the principal foundation of their authority. The crania of the Inca race show a decided superiority over the other races of the land in intellectual power; and it cannot be denied that it was the fountain of that peculiar civilization and social polity, which raised the Peruvian monarchy above every other state in South America. (Prescott 1847, 38–39)

Based on earlier work on Inca nationalism and its central place in Peruvian history, I once suggested, countering Bruno Latour's (1993) famous manifesto against modernity, that from a certain point of view the Inca have always been modern (Greene 2007a). Here, by resituating that argument within global racial discourses about Peru's ostensible place in the Eurocentric version of world history, I've been trying to suggest something that is related but slightly different: the Inca have also always been white.

Indeed, the comment from President Garcia that opened this chapter about copper-colored men as the "real Peruvians" could easily be read as a recent manifestation of this old and complicated fusion of ideas about the relation between whiteness and Incanness in Peru. And so a question arises about what other aspects of contemporary state discourse might continue to reflect the way the ideology of Inca whiteness is used to marginalize other race-based claims to citizenship. The peculiar notion of Inca whiteness governs Peruvian nationalism. In other words, Inca whiteness is a form of hegemony in which the Inca continue to be implicitly white and thus the implicit standard by which all Peruvians are judged, including those, Afro-Peruvians, for example, who are necessarily constituted as racially and culturally different.

White Liberal Incas within Peruvian Congressional Committees

Compared to other Latin American countries, for example Ecuador or Colombia, where significant constitutional changes have taken place in recent years, Peru's multicultural reforms are largely superficial. Yet in large part influenced by such regional trends and neighboring cases, debate among civil society actors and certain state institutions on such issues has become a constant. Indeed, it has taken on newly institutional forms in Peru since the election of Alejandro Toledo in 2001.

Largely the work of the first lady, Eliane Karp, the Toledo administration oversaw the creation of two arenas of state discussion over indigenous and Afro-Peruvian issues. The first is the Instituto Nacional de Desarrollo de los Pueblos Andinos, Amazónicos, y Afroperuano (Institute for the National Development of Andean Peoples, Amazonians, and Afro-Peruvians; INDEPA). It is an institution with ministerial ranking that includes state-appointed officials and ethnic representatives from Peru's Amazonian, Andean and Afro-descendant populations. Most activists and NGOs working on indigenous and Afro-Peruvian issues view INDEPA as an inefficient and mostly symbolic effort. A controversial past, frequent budgetary woes, a marginal status within the ministerial rankings, and an increasingly passive role on issues of racism and cultural recognition make it an incredibly weak institution. But INDEPA is nonetheless a state institution that continues to play a role in Peru's multicultural and race politics (see Greene 2007a).

Issues of racism, multicultural reforms, and indigenous and Afro-Peruvian issues are routinely debated in a second governmental context in Peru. Since 2004, the Peruvian Congress has had a committee that oversees debate and proposed legislation dealing with Andean, Amazonian, and Afro-Peruvian claims. To my knowledge the work of this committee has yet to be analyzed. Below I present an initial examination of the committee's work with a particular emphasis on the fact that although Afro-Peruvian issues are rarely discussed, Inca whiteness often appears. My analysis relies on transcripts of the committee's meetings from 2004 to 2008.

The name of the committee, which originally was the Committee on Amazon, Indigenous and Afro-Peruvian Affairs (Comisión de Amazonía, Asuntos Indígenas y Afroperuanos), was later changed to the Committee on Andean, Amazonian and Afro-Peruvian Peoples and Ecology and Environment. The change brought the name into alignment with INDEPA's specific regional demarcation of Andean, Amazonian, and Afro-Peruvian (who are implicitly coastal) populations. It also reflects the fact that the committee merged with another committee that had previously dealt exclusively with environmental issues, both urban and rural. This makes the committee a strange place for debate at times. Sometimes the environmental and indigenous themes coincide, particularly regarding environmental issues in the Amazon. But sometimes they do not, as for example when entire sessions are dedicated to discussing contamination in factories or the need for more green space in Lima.

The debate within the committee represents a microcosm of Peruvian political ideologies and party positions. During its existence Congress members from across Peru's party spectrum have participated, ranging from loyal Fujimoristas and cosmopolitan independents to Apristas and politicians with rural roots in the Peruvian provinces.[4] The committee is a particularly interesting space of debate because of the participation of three Congresswomen who openly identify as representatives of Peru's ethnic and racial minority populations. Martha Moyano Delgado, a devout Fujimori supporter and sister of the shantytown activist Maria Elena Moyano (who was killed by the Shining Path in 1992), openly identifies as Afro-Peruvian. Congresswoman Paulina Arpasi was on the committee during its first two years of existence. She was very active until 2006, when she left Congress. Arpasi is an Aymara speaker and longtime Andean peasant activist from Puno with a history of participation in the Confederación Campesina del Perú. In 2006 an indigenous woman from Cuzco, Hilaria Supa Huamán, was elected to Congress and is now also a member of the committee in its more recent manifestation.

Much like the multicultural INDEPA, this congressional committee is relatively superficial. While Congress members do discuss deep historical problems related to racism and ethnic marginalization, the solutions they propose are inevitably more symbolic than structural. In its five years of existence the committee has seen almost no major legislation passed regarding indigenous or Afro-Peruvian issues. The legislation regarding indigenous land rights, bilingual education, and minimal legal autonomy that pertains to Peru's titled Andean and Amazonian communities has been on the books for decades; these laws are clearly the product of a different historical era (see Greene 2009). And the various proposals for new legislation dealing with cultural and linguistic rights and constitutional reform put forth by indigenous organizations have effectively gone nowhere.

One important exception in terms of new legislation the committee has overseen in the last few years is Law #28761. Passed in 2006 at the initiative of Moyano Delgado, the law declares June 4 Afro-Peruvian Culture Day. Modeled a bit like the Martin Luther King Jr. holiday in the United States, it is meant to promote Afro-Peruvian contributions to Peruvian culture and recognize the struggles of Afro-Peruvians against racism. It does so by commemorating a memorable Afro-Peruvian icon and intellectual. June 4 is the birthday of Nicomedes Santa Cruz, a folklorist and ethnomusicologist who spearheaded the initial renaissance of Afro-Peruvian cultural expression in the 1950s and 1960s (see Feldman 2006 and in this volume). As a result of the recent legislation June 4 now marks a day when Afro-Peruvian NGOs and community leaders organize various public cultural events to celebrate Afro-Peruvian culture and to debate current black struggles in Peru. But the legislation was passed without much discussion in committee or in the assembly because it in effect represents merely symbolic change.

Despite the relative absence of new legislation passed on issues of multiculturalism and racism, the committee is an interesting space because it allows us a glimpse into the ways that race, culture, and nation are being debated by state officials in the political body that represents the nation at large. Some members represent themselves as part of Peru's ethnic minority groups, while others do not. But as a matter of political positioning and posturing, all have to maintain a constant engagement with nationalist discourse as members of Congress and participants in the process of defining the nature and importance of Peruvianness.

I have several impressions of the committee as a result of having read and analyzed its work from 2004 to 2008 with regard to Afro-Peruvians. The first is that despite the passage of the Afro-Peruvian Culture Day act in 2006, Afro-Peruvian issues are in fact rarely discussed. Although indigenous community and environmental issues are the mainstay of the committee, the issue of blackness typically only comes up when Moyano Delgado brings it up. And more often than not, when she does so, it provokes no real debate or even a complete unwillingness to engage with the issue. In other words, the basic strategy of the other Congress members is simply to ignore blackness as an issue. And yet when the issue of Andean indigeneity emerges, as it often does in the committee, it tends to lead toward an ideological free-for-all whereby all members discuss what it means to be indigenous (or more specifically Inca) as a way of talking about what it means to be Peruvian.

A particular example will demonstrate this point. At an early stage in the committee's history there was a lengthy and important meeting to discuss the creation of INDEPA as well as proposals for constitutional reforms that would create certain mechanisms of recognition for Afro-Peruvian and indigenous communities. This meeting, which was held on September 29, 2004, included the participation of architect Luis Huarcaya. A history and archaeology fanatic, Huarcaya has worked at the National Institute of Culture and was named director of INDEPA by Alejandro Toledo. He had thus come to participate in the discussion and help define a formal relationship between INDEPA and the committee. Notably, according to his personal blog he is also apparently a self-described "Ancestral Wiseman and Descendant of the Inca" (see http://luishuarcaya.blogspot.com).

After Huarcaya's presentation on how he envisioned INDEPA's work, Congresswoman Moyano Delgado intervened with two remarks that referred to two key issues that Afro-Peruvian activists have been debating about for years. The first was a question about different kinds of ethnic terminology and the political implications for self-representation of such language in the law that would create INDEPA. Moyano Delgado said:

> We . . . I say this because there is a group of Afro-descendants that has entered into debate about whether or not we Peruvian Afro-descendants consider ourselves black. There's a debate, for example, about the word "black" that was a concept, a word, a pejorative insult that slave-traders gave to us to treat us as just a thing, like fourth-class persons, or not even persons but just animals. And there's another concept that is all over this legislative proposal [to create INDEPA] [problem in the recording] . . . language where people identify as Andean persons and speak of the concept of "indigenous." (Committee on Amazon, Indigenous and Afro-Peruvian Affairs, September 29, 2004).[5]

Notably, neither Huarcaya nor anyone else responded to the question of being black versus being Afro-Peruvian, a key terminological distinction and cause for constant debate in diaspora contexts over issues of racism, ideology, and political correctness. The key question of whether the word black, or "negro" in this case, necessarily entails a racist ideology or can in fact be overcome by revalorizing the word was left aside entirely.

However, the comment sparked a long conversation about the implications of the words *indígena* and *originario* (indigenous and first peoples) versus *campesino* (or peasant). Huarcaya and several Congress members including

Paulina Arpasi, Valderrama Chavez, Molina Almanza, and Santa María del Águila, the president of the committee, all chimed in. While there were certain differences in opinion—most notably Molina Almanza insisted he does not accept use of the word "*indígena*"—the basic consensus pointed to a strategic compromise. Multiple members of the meeting recognized that *indígena* is a problematic term because of its colonial connotations generally and more specifically because in some parts of the Peruvian Andes communities consider themselves campesinos and actively reject the term indigenous. Yet the consensus points to the fact that ultimately the word indigenous is internationally recognized and thus must remain as the official terminology. As Huarcaya put it, "I don't like the word indigenous because nobody likes it, neither Paulina nor Martha, nobody likes it. But it is accepted in international agreements" (Committee on Amazon, Indigenous and Afro-Peruvian Affairs, September 29, 2004).

The discussion over the word campesino then provoked Moyano Delgado to raise another major point of debate within Afro-Peruvian activist circles. She remarked:

> For example, when someone says representative of a peasant community [*comunidad campesina*] or when we speak of peasant communities we are always referring to the Andes. Sir, on the coast there are peasant communities, Afro-Peruvian peoples worked basically on the land on the coast and there are Afro-Peruvian peasants. So there's an error in our concept here. No? (Committee on Amazon, Indigenous and Afro-Peruvian Affairs, September 29, 2004)

Moyano Delgado was alluding to a long-standing argument within black activist circles about the invisibility of rural or small-town Afro-Peruvian communities, such as those around Chincha in the south or small towns such as Morropón and Yapatera in the north. Many of the members of these towns continue to be small landowners or are primarily involved in low-level agricultural labor. More important, in cases such as Morropón, Yapatera, and Chincha, descendants of Afro-Peruvians historically worked on large haciendas in conditions of servile labor until the agrarian reforms of 1968 effectively abolished such forms of land tenure. In other words, she was trying to make an important historical point about the existence of a black rural class that is overshadowed by the national image of the peasant as an essentially indigenous Andean farmer. Again there was no engagement with the issue she brought up. Instead, Congressman Valderrama Chavez intervened and pushed the president to move immediately toward a vote to approve the INDEPA law. Committee president Santa María de Águila did so and Moyano Delgado's comment was ignored entirely.

Of course it is one thing to pay attention to how blackness is being made invisible by ignoring it in practice within state arenas, and it is another to pay close attention to the kind of national discourses that continually overshadow blackness. Two very important discourses emerge in this context, both of which are linked by their appeal to Peruvian nationalism. The first is the classical discourse of liberal political democracy, an old abstract idea that obeys the logic of "if we are all citizens then we must all be equal." And yet it is used ideologically as a form of political discourse with which to dismiss the legitimacy of claims for social and historical justice. In other words, it is just the kind of perfect ideological cover for real and more hidden structural inequality that Marx and Du Bois, with their respective emphases on class and race, were talking about.

The political utility of liberal democratic discourse becomes most obvious when political proposals for structural or significant institutional changes are being debated. This became obvious in the September 29 committee meeting. When INDEPA was being created, several proposals circulated to reform the Peruvian constitution to recognize a specific set of ethnic and cultural rights for Peru's minority populations. Eliane Karp spearheaded one of the initial proposals in April 2002. Her efforts resulted in a text prepared for circulation within the committee that discussed constitutional issues and became a point of reference within the committee on Andean, Amazonian, and Afro-Peruvian affairs as well (see Comisión de Constitución, Reglamento y Acusaciones Constitucionales 2002). A year later a large group of Andean and Amazonian activists from all the major indigenous rights organizations in Peru organized a national-level consultation with community representatives. They formulated their own proposal for constitutional reform and produced a document that was also circulated to Congress members (COPPIP 2003).

From the point of view of the Committee on Amazon, Indigenous, and Afro-Peruvian Affairs the most controversial issue that came up in the proposals was the one dealing with ethnic quotas in Congress. The two proposals clearly followed the precedent set by Colombia's 1991 Constitution, which mandates two seats in the upper house for indigenous representatives and two seats in the lower house for Afro-Colombian representatives. The proposal circulated by Andean and Amazonian representatives talks in general terms about the need for "direct political participation in the Parliament of the Republic as happens in other countries" and remarks that this participation "will permit the society and the Peruvian state to broaden the margins of equality and foment an exercise in true citizenship" (COPPIP 2003, 6–7). The text proposed by the Comisión de Constitución, Reglamento y Acusaciones Constitucionales, which oversees constitutional affairs, in which Karp had a hand, actually goes further. In a short book published by the Congress the committee proposes that 10 percent of members of Congress should be specially elected by indigenous and

Afro-Peruvian populations (Comisión de Constitución, Reglamento y Acusaciones Constitucionales 2002, 61).

In following the trend set by Colombia for ethnic quotas, indigenous activists and supporters such as Karp pushed the state to contemplate what Mala Htun (2004) has called the need to instate a "self-perpetuating" logic of ethnicity in many countries. The idea is that by inscribing such multicultural measures into a document such as the constitution, which is after all the text that literally constitutes the nation, one perpetuates the existence of a nation that is permanently divided along ethnic lines. In attempting to address historical grievances and recognize past wrongs, such measures challenge the classic nationalist ideologies about a singular and homogeneous national body. But they also contribute to the hardening and often the institutionalization of ethnic boundaries that are in reality rather porous. In short, to elect an indigenous or Afro-descendant representative, one has to first explicitly define who is and who is not indigenous and Afro-descendant.

This kind of debate about ethnic quotas emerged in the Committee on Amazon, Indigenous, and Afro-Peruvian Affairs during another session devoted to discussing INDEPA and its legislative implications on March 16, 2005. It is unclear to me which of the various legislative or constitutional reform proposals they were discussing. In the transcript, there appeared to be some confusion among the Congress members themselves as they discussed the possibility of reserving two or four seats for Peru's ethnic minority populations. But the frequent references to classic liberal democratic tenets about the inherent equality of all citizens under the law were very clear. They were used repeatedly as a justification for not supporting ethnic quotas and for suggesting that in fact such quotas would do harm to Peru's ethnic minority communities.

Several examples display this clearly. Congressman Valdez Melendez intervened in the debate by saying:

> For example, how would these first peoples elect national representatives? Would it be Amazonians? Would it be Andeans? Would it be those from the North? Would it be people from Cuzco? Would they be from the central jungle? How would it be done, Mr. President [of the Committee]? And, finally, the Constitution guarantees equality before the law. If this is true then all communities, all social groups and all persons have access to the Congress, Mr. President. I think this . . . should not be approved and it seems to me even a bit demagogic. (Committee on Amazon, Indigenous, and Afro-Peruvian Affairs, March 16, 2005)

The logic here is clear. In a liberal democracy all social groups have equal access to the law and equal access to political representation. What is also clear is the unintentional space Valdez Melendez's language created. His use of the phrase "if this is true" implicitly revealed that equal access is in fact precisely what is in question for ethnic constituencies that seek to implement such quotas. For ethnic minorities in Latin American countries, black and indigenous alike, liberal political practice is completely out of sync with liberal political theory. Marx, as modified by Du Bois, was right. Equality exists in theory but not in practice.

Later in the same discussion Congressman Valderrama Chavez made a similar argument. He said that the logic of a fixed number of ethnic seats is "segregationist because it's as if they [ethnic groups] are being excluded or have a lesser value. And, so by this criteria one should also put a set number for women, a set number for young people; I think it distorts the principle of equality and antidiscrimination that should exist according to the Constitution" (Committee on Amazon, Indigenous, and Afro-Peruvian Affairs, March 16, 2005). Here once again the overriding logic is one of an imaginary equality that the constitution of a liberal democracy such as Peru upholds. Yet his comment adds an important dimension by clarifying that such a policy of ethnic quotas would open the door to many other political interest groups. The subtext of his words implicitly recognizes that there are in fact multiple forms of political marginalization in Peru that stretch well beyond ethnicity and race. Yet the universal ideological recipe for dismissing the claims of such political interest groups is a constant appeal to the myth of liberal democratic equality.

The participation of Congresswomen Moyano and Arpasi in this debate reveals just how complex ethnic politicking is in a country like Peru. Moyano said that she supported the idea, particularly if it includes a seat for Afro-Peruvians but that she also thought they had to be "serious" and "responsible" in debating this issue. Her desire to not be perceived as an ethnic hardliner is palpable; she argued for indefinite postponement. She concluded by suggesting that there are unresolved issues in the proposals because it was unclear whether the ethnic seats would be in addition to the current 120 seats in Parliament (which would require a constitutional change) or would be part of that 120. She then suggested that the timing was not right, saying, "One would have to pick up on how it's being done in international legislation and apply it to us, but now's not the time. I don't want this idea to be abandoned. I defend the idea that there should be representation, but we have to let it mature, Mr. President, for later on" (Committee on Amazon, Indigenous, and Afro-Peruvian Affairs, March 16, 2005).

Congresswoman Paulina Arpasi provoked a discussion that reveals quite a bit about how liberalism and indigenism are deeply, if contradictorily, connected in Peru. Confronted with the apparent disapproval of quota-based representation, she embarked on a personalized diatribe that implicated the other members of the committee.

Truthfully, I feel like I'm being alluded to. I hope that's not the case because I represent, I feel like a representative. . . . I too have questions:
When are we going to include these first peoples? When? Never? It would
be better just to say, ok, never, that they should leave Peru because that's
what this is leading to. And, yes, I am going to ask that somebody tell us
where we're from. I'm only going to feel ok when finally they just tell me:
Where are you from? You're not from Peru. So, let's [i.e., us indigenous
people] just leave. I think everybody would accept that because I feel like
they don't want us to be here. But we already have it [i.e., indigenous rep-
resentation] in Bolivia; we have it in Colombia; we have it in Ecuador; we
have it in all those countries. But I don't know in Peru. I'll tell you what's
more. People always say to me: Paulina, what is it you want to do? You
want to divide the country into two nations: Peru and its mestizaje part?
For me Peru is not mestizaje. Peru belongs to the Inca. We have to get to
that point without denying it. We are all indigenous people here; maybe
10% are not indigenous. We are all indigenous but unfortunately nobody
wants to recognize that because we are first peoples and they don't want to
see us. (Committee on Amazon, Indigenous, and Afro-Peruvian Affairs,
March 16, 2005)

One could easily take this discourse as an indication of Arpasi's inarticulate
Spanish. Indeed, as an Aymara speaker operating in a Spanish-dominated state
context this was a major point of debate as well as cause for racist ridicule on
popular Peruvian radio shows throughout her time as a Congress member. Yet
her speech here clearly articulates some of the core contradictions in Peruvian
nationalism and identifies the ethnic others against which it is pitted. The version of Peruvian nationalism that Arpasi railed against illustrates the contradictions of Andean indigeneity and shows how it makes Afro-descendants in Peru
invisible. Arpasi applies the difficulties this ideology creates both for herself as
an Aymara woman from Puno who made it to Congress and for the Peruvian
nation at large. These difficulties are summed up by the contradiction in the last
sentence: "We are all indigenous" alludes to an ideal of national inclusion rooted
in indigeneity. Yet this ideal is contradicted by the idea of a permanently divided
nation, a nation where "they don't want to recognize us." Here she includes herself in the historically excluded "us"—Peru's first peoples.

Yet the importance of this statement becomes clear only when one pays attention to which particular ideology and identity of indigeneity she identifies as the
one that is inclusively and homogenously Peruvian. It is not just any indigeneity.
It is specifically the indigeneity of the Inca. This is what she alludes to directly
by saying, "For me, Peru is not *mestizaje*. Peru belongs to the Inca." Indigeneity

is fully inclusive and fully nationalistic only when it appears in its idealized, abstract, and of course imperial form: in other words, in its Incaic version. Hence, from the point of view of Peruvian discourses on the nation, the issue is not that "we are all indigenous" but rather, and quite clearly, that "we are all Inca." When she recognizes her Aymaraness, and implicitly her "everyday" peasant indigeneity, she feels excluded with all the other "actually existing" Andean peoples. But when she stakes a claim on deep Peru, that ancient and powerful Peru of Tuantinsuyo, she is forced to include all Peruvians, implicitly including herself. Why? Because, as she says, "Peru belongs to the Inca."

Notably, at least two other Congress members followed her lead and tried to wrestle with the problem of their own indigeneity as Peruvians. Valderrama Chavez, who is from Arequipa, said, "Paulina feels alluded to here as if she was the only indigenous person. . . . I also feel indigenous because it is an emotional state or a conviction that leads one to recognize oneself as indigenous or a descendant of indigenous people without leading one to identify with indigenism [indigenismo] but rather as indigenous. So she doesn't have to feel alluded to or that we direct ourselves at her" (Committee on Amazon, Indigenous, and Afro-Peruvian Affairs, March 16, 2005). Congressman Valdez Melendez, who represents the Amazonian province of Ucayali, made the Incaic dimensions of Peru's indigenous nationalism crystal clear by remarking on the Congress members' respective provincial origins and their relative places in Peru's indigenous hierarchies:

> Mr. President, I would like to say clearly to all my colleagues, that when I look in the mirror I see an Indian from Ucayali; when I look at you, president of this dignified committee, I also see an Ucayali Indian . . . when I look at Hipolito Valderrama I'm looking at an Arequipa Indian. And when I look at Mario Molina I'm looking at an imperial Indian; and when I look at Paulina I'm also seeing an Indian from Puno. (Committee on Amazon, Indigenous, and Afro-Peruvian Affairs, March 16, 2005)

Valdez Melendez made an important distinction that illustrates how Incaic indigeneity is inherently hierarchal and serves to perpetuate exclusion. He marked himself and other Congress members as provincial Indians from the departments of Ucayali, Arequipa, and Puno. Notably, none of them except Arpasi speak an indigenous language or have direct ties to the titled Andean or Amazonian communities located in their respective departments. As provincial Indians, they are also implicitly in a relation of historical subordination to an imaginary Inca leader, or what Valdez Melendez calls an "imperial Indian." Congressman Mario Molina hails from and represents Cuzco, which is of course in many ways more of a center than a provincial periphery within the Peruvian imagination.

Aside from the fact that it served as the political center of Tuantinsuyo before the Spanish arrived, it is also a mythic center of Peruvian nationalism in Peru's *indigenista* traditions (see De la Cadena 2000). It thus continues to be a site from which various Cusco-centric claims on Peruvianness, at least in its Incaic version, are made. I see this as another manifestation of that never-ending return to the idea of the ancient Andean emperor who will one day return to rule (see Greene 2006). Valdez Melendez slipped Molina into the Inca slot and he suddenly represented the mythical leader of all Peru's Indians. Implicit in all of this is the idea that Molina is also momentarily the leader of all Peruvians since, as this discourse on indigeneity among a motley crew of Peruvian politicians makes clear, from a certain logic all Peruvians are Indians waiting to be led by an arriving Inca.

While Valdez Melendez's remarks make Peru's Incaic nationalism clear enough, one need only return to the thought of Luis Huarcaya to see how deeply rooted and labyrinthine Inca ideologies can be. Some of Huarcaya's remarks during the session he attended to introduce the mission of INDEPA to the Committee on Amazon, Indigenous, and Afro-Peruvian Affairs are worth noting. Take these, for example:

> And why isn't history better known? It isn't correct to say that the Conquest was just the killing of savage Indians. Those savage Indians were wise men and they had five thousand years of history. It hasn't been convenient to say that, hasn't been convenient. But all this is coming to light with the archaeological discoveries that are being found every day. I think, just as is thought in other places, in Egypt, that in archaeology only 20 to 25% of what we have has been discovered. So there is still a lot of work to do.... The Inca traveled with 150 boats throughout the entire world in the era of the *amautas* [wise man or philosopher]. Is that in the books? No. It's in the books of the Jesuits. It's in the Archive of the Indies in Seville. But it's not in Peruvian education and so we are not proud of anything. We have no identity because we are not proud of anything but we have so many things to be proud of. How many types of potato do we have? So much time has passed to domesticate the potato, to domesticate vicuñas: five thousand, six thousand years. And that's not in the history. In the universities they teach that there were 14 Incas and there were 108 Incas. We are going against our true soul and our true spirit. (Committee on Amazon, Indigenous and Afro-Peruvian Affairs, September 29, 2004)

Two things about Huarcaya's comments to the committee are important. First, he is incorrect in his remarks about the place of the Inca in Peruvian history books and higher education. It is clear from those who have studied how Peruvian history is taught in Peru that the Inca are in fact at the center of the national narrative. As early as primary school, Peruvian children from all different regions, ethnicities, and classes memorize basic dates, facts, and figures about the Inca. There's even a popular children's song to help them memorize the names of the fourteen Inca rulers. Other lesser and more provincial Indians and other ethnic groups such as Afro-Peruvians fare considerably worse in terms of representation in official history texts (see Portocarrero and Oliart 1989). To the extent to which Afro-Peruvians are mentioned at all in school textbooks they are usually relegated to a section on the history and eventual abolition of slavery. Relegating them to a period in the past effectively erases them from the present. Huarcaya's portrayal of a lack of Inca history in the history books is deeply self-interested. Clearly, his intent is to put forth a passionate plea to expand such teaching even further and to do so in a way that draws on his own peculiarly Inca-centric view of Peru and the world.

This brings us to the second and crucial point. Huarcaya did not wholly invent his Incaic utopianism; much of it was already invented for him long ago. And his way of speaking about the Inca makes it clear that from a certain ideological point of view the Inca should be represented as more than just a civilization central to Peruvian history. From the point of view of this ideology, they should be portrayed as central to the history of the entire world and part of Europe's invented and white privileged centrality within that history. His reference to Egypt as a great world civilization is crucial to the historical narrative of Europe's "whiteness" and to its ostensible legacy of civilizational "greatness." His statement about Egypt implicitly refers to the well-known controversies Egyptology has generated. The discipline has a complex history of deeply racist claims about the ostensibly Aryan basis of ancient Egyptian civilization and the ostensibly inferior and servile nature of "black" Africans.

Huarcaya is drawing on a long and complex intellectual tradition that I do not have space to detail here but is at the foundation of his Incaic vision of Peru and its rightful place in Europe's whitened version of world history. He explicitly seeks to whiten the Inca and configure Peru as central within that particular Eurocentric narrative that sees Europe at the center of all world historical progress (see Chakrabarty 2000). In fact, in some of his own writings Huarcaya goes so far as to Incanize Europe's claims to whiteness by claiming Inca society as a world historical and thus a standardizing form of universal civilization. In promoting one of his many books, *Mil Años Viajando por el Mundo Antiguo*, on his website Huarcaya writes:

This book shows definitively that the Inca civilization located in South America has been one of the most advanced in the world and that it in fact gave birth to civilizations like those of China and Egypt. The erroneous concept that globalization is new is false because it was practiced by various civilizations in very ancient epochs. (Huarcaya 2009)

In short, Huarcaya, notably the intellectual figure appointed to represent a multicultural Peru, clearly sees himself as the inheritor of a long-standing hegemony of Inca whiteness in Peru, so much so that he stops just short of explicitly calling himself a white Inca. Or, actually, that is the point. It need not be said, because the privileges associated with Inca whiteness make it such that it is already understood.

Conclusion

By this point the reader will be wondering what all this analysis of Inca whiteness and the hierarchical forms of indigeneity found in Peruvian nationalism have to do with blackness. My answer is quite a lot. The complex and contradictory interplay between ideologies of race and ideologies of the liberal and civilized citizen play into a deeply historical logic that is specific to Peru's Andean context. Central to that specificity is an idea about the Inca's rightfully powerful and privileged position in the Peruvian imaginary. It is a curiously contradictory idea that nonetheless continuously surfaces in discourses of state and nation. It is an implicit hegemonic idea that the Inca are both the rightful and yet also the whitened rulers of what is presumed to be an essentially indigenous, essentially Andean country.

As many authors have noted, this overwhelming emphasis on the Inca discourse creates many problems for Peru's actually existing Andean populations (see De la Cadena 2000; Degregori 1998; Mendez 1996). But it also leaves aside almost entirely any mention of blackness as a position from which to construct alternative ideas of Peruvian citizenship or a Peruvian historical subject. I believe that this is a defining feature of the struggles of contemporary blacks as they have evolved within these specific constraints of Peruvian history. In Peru the fight is not simply one against the global doctrine of white supremacy. More specifically, the struggle is to make blackness visible within a space already characterized by a complex fusion of discourses about the white supremacy of the Incas. The global logic of whiteness is indeed manifest in the idea of Peru as a modernizing liberal republic eager to cast out racialized others, including, of course, the masses of "ordinary" Andean Indians. However, this same history of national modernization continues to reserve a special place for the clearly "superior" Indian: the white Inca. And it is in the shadow of this imagined white Inca that Afro-Peruvians continually find themselves fighting to achieve a semblance of black visibility.

Notes

1. The translation "white yuppie" is necessarily a compromise since the term *pituco* in Peruvian Spanish does not directly index skin color the way the adjective "white" does. However, when uttered in context whiteness is often implied. *Blanco* (white) is in fact used in Peru but not nearly as commonly as *pituco*.

2. While they are beyond the scope of this essay, explicit comparisons can be made in this regard to Mexico in the context of the confrontation between the Spanish and the Aztecs and the eventual usage of Aztec symbols in Mexican nationalism (see Earle 2007).

3. There is no adequate English translation of the term *encomendero*. The Spanish crown granted *encomenderos* authority to exact tribute from indigenous populations in exchange for their promise to act as moral guardians of those populations, including instructing them in the Christian faith.

4. Apristas refers to members of the APRA (Alianza Popular Revolucionara Americana; American Populist Revolutionary Alliance), one of the only historical political parties still functioning in Peru. Originally founded by Victor Raúl Haya de la Torre in the 1920s with a strong socialist bent, it has since increasingly moved toward the right, particularly during the second period of President Alan García.

5. Official transcripts of sessions of the Committee on Amazon, Indigenous and Afro-Peruvian Affairs are obtainable through the Area de Transcripciones of the Congreso de la Republica in Lima, Peru. Transcripts are cited by date of session within parentheses.

Bibliography

Chakrabarty, Dipesh. 2000. *Provincializing Europe*. Princeton, N.J.: Princeton University Press.

Comisión de Constitución, Reglamento y Acusaciones Constitucionales. 2002. *Anteproyecto de ley de reforma de la Constitución: Texto para el debate*. Lima: Congreso de la República.

COPPIP (Coordinadora Permanente de Pueblos Indígenas del Perú). 2003. "Consulta Indígena sobre la Reforma Constitucional" Unpublished document circulated to Peruvian Congress. Lima.

De la Cadena, Marisol. 2000. *Indigenous Mestizos*. Durham, N.C.: Duke University Press.

Degregori, Carlos Iván. 1998. "Movimientos etnicos, democracia y nación en Perú y Bolivia." In *La construcción de la nación y la representación ciudadana en México, Guatemala, Perú, Ecuador, y Bolivia*, ed. Claudia Dary, 159–226. Guatemala: FLACSO.

Earle, Rebecca. 2007. *The Return of the Native*. Durham, N.C.: Duke University Press.

El Comercio. 2008. "Presidente critica a las ONG y a los simpatizantes de izquierda." December 7. Available at http://www.elcomercio.com.pe/ediciononline/HTML/2008-12-07/presidente-critrica-ong-y-simpatizantes-izquierda.html. Accessed May 10, 2009.

Feldman, Heidi. 2006. *Black Rhythms of Peru: Reviving African Musical Heritage in the Black Pacific*. Middletown, Conn.: Wesleyan University Press.

Flores Galindo, Alberto. 1988. *Buscando un Inca*. Lima: Editorial Horizonte.

Garcilaso de la Vega, El Inca. 2004. *Comentarios reales de los Incas*. Lima: Editores Importadores.

Gilroy, Paul. 1993. *The Black Atlantic*. Cambridge, Mass.: Harvard University Press.

Goad, Jim. 1997. *The Redneck Manifesto*. New York: Simon and Schuster.

Gould, Stephen Jay. 1981. *The Mismeasure of Man*. New York: W. W. Norton and Co.

Greene, Shane. 2006. "Getting over the Andes: The Geo-Eco-Politics of Indigenous Movements in Peru's 21st Century Inca Empire." *Journal of Latin American Studies* 38 (2): 327–54.

———. 2007a. "Entre lo indio, lo negro, y lo incaico: The Spatial Hierarchies of Difference behind Peru's Multicultural Curtain." *Journal of Latin American and Caribbean Anthropology* 12 (2): 441–474.

———. 2007b. "Introduction: On Race, Roots/Routes, and Sovereignty in Latin America's Afro-Indigenous Multiculturalisms." *Journal of Latin American and Caribbean Anthropology* 12 (2): 329–355.

———. 2009. *Customizing Indigeneity: Paths to a Visionary Politics in Peru.* Palo Alto, Calif.: Stanford University Press.

Hale, Charles. 2006. *Mas que un indio: More Than an Indian.* Santa Fe, N.M.: School for Advanced Research.

Hooker, Juliet. 2005. "Indigenous Inclusion/Black Exclusion: Race, Ethnicity, and Multicultural Citizenship in Latin America." *Journal of Latin American Studies* 37 (2): 285–310.

Htun, Mala. 2004. "Is Gender Like Ethnicity? The Political Representation of Identity Groups." *Perspectives on Politics* 2 (3): 439–458.

Huarcaya, Luis. 2009. Online comment on *Mil años viajando por el mundo Antiguo.* Available at http://luishuarcaya.blogspot.com/search/label/OBRA%20I N%C3%89DITA. Accessed October 10, 2009.

Latour, Bruno. 1993. *We Have Never Been Modern.* Cambridge, Mass.: Harvard University Press.

Lipsitz, George. 1998. *The Possessive Investment in Whiteness.* Philadelphia, Pa.: Temple University Press.

López, Vicente Fidel. 1871. *Les races Aryennes du Perou.* Paris: Imprimerie Jouaust.

Marx, Karl. 1977. *Capital.* Vol. 1. New York: Vintage.

Mendez, Cecilia. 1996. "Incas sí, indios no: Notes on Peruvian Creole Nationalism and its Contemporary Crisis." *Journal of Latin American Studies* 28:197–225.

Palma, Clemente. 1897. *El porvenir de las razas en el Perú.* Imprenta Torres Aguirre: Lima.

Portocarrero, Gonzalo, and Patricia Oliart. 1989. *El Perú desde la escuela.* Lima: Instituto de Apoyo Agrario.

Prescott, William H. 1847. *History of the Conquest of Peru.* New York: Harper and Brothers.

Sinclair, Thomas. 2003. *We Alone Will Rule.* Madison: University of Wisconsin Press.

Villamil de Rada, Emeterio. 1939. *La lengua de adan y el hombre de Tiaguanaco.* La Paz: Imprenta Artistica.

14

Sociology and Racial Inequality

Challenges and Approaches in Brazil

ANTÔNIO GUIMARÃES

History presents a challenge for sociological theory because of the contingencies it contains. Inequality, ethnocentrism, and racism are universal phenomena, but they develop differently within different national, political, and economic contexts. Across such differences we may detect commonalities forged by empire, colonialism, migration, and the encounter with cultural difference. The aim of this chapter is to discuss how Brazilian social theorists have explained relations between whites and blacks since the middle of the nineteenth century. My premise is that understanding these sociological explanations enriches social theory in general and public policy in particular.

Sociology began its institutionalizing process in Western universities in the late nineteenth century with the rejection of race, climate, and other natural forces as causal explanations for social phenomena. This rejection did not translate immediately into the understanding that race was a social, cultural, and historical construct; that occurred only after World War II. Although some scholars such as W.E.B. Du Bois and Max Weber used race occasionally as a nonbiological socioanalytical term, the concept maintained its strong biological meaning until the mid-twentieth century. As a result, in its early years, sociology exercised little influence on state policies vis-à-vis the Brazilian black population. At the time, academic thought about race was centered in schools of medicine and law. Public hygiene, eugenics, criminology, legal medicine, and other applied sciences were deployed by the state to construct policies regarding sanitation, education, health, and security that pertained to black Brazilians. Until the second decade of the twentieth century, the most advanced theory that sought to integrate African descendants and counter the view that blackness is an impediment to national development and growth was the claim that continuous miscegenation would introduce white biological virtues into the Brazilian nation (Skidmore 1974; Schwarcz 1993).

Beginning in the 1930s, Gilberto Freyre, Arthur Ramos, and other sociologists began to disseminate another understanding of how the state should develop and implement policies regarding blacks. Strongly influenced by the cultural anthropology of Franz Boas in its distinction between race and culture and downplaying the influence of race in human affairs, Freyre and his generation advanced the thesis that racial and cultural miscegenation among European, African, and indigenous peoples gave Brazil a solid basis upon which to build an advanced ("tropical") form of civilization and democracy. However, their thesis left the idea of miscegenation as whitening alive, albeit in a surreptitious form. The continuing whitening ideal partially explains the general acceptance of their thesis by Brazilian intellectuals over the next five decades. Influenced by this idea, state policies of cultural integration championed the national embrace of black subcultures and encouraged racial tolerance and coexistence in laws and social practices.

Brazil came to be viewed on the world scene not only as a mixed-race nation but also as a racial democracy, even in the face of great racial inequality. For decades, the state avoided articulating a specific policy about blacks, for such a policy would have had to acknowledge the existence of a racial inequality that it had ideologically defined out of existence. The erasure of race as a political concept also unfolded at the popular level. For the fifty years from 1930 to 1980 (except for the cultural politics of some intrepid black organizations), popular resistance against inequality was articulated almost entirely in class terms.

One of the first economic and demographic facts to catch the attention of Brazilian sociologists was that Brazil was colonized by Europeans who did not form residential settlements; instead, Brazil's colonizers built productive plantations (Prado 1937). Where colonizers formed settlements, indigenous populations were almost completely exterminated and Europeans dominated demographically. But where colonizers lived only on plantations, Europeans were the minority, outnumbered by *brancos da terra*,[1] *mestiços* (mixed-race individuals), and enslaved men and women. Slavery was abolished late in the nineteenth century (1888), but then, during the First Republic (1889–1937), ex-slaves and the black population were replaced by European immigrants as a labor force for the coffee *fazendas* of São Paulo. Thus, while in the first 300 years of Brazil's history, planters imported 6 million Africans, the country received, in only fifty years, 3 million European immigrants.

Three factors shaped Brazilian sociological thought. First, *mestiçagem* (racial mixing) between Europeans, the indigenous population, and Africans occurred on a massive scale. Because of the small European presence during the first centuries of settlement, this pattern gave rise to a large number of *mulatos* (individuals of mixed African and European descent) and *mestiços*, and together these two groups acted as an intermediate social group between slaves and the masses, on the one hand, and officials and landowners/slave masters, on the other. Racial mixing and the formation of a *mestiço* social stratum was evident in almost all important cities in the country (Carvalho 1998), particularly in Salvador, Recife, Rio de Janeiro, São Luis, Belém, and the cities of the states of Minas Gerais. Massive miscegenation was not limited to a single city or region, and the recognition and integration of *mestiços* was thus a major challenge for the ideologists of the new nation (Freyre 1936). The racism and ethnocentrism that had characterized European imperial expansion from the seventeenth century had to be reconfigured in the face of this reality (Skidmore 1974).

The second fact is that although the large European immigration at the start of the twentieth century was sponsored by the Brazilian state and was expected to provide a workforce for coffee cultivation to replace slaves after abolition, it was also a project for the racial reconstruction of the nation (Schwarcz 1993). Consequently, the ethnic intolerance that each new wave of immigrants faced in the United States did not occur in Brazil, at least not with the same degree of intensity. There was no displacement or competition between new immigrants and immigrant groups that were already established. However, there was tension between immigrants, on the one hand, and landowners and the Brazilian middle class, on the other. Immigrants felt the need to differentiate themselves from the mixed and black populations that constituted the core of the slave system (Fernandes 1965). The ideological project of whitening and Europeanizing Brazil led these immigrants to be quickly absorbed by the country's middle classes (Nogueira [1955] 1998).

A third fact is that this historical process left profound regional idiosyncrasies that only recently, with the growing mobility of the workforce across regional employment markets, have started to wane. The east, north and west of the country continued to have a large indigenous or *caboclo* (indigenous-European) population and no significant influx of European immigrants. Areas of older colonization, which did not have a large presence of European immigrants—including the northeast and the coffee cultivation areas in the state of Rio de Janeiro—have a large black population and a strong *mulato* cultural identity. Only São Paulo and the south of Brazil, the more dynamic areas of the modern Brazilian economy, saw a large influx of Europeans at the beginning of the last century.

Mestiçagem and Racial Democracy

The growing presence of *mulatos* and *mestiços* among the urban middle classes (intellectuals, public servants, artists, and craftsmen) soon became a theme for

Brazilian sociology (Freyre 1933, 1936). However, Skidmore (1974) was perhaps the first to see the connection between whitening[2] ideology and the demographic and social importance of the *mulato* middle class. For Skidmore, the doctrine that white blood and European culture would, through *mestiçagem*, end up prevailing over African and indigenous blood and cultures was crucial for the architects of the young Brazilian nation, who, in face of the legitimacy of the quasi-scientific racialist doctrines of the nineteenth century, needed to carve out a place for Brazil among the "civilized" nations of the world.

Freyre saw *mestiçagem* as a process that would prevent the nation's fragmentation into races, promote the social ascension of *mestiços*, and contribute to Brazil's democratization. Yet this vision encountered two barriers. First, as only different things can be mixed, the persistent discourse of *mestiçagem* implies the continuing reproduction of the two key elements of this mixture: black and white. Second, to propose the extinction of blacks and whites through mixing presupposes their real and factual existence as natural phenomena, which exempts this sociology from the task of examining the symbolic reproduction of these groups.

From the mid-1930s to the early 1950s, Brazilian sociology was tethered to the dilemma of *mestiçagem* and was in close dialogue with structural-functionalism. Two new concepts that developed from this dialogue became central to this sociology: racial democracy and color. Even though they were not being strictly analytical, racial democracy and color became central to Brazilian social analysis. Both were introduced into academic discourse, together with the concepts of ethnicity and culture, with the explicit aim of superseding the concepts of race and whitening, which had been cultivated by the earlier generation of Brazilian social thinkers, such as Vianna ([1932] 1959).

It is worth noting that racial democracy, which can be summarized as the claim that whites and nonwhites can interact without restricting the rights and life chances of nonwhites, suffers from the contradiction that it reaffirms the existence of races: it is about races coexisting in democracy.[3] To overcome races, the doctrine has to explain inequalities between whites and blacks as being only differences in color or status, whether these differences are the result of slavery or differences in social class between groups of individuals (Pierson 1942; Azevedo 1953; Harris 1956; Harris and Kotak 1963; Wagley 1968).

Color, an integral part of the discourse of social agents and the foundation for multiple distinctions, was taken as a given in this discourse and referred to as a natural reality—the color of the skin. For this reason, the post–World War II generation of Brazilian social scientists had to unravel the social meaning of differences and distinctions based on the color and social class of Brazilians, since race was not included in Brazilian social classifications and did not have any analytical purpose. In the three decades from the 1930s to the 1960s, it became well established in Brazilian sociology that within the social and symbolic universe of Brazilians there were no social groups that could be called races, either as descent groups, such as North American Negroes or blacks, or as ethnic groups that could be recognized by their cultural markers. On the other hand, stereotypes, prejudices, and the categories used for classification employed the concept of color. These colors were open-ended and malleable and had almost no capacity to mobilize people for political action, particularly in the northeast, north, and west of the country.

What could color be, therefore, if not reduced to natural reality? Much of the research conducted during the 1950s and 1960s, mainly in Bahia and the northeast, unmasked the social construction of color, which encompassed various physical attributes (skin, hair, nose, lips) and cultural practices (gestures, language, titles) (Azevedo 1953; Wagley 1968; Harris 1956; Nogueira [1955] 1998). Appearance, not origin, was the basis of these color groups, some of which were already firmly established in government language and with social categories such as white, preto,[4] negro, pardo, and moreno. Following a suggestion by Mário de Andrade (1938), for whom color prejudice was nothing more than a superstition rooted in Western thinking and feeling, Roger Bastide (1967) insisted on the symbolism of color within Christianity and its resulting stereotypes of blacks as missing moral and spiritual vivacity and transparency. He suggested that color distinction in Brazil was based on the long Christian tradition of the Portuguese colonizers that had preceded and survived the racist theories of the nineteenth century. For Bastide, even if Brazilians developed the same stereotypes about blacks that derived from the social stigma of slavery, Catholicism prevented them from developing a segregationist racism, as had developed in the United States, since they did not have the ethos of a chosen people that is peculiar to Protestant Christianity. Some authors of this generation—such as Bastide and Fernandes (1955), Nogueira ([1955] 1998), Costa Pinto (1953), and Azevedo (1975)—recognized that color or racial prejudice coexisted with the ideal of mestiçagem and racial democracy. Nevertheless, there was an academic consensus that there were no ethnic-racial groups in Brazil and that social groups of color coexisted in competition, albeit in a nonviolent way, struggling for their social rights but defining themselves more by color than by race. It was not until the 1960s and 1970s that Brazilian sociology, in particular at the University of São Paulo, returned to the subject of race relations, leaving behind the paradigm created by Robert Park and Ernest Burgess in the 1920s. It also freed itself from Freyre's paradigm, which made biological and cultural miscegenation the key explanation for race relations in Brazil.

The object now was to study the integration of blacks as part of the proletariat of a new society of classes that was emerging in Brazil as a result of the industrialization of São Paulo. The *negro* (black) became the object of prejudice in the 1890s and was displaced from the workforce of the emerging capitalist society. What Fernandes called the bourgeois revolution—that is, the transformation of the slave order and status into a capitalist order, now steered by a bourgeois and business ethos—would ensue and Brazil's social and economic development would follow. In following this path, blacks, as an archaic racial group that belonged to the slave order, would also transform themselves. The analyses of Fernandes and his disciples were developed along two axes—the first was the refusal to explain social phenomena such as racial prejudice, class position, or life opportunities as attributable to social interaction, the values or attitudes of social agents, or even the use of the universe of cultural symbols in which agents are immersed. All important scientific determination was of a structural order. The second axis was the belief in a typical-ideal bourgeoisie in which universalist values and attitudes of merit would prevail without taking into account any forces of a non-economic nature. Thus, the "prejudice of 'race' or 'color' was an organizational component of a caste society" (Cardoso 1962, 281) and was functionally inappropriate in a class society. In the same way, racial prejudice, which was more prominent in São Paulo than in other large Brazilian cities, could not be explained as something that belonged to the personality and culture of the new European immigrants who formed the first *paulista* (from São Paulo) proletariat and who at that time (that is, by the 1960s) constituted the city's middle class. Racial prejudice was symptomatic of an incomplete bourgeois order. The revolution was unfinished because it had preserved the aristocratic ethos of castes, and the new order proved itself incapable, in 1964, of ensuring the political representation of classes. Racial democracy, therefore, was no more than a myth that tried to affirm as an ideology what the system neutralized in its political practice (Fernandes 1965). Thus, the second wave of sociological studies about race relations in Brazil (Cardoso and Ianni 1960; Cardoso 1962; Ianni 1962; Fernandes 1965) ended in dialogue with structural-functionalist sociology and was influenced by Marxist dialectics and research on Latin American underdevelopment that had been influenced by readings of contemporary European Marxism. It is worth emphasizing that all this theoretical development was being closely observed by black social movements and intellectuals, who used these theories in their social and political demands. The influence of some of these researchers—such as Ramos and Freyre during the 1940s and Bastide, Fernandes, Azevedo, Cardoso, and Ianni in the following decades—cannot be denied.

In the 1970s, some Brazilian sociologists, forced into exile by political repression, circulated internationally. This period is marked by two theoretical blocs that came to nurture each other: on the one hand, the theories of dependency and underdevelopment, which attempted to explain the social and economic development of Latin American as well as postcolonial imperialist relations; and on the other hand, theories of institutional racism, racial inequality, and the relations between races and capitalism (Fernandes 1972; Ianni 1972, 1978; Hasenbalg 1979).

Racial Inequalities and the Politicization of the Academic World

In Brazil, the 1970s and 1980s were marked by profound criticism not only of Brazilian democracy as experienced during the pretense of parliamentary democracy that the military regime installed (1964–1985) but also of democracy during the Second Republic (1945–1964). The watchword used by social movements and parties in opposition to the authoritarian regime was "reclaiming citizenship," a phrase that was incessantly repeated in party political discourses and articles in the mainstream press. Criticism was focused on the absence in practice of not only the political but also the civil and social rights of the Brazilian population, which was being treated in an authoritarian manner by the state. Groups advocating for human rights, many of which emerged during this period, sought to mobilize civil society against state authoritarianism and to take forward the social reforms that the military had aborted in 1964.

During the military period, groups of black activists joined cultural associations geared toward cultivating African or diasporic traditions in organizations to combat racism that were in sympathy with anti-colonialist and anti-apartheid struggles in Africa and in sections of clandestine Marxist parties sheltered within the large legal opposition party, the MDB (Brazilian Democratic Movement). During this period black militants came together to denounce the pernicious character of Brazilian racism, converging under the banner of unmasking racial democracy.

Racial studies by academics in the 1970s and 1980s were marked by attempts to show that the reality or effectiveness of racial democracy was false and demonstrate the increasing social inequalities between whites and blacks that validated the thesis of black activists that racism was an active and colossal force in Brazil. Studies about inequality in Brazil were supported methodologically by multivariate analysis of aggregated data using relatively refined models in the 1980s and 1990s. These studies provided ample empirical evidence of the existence of institutional racism in Brazil (Hasenbalg and Silva 1988, 1992; Hasenbalg, Silva, and Lima 1999), and they inspired others (Guimarães 2004; Silva 1995, 1997) to attempt to reveal the mechanisms through which the competition between people of different colors in markets and situations that followed apparently egalitarian universalist rules always ended up putting black people at a disadvantage.

Unexpected and growing attention started to be given to the ethnicization of the fight against racism. That is, the struggle for social and political integration, which had always emerged in the political sphere—Abolicionism (1870–1888); the Frente Negra Brasileira (Black Brazilian Front; 1931–1937); the Teatro Experimental do Negro (Black Experimental Theater; 1944–1964)—started to demand its own cultural identity—black, African, or diasporic. Thus, the creation of groups in Brazil that cultivated black ethnic-racial identities organized into private associations that developed their own political demands and sought dialogue with governmental bodies. This development began to become clear to analysts in the 1990s. The political importance of these groups is clear in the role they play today in the ongoing reform of universities, such as the demand that universities adopt quotas for blacks. During the Lula administration, they were also successful in their demand for the creation of a Special Secretary for the Promotion of Racial Equality, which has the status of a ministry. Members of these groups were nominated for important positions in other areas of the Brazilian state.

The response of social scientists to these events has been varied. On the one hand, some have revisited the findings of the social anthropology of the 1950s and 1960s to give them contemporary meaning (DaMatta 1990; Fry 1998; Maggie 1996). The anthropological studies of the 1950s and 1960s, however, were backed by a limited amount of new data that generally were restricted to a particular geographic region, the Northeast. The anthropologists of the 1990s attempted to redefine racial democracy as a structuring myth of Brazilian nationality that continues to guide the daily conduct of blacks and whites even though it has been denounced as false by black political activists. Other studies, along the same lines, tried to demonstrate that the Brazilian color system remains the same as that observed in earlier decades; such studies were characterized by the same ambiguous logic of earlier ones (Schwarcz 2003). These studies, because they are founded on a denial of races, remind us that color in Brazil is a kind of social classification, but they fail to analyze the relationships between racial discrimination, the system of color classification, and the systematic reproduction of racial inequalities. More important, they avoid a central question: Why, after centuries of cultural and biological *mestiçagem*, do so many individuals continue to define themselves in relation to color groups—blacks and whites—or in relation to races?

There are also a number of contemporary authors who appeal to vague explanations, such as North American cultural imperialism (Bourdieu and Wacquant

1998), when challenged to explain the paradox of why the black movement with its small number of activists has been so influential, for example by achieving victory with the adoption of quotas for blacks at universities. By limiting their theoretical thinking to the relationship between races and nationality, they fall back on the defense of principles such as the nonexistence of human races, the inadequacy of racial classification by state organs, suspicion of the categories used in the Brazilian census (Harris et al. 1993), and so forth—all without incorporating a more careful analysis of the contemporary political scene. An example of this was the 2008 manifesto against the introduction of racial quotas in Brazilian universities, "*Cento e treze cidadãos anti-racistas contra as leis raciais*" (One hundred thirteen anti-racist citizens against the racialist laws), which was published in the mainstream press.[5] This manifesto is based on the construction of an ideal of *mestiço* nationality and challenges the legitimacy of the category *race*. One of its main arguments is that the state's recognition of classificatory categories of color is equivalent to the institutionalization of races in Brazilian society, thus making color categories impervious and closed. The manifesto also presents compensatory policies in education as a foreign imposition of American solutions by international agencies, thus exploiting the anti-Americanism of the middle classes.

These arguments are based on two premises: 1) the denial of the existence of human races by science; and 2) the claim that the color of the skin of human beings is a biological phenomenon that bears no relation to racial classification. Because the policy of access to universities is directed at young people who call themselves *pretos, negros,* or *pardos*, those who oppose quotas suggest that by institutionalizing color, these policies institutionalize the concept of races. They call this the racialist position—understood as the belief in the existence of human races. In fact, however, the object of quota regulations is "color," not "races." Even in extreme cases where commissions have been created to verify the self-declaration of the color of those who attempt to participate in the university quota system, what the commission investigates is "color" and the sentiment of ethnic belonging of those who apply, not "race."

From a theoretical point of view, it is a mistake to set apart "races" and "color," as if one were a social fallacy and the other a biological fact. If it is true that "races" are nothing more than the product of social classification based on cultural prejudice and stereotypes, even though they are based on natural aspects and human phenotypes,[6] the same is true of a person's color. When we use color—white, *negro, preto, pardo, amarelo*,[7] and so forth—to refer to someone, we are not just indicating the color of their skin, as biologists would do. These colors are also classifications that enclose people in groups, using other phenotypical characteristics (hair, lips, nose, etc.), including cultural characteristics, as we saw earlier. Therefore race and color constitute social status; that is, both are markers that serve equally as a basis for discrimination.

Certainly, observers would be right in claiming that "race" is a more rigid social construction than "color." Paradoxically, because "race" lacks any natural justification, it is totally arbitrary and therefore undeniable, as there is no physical basis on which we can decide someone's race. Color, on the other hand, because it has a clearly visible referent, can be manipulated, both biologically and socially. This is true in the Brazilian case. The Instituto Brasileiro de Geografia e Estatística has collected statistics that show that in the last decades there has been an important change in the classification of the Brazilian population by color. According to the Brazilian National Household Sample Survey data, the number of "pretos" in Brazil increased from 4.9 percent in 1995 to 6.5 percent in 2008 (Fundação Instituto Brasileiro de Geografia e Estatística 1995, 2008).

But by appealing to the biological reality of colors, those who oppose quotas are in fact moving away from a sociological position—the social fantasy of what we call color—and instead seeking refuge in genetics, the physical basis of color, only to claim a tautology that to discriminate is to discriminate, either positively or negatively. But the crux of the question is whether and how a self-consciously discriminatory policy (affirmative action) that seeks to remedy existing social inequalities based on perceived "race" or "color" can be equated with the social discrimination that created those inequalities in the first place.

Another logical consequence of the use of color categories by the state, according to the manifesto, is that this "racialism" would be the first step toward racism, understood as the cultivation of hatred between races. The argument is complex. Certainly there would be a cultivation of color differences, since these differences would be socially more widely accepted and used than before, but this is not racism and it does not have any logical or necessary link with racism. This would be at most "colorism." Does treating people of different colors differently induce hatred between them? If this is so, where, through the centuries, is the hatred in Brazil? Furthermore, unequal treatment does not necessarily promote hatred between races. First of all, for this to occur, there must be race, something that—as those who argue against quotas recognize—is not a natural phenomenon and something that would require a huge social project to create. Is this the Brazilian case? I cannot find any racist discourse in Brazil, either against whites or against blacks, on the part of those proposing affirmative action.

The racialism that is validated by empirical facts and evidence is that which claims that color is used, in Brazil, to attribute racial and racist characteristics to people. The argument that the state creates a legal foundation for perpetuating racial discrimination by applying categories of color used on a day-to-day basis is ingenious. But is it true? There is no empirical evidence for the conclusion that positive discrimination will perpetuate social inequality between the social groups in question, either as races or colors. The argument that in recognizing social races and social colors in its policies the state institutionalizes and reinforces racial classifications quite simply lacks empirical support. Races and colors have existed for centuries, and laws have not been able to transform society. It is always possible to imagine, for example, that racial demands in present-day Brazil will run their course as the state satisfies them. To suppose that a logic of racialization is embedded within these demands is to restrict the debate to the moral field. It is plausible to argue that it is a question of justice and that all national states should try to correct inequalities in access to education because of race or ethnicity. In the same way, at a political level, we cannot forego the use of concepts and categories that belong to this world. In their efforts to correct racial and social inequalities and injustices, politicians and jurists must use the words and concepts that make sense to their citizens.

Race and Mobilization

Despite the flaws and risks I have identified, a broad social scientific research agenda has arisen in Brazil that includes diverse studies on prejudice and discrimination (not only against blacks but against other social groups as well), racial classification, the relationship between color and race, multiculturalism, black social movements, and the reproduction of racial inequalities in situations of apparent equality of rights (Guimarães 1999, 2002; Telles 2003; Costa 2002, 2006; Souza 2006; Fry 2005).

This trend of rethinking race relations within the context of the expanding nature of the Brazilian democracy has been reinforced by the growing number of researchers in the fields of the social sciences, history, and education who are attuned to the agenda of black social movements (Munanga 1986, 1999; Queiroz et al. 2000; Bacelar 2001; D'Adesky 2001, 2002; Nascimento 2003; Silvério 2003, 2006; Domingues 2004, 2007; Paixão 2006). These researchers have focused on the reemergence of Brazilian black social movements, the assessment of public policies such as affirmative action, and the introduction of multicultural reforms to the Brazilian educational system. The majority of those who fight for racial quotas in universities consider themselves to be members of a race, even as they question the objective existence of biological race. Why, for blacks, does race seems to be an inescapable cognitive category?

Unlike other people formed in a diaspora, such as Jews, or immigrant communities, such as Indians, the millions of descendants of the Africans who were brought to the Americas as slaves did not, in these new countries, constitute ethnic or religious groups. Instead, they constituted a race. The same could be said for those who, centuries later, emigrated of their own accord from the young African nations in search of work in the West. Like the descendants of those who were brought to the Americas, Africans today are also generally defined negatively (by others) or positively (by themselves) through physiognomic and phenotype characteristics and not by their native culture or nationality. In the Americas—even in Brazil or Cuba, where traces of African cultures have deeply influenced popular culture and fused into national and regional culture—these people were able to advance in their civil rights claims only by mobilizing around race. Thus, for blacks, as Du Bois (1986) argued, the double consciousness of race and nationality was, from the start of citizenship, a condition for social and political integration.

This fact marks the difference between blacks and other diasporic communities, who, in contrast to people of African descent, constituted themselves as ethnic or religious minorities in modern Europe. Jews, for example, resisted the process of racialization imposed on them. Religion and the culture developed around it served as the basis of their identity rather than phenotype. The existing "doubleness" of consciousness in the Jewish case arises from a heritage of self-affirmation in the face of persecution. Like blacks, descendants of Japanese who emigrated to the Americas are differentiated phenotypically from other Americans and Brazilians, depending on the degree of miscegenation among their ancestors. However, they did not mobilize in terms of racialization: preserving a reference to their original nationality was a much stronger tool against the designation of "yellow race" the racist imagination sought to impose upon them. Thus, instead of yellow, they were and continue to be Japanese, Chinese, Korean, or Indian.

In the Americas there were strong attempts to make nationality, and not race, the principal marker of black identity, such as the national identities that were consolidated from the 1920s to the 1950s in the Caribbean and South America. The majority of Caribbean and Latin American nations forged for themselves a new supra-racial identity that transformed the stigma of *mestiçagem* to a positive marker. As this occurred blacks were urged to move away both culturally and sentimentally from their continent of origin to become 100 percent nationals of the new American states. Guerreiro Ramos (1954) noted that black people were not but Brazilians—those who could not claim any other nationality or culture. However, the strength of racial stereotypes that identify black people as black, as if color was something insurmountable—a definition attributed by others—has always emerged on a par with the national definition attributed by oneself.

Race and color, as well as nationality, were the key points of reference for these movements. The old African nations of the slave trade period were abandoned, preserved only as colonial denominations or as instruments of cultural genealogy.

It is also true that culture and religion, in the case of blacks, have served as a nucleus from which racial identity could develop and solidify. Food and leisure customs—such as *feijoada*, made into a national mainstream dish by black cooks, and *samba*—or religious rites, such as devotion to a particular saint or to Candomblé, *xango*, or *batuque*—served as a means of bringing together people who were socially diverse but whose "color"—that is, the race attributed to them—was a trait that was negatively valued by the dominant ethnic group. While culture clearly contributed to the development of black ethnoracial identity, the source of identity for other diasporas has been much more about their cultural symbols than their phenotype or presumed genotype. In contrast, for people of African descent, phenotypes and presumed genotypes have been the primary markers of their collective identity.

The process of *mestiçagem* was, up to a point, successful, if we consider the fact that a large number of *mestiços* abandoned African or indigenous cultural references and light-skinned *mestiços* assimilated into a Latin American "Europeanness." I use the term "Europeanness" because the Latin American *mestiço* worlds have preserved European values as a key standard by which to measure themselves. What remained of "African culture" or indigenous culture was gradually absorbed by national cultures. Accompanying this process was a feeling of *mestiço* inferiority, color prejudice, and a widening of social inequalities between blacks and whites. Race has thus continued to be an important marker with regard to feelings of inferiority, the existence of discrimination, or the construction of positive racial identities, such as the Frente Negra Brasileira (1930s), Teatro Experimental do Negro (1950s), and the Movimento Negro Unificado (1980s).

This historical phenomenon helps us understand the dilemma of Brazilian blacks today, when they are urged to embrace universalist and republican norms of citizenship and reject public policies that might benefit them as a race. The problem is that history has bequeathed only one main marker that can serve as a strong basis of collective identity for them: the notion of race.

The reasons blacks have not managed to abandon their putative "race" are, as I have suggested, mainly historical and sociological. In the past the members of African "nations" who were brought to Brazil sustained different forms of ethnic solidarity (Reis 2003). But these "nations" were superseded by the emergence of a national identity, an emergence that accelerated after independence and abolition. What remained was a nationalist African sentiment that was limited to the religious sphere (the Candomblé nations). In the search for uniformity and the homogenization of the national culture, African languages and customs were swept away, sometimes through violent political repression, giving rise to

Brazilian-based regional and cultural identities. In addition, modern African nation-states arose after Brazilian nationalism had already come into being and consolidated, leaving little space for the descendants of enslaved peoples to identify themselves or to be identified with their ancestors' places of origin.

What remained after the process of domination to which the enslaved African peoples were subjected were physical and corporal marks that were synthesized into color and the notion of race. That is why social movements have theoretically reworked the concept of race, in order to strip it of racist overtones, moving from negative generalizations about moral, biological, or social flaws of race as defined by others to race defined by oneself, turning it into a positive cultural marker.

The goal of transcending racial and cultural distinctiveness and becoming "one hundred per cent Brazilian" proved to be impossible, partly because most Brazilians do not want to be black. We are Brazilians, but we are also Bahians, *paulistas*, men and women, rich and poor, black and white, Catholic, Protestant, and so forth. Given these multiple and hybrid identities, all subsumed under the national umbrella, it is difficult to mobilize against racial discrimination without embracing race or color.

Some Afro-Brazilian intellectuals in the 1940s and 1950s embraced socialism in order to be consistent with the universalism and nationalism expected of black people in Brazil. These intellectuals theorized that the consequences of discrimination provoked by color were a major contributing factor to black people's poverty, exploitation, and political marginalization. This view found many sympathizers among twentieth-century black Brazilians, European communists, and North American and Latin American black communists.

It is difficult to explain why this universalist view has given way, over the past few years, to mobilizations that are clearly more racial. A similar phenomenon has taken place all over the Western world since the 1970s, leading to what sociologists call "new social movements." In the case of blacks, it is worth remembering that race (through color) has been a key marker, shaping the personal fate of most blacks in Brazil. Thus, upward social mobility, joining the bourgeoisie, personal success, fame, personal cultivation of European culture—none of these has ever prevented a black person from being regarded socially as black.

"Race" has been used by racists of all times to identify their own social group and distinguish it from others. The effect and motivation of this process has been the oppression and economic, sexual, and cultural exploitation of certain social groups. Yet people of African descent in the Americas and Europe use "race" (and sometimes "color") for political mobilization and to draw attention to racial injustice. These groups clearly have no capacity or intent to develop the power to dominate, oppress, or exploit other groups. The process of racial formation in Brazilian blacks is similar to that of any other group, but from a sociological point of view, it seems to be developing in reverse: defense instead of attack, equal opportunities instead of calling for social inequality. Bourdieu (1990) reminds us that ideas get reinterpreted and appropriated by different actors who are entrenched in their group interests and their respective social power. This seems to be what is happening when Brazilian blacks fight for affirmative action, even though they use the rhetoric of race.

Where We Are

To limit the academic debate to the mythic character of claims of "racial democracy," to whether or not "races" are real, or to claims that miscegenation resulted in a lack of social barriers is to go round in circles and become caught up in the logic of re-creating national myths. We need to face the question of why and how a national population that believes itself to be highly mixed and culturally homogeneous periodically re-creates itself into black and white, into racial or ethnic-racial groups, in contrast to today's Europe, where the same ethnic and discriminatory phenomenon takes place under the apparent natural reality of differences between customs, religions, and colors. In Brazil, the ethnic and racial phenomenon reproduces itself in an environment of apparent cultural tolerance and homogeneity, the illusionary twilight of *mestiçagem*. We need to experiment with public policies that recognize the existence of social races and reflect on the limitations and pitfalls of identity politics.

In contrast to Europe and the United States, ethnic or racial conflicts in Brazil carry less weight in the political-electoral system because they are almost exclusively focused on equal opportunities and access to goods and services, and do not permeate all other social realms, such as religion, and cultural identity. We may thus avoid the temptation of thinking of these things as "natural" categories.

Notes

A first version of this text was presented in a work group meeting between the British Academy of Social Sciences and the Brazilian Federal Agency for the Support and Evaluation of Graduate Education (CAPES), held in Rio de Janeiro, November 5–7, 2008.

1. *Brancos da terra*—very light-skinned *mulatos* (individual of mixed African and European descent).

2. For further details of the discussion about whitening in Brazilian sociology, see Guimarães (1999).

3. I have discussed in greater detail the concept of racial democracy in Guimarães (2005).

4. *Preto*—dark or black individuals of African descent; *negro*—all black individuals including mixed-race individuals of all types; *pardo*—dark or brown individuals; and *moreno*—an imprecise term that could mean dark white or light brown or black.

5. See "Manifesto: Cento e treze cidadãos anti-racistas contra as leis raciais," a letter presented to the president of the Supreme Court on April 30, 2008. Reprinted at Época, May 5, 2008, at http://revistaepoca.globo.com/Revista/Epoca/0,,EDR83466-6014,00.html.

6. Charles Wagley (1968) called these groupings "social races."

7. *Amarelo* means "yellow" or an individual of East Asian descent.

Bibliography

Andrade, Mario de. 1938. "A superstição da cor preta." *Boletim Luso-Africano* (dezembro).

Azevedo, Thales de. 1953. *Les élites de couleur dans une ville brésilienne.* Paris: UNESCO.

———. 1975. *Democracia racial.* Rio de Janeiro: Vozes.

Bacelar, Jeferson. 2001. *A hierarquia das raças. Negros e brancos em Salvador.* Rio de Janeiro: Pallas.

Bastide, Roger. 1967. "Color, Racism, and Christianity." *Daedalus* 96 (2): 312–327.

Bastide, R., and F. Fernandes. 1955. *Relações raciais entre negros e brancos em São Paulo.* São Paulo: Anhembi.

Bourdieu, Pierre. 1990. "Les conditions sociales de la circulation des idées." *Romantischezeitshrift für Literaturgeschichte* 14: 1–10.

Bourdieu, Pierre, and Loïc Wacquant. 1998. "Sur les ruses de la raison imperialiste." *Actes de la Recherche en Sciences Sociales* 121: 109–118.

Cardoso, F. H., and Octávio Ianni. 1960. *Cor e mobilidade social em Florianópolis: aspectos das relações entre negros e brancos numa comunidade do Brasil Meridional.* São Paulo: Cia. Editora Nacional.

Cardoso, Fernando Henrique. 1962. *Capitalismo e escravidão no Brasil meridional.* São Paulo: Difusão Européia de Livro.

Carvalho, Maria Alice R. de. 1998. *O quinto século, André Rebouças e a construção do Brasil.* Rio de Janeiro: Revan.

Costa, S. 2002. *As cores de Ercília: Esfera pública, democracia, configurações pós-nacionais.* Belo Horizonte: UFMG.

———. 2006. *Dois Atlânticos. Teoria social, anti-racismo, cosmopolitismo.* Belo Horizonte: UFMG.

Costa Pinto, Luis Aguiar. 1953. *O negro no Rio de Janeiro: relações de raças numa sociedade em mudança.* Rio de Janeiro: Cia. Editora Nacional.

D'Adesky, J. 2001. *Racismes et antiracismes au Brésil.* Paris: L'Harmattan.

———. 2002. *Racismo, preconceito e intolerância.* São Paulo: Atual.

DaMatta, Roberto. 1990. *Relativizando, uma introdução à antropologia social.* Rio de Janeiro: Rocco.

Domingues, Petrônio José. 2004. "A nova abolição. A imprensa negra paulista (1889–1930)." *Estudos Afro-Asiáticos* 27 (3): 89–122.

———. 2007. "Movimento Negro Brasileiro: alguns apontamentos históricos." *Revista tempo* 12: 100–122.

Du Bois, W.E.B. 1986. "On the Meaning of Race." In *Du Bois: Writings*, ed. Nathan I. Huggins. New York: Library of America.

Fernandes, Florestan. 1965. *A Integração do Negro na Sociedade de Clases.* São Paulo: Cia. Editora Nacional.

———. 1972. *O negro no mundo dos brancos.* São Paulo: Difel.

Freyre, Gilberto. 1933. *Casa grande e senzala.* Rio: Schmidt.

——. 1936. *Sobrados e mucambos*. Rio de Janeiro: Cia. Editora Nacional.

Fry, Peter. 1998. "O que a Cinderela Negra tem a dizer sobre a 'política racial' no Brasil." *Revista da USP* 28: 122–135.

——. 2005. *A persistência da raça: ensaios antropológicos sobre o Brasil e a África austral*. Rio de Janeiro: Civilização Brasileira.

Fundação Instituto Brasiliero de Geografie e Estatistica. 1995. *Pesquisa Nacional por Amostragem de Domicílios*. Rio de Janeiro: Fundação Instituto Brasiliero de Geografie e Estatistica.

——. 2008. *Pesquisa Nacional por Amostragem de Domicílios*. Rio de Janeiro: Fundação Instituto Brasiliero de Geografie e Estatistica.

Guerreiro Ramos, Alberto. 1954. *Cartilha Brasileira do aprendiz de sociólogo*. Rio de Janeiro: Andes.

——. 1995. *Introdução crítica à sociologia Brasileira*. Rio de Janeiro: UFRJ.

Guimarães, A.S.A. 1999. *Racismo e anti-racismo no Brasil*. São Paulo: Editora 34.

——. 2002. *Classes, raças e democracia*. São Paulo: Editora 34.

——. 2004. *Preconceito e discriminação*. 2nd ed. São Paulo: Editora 34.

——. 2005. "Racial Democracy." In *Imagining Brazil (Global Encounters)*, ed. Jessé Souza and Valter Sinder, 119–140. Lanham, Md.: Lexington Books.

Harris, Marvin. 1956. *Town and Country in Brazil*. New York: Columbia University Press.

Harris, Marvin, and Conrad Kotak. 1963. "The Structural Significance of Brazilian Categories." *Sociologia* 35 (3): 203–208.

Harris, Marvin, Josildeth Gomes Consorte, Joseph Lang, and Bryan Byrne. 1993. "Who Are the Whites? Imposed Census Categories and the Racial Demography of Brazil." *Social Forces* 72 (2): 451–462.

Hasenbalg, Carlos. 1979. *Discriminação e desigualdades raciais no Brasil*. Rio de Janeiro: Graal.

Hasenbalg, C., and N. V. Silva. 1988. *Estrutura social, mobilidade e raça*. Rio de Janeiro: Vértice/ IUPERJ.

——. 1992. *Relações raciais no Brasil contemporâneo*. Rio de Janeiro: Rio Fundo.

Hasenbalg, C., N. V. Silva, and M. Lima. 1999. *Cor e Estratificação Social*. Rio de Janeiro: Contracapa Livraria.

Ianni, Octávio. 1962. *As metamorfoses do escravo: Apogeu e crise da escravatura no Brasil Meridional*. São Paulo: Difusão Européia do Livro.

——. 1972. *Raças e classes sociais no Brasil*. Rio de Janeiro: Civilização Brasileira.

——. 1978. *Escravidão e racismo*. São Paulo: Hucitec.

Maggie, Yvonne. 1996. "Aqueles a quem foi negada a cor do dia: as catogorias de cor e raça na cultura brasileira." In *Raça, Ciência e Sociedade*, ed. Marcos C. Maio and Ricardo V. Santos, 225–234. Rio de Janeiro: Fiocruz/Centro Cultural Banco do Brasil.

Munanga, Kabengele. 1986. *Negritude. Usos e Sentidos*. São Paulo: Ática.

——. 1999. *Rediscutindo a mestiçagem no Brasil. Identidade nacional versus identidade negra*. Petrópolis: Vozes.

Nascimento, Elisa L. 2003. *O sortilégio da cor*. São Paulo: Summus.

Nogueira, Oracy. (1955) 1998. *Preconceito de marca: As relações raciais em Itapetininga*. São Paulo: Edusp.

Paixão, Marcelo. 2006. *Manifesto anti-racista: Idéias em prol de uma utopia chamada Brasil*. Rio de Janeiro: DP&A.

Pierson, Donald. 1942. *Negroes in Brazil: A Study of Race Contact in Bahia*. Chicago: University of Chicago Press.

Prado, Caio, Jr. 1937. *A formação do Brasil contemporâneo: Colônia*. São Paulo: Brasiliense.

Queiroz, D. et al. 2000. *Educação, racismo e anti-racismo*. Salvador: Novos Toques.

Reis, João. 2003. *Rebelião escrava no Brasil*. São Paulo: Cia. Das Letras.

Schwarcz, L.K.M. 1993. *O espetáculo das raças: Cientistas, instituições e questões raciais no Brasil (1870–1930)*. São Paulo: Companhia das Letras.

———. 2003. *Neither Black, nor White: Culture, Race and National Identity in Brazil*. Working Papers, Oxford.

Silva, A. C. da. 1995. *A discriminação do negro no livro didático*. Salvador: EDUFBA/CEAO.

Silva, P. C. da. 1997. *Negros à luz dos fornos: Representações do trabalho e da cor entre metalúrgicos baianos*. Salvador: Dynamis.

Silvério, Valter Roberto, ed. 2003. *Educação e ações afirmativas: Entre a injustiça simbólica e a injustiça econômica*. Brasilia: INEP/MEC.

———. 2006. *Trabalhando a diferença na educação infantil*. São Paulo: Moderna.

Skidmore, Thomas E. 1974. *Black into White: Race and Nationality in Brazilian Thought*. New York: Oxford University Press.

Souza, Jessé, ed. 2006. *A invisibilidade da desigualdade brasileira*. Belo Horizonte: UFMG.

Telles, Edward. 2003. *Racismo à brasileira*. Rio de Janeiro: Relume-Dumará.

Vianna, José de Oliveira. (1932) 1959. *Raça e assimilação*. Rio de Janeiro: J. Olympio.

Wagley, Charles. 1968. "The Concept of Social Race in the Americas." In Wagley, *The Latin American Tradition*. New York: Columbia University Press.

15

Black—but Not Haitian

Color, Class, and Ethnicity in the Dominican Republic

ERNESTO SAGÁS

Injustice anywhere is a threat to justice everywhere.

Martin Luther King Jr., "Letter from a Birmingham Jail," April 16, 1963

On the surface, the Dominican Republic seems like a racial democracy. It is one of the most racially mixed countries in the world. An estimated three-fourths of the population is classified as mulatto (the offspring of whites and blacks), and the color of black and white minorities is more a matter of convenience for classification purposes than a reflection of their racial "purity."[1] Blacks and mulattos have made it to positions of power, particularly in politics and the military, and the current president, Leonel Fernández (a light-skinned mulatto), is the latest in a long list of nonwhites who have reached the presidency. Historically, slavery declined precipitously after the end of the sixteenth century's plantation boom, and its final abolition in 1844 affected a proportionally small number of blacks. As such, there is no divisive legacy of exploitation or historical resentment between blacks and whites over the issue of slavery. Dominican culture is strongly influenced by African legacies, and Dominicans do not shy away from extolling the syncretic nature of their food, music, and speech patterns. Afro-Dominicans are quite visible in most spheres of society, and Afro-Dominican baseball players (some of them descendants of English-speaking black immigrants from the British Lesser Antilles) are a source of national pride for their exploits in the U.S. major leagues.

Alas, there is trouble in paradise. Class and color cleavages tend to run deep in Dominican society: white and light-skinned elites occupy the upper echelons of the socioeconomic pyramid, while dark-skinned Dominicans are still at the bottom. A light skin tone literally opens many doors in the Dominican Republic, as evidenced by recent (albeit isolated) cases of racial discrimination in some Dominican discotheques. European beauty standards are still prevalent: from bank tellers to TV personalities, Afro-Dominicans are conspicuously absent from the public eye.[2] Literature and "high culture" are still the realms of light-skinned Dominicans, as are many of the well-paying professions and the entrepreneurial sector. But where racial inequality truly rears its ugly head is in the treatment of the Dominican Republic's largest ethnic minority: Haitians. *El problema haitiano* (the Haitian problem), as many Dominicans writers describe it, is a vexing issue for a nation that otherwise prides itself on its racial harmony. Haitians and their offspring—mostly poor, black, and "foreign"—are routinely subjected to racial and ethnic discrimination, and their human rights have historically been ignored and blatantly violated. Being a Haitian in the Dominican Republic means being a foreign pariah, easily identified by your foreign-sounding name, by your accent, and, more often than not, by your black skin.

This chapter examines the current status of blacks in the Dominican Republic, including not only Afro-Dominicans but also Haitian immigrants and their offspring (who technically, by virtue of being born in the Dominican Republic, are Afro-Dominicans too). I argue that in spite of the major strides Dominicans have made toward a more egalitarian, racially inclusive society, major problems persist. In general, the socioeconomic gap between whites and blacks still gives light-skinned Dominicans a privileged place in society when it comes to opportunities, recognition, and even the application of the rule of law. More specifically, the mistreatment of Haitians and the persistent denial of their rights (thus turning them into a veritable underclass in Dominican society) remains a serious problem for the country.

Two Nations, One Small Island

The Caribbean island of Hispaniola is a geopolitical oddity. Not only are there very few islands in the world that are divided by political boundaries (other examples include St. Martin and Cyprus), but in this particular case the small island of Hispaniola has long been divided into two independent states (dating back to 1844) with widely different backgrounds. While the island was conquered and colonized by the Spanish in the late fifteenth century (who briefly tried their hand at gold mining and sugar production), by the late sixteenth century it had been bypassed for other more profitable mainland territories, leaving behind a languishing colony of Spanish officials, poor whites, mixed-race mestizos and mulattos and a large number of blacks, mostly slaves remaining from the sugar industry's boom and subsequent bust. The French Crown, eager to expand its colonial possessions in the New World, soon gained a foothold in western Hispaniola, and by the seventeenth century the French colony of

Saint-Domingue was fully established. The contrast between French Saint-Domingue and Spanish Santo Domingo could not have been starker: while Saint-Domingue thrived as a plantation colony in which the French grew and exported sugar, coffee, and other tropical crops, Santo Domingo remained a backwater of the Spanish empire and its inhabitants eked out a living by raising cattle and trading with (or selling contraband to) the French. Different economic activities also led to widely different social formations in the two colonies. French Saint-Domingue developed into the typical plantation society where a minority of white plantation owners and poor whites lived off the toil of the large slave population. Sandwiched in between were the mulattos (*affranchis*), often wealthy slave owners themselves, but always a notch below whites because of their skin color. Strict social divisions were the norm, and a draconian Code Noir (Black Code) ruthlessly enforced them. Spanish Santo Domingo, on the other hand, endured centuries of poverty and neglect, leading to widespread racial mixing among most social sectors, much to the dismay of the Spanish authorities.[3]

The Age of Revolutions upset the colonial social order. In 1804, after years of slave revolts, civil war, and an anti-colonial struggle all wrapped into one, Haiti became an independent nation. A black majority made up of former slaves now shared power with a mulatto elite in a country almost devoid of whites, to the horror of European colonial powers. Santo Domingo was also dragged into conflict. After interventions and occupations by French, Spanish, and Haitian armies, in 1844 the former Spanish colonial subjects declared independence (from Haiti) and created a sovereign state called the Dominican Republic. The two new nations were as different as the two old colonies had been: on the one hand, Haiti, which was Creole and French-speaking, mostly black, and impoverished by revolution and the collapse of the plantation economy, had a military leadership bent on preventing an European takeover (to the point of paranoia) and was seen as a pariah by "civilized" nations. On the other hand, the Dominican Republic, which was Spanish-speaking, mostly mulatto, and impoverished by war and colonial neglect, had a leadership bent on protecting its independence from Haiti and was coveted by European powers. These conflicting foreign policy goals led to intense suspicion and animosity between Haiti and the Dominican Republic at least until the last decades of the nineteenth century—a fact not helped by the former's repeated attempts to reconquer the latter and the latter's repeated attempts to seek a foreign protector from the former.

By the early twentieth century, Haiti and the Dominican Republic, although they shared the small island of Hispaniola, continued to develop into very different societies. Haiti was a nation of black peasants with a mulatto elite, both of whom depended on coffee as the major export crop. Class and color were closely intertwined: most blacks were poor peasants who grew coffee as a cash crop, while the mulatto elites were large landowners, coffee middlemen and exporters, or French-speaking urban bureaucrats. Still, in a nation proud of its antislavery struggle and black identity, some social mobility was possible, and by the mid-twentieth century a large black middle class had developed and had started challenging the economic dominance of the mulatto elite—often marrying into it (Nicholls 1996). The Dominican Republic, on the other hand, had developed an incipient sugar industry in the nineteenth century, and by the mid-twentieth century it was in full bloom. In an ironic twist, Haiti, once the hemisphere's wealthiest colony, had become one of its most impoverished nations, while the Dominican Republic, once a backwater of the Spanish empire, now thrived as a sugar exporter. To add insult to injury, Haitians, who decades ago had brought down the plantation system in Saint-Domingue, now flocked east to perform backbreaking work as field hands in the Dominican Republic's sugar plantations.

A third element forcefully came into play in the development of these two countries in the early twentieth century: the United States. Already a diplomatic and economic player since the late nineteenth century, the United States became the region's military superpower after the 1898 Cuban-Spanish-American War and its takeover of Cuba and Puerto Rico. Soon thereafter, the United States started building the Panama Canal and protecting it through the establishment of military bases throughout the region (Guantanamo Bay, the Canal Zone, etc.) and military interventions in Mexico, Central America, and the Caribbean. Besides brief skirmishes and saber-rattling, the U.S. Marines occupied Haiti and the Dominican Republic for longer periods (1915–1934 and 1916–1924, respectively). The U.S. military interventions upset these countries' social orders and strengthened groups that identified themselves with the foreign occupiers. New local elites thus made it to power thanks to the occupiers, who in turn made sure that their interests were well protected. The U.S. military occupations also brought in foreign notions of white racial superiority. Jim Crow laws were alive and well in the United States, and even light-skinned elites in Haiti and the Dominican Republic felt the sting of racial prejudice at the hands of U.S. Marines (Calder 1984; Schmidt 1995). In addition, the U.S. forces implemented segregationist practices and policies, such as favoring light-skinned individuals over blacks, and even revived the old *corvée* law in Haiti, which allowed the U.S. Marines to use Haitian peasants as forced laborers to build roads.

U.S. dollars followed the military's guns, and U.S. economic investments grew in Hispaniola. Particularly in the Dominican Republic, most sugar plantations were owned by U.S. companies, and soon a familiar socioracial pattern developed in which (white) U.S. companies owned the plantations, (mostly mulatto) Dominican overseers and semi-skilled workers ran them, and (black) Haitian field hands performed the backbreaking labor of cutting cane (Hernández 1976). Soon Haitians and Dominicans were (re)defining their socioracial identities, not only vis-à-vis each other, but also in reference to "the Americans."[4] However, neither Haitians nor Dominicans were totally innocent bystanders. While some members of the native elites refused to cooperate with the U.S. military authorities, others caved in and benefited from their new partnerships. Furthermore, the U.S. Marines did not "invent" racial and class prejudices in Hispaniola; they were both well established in the island, particularly among its elites. The U.S. occupation forces just added a new layer of complexity and virulence to it. For example, mulatto elites in Haiti thought of black peasants as uneducated, superstitious oafs, and upper-class blacks and mulattos eventually went into the profitable business of providing cheap labor for sugar plantations in the Dominican Republic.[5]

Dominican elites did not do any better. Like their counterparts throughout Latin America, they were obsessed with Social Darwinism and concerned about racially mixed, uneducated lower classes. Late nineteenth-century and early twentieth-century Dominican literature pins the blame for the country's chronic political instability and economic "backwardness" on the malnutrition, indolence, superstitions, penchant for gambling and drinking of the lower classes, and, not the least, on the non-European ancestry of that group (López [1896] 1955). To make matters worse, Dominican elites felt trapped on a small island they had to share with a non-Hispanic, culturally alien black neighbor. Haiti's geographical proximity and the fact that many lower-class Dominicans were not that different in skin tone from Haitians were constant sources of apprehension.

Dominican elites responded by concocting a new national identity, not only vis-à-vis Spain but particularly in opposition to Haiti.[6] As was the case in other Latin American nations, Dominican elites looked back to the original inhabitants of the land in order to stake a claim of nativity. Unfortunately for them, the native Taíno Indians had been wiped out and absorbed by the Spanish conquerors centuries earlier. In spite of the time gap and the historical stretch, Dominican elites began "imagining"[7] the nation's citizens as *indios*, the racially mixed descendants of valiant Taínos and dashing Spaniards—thus helping to explain the obvious lack of whites. This new identity reinforced—and was in turn reinforced by—the lower classes' predilection for imagining themselves as such. Little mention, if any, was made of African slaves and blacks.[8] Dominican identity formation (as defined by the nation's elites) became a convoluted process that got even more complicated when the country went under U.S. military occupation in 1916, and by the mid-twentieth century, at the height of the Rafael Trujillo dictatorship, blackness as a cultural element was virtually eradicated from Dominican society. General Trujillo and his ideologues embarked on a nation-building process that included a major "whitening" component: not only did his ideologues promote the Dominican *indio* identity and suppress all perceived black cultural elements (which now became associated with Haiti) but government policies also actively promoted white immigration.[9] In short, Haitians were the only blacks in Hispaniola; Dominicans were anything but (Sagás 2000). The zenith of anti-Haitian thought was reached shortly after the 1937 massacre, when thousands of Haitian immigrants (and dark-skinned Dominicans who looked "suspicious" to the authorities) were murdered under orders from Trujillo, who was bent on "whitening" the Dominican population. El Corte ("The Cut")—as it is popularly known—was carried out by the Dominican military and civilian accomplices using machetes and clubs so as to not show the hand of the government (few civilians owned guns at the time). It is estimated that between several hundred to as many as 35,000 (although 10,000–12,000 is the most accurate number) Haitian men, women, and children were murdered in what became the bloodiest incident between the two nations since the nineteenth-century Haitian-Dominican wars (Vega 1988, 385–387). Trujillo, however, was careful not to murder Haitians living on U.S.-owned sugar plantations and limited most of the massacre to the border region and towns in the interior. The massacre was followed by a state-led anti-Haitian campaign that featured some of the regime's brightest ideologues, such as Joaquín Balaguer and Manuel Arturo Peña Batlle. These ideologues framed the massacre as a regrettable but perhaps unavoidable incident as Dominicans tried to defend their right to exist as a sociocultural entity apart from Haiti. In the end, the Dominican government ended up paying a small compensation to the survivors of the massacre—without ever acknowledging guilt. The 1937 massacre has since remained a bone of contention between Haitian and Dominican political ideologues.

The thirty-one years of the Trujillo dictatorship (1930–1961) still weigh heavily on Dominican society. Trujillo's ideologues, including Joaquín Balaguer, continued to influence Dominican society for decades after the collapse of the regime.[10] Entire generations of teachers were educated under Trujillo or Balaguer and continued to reproduce distorted versions of Dominican history, in spite of the efforts of new generations of Dominicans who sought to revisit their history and identity formation process.[11] Though anti-Haitian bias (and by extension, anti-black prejudice) is not as prevalent today as it was during the heyday of the Trujillo era, it still runs deep in Dominican society.

As seen from this historical overview, Dominican identity formation is a complex, multilayered process that to this day is burdened by the heavy legacies of nineteenth-century elite formulations and Trujillo's (and Balaguer's) grandiose nation-building agendas. A strong anti-Haitian component is an inherent part of contemporary Dominican identity, and it seeps into and influences Dominican perceptions of its black/African heritage.

Black—but Not Haitian

In most societies, poor immigrant laborers live precarious lives. Not only do they perform the toughest jobs in the host society and are usually discriminated against but the demand for their labor tends to be cyclical and ebbs and flows with the vagaries of the local economy. The Dominican Republic is no exception: it craves Haitian labor (which has become indispensable in some economic sectors such as agriculture and construction), yet it looks down on the dirt-poor Haitian laborers and quickly pins the blame on them when the economy goes sour. And as if class prejudices were not enough, poor Haitian immigrants carry the additional burden of being black, poorly educated (often illiterate), and usually not fluent in Spanish.[12] All these factors combine to make the Dominican Republic's largest ethnic minority its most stigmatized.

No one knows for sure how many Haitians (and their descendants) currently reside in the Dominican Republic. Alarmist newspapers and right-wing groups speak of a "flood" of Haitians into Dominican territory and usually tout figures that range from half a million to a million Haitians to make their case. According to the 2002 census, the population of the Dominican Republic was slightly over 8.5 million inhabitants (ONE 2002).[13] If these wildly ranging estimates are to be believed, then close to one in eight inhabitants is a Haitian citizen. In reality, there is no way to know. The 2002 census counted 61,863 Haitians—that is, 0.72 percent of the population and much lower than the estimates quoted above. However, the same census listed 551,508 persons of "undeclared" origin—that is, individuals who did not answer the census question about origin or individuals the census takers could not contact.[14] Are they the "half million Haitians" that the Dominican press often quotes? Or is this number just a reflection of methodological shortcomings? (It is simply impossible to contact every individual at home over the course of just a few days.) The answer is complex. Anecdotal evidence and studies clearly show that there are over 61,863 Haitians in the Dominican Republic and that this figure is a significant undercount. But half a million Haitians also seems like an overblown figure and probably includes thousands of individuals that the census takers were not able to reach and therefore could not answer questions. A better estimate is provided by the Catholic Institute for International Relations (CIIR), a nongovernmental organization that works with Haitian laborers in the Dominican Republic. According to CIIR estimates, there are about 380,000 Haitians in the Dominican Republic (Wooding and Moseley-Williams 2004). This estimate takes into account the growth in Haitian migration to the Dominican Republic as well as the effect of periodic massive repatriations. Based on this estimate, Haitians make up less than 5 percent of the Dominican population.

The number of Haitian-Dominicans, the offspring of Haitian immigrants, is even harder to quantify. First of all, who is a Haitian-Dominican? How many generations does it take them to become full-fledged "Dominicans"? And what about those who have one Dominican parent? Are they more "Dominican" and less "Haitian"? Again, the 2002 Dominican census is of no help, as it lists hundreds of thousands of respondents' parents as being of "undeclared origin." From a legal standpoint, the *jus soli* provisions of the Dominican Constitution extended Dominican citizenship to all children born on Dominican soil—that is, until the recent landmark decision of the Dominican Supreme Court of Justice that stripped Haitian-ancestry children of Dominican citizenship by right of birth.[15] As in the case of their immigrant parents (or ancestors), one thing remains constant: whether in theory or in practice, most Haitian immigrants and their descendants in the Dominican Republic are on shaky legal ground and can expect little if any protection from the authorities.

Haitians in the Dominican Republic are employed in the lowest-paid sectors of the Dominican economy, such as agriculture, construction, and the informal economy (Martínez 1995). These are economic sectors that lower-class Dominicans abandoned long ago (e.g., cutting cane in sugar plantations) or more recently (e.g., coffee harvesting or construction work), for better jobs in urban areas (such as factory work in the free trade zones) or overseas.[16] Moreover, Dominican employers in these sectors actively recruit Haitian workers since they will work for lower wages and because if they prove to be troublesome, they can always be reported to the authorities, who will round them up and deport them. Thus, Haitian immigrant laborers are caught between a rock and hard place; resented by lower-class Dominicans who accuse them of "stealing" their jobs and in fear of employers who could turn them over to the authorities on a whim. Additionally, the employment of Haitian immigrant laborers in certain sectors of the Dominican economy has created a "pull" effect that attracts more Haitians into that sector and has led to the ethnicization of entire sectors of the Dominican economy, making them less attractive to Dominican workers, who stereotype the Haitians employed in them. While there is a decades-old connection between Haitian immigrant laborers and the Dominican sugar industry, nowadays entire sectors of the economy (such as construction and agriculture) are spurned by Dominican workers as being *trabajos de haitianos* (i.e., jobs only a Haitian would take). This ethnic division of labor stigmatizes and isolates Haitians into "labor ghettoes" where they are subject to economic exploitation. There is ample evidence to show that Haitians are paid less than Dominicans (for the same jobs), routinely denied labor benefits, cheated in economic trans-actions (since many of them are illiterate and not fluent in Spanish), harassed by the authorities who demand bribes, physically abused and sexually harassed, and, ultimately, deported once they have outlived their usefulness.[17] Generally, when Haitian immigrant laborers seek redress from these abuses, they are ig-nored by the Dominican authorities, and, in the worst of cases, they are arrested and deported for daring to complain. Most Haitian immigrant laborers have learned to simply keep quiet and remain as inconspicuous as possible.

The situation of Haitian-Dominicans is even more worrisome, as most of them technically are (or were) Dominican citizens. Yet their rights are routinely ignored. The poorer, darker, and more "Haitian-looking" a Haitian-Dominican is, the harder it will be for her/him to get her/his rights recognized by Do-minican society. There are documented cases of Haitian-Dominican children whose parents have been unable to get them birth certificates, as the authorities claim that they are Haitians by blood and should be legally registered in Haiti. Their case was taken to the Inter-American Court of Human Rights, where the court ruled in their favor—only to have the ruling ignored and criticized by the Dominican authorities (Inter-American Court of Human Rights 2006). The cost and bureaucratic procedures involved in getting a birth certificate and a Dominican ID card are also major obstacles for a poor immigrant population when it comes to legalizing their children's status. As a result, hundreds of Hai-tian-Dominican children live in a legal limbo because they lack documents, and they are often deported with their parents in periodic repatriation campaigns carried out by the Dominican authorities. Others, in spite of having Dominican birth certificates and ID cards, have been rounded up and deported to Haiti—a country many of them do not even know—with the commonly used admoni-tion: "Your documents may be Dominican, but you are not." The recent decision by the Dominican Supreme Court of Justice (and now clearly restated in the 2010 Constitution) that strips the children of "those in transit" of Dominican citizenship does not bode well for the future of Haitian-Dominicans, as it makes even those who have lived in the Dominican Republic since birth (and often for decades) potential targets for deportation.[18]

What are the factors behind the mistreatment and discrimination of Hai-tians (and their descendants) in the Dominican Republic? The first factor is race. Haitian immigrants are mostly black; most Dominicans do not see them-selves as such. Dominican ID cards identify the country's citizens using a pano-ply of racial euphemisms that go to great lengths to avoid using the racially charged term *negro* (black). Dominicans of all shades are described in ID cards using shades of *indio* (light, dark) or similar terms (e.g., *moreno*), while reserving *negro* mostly for Haitians. Obviously, many Dominicans are as black as most

Haitian immigrants, so why avoid using the term *negro?* The answer again lies in the complex process of Dominican identity formation (in which African origins were officially downplayed) and on the relative "usefulness" of color as an identifier. If Dominicans are *indios* and Haitians are blacks, then most blacks in the Dominican Republic ought to be Haitian, or so the reasoning goes. Thus Haitians, the "other" in Dominican society, the useful scapegoat during hard times, can be easily spotted by their color. But then what about black Dominicans? Afro-Dominicans typically go to great lengths to make others aware of their Dominican nationality so they will not be confused with Haitians. I have personally witnessed Afro-Dominicans deny vehemently that they are black while remarking: "Only Haitians are black." Not surprisingly, some of the most discriminatory attitudes toward Haitians are to be found among lower-class Afro-Dominicans, as they are the ones most likely to be confused with Haitians (and suffer the consequences of misidentification). Afro-Dominicans (not of Haitian ancestry) have even been deported to Haiti by overzealous government officials who thought that they were Haitians who were fluent in Spanish and were trying to "pass" as Dominicans. A well-known anecdote from the Haitian-Dominican wars of independence sums up the plight of Afro-Dominicans: before battle, Dominican officers admonished their troops that "whoever is black better speak clearly" (Balcácer 1977, 26).

The second factor is class. Haitian immigrant laborers are poor and come from the poorest country in the Western Hemisphere. Though the Dominican Republic is no paradise for them, emigration is more often than not the lesser of two evils when it comes to making hard economic choices, and it is usually undertaken as a temporary or seasonal strategy until a short-term economic goal is met or things improve back home (Martínez 1995). Being poor makes it even harder for Haitian immigrants to navigate class-conscious Dominican society. As mentioned before, while many doors open to wealthy, elite Haitians, poor Haitians are often seen as less than human. Illiterate, resourceless, and powerless, poor Haitian immigrants are easy targets of class-based discrimination. While an aristocracy has never existed in the Dominican Republic, there is certainly an entrenched upper class in the country—a veritable oligarchy.[19] These are well-known families who are often easy to identify by their surnames. Dominicans are very aware of their station in the class pyramid, and conversations between strangers usually involve delicate "maneuvering" until both parties can ascertain with whom they are *really* talking. Haitian immigrant laborers, poor and connectionless as they are, do not stand a chance in this system. Moreover, regardless of how poor a Dominican is, s/he can always feel a notch above a Haitian immigrant. Thus, it is not surprising that it is precisely the poorest of Dominicans that tend to discriminate against Haitians the most. They are too close for comfort (in terms of class and color), to use the popular expression. In practice, poor Dominicans often treat Haitians the same way they are treated themselves by upper-class Dominicans: with disdain and thinly veiled contempt. I have seen poor Dominicans make Haitians stand in line outside of the back entrance of their wooden shacks while their equally poor Dominican "equals" walk in through the front door without as much as wiping their shoes. In Dominican society, the oppressed can also become the oppressors.

Some Dominican writers (notably Joaquín Balaguer) have argued that there is no racial prejudice in the Dominican Republic, just class prejudice. Thus, they argue, Haitian immigrants are discriminated against not because they are black but because they are poor (Balaguer 1947). Unfortunately, this view is as simplistic as saying that Haitian immigrants are discriminated against *just* because they are black. In Latin America, race and class go hand in hand, and the Dominican Republic is no exception. Since colonial times, race has determined class, and even nowadays, race tends to be a good predictor of one's class. So being poor and black—as most Haitian immigrants are—is a double whammy that puts many Dominicans at the bottom of the hierarchy to begin with. For Haitians, it is even worse, as they are foreigners, too.

The third factor is ethnicity. Haitians come from a foreign country; they are less-than-desired aliens in a society that does not look on them kindly. And for Dominicans, Haiti is no ordinary country. Haiti repeatedly invaded the Dominican Republic in the early nineteenth century, Dominicans obtained their independence from Haiti after twenty-two years of annexation, and then Dominicans fought Haitians in a series of bloody conflicts as Haitian leaders tried to recover their erstwhile "province." While other neighboring countries have fought even more bitter and protracted wars (e.g., France and Germany), entire generations of Dominican writers have made sure that Dominicans learned their own particular version of history and that they do not forgive or forget the Haitian people. On top of that (these writers argue), Haitians, the old nemesis of Dominicans, now come as poor, desperate immigrants willing to work for hunger wages. Some Dominican writers and political leaders go as far as suggesting that Haitian migration is part of a Machiavellian plan conceived to recover the eastern part of the island for Haiti, a silent invasion of destitute migrants who eventually will bring about a major demographic shift in the Dominican Republic. This *reconquista* (reconquest) strategy, they argue, is supported by the Haitian government and treasonous Dominicans who greedily benefit from cheap Haitian labor without realizing the potential consequences of their misguided actions (Núñez 1990; Pérez 1990).

A fourth factor is gender, which I did not originally include among the three factors that "separate" Haitians from Dominicans because gender cannot be used to distinguish Haitians from Dominicans. But there is certainly a gendering of Haitian migrants in the Dominican Republic that reinforces stereotypes about their perceived moral attributes and character. For example, Haitian men are perceived as untrustworthy, sneaky, sexually rapacious, disease-ridden, and prone to violence, while Haitian women are objectified as sexually promiscuous, prolific, unfaithful, unclean, and as practitioners of witchcraft. Moreover, unlike Dominican women, who are oftentimes visualized as gentle and docile (and even as somewhat "innocent"), Haitian women are seen as assertive, aggressive "pros" who are in the Dominican Republic with the sole purpose of making money (Gregory 2007, 185). Haitian women are commonly accused of coming to the Dominican Republic to work as prostitutes or to send their children out into the streets to beg, in total disregard for their health and safety. While some Haitian women do engage in prostitution and Haitian children can be seen begging in the streets of major cities in the Dominican Republic, the situation is blown out of proportion in order to make the case that Haitians are inferior. I have heard discussions of rape cases involving Haitian immigrant women in which people would comment: "It's no big deal. They're used to that." To make matters worse, the high rates of individuals infected with the HIV/AIDS virus in Haiti further reinforce the stereotype that Haitians (and particularly Haitian women) are dirty, promiscuous, and disease-ridden and lack moral standards. To illustrate this stereotype, a Dominican woman who marries a Haitian man is commonly seen as lowering her standards and fouling herself by sleeping with a Haitian (unless she happens to marry a wealthy, upper-class Haitian, of course). These views reinforce stereotypes about the supremacy of Dominican women over Haitians as wives and mothers and serve as additional reasons to "justify" mistreating and violating the human rights of the latter. Gender thus becomes another tool in the hands of the majority to discriminate against the country's largest minority.

All these factors converge in *antihaitianismo*, a decades-old dominant ideology that portrays Haiti and Haitians as racially, ethnically, and culturally inferior to Dominicans and thus seeks to justify the exploitation of the former by the latter. *Antihaitianismo* ideology originated deep in the Dominican Republic's past. It began with Spanish notions of racial superiority and justifications for enslaving Africans, was further reinforced by the traumatic separation of Santo Domingo from Haiti, and then was reshaped by late nineteenth-century and early twentieth-century Dominican writers who sought to (re)create Dominican identity by reaching back to the country's Amerindian past. But it was during the Trujillo dictatorship that *antihaitianismo* reached its zenith, becoming a state-sponsored ideology that was imposed on generations of Dominicans through Trujillo's vigorous nation-building agenda (Sagás 2000). Trujillo's death and the collapse of his dictatorship did not mean the end of *antihaitian-ismo*. It continued through other means. Balaguer and many other Trujillistas remained in positions of power, and for the next four decades they continued their work—this time as "democratic" leaders. For over seventy years, *antihaitianismo* was the norm, and few individuals or groups deviated from it. Not surprisingly, nowadays most Dominicans still subscribe to erroneous historical notions about Haitian-Dominican relations and express opinions that are consistent with *antihaitianismo* ideology (Equipo ONE-RESPE 1995).

Afro-Dominicans?

The term "Afro-Dominican" is rarely—if ever—used by most Dominicans, and the same goes for *negro*, which is usually reserved for Haitians and is often used as a derogatory term. Most black Dominicans use the more socially acceptable terms *indio oscuro* or *moreno*. Does this mean that Dominicans are somewhat "confused" or are in denial about their blackness and "pretend" to be something else? Not necessarily (Torres-Saillant 1998). Particularly in the last two or three decades there has been a resurgence among Dominican intellectuals and performers who emphasize the African roots of Dominican culture, and probably every Dominican schoolchild can recite that Dominicans are the product of three groups (or "races"): Taíno Indians, Spaniards, and Africans. Still, racial self-identification in the Dominican Republic is different from that in other nations in the Caribbean and tends to rest more on the nation than on race or ethnicity. In other words, most Dominicans think of themselves as "Dominicans" for national *and* racial purposes. Thus, *indio* has become a new sort of "race" by which Dominicans identify themselves and that describes the veritable racial melting pot that is the Dominican Republic—a place where it is hard to tell one "race" from the other and where almost no one can make a valid claim to belonging to one "race." Just as José Vasconcelos coined his term *raza cósmica* to describe the mestizaje of the Mexican people, Dominicans have come up with their own, very Dominican way of describing themselves and their "race" as *indio*.

The development of the term *indio* thus comes as no surprise in a country bent on achieving racial and national unity in the face of regional cleavages (which were quite significant until the early twentieth century) and real or perceived threats from neighboring Haiti. What is really disturbing about the use of the term *indio* is not its perceived racial "denial" but its political manipulation over the course of several decades to homogenize a people, to stifle dissent when it comes to discussions of race and national identity, to preempt race-based sociopolitical movements, and, in the worst of cases, to use as a "racial" marker to differentiate between Dominicans and unwelcome aliens (i.e., Haitians). Thus, unlike other parts of the hemisphere, there have never been significant black social movements in the Dominican Republic.[20] Blackness is tolerated in the cultural arena, but when it comes to national identity, being Dominican trumps everything.

As in the rest of Latin America, race and class go hand in hand in the Dominican Republic. Though Dominican censuses nowadays do not classify people on the basis of race, even casual observers can easily witness the connection: the Dominican upper classes tend to be white or light-skinned, while the middle and lower classes tend to have a greater proportion of black or dark-skinned Dominicans. So, in general, dark-skinned Dominicans live in the poorest neighborhoods and have lower-paying jobs. Though being black in the Dominican Republic is not a major handicap per se (as it depends on your "looks," i.e., the tone of your skin, hair texture, and facial features), being black and poor (as is often the case), places many Dominicans at a disadvantage. Dominican beauty standards still tend to be Eurocentric, and it is not uncommon for employers to post classified ads asking for "young females of good presence" (i.e., light-skinned and straight/soft haired) for jobs as secretaries, receptionists, and bank tellers. Moreover, many employers still ask job applicants to include a recent picture with their résumés. Though Dominican labor laws ban racial discrimination, these are rarely—if ever—enforced and those who experience discrimination have little recourse in a country where the rule of law is still weak.

It is also rare, though not uncommon, to find overt cases of racial discrimination in a country where there has never been any official segregation or Jim Crow laws. For example, in 2007–2008 some Dominican discos were publicly accused of barring dark-skinned patrons from entering their establishments (a practice that had been sporadically taking place for years at other discos in Santo Domingo and Santiago). In one of these cases, at Tonic disco in Santo Domingo, some African American employees of the U.S. consulate were denied admission. This case sparked a major scandal when the U.S. consulate took action by issuing a communiqué deploring the disco's discriminatory practices and asking its employees to refrain from patronizing that particular establishment ("Embajada de EE.UU."). Similar incidents have also taken place at other discos and bars in Santo Domingo and Santiago. In most of these cases, the owners of the establishments have defended themselves by alleging other reasons for denying admission, such as arguing that the black patrons were not properly dressed. Yet in most of these cases, other lighter-skinned patrons in similar clothes had been allowed to enter the discos. While Dominican public opinion widely condemned these practices and media commentators seemed perplexed by such practices in a country where most people have some black ancestry, the issue never went beyond that. There were no protests or organized boycotts against these establishments.

Though these incidents may appear to be trivial in comparison with ongoing large-scale racial discrimination in other countries in the Americas, we must keep in mind that the Dominican Republic is one of the most racially mixed countries in the world. Moreover, for centuries slavery was a relatively marginal institution in the colony and when it was finally abolished in the early nineteenth century, slaves made up only a small minority of black Dominicans. If there is a country in the Americas where there should be little or no racial discrimination against its black citizens, it should be the Dominican Republic. Neither its historical record nor its racial composition should allow for it, yet it still happens, often in the most subtle of ways.

Finally, one of the most perplexing phenomena for the casual observer—in the face of these egregious violations of human rights—is the dearth of race- or ethnic-based organizations in the Dominican Republic. There are some, most notably the Movement for Dominican Women of Haitian Descent (Movimiento de Mujeres Domínico-Haitianas; MUDHA), but their impact on Dominican public opinion has been marginal at best, and in some cases, it has backfired. For example, in 2005 MUDHA took the cases of two Dominican minors of Haitian ancestry who were being denied birth certificates by the Dominican authorities to the Inter-American Court of Human Rights. In 2007, the Court ruled against the Dominican Republic and ordered its government to issue birth certificates to the minors and pay for their legal costs. Though the legal reasoning of the court was clear, Dominican public opinion mostly rallied against Sonia Pierre, MUDHA's director (Lacey 2007). Pierre, now considered a treacherous foreigner by many Dominicans for taking the case to the Inter-American Court of Human Rights, has received numerous threats and there was even a campaign to have her deported to Haiti under the terms of the 2005 ruling of the Dominican Supreme Court of Justice (Cruz Tejada 2009).

One of the obstacles for these organizations is that their work in defense of human rights for Haitians and Afro-Dominicans is often portrayed by the media and public opinion makers as anti-Dominican and racially divisive. Pierre is often portrayed as a Haitian who is conspiring to "Haitianize" Dominican society by manipulating the law against Dominican national interests. The fact that she was awarded the 2006 Robert F. Kennedy Human Rights Award only served to add more fuel to conspiracy theories about foreign powers trying to unify the two nations of the island of Hispaniola into one. Thus, human rights groups such as MUDHA have to walk a fine line in their struggle. They can be easily accused of defending foreign interests or of espousing divisive ideas and inciting a "race war." These hurdles, together with threats from individuals and fringe groups and a long-standing history of state repression, account for the dearth of race- or ethnicity-based movements in the Dominican Republic. Race

and ethnicity have been seen as "dangerous" developments throughout Dominican history, and the use of them as categories to organize society is actively discouraged. As a result, calls for Afro-Dominican political movements have never
gone beyond the voices of a handful of radical intellectuals.

Conclusion

It is ironic that on the island where African slavery was born in the Americas—
and where it was first abolished centuries ago—individuals of African descent
are, in so many ways, still treated as second-class citizens. Not only are Afro-
Dominicans excluded from full enjoyment of their rights (often in the most
subtle of ways), but Haitians—the country's largest ethnic minority—are sys-
tematically targeted because of their skin color and appearance and are subjected
to widespread and overt discrimination. The irony is further reinforced by the
fact that Hispaniola is also the birthplace of *mestizaje* in the New World and the
Dominican Republic is a mulatto nation; thus, in many cases, it is blacks who
are discriminating against other blacks. For example, the doorman at the disco
that excluded black patrons also happened to be black, and so are many of the
Dominican soldiers who routinely blackmail, beat up, and/or round up Haitian
migrants in order to extort money from them. The underlying explanation for
this irony lies in the unique racial consciousness (or lack thereof) among Dominicans, who emphasize national allegiance over racial identity (as is common
throughout the Hispanic Caribbean). *Indio* identity thus "insulates" Dominicans from race-based identities that are perceived as "divisive" while justifying
discrimination against those who do not fit the national mold (e.g., Haitians).

However, the popularity of Dominican *indio* identity does not, by itself, explain the sorry state of human rights for Haitian migrants and even some Afro-
Dominicans in the Dominican Republic. The Dominican state deserves also
much of the blame. While decades of dictatorship (Trujillo) and semi-author-
itarian regimes (Balaguer) contributed to forming a hostile mentality toward
Haitians and things African, the recent (post-1978) democratic administrations
have done little to reverse the tide of prejudice and discrimination.[21] The liberal
administrations of Antonio Guzmán (1978–1982) and Salvador Jorge Blanco
(1982–1986), for example, continued the widely criticized practice of signing labor agreements with Haitian dictator Jean-Claude Duvalier to import Haitian
laborers. A slightly more moderate ten-year period of Balaguer rule (1986–1996)
restored the status quo regarding the Haitian presence in the Dominican Republic and took it a step further by engaging in massive repatriations and a
smear campaign against black presidential opposition candidate José F. Peña
Gómez.[22] The mud-slinging campaign against Peña Gómez during the 1994
presidential campaign brought out the worst in xenophobia and negrophobia

among Dominican politicians, journalists, and other makers of public opinion.[23] The election of Leonel Fernández in 1996 brought back a repeat of the "dirty campaign" against Peña Gómez (who ran for the presidency one last time) and little if any change in the government's position regarding Haitian migrants.

The last two presidential administrations (Hipólito Mejía, 2000–2004; and Leonel Fernández, 2004–present) have, if anything, made it harder for Haitians to live and work in the Dominican Republic. While apathy typically characterized the position of previous Dominican administrations regarding Haitians (the government often just looked the other way), since 2004 the Dominican state has taken a more proactive position by drafting a new migratory law (Law 285-04) that reinforces the infamous "in transit" legal status of Haitian migrants, regardless of how long they have resided in the Dominican Republic. The law's constitutionality was recently ratified by the Dominican Supreme Court of Justice in its 2005 landmark decision, and it is now endorsed by the new 2010 Constitution. While in the past Haitian migrants felt relative safety in the ambiguity of the Dominican Constitution regarding the right to automatic Dominican citizenship for their children via *jus soli*, that safety net is now gone. Nowadays, Haitian migrants and their children do not have even a shred of legal protection; they can be arrested and deported by the Dominican authorities without legal recourse.

This recent legal decision has emboldened anti-Haitian groups in the Dominican Republic and ratcheted the level of xenophobia against Haitians to new heights. Even worse, the Dominican state has largely ignored foreign criticism regarding the treatment of Haitians and has responded to arguments that the new immigration law violates human rights by resorting to arguments that emphasize the right of sovereign states to control their borders. This tactic, unfortunately, is in large measure modeled after similar ones in the United States and some European nations. In the past, the Dominican state simply ignored foreign criticism without fully realizing how damaging that strategy could be to its international public image. Nowadays, the Dominican state (particularly under the "globalized" administration of Leonel Fernández) is very conscious about its public image and is very keen on controlling its image. For example, while in the past press secretaries were simply mouthpieces for the president, the current Fernández administration has a dedicated, professional team of speech writers, media consultants, spin doctors, and "embedded" journalists who defend the government's position. In the Internet age, where human rights violations can be recorded and shared with millions of viewers online, the Dominican state can no longer afford not to respond. And it responds in the same way it sees other developed nations responding: by invoking sovereignty.

While many Dominicans simply shrug off these human rights violations because, as many of my interviewees in the past have told me, "they're Haitians," the truth of the matter is that the mistreatment of Haitian migrants has potentially negative consequences for all Dominicans. Not only does the negative publicity taint the international image of the country and may even subject it to international condemnation (and possibly sanctions), but it also undermines the quality of democracy in the Dominican Republic. The protection of human rights is a major achievement for generations of Dominicans who fought bravely against decades of cruel dictatorships—often paying the ultimate price. So why deny these universal rights to the Haitian "Other" just because s/he is perceived as "different"? Not only is that a disservice to the cause of Dominican democracy, but the survival of these authoritarian practices imperils hard-fought democratic gains by establishing a dual standard: one for Haitians; and an entirely different one for Dominicans. From there, it is very easy to move into the slippery legal ground of justifying authoritarian excesses just because the abused parties are Haitians.[24] Not until the human rights of all individuals in the Dominican Republic are recognized and respected will Dominicans be able to speak of living in a truly democratic regime.

The position of the Dominican state regarding Haitian migrants also affects Afro-Dominicans, both those who are of Haitian ancestry and those who are not. As mentioned above, Haitian-Dominicans have to face many legal obstacles and unofficial discriminatory practices in their efforts to become full-fledged members of the Dominican nation. In the case of Afro-Dominicans (not of Haitian ancestry), their skin color places them perilously close to the Haitian "Other" and their lives often become a constant process of identity (re)affirmation in the face of social questioning about their nationality. Thus, no black Dominican is exempt from ever being confused with a Haitian and having her/his rights violated. Moreover, the violation of human rights for black Haitians easily translates into the violation of human rights for black Dominicans. As color has become the unofficial marker that determines a person's standing in society, black Dominicans are never entirely safe. For example, black Dominicans in the borderlands are routinely accused by soldiers of being Haitians just so they can extort some money from them. If they refuse to pay, they can be arrested until their identity can be proven (at their own expense).

Finally, a society in which blackness is equated with the foreign "Other" has little space—or sympathy—for sociopolitical expressions of blackness. Although black cultural expressions are now more commonplace in the Dominican Republic than ever before, they are still seen as suspect by many Dominicans who see "Haitian" roots in them rather than African roots, and even African roots are often seen as inferior. In a society where white beauty standards prevail and the United States and European nations are the main role models to emulate, being black puts a person at a disadvantage. Therefore, any form of discrimination against Haitians in particular is a form of discrimination against

Afro-Dominicans in general. While dark-skinned Dominicans can always latch on to their *indio* identity, they cannot change their color of their skin, and that makes them as vulnerable to racial discrimination as any Haitian (even at the hands of other black Dominicans). I have argued elsewhere (Sagás 2000) that *antihaitianismo* is the perfect "divide and conquer" strategy. Not only does it rally Dominicans of all colors together in a common rejection of Haiti and things Haitian, it also keeps Afro-Dominicans from overtly emphasizing their blackness because doing so would place them perilously close to the foreign "Other." Though *antihaitianismo* is ostensibly aimed at a foreign population, it is really an ideology designed for domestic purposes. And it has done its job very well.

Notes

1. These percentages are widely used estimates for two reasons: first, Dominican censuses over the past few decades have not asked respondents for their "race"; and second, in a highly racially mixed society in which there are no discrete color categories it is an exercise in futility to try to determine clear-cut racial lines beyond which, say, one is no longer considered black and "becomes" a mulatto.

2. An exceptional case—that serves to confirm the trend—is TV show host and media entrepreneur Rafael Corporán de los Santos, a black Dominican of humble origins who worked his way to the top.

3. There were so few whites in Santo Domingo that Spanish authorities had to constantly ask for exceptions in the appointment of bureaucrats, leading to the breaking down of social barriers as mulattos and other nonwhites made it to positions of authority. Of course, the appointment of a few nonwhites to political offices did little to mitigate the personal prejudices of the majority of European residents (Sagás and Inoa 2003, 46–47). This decision was recently restated in Article 18 of the 2010 Dominican Constitution, which in addition denies Dominican nationality to those that did not have it before the new Constitution went into effect (República Dominicana 2010). In other words, the thousands of Dominican-born descendants of Haitian migrants that had been unable to get Dominican documents are now being denied that opportunity permanently.

4. A similar phenomenon took place in Cuba, where the locals, having defined themselves vis-à-vis the Spanish in the nineteenth century, (re)defined Cuban nationality vis-à-vis the Americans in the twentieth. See Pérez 2007 for the deepest analysis of the Cuban case.

5. The profitable business of providing Haitian workers for Dominican sugar plantations reached its zenith during the regime of the Duvaliers (the notorious Papa Doc and Baby Doc). They signed agreements with Dominican authorities that not only paid them for each worker they provided but also took money out of the workers' salaries for a savings fund to be held by the Haitian authorities. Of course, not a single worker ever received a cent from this fund or was naive enough to demand it.

6. Technically, the nation known today as the Dominican Republic has achieved independence three times: in 1821 from Spain, but independence was quickly crushed when Haiti annexed the new state; in 1844 from Haiti, after twenty-two years of annexation; and in 1865 from Spain, after Dominican dictator Pedro Santana turned the country over to the Spanish Crown in 1861.

7. I am borrowing the term from Benedict Anderson's classic work on nationalism, *Imagined Communities: Reflections on the Origin and Spread of Nationalism* (1991).

8. Though many of these elements of Dominican identity formation may appear to modern observers as preposterous concoctions (i.e., blacks and dark-skinned mulattos trying to pass as *indios*), they must be seen in their proper historical context. Neighboring Haiti was a pariah nation, and Dominican elites did not want their nation (or themselves) to be linked to it in any way. Slavery was a shameful legacy that most islanders wanted to forget, and whites (Americans and Europeans) ruled the world and imposed their cultural values, norms, and standards of "civilization" on others. When given the choice to claim as ancestors either brave Taínos who rebelled and fought gallantly against the Spanish or Africans who came to the New World in chains and were degraded into something less than human, the choice for most Dominicans was quite clear.

9. One of the most famous immigration schemes was Trujillo's offer to accept thousands of Jewish refugees from Europe. A few hundred arrived, only to realize that they had exchanged one dictatorship for another, and they quickly moved on.

10. Balaguer himself was president of the Dominican Republic on six occasions in the period 1966 to 1996.

11. As in the United States, the 1960s and 1970s were years of cultural upheaval in the Dominican Republic, a period when Dominicans "rediscovered" their blackness and revisionist historians tried to undo the effects of Trujillo's ideological legacy. Still, it was not until the late 1990s (after Balaguer was no longer president) that Dominican history textbooks were finally replaced with new texts that portray a more accurate and objective interpretation of Haitian-Dominican relations.

12. I deliberately emphasize the use of the word "poor" to describe immigrant Haitian laborers, as wealthy Haitians are seen in a different light by most Dominicans. Many upper- and middle-class Haitians study in Dominican universities, vacation in Dominican resorts, and maintain an active business presence in the Dominican Republic, constantly rubbing elbows with Dominican economic, political, and diplomatic elites. As many of my Dominican interviewees have told me: "Well, sir, those [the Haitian elites] are *other* types of Haitians." This quote and others used in this chapter are from fieldwork that I carried out in the Dominican Republic in the late 1980s and throughout the 1990s. These interviews provided some of the material for my doctoral dissertation and for *Race and Politics in the Dominican Republic* (Sagás 2000).

13. The 2002 Dominican census has been widely criticized for its inaccuracies. Critics point to the lack of planning, training, and funding that characterized the whole process and to the last-minute decision of the Hipólito Mejía administration to carry out the long-overdue census in spite of the fact that the country was undergoing a major economic crisis.

14. In the Dominican Republic, thousands of census takers are sent throughout the country to interview people in their homes. The whole process takes only a few days, and usually respondents are not allowed to fill out the forms themselves.

15. While Dominican laws are not applied retroactively, the ruling of the Dominican Supreme Court of Justice is only an interpretation or clarification of an article of the Dominican Constitution that has been in place for decades. Thus, in theory, Haitian-Dominicans who were born in the Dominican Republic several decades ago could be stripped of their Dominican citizenship and rendered "stateless."

16. Ironically, Dominican migrants do many of these same jobs overseas—albeit for comparatively better wages—in places such as Puerto Rico, the United States, Canada, and Europe.

17. See dozens of documented cases of mistreatment of Haitian immigrants in the Dominican Republic at Amnesty International's website, http://www.amnesty.org/en/region/dominican-republic.

18. To make matters worse, the overwhelming majority of Haitian deportees never get to see

an immigration court. They are simply rounded up (often by the Dominican military), put in trucks, and taken to the border. Deportees rarely get the chance to collect their belongings and are often shaken down by the same authorities that deport them. Once they are across the border, they receive no help from the Haitian government. For those who know no nation but the Dominican Republic, it is a traumatic experience; and once they are in Haiti, it becomes quite an ordeal for them to cross the border back "home."

19. Mass migration, modernization, and globalization have undermined the traditional class structure of Dominican society. With the decline of agriculture as the main economic activity, the old land-based oligarchy has seen its power and influence wane somewhat. Many lower- and middle-class Dominicans have also "made it" in the United States and return to the Dominican Republic flush with cash to spend—notably the Major League Baseball players. These recent trends have led to friction between "old money" and "new money," particularly as those with "new money" seek entry into the country clubs of the elite and are blackballed.

20. The Dominican Republic does not stand alone in this respect. Black sociopolitical movements were harshly crushed in early-twentieth-century Cuba in the name of unity and *cubanidad* (Cubanness) (Helg 1995), while in Puerto Rico race is not seen as a significant issue and is ignored in the official discourse (Zenón Cruz 1975).

21. Revolutionary Cuba serves as an interesting contrast. While racial attitudes in pre-revolutionary Cuba were not that different from those in the Dominican Republic at the time, the revolutionary government made a concerted effort in the 1960s to stamp out all forms of racial discrimination (Fuente 2001). While the campaign's success may be overstated, the effort was certainly laudable and unparalleled in the Hispanic Caribbean.

22. In 1991, the Balaguer administration carried out widespread repatriations of Haitians that were politically motivated. Just weeks before, Haitian president Jean-Bertrand Aristide had publicly denounced the Dominican Republic at the United Nations for the slave-like treatment of Haitian field laborers in the Dominican sugar industry. Balaguer replied by deporting thousands of poor Haitians back home, thus creating a crisis for Aristide, who had to deal with a massive flow of needy deportees.

23. See Sagás (2000, 133–140) for some infamous examples of anti-Haitian and anti–Peña Gómez propaganda.

24. Paradoxically, some Dominican writers can extol democracy at the same time that they condone Trujillo's massacre of thousands of Haitians in 1937 as an "excessive, but necessary evil" (Cornielle 1980).

Bibliography

Anderson, Benedict. 1991. *Imagined Communities: Reflections on the Origin and Spread of Nationalism*. London: Verso.

Balaguer, Joaquín. 1947. *La realidad dominicana: Semblanza de un país y de un régimen*. Buenos Aires: Imprenta Ferrari Hermanos.

Balcácer, Juan D. 1977. "Los dominicanos y la discriminación racial." *¡Ahora!* 695: 25–27.

Calder, Bruce J. 1984. *The Impact of Intervention: The Dominican Republic during the U.S. Occupation of 1916–1924*. Austin: University of Texas Press.

Cornielle, Carlos. 1980. *Proceso histórico dominico-haitiano: Una advertencia a la juventud dominicana*. Santo Domingo: Publicaciones América.

Cruz Tejada, Miguel. 2005. "Sonia Pierre denuncia amenazas contra ella y sus hijos por campañas contra el gobierno." *El Nuevo Diario*, October 28.

"Embajada de EE.UU. prohíbe a empleados visitar discoteca por discriminación." 2008. *El Nuevo Diario*, January 30. Available at http://elnuevodiario.com.do/app/article.aspx?id=88836.

Equipo ONE-RESPE. 1995. *Informe de investigación acerca del prejuicio antihaitiano en la ciudad de Santiago, de la República Dominicana: Un aporte a la comprensión y al acercamiento de dos pueblos*. Santo Domingo: Editora Búho.

Fuente, Alejandro de la. 2001. *A Nation for All: Race, Inequality, and Politics in Twentieth-Century Cuba*. Chapel Hill: University of North Carolina Press.

Gregory, Steven. 2007. *The Devil behind the Mirror: Globalization and Politics in the Dominican Republic*. Berkeley: University of California Press.

Helg, Aline. 1995. *Our Rightful Share: The Afro-Cuban Struggle for Equality, 1886–1912*. Chapel Hill: University of North Carolina Press.

Hernández, Frank M. 1976. *Inmigración haitiana y producción azucarera en la República Dominicana*. Santo Domingo: CEPAE.

Inter-American Court of Human Rights. 2006. *Case of the Girls Yean and Bosico v. Dominican Republic*. See documents associated with this case at http://www.escr-net.org/caselaw/caselaw_show.htm?doc_id=409688.

Lacey, Marc. 2007. "A Rights Advocate's Work Divides Dominicans." *New York Times*, September 29.

López, José R. [1896] 1955. "La alimentación y las razas." *Revista Dominicana de Cultura* 1 (1): 73–112.

Martínez, Samuel. 1995. *Peripheral Migrants: Haitians and Dominican Republic Sugar Plantations*. Knoxville: University of Tennessee Press.

Nicholls, David. 1996. *From Dessalines to Duvalier: Race, Colour, and National Independence in Haiti*. New Brunswick, N.J.: Rutgers University Press.

Núñez, Manuel. 1990. *El ocaso de la nación dominicana*. Santo Domingo: Alfa y Omega.

ONE [Oficina Nacional de Estadística]. 2002. *VIII Censo Nacional de Población y Vivienda 2002*. Santo Domingo: ONE.

Pérez, Louis A., Jr. 2007. *On Becoming Cuban: Identity, Nationality, and Culture*. Chapel Hill: University of North Carolina Press.

Pérez, Luis J. 1990. *Santo Domingo frente al destino*. 2nd ed. Santo Domingo: Taller.

República Dominicana. 2010. "Constitución de la República Dominicana." *Gaceta Oficial* 10561: 1–102.

Sagás, Ernesto. 2000. *Race and Politics in the Dominican Republic*. Gainesville: University Press of Florida.

Sagás, Ernesto, and Orlando Inoa, eds. 2003. *The Dominican People: A Documentary History*. Princeton, N.J.: Markus Wiener Publishers.

Schmidt, Hans. 1995. *The United States Occupation of Haiti, 1915–1934*. New Brunswick, N.J.: Rutgers University Press.

Torres-Saillant, Silvio. 1998. "The Tribulations of Blackness: Stages in Dominican Racial Identity." *Latin American Perspectives* 25 (3): 126–146.

Vega, Bernardo. 1988. *Trujillo y Haití, Volumen I (1930–1937)*. Santo Domingo: Fundación Cultural Dominicana.

Wooding, Bridget, and Richard Moseley-Williams. 2004. *Inmigrantes haitianos y dominicanos de ascendencia haitiana en la República Dominicana*. Santo Domingo: CID-SJR.

Zenón Cruz, Isabelo. 1975. *Narciso descubre su trasero: El negro en la cultura puertorriqueña*. Humacao, P.R.: Editorial Furidi.

Contributors

Volume Editors

Kwame Dixon is assistant professor of African American studies at Syracuse University. His research focuses on human rights, democracy, and social movements in the Americas.

John Burdick is professor of anthropology at Syracuse University. He is author of *Blessed Anastacia: Women, Race and Popular Christianity in Brazil* and several other books.

Chapter Contributors

Angela N. Castañeda is associate professor of anthropology and Latin American and Caribbean studies at DePauw University. Her research and teaching focus on identity formation, religion, and performance in Latin America.

Heidi Carolyn Feldman is an ethnomusicologist and a lecturer at the University of California, San Diego, and San Diego State University. Her award-winning book, *Black Rhythms of Peru: Reviving African Musical Heritage in the Black Pacific*.

Sujatha Fernandes is assistant professor of sociology at Queens College and the Graduate Center of the City University of New York. She is the author of *Cuba Represent! Cuban Arts, State Power, and the Making of New Revolutionary Cultures* and *Who Can Stop the Drums? Urban Social Movements in Chavez's Venezuela*.

Shane Greene is assistant professor of anthropology at Indiana University. His research is based in Peru, and he has published a number of articles on indigenous and Afro-descendant social movements. He is the author of *Customizing Indigeneity*.

Antônio Guimarães is currently chair and professor of sociology at the University of São Paulo. His research focuses on racial, national, and class identities; black social movements, affirmative action, and black intellectuals.

Juliet Hooker is associate professor of government and African and African Diaspora studies at the University of Texas at Austin and associate director of the Teresa Lozano Long Institute of Latin American Studies (LLILAS). She is the author of *Race and the Politics of Solidarity*.

Ollie A. Johnson III is associate professor of Africana studies at Wayne State University. His research focuses on Afro-Brazil and Afro-Latin American politics.

Elizabeth Morán is assistant professor of art history at Christopher Newport University in Newport News, Virginia. Her areas of specialization include pre-Columbian, African, and Caribbean arts.

Judith A. Morrison has extensive experience designing policies and researching inclusive development through such institutions as the Inter-American Dialogue, the Inter-American Development Bank, and the Inter-American Foundation. She was a founding member and executive director of the Inter-Agency Consultation on Race in Latin America.

Bettina Ng'weno is associate professor of African American and African studies at the University of California, Davis.

Keisha-Khan Y. Perry is assistant professor of Africana studies at Brown University. Her anthropological research focuses on black women's grassroots organizing in Brazilian cities and throughout the African diaspora.

Jean Muteba Rahier is associate professor of anthropology and director of the Africa and African Diaspora Program at Florida International University.

Ernesto Sagás is associate professor of ethnic studies at Colorado State University. He is the author of *Race and Politics in the Dominican Republic* and co-editor of *The Dominican People: A Documentary History* and *Dominican Migration: Transnational Perspectives*.

Patricia de Santana Pinho is assistant professor of Latin American and Caribbean studies at SUNY Albany. Her research and teaching focus on the topics of blackness, whiteness, racism, and forms of resistance to racism in Brazil and in Latin America. She is the author of *Mama Africa: Reinventing Blackness in Bahia*.

Peter Wade is professor of social anthropology at the University of Manchester. His recent publications include *Race and Sex in Latin America* and *Race and Ethnicity in Latin America*.

Howard Winant is professor of sociology at the University of California, Santa Barbara. He has written extensively on the process of racialization.

Index

Imbabura, Ecuador, 176
Import-substitution industrialization, ix
INAPE. *See* Institute of Afro-Peruvian Investigations
Inca, 13; Aryan race and, 287; history in history books, 300–301; indigeneity of, 298–99; lineage, 288; measurements of, 288–89; representation, 283; Spanish authorities and, 285; utopianism and, 301
Inca whiteness, in Peru, 282–302; Peruvian Congressional Committees and, 290–302; race and class theories and, 284–90
INDEPA. *See* National Institute for the Development of Andean, Amazonian, and Afro-Peruvian Peoples
Indígena, 141; in Peru, 293–94
Indigenous Colombians, 141, 143, 166–67; tie to land, 165
Indigenous costeños, 279; Creoles and, 273–74
Indigenous Latin Americans, 11, 199; autonomy, 173; Caribbean populations of, 65n11; collective rights and, 12, 267; Cuban populations of, 65n11; culture in black Pacific, 59–60, 65n11; labor and, 6; state recognition of, 157–58. *See also* Caboclo; Mestiçagem or mestiço; Mestizaje or mestizo; *specific groups*
Indigenous nationalities of Ecuador, 176–77, 179; in Constitution, 201, 212; land rights and, 184–85; political activism, 202. *See also* Zambo community
Indigenous Peruvians, 56, 64n2, 65n11, 302; Afro-Peruvians and, 65n11, 290; liberalism, indigenism and, 297–99. *See also* Amazonians, in Peru; Andeans, in Peru
Indigenous social mobilization, 1
Indio permitido (permitted Indian), 198
Informal economy, 90; in Venezuela, 82–86
Institute of Afro-Peruvian Investigations (INAPE), 61
Institutional racism, 311–12
Instituto Palmares, 261n4
Integral Peasant Association of the Atrato River, 141
Integrated social movements, 1900–1960s, 250–51
Inter-American Court of Human Rights, 331
Intercultural, 157
International Labour Organization (ILO), 39n23; Convention 169, 157, 174n1
International policies, 259
Interracial unions, 150

Inventory of the Communities of African Heritage in Salvador, 32
Iraci Isabel da Silva Health Center of Gamboa de Baixo, 238–39
Írime dancer, 125
Isabel (Princess), 239n2
IVEC. *See* Veracruz Institute of Culture

Japanese, 316
JAPER. *See* United States–Brazil Joint Action Plan to Eliminate Racial Discrimination
Jaranas, 64n6; in Lima, 45–46
Jeje Candomblé, 23
Jewish diaspora, 316, 342n9
Johnson, Ollie, 11
Jongos dance and music, 26, 38n13
José Francisco (Landaluze), 118, *120*, 121–22, 128, 131
Junior Leon, Victor, 189, 191

Karp, Eliane, 62–63, 290, 295–96
Katherine Dunham Company, 46–47
Kelley, Robin, 79–80, 82
Kenyatta, Jomo, 219, 229
Ketu Candomblé (Yoruba), 23, 33, 38n8
Kikongo people, 3
Kikoongo, 22–23, 26
Kimbundo, 22–23
Kimbundu, 26
King, Martin Luther, Jr., 323
Kitaanda Bantu, 33
Kizoonga Bantu, 34
Klein, Herbert, 122
Knowledge: ancestral, 26–27; performance and, 101–2; production, 32
Kôdya Network, 28
Konmannanjy, Raimundo, 30, 34–35

Labor movement, 250
Lacreo, 90n9
Land: African diaspora politics and, 227–31; class and, 228; ownership, 147; as symbol, of freedom and resistance, 165, 228, 229, 249. *See also* Territory
Landaluze, Victor Patricio de, 7, 114; Aguilera image by, 120; curros representations, 130; depictions of Afro-Cubans, and Africans, 116–31; Havana arrival, 116–17; Rigol on, 121; white Cubans in paintings, 126–28. *See also specific works of art*

Rowell, Charles, 98, 100
Royce, Anya, 101
Rural Afro-descendants, 269–70

SACI. *See* Sociedade Afrosergipana de Estudos e Cidadania
Saint-Domingue, French, 325
Salas, Yolanda, 78
Salvador, Bahia, 12, 28; Afro-Brazilian women as community leaders in, 231–33; political organization of women in, 230; redevelopment process, 221, 230; reurbanization practices in, 223; urban land rights struggle in, 219–39
Samba de roda, 34
Samba landó dance and music, 49, 65n10
Samba-lundú dance and music, 49
Samba Malató, 65n10
"Samba Malató" (Santa Cruz, N.), 50
Sanchez, Margarita, 249
Sanchez R., Magaly, 86
Sanders, James E., 166
Sandinista revolution, 1979, 272, 280n5
San José, Chincha, 55
Sanjuán, María, 73
San Regis, Chincha, 55
Santa Cruz, Nicomedes, 46–47, 47, 50–51, 61–62, 63, 64n7, 65n10, 292; décima, 65n8; marinera origins theory, 48, 48–49
Santa Cruz, Victoria, 46–47, 52, 65n10; ancestral memory and, 51–55; studies, 65n9
Santa Marta, 169–70
Santería, 7; in Afro-Caribbean Festival, 104–5, 107–8. *See also* Regla de Ocha
Santo Amaro da Purificação, 39n18
Santo Domingo, Spanish, 325, 341n3
Santos, Edson, 256
Santos, Juana Elbein dos, 24
São Paulo, Brazil, 307, 310
Savoia, Rafael, 183, 185–86, 187, 205; departure from Ecuador, 188
Self-help networks, 248
Self-identified ethnicity, 137, 147–48, 246, 252, 262n8
Selma, Dona, 219
Sena, Telma, 219–23, 228
SEPPIR. *See* Políticas de Promoção da Igualdade Racial
Shantytowns. *See* Barrios
Silent racism, 42–45
Skidmore, Thomas, 308

Skurski, Julie, 88
Slavery, 74–75, 248; abolition of, 165–66; in Brazil, 74–75, 239n2, 306; citizenship and, 165; in Colombia, 136–38; consequences of, 23; in Cuba, 7, 74–75, 121; in Dominican Republic, 323, 338, 342n8; land and freedom from, 229; Mexican labor, 94; organizations approved by Catholic Church, 3; in Venezuela, 74–75; in Veracruz, 103. *See also* African diaspora; Cimarrones; Coartación
Slave trade: Atlantic, ix, x, 3, 44, 54, 93, 94; fugitive settlements, 94
Slavocracy, xiiin2
Slum clearance, 230
Smith, Barbara, 219
Smith Córdoba, Amir, 140
Social change, music's power to affect, 60–63
Social Christian Party (PSC), 181, 200
Social inclusion policy initiatives, 260
Social invisibility, 44, 139, 283–84, 294–95, 298
Social movements, 1, 8, 9–10, 11, 12, 14, 247. *See also specific social movements*
Sociedade Afrosergipana de Estudos e Cidadania (SACI), 251
Socioeconomics, 177–78; gaps, 138, 244–47
Sociology, 305. *See also* Brazilian sociology
Sociospatial exclusion, 223–27; hierarchies and, 224
Solar do Unhao, 234–36
Somoza family, 272
Son de los diablos dance, 62
Soul Parties, 66n14
South Atlantic Autonomous Region (RAAS), 273, 279n1; Rama-Creole Territory in, 275–76
Southern Cone, 254, 260
Soweto, 139
Spanish authorities, 115; cabildos and, 116, 123, 128; Inca lineages and, 285; independence movements against, 116
Stereotypes, 57; of criminals as racialized, 87, 88, 89; racist, 2; rap and, 82
Structural racism, xi, 162
Stutzman, Ronald, 96
Sudan, 22–23
Sudanese, 22–23, 24. *See also* Yoruba
Sugar economy, ix; in Cuba, 114, 121; in Dominican Republic, 326–27, 330–31, 341n5
Sugrue, Thomas, 231

Tadeo, Alonso, 181–82
Taíno Indians, 327

CPSIA information can be obtained
at www.ICGtesting.com
Printed in the USA
FFOW02n0225160317
33468FF

9 780813 049625